ANIMAL-ASSISTED COUNSELING AND PSYCHOTHERAPY

NEW DIRECTIONS IN THE HUMAN-ANIMAL BOND

A dynamic relationship has always existed between people and animals. Each influences the psychological and physiological state of the other. Published in collaboration with Purdue University's College of Veterinary Medicine, New Directions in the Human-Animal Bond expands our knowledge of the interrelationships between people, animals, and their environment. Scholarly works, memoirs, practitioner guides, and books written for a general audience are welcomed on all aspects of human-animal interaction and welfare.

SERIES EDITOR

Alan M. Beck, Purdue University

OTHER TITLES IN THIS SERIES

A History of the Development of Alternatives to Animals in Research and Testing
John Parascandola

Fine Horses and Fair-Minded Riders: Modern Vaquero Horsemanship
JuliAnna Ávila

My One-Eyed, Three-Legged Therapist: How My Cat Clio Saved Me
Kathy M. Finley

Identity, Gender, and Tracking: The Reality of Boundaries for Veterinary Students
Jenny R. Vermilya

Dogs and Cats in South Korea: Itinerant Commodities
Julien Dugnoille

Assessing Handlers for Competence in Animal-Assisted Interventions
Ann R. Howie

The Canine-Campus Connection: Roles for Dogs in the Lives of College Students
Mary Renck Jalongo (Ed.)

Pioneer Science and the Great Plagues:
How Microbes, War, and Public Health Shaped Animal Health
Norman F. Cheville

Cats and Conservationists: The Debate Over Who Owns the Outdoors
Dara M. Wald and Anna L. Peterson

That Sheep May Safely Graze: Rebuilding Animal Health Care in War-Torn Afghanistan
David M. Sherman

ANIMAL-ASSISTED COUNSELING AND PSYCHOTHERAPY

A Clinician's Guide

Linda Chassman Craddock
and Ellen Kinney Winston

Purdue University Press, West Lafayette, Indiana

Cataloging-in-Publication Data is available from the Library of Congress.
978-1-61249-999-4 (hardback)
978-1-62671-089-4 (paperback)
978-1-62671-090-0 (epub)
978-1-62671-091-7 (epdf)

All photos courtesy of Animal Assisted Therapy Programs of Colorado unless otherwise noted.

Cover images courtesy of Animal Assisted Therapy Programs of Colorado.

*Dedicated to the humans and animals at
Animal Assisted Therapy Programs of Colorado.
For all your inspiration and amazing work.
Thank you.*

CONTENTS

INTRODUCTION

"The greatness of animals is that they are just themselves."

—*ALICE WALKER*

WHY DID YOU BUY THIS BOOK?

You ...

- are a mental health clinician with an animal that you believe will make a great therapy animal and will help your clients.
- bring your animal to work sometimes and see how they positively impact clients, but also are not exactly sure what to do with your animal.
- are a student in an early stage of your educational journey and are considering integrating animals into your future occupation.
- have some knowledge about animal-assisted counseling but are not sure what to do next.
- have been doing animal-assisted therapy work for a while but feel stuck in creating more ways to integrate your animal.
- are working with one animal but are considering getting more and are not sure how to incorporate them.
- do not know how to develop and provide a variety of stimulating and effective interventions with your animal.
- see how your animal helps in supportive counseling but want to learn to dive deeper with clients in psychotherapy.
- have a thirst for learning about animal-assisted work!

THE STORIES WE HEAR

June has been a clinician for over 15 years and recently adopted Sadie, a three-year-old Labrador retriever mix that shows some aptitude for helping others. June has started bringing Sadie to work and sees how great she is with her clients and how her clients open up when Sadie is present. June knows there is more she can do with Sadie to help her clients, but she is not sure what that is or where to learn about it.

Pete has heard about animal-assisted psychotherapy and wants to adopt a puppy that he can train to work with him in his practice with couples, but he is not sure where to start.

Inga has been working as a clinical social worker for 20 years but is getting burned out in her job and private practice. She has horses on her suburban farm and wonders if they would be appropriate in helping her transition to doing animal-assisted work at home.

Mitra is an undergraduate student in psychology and has heard about animal-assisted therapy. She is curious if she wants to pursue this specialty field.

If you relate to any of these descriptions or stories, then you are reading the right book.

WHY WE WROTE THIS BOOK

The idea for this book began years ago, when we noticed that we were frequently asked questions about animal-assisted counseling and psychotherapy, and that there was not a comprehensive book on the topic. We wanted to write a book that describes the *how* of doing animal-assisted clinical therapy work. This book describes not only what animal-assisted work is, but how we actually integrate our animals with clients of all ages. We review the various terms and types of animal-assisted work; address important legal and ethical issues unique to this field; describe the interventions you can do with your animal(s); discuss how different animals can work with varied populations; and provide resources for ongoing use, including a reference document for interventions. We hope that in the process of reading this book, we stimulate your creativity and excitement about including animals in your own therapeutic work.

Most of the books written in this field are about animal-assisted activities (AAA) or animal-assisted interventions (AAI). These are activities conducted by volunteers with their trained and certified pets. Teams doing AAA and/or AAI typically visit people in hospitals, schools, assisted living facilities, or other settings so that their pets can provide a temporary, positive benefit. These volunteer programs are notable and beneficial to many, but are quite different than the work we do in several ways: (1) all of our sessions are facilitated by a professional mental health clinician or graduate-level intern; (2) clients receive their care either in person or via Zoom at our ranch; (3) our animal partners are directly involved with our clients in an intentional way to meet specific therapeutic goals; (4) all dogs and clinicians are trained, certified, and evaluated through an organization specifically evaluating mental health professionals and their dogs; (5) animals are seen as partners and are always given the choice about when and how they will be involved with a given client; and (6) most importantly, we are professional mental health clinicians first, practicing with ethics and competency in our field of training. We include animals in our work to the extent that it fits with our theoretical orientation and training, the client's treatment goals, the needs of the client, and the needs and desires of the animal. We are always conscious and mindful about how the animal is impacting the client and the session, whether or not the animal is directly involved.

When we began to research animal-assisted therapy, we found many excellent resources on the human-animal bond, animal-assisted activities, and visiting animal programs; however, we also noticed a surprising scarcity of information that described our specific work and its results. We realized that we were among a small—but growing—number of professionals working with animals in a new and exciting way. We also realized that many more professionals and students wanted to do similar work but were having difficulties finding resources or they were including animals in their work with clients but without any training. In response, we decided to take our years of education and practical experience and start a training program to help mental health professionals learn how to do this work in an ethical, mindful, professional, and safe way.

Our in-person training courses and clinical work ultimately led to our international online certificate program in animal-assisted psychotherapy (CAAP) and this book. It is our goal to give readers the information to understand how to conduct animal-assisted psychotherapy in a safe, ethical, and professional manner, but also to encourage them to develop client-focused interventions that deliberately incorporate animals. We also hope that the growing number of specialists in AAP will contribute to the research in the field.

While there are no federal or state regulations on animal-assisted clinical work, the American Counseling Association (ACA) developed the term *animal-assisted therapy in counseling* (AAT-C) and issued the first set of competencies, or guidelines, to help legitimize this specialty (Stewart, 2014; Stewart et al., 2016). Professional groups around the world are now developing their own educational standards and competencies, which may include information about the history of animal-assisted work in mental health, animal-specific ethology, legal and ethical issues specific to animal-assisted work, theoretically appropriate skills, and safety and animal welfare issues. (Please refer to Stewart et al., 2016 for a complete list of AAT-C competencies.) States are also holding counselors accountable for issues that may arise when an animal is included in therapy without the clinicians' proper training and experience (Lien, 2017).

This book alone is not intended to meet the competencies for animal-assisted psychotherapy or counseling, as outlined by ACA. Animal Assisted Therapy Programs of Colorado (AATPC), the program that we developed in 2010, has a certificate program that does meet those competencies. There are a handful of other training programs that meet the competencies as well, many run by training institutions.

When we began writing this book, we chose the term *animal-assisted counseling and psychotherapy* (AACP), as we felt it encompassed the work done with animals integrated in mental health counseling or psychotherapy. In 2024, several prominent educators, clinicians, and authors in the field proposed a new terminology system for all animal-assisted work and developed the acronym AATx-P, which refers to *professional animal-assisted treatment* (Johnson Binder et al., 2024). While we do hope to unify this field and respect the opinion and research of those authors, we will be using the acronym AACP throughout our book because we feel it best describes the work we are doing. We go into more depth on terminology in the following chapter, but we want to acknowledge that the field is always growing, adapting, and changing, and the terminology is no exception.

We will be referring to animal-assisted counselors, clinicians, psychotherapists, social workers, and so forth as *clinicians*. While many clinicians provide both counseling and psychotherapy, we distinguish counseling as the work with clients that is primarily done on a conscious level, is relatively short term, and may address a certain issue or life circumstance. We use the term *psychotherapy* to identify treatment that addresses both the conscious and unconscious, focuses on ingrained patterns of behavior, and is longer term therapeutic work. This characterization of the work and how it is delineated will be described further in this chapter.

Our goal for this book is to inspire clinicians to expand their work with animals in clinical settings. We hope these ideas will stimulate professionals to be creative, have fun, and document the impact of this approach, thus expanding the evidence-based practice.

THE AUTHORS

Ellen and Linda have over 40 years of combined experience in animal-assisted counseling and psychotherapy, though it is a relatively new field. Linda started working in this field in the 1980s, before it was an officially recognized practice. Ellen was motivated to become an animal-assisted clinician before she attended graduate school. We found that the most useful knowledge came from our own practice, within our clinical framework and ethical guidelines. Linda has an object relations background and sees clients through a developmental lens. Ellen's focus was in child and family therapy, emphasizing play and familial relationships.

When AATPC was founded in 2010, it was among the first programs in the world to provide animal-assisted counseling and psychotherapy, with a variety of animals, clients, and professional mental health clinicians trained in the specialty. We became a nonprofit organization to enable us provide therapy to a wider range of communities. AATPC's mission is to provide and promote animal-assisted psychotherapy to facilitate healing for all people in need and for rescued animals through our counseling and training programs. Linda and Ellen have been involved with over 1,000 clients and hundreds of student clinicians working with a variety of animals, qualifying us as some of the most experienced clinicians and trainers in the field. Our training focus is professionals and graduate students in mental health, counseling, social work, psychology, or other mental health disciplines who wish to find innovative, fun, safe, and ethical ways to incorporate animals into their clinical work.

LINDA

My favorite movie growing up was *Dr. Doolittle* (the first one with Rex Harrison). I was certain that I was Dr. Doolittle and talked to all the animals, and of course they talked to me! Every family vacation was met by scolding from one of my parents for touching an animal, whether it was a chipmunk, cow, stray cat, or—when I was older (with my husband)—lion cubs and Tasmanian devils. I have volunteered at zoos and wild animal shelters, and have fostered feral kittens. I am proud of being fearless around animals and have a secret wish to cuddle with a baby tiger.

My professional background includes being a psychotherapist, supervisor, educator, researcher, writer, lecturer, and consultant. I have worked mostly in nonprofits but also had a private practice, seeing mostly clients with trauma and addiction issues. I got started in this work by accident while working at my home-based private practice. When I adopted my little orange kitten, Norman, he started working his way into sessions, first by cuddling up to clients when they were waiting and then insisting he be included in the session itself. At the same time, I was working at a group home for severely abused and neglected adolescents. I started to bring Norman to work with me and was amazed at the things he taught me.

This was in the mid-1980s and animal-assisted counseling did not exist, but I knew that Norman wanted to come to work with me every day and that my clients wanted him to be there. Moreover, something special was happening in my sessions as a result. I started to be more creative, as I saw how Norman behaved with different clients, and as a result, I was able to see my clients more clearly. Norman was a great mirror and helped clients to see themselves in a different light and examine their own behavior in ways that would have been too confrontational if I had done it. Finally, clients wanted to come to session! They laughed more, expressed more, and worked more when Norman was involved. They also got cuddles whenever they needed.

Many years later, we moved from California to Colorado, and I was feeling burned out, so I "retired" from counseling. I was also struggling with depression and feeling listless from being a stay-at-home mom after years of independent and productive work. Being a new mom to a toddler challenged me in every way possible. Then in 2009, I fostered a litter of feral (wild) kittens and met my soul cat, Mazey. She was my solace and my comfort; Mazey was the one creature who gave to me without demanding anything for herself. I could see her gift for love and saw how she wanted to share her love with others. Mazey was my muse and helped me to imagine the program I would develop with Ellen in 2010.

Sadly, Mazey passed away at only 14 months from feline infectious peritonitis (FIP), which is always fatal. Norman was still with me, and although quite old, had come back to work with me for a short time. He loved working with my clients, but got carsick, so I let him retire. I eventually rescued my therapy dog, Rupert, who is still with me.

Even though in California I worked with various animals for years, I had no formal training and felt uncertain at times. I learned by trial and error and the animals really showed me what they were capable of doing with clients. In my search for knowledge on the topic, I read every book I could find, yet I never

Linda's cat, Mazey.

felt satisfied. It was not until years later that I heard about animal-assisted psychotherapy, and then it was several more years before I received any formal training.

I am a licensed marriage and family clinician and both Norman and my therapy dog, Rupert, were an integral aspect of my work with adult couples and families; yet, as of this writing, there is little research or description in the literature about how animals can be beneficial with these clients. My drive for writing this book is the same that inspired me to develop our training program: I believe in this work and hope to encourage others to develop their skills and the specialty so that they can help clients who may not be helped in any other way. I also believe in providing this work only when it is ethical. To me, this means that the animal is well-suited to working with others and is always given a choice as to when and how to work with clients. Clients must also give consent and be comfortable with the animals involved.

I want to clarify that this book does not teach all that is necessary to be a competent and ethical animal-assisted clinician, but my hope is that this book will inspire both new and experienced clinicians to learn more about animal-assisted work and to provide additional tools to further develop their craft.

ELLEN

I have always loved animals and some of my earliest memories involve animals. Growing up, I would rescue worms, bugs, and baby birds, sometimes bringing them into school, which took many teachers by surprise. My sister and I had hamsters and rats as pets, and we would create mazes, obstacle courses, and even made leashes and harnesses for our rats so we could take them on walks.

After years of hoping and hours researching dogs, my family got a black Labrador retriever named Cassie, who was my responsibility. Part of that responsibility meant crate training her at night; she lasted about three minutes that first night until she was sharing my bed, where she slept for years. Cassie was a comfort to our entire family and had a special bond with each of us. Some of my most formative memories involve Cassie: taking her on daily walks and playing with her on playgrounds, seeing her comfort my sister after a car accident, and watching the strong bond that developed between her and my dad after I left for college. She was an incredible family pet and I will always think of her with a smile.

During and after college, I worked in various animal shelters, dog day cares, and a residential treatment facility for adolescent girls. During a time in my life when I was struggling with my own self-image and confidence, I felt comfortable and at ease when I was walking the shelter dogs or giving them much needed care and affection. I also noticed that there was a significant overlap in my work with humans and animals. I was learning to pay attention to subtle cues and changes in body language and behavior, rather than verbal interactions. I was working with both people and animals who had spent much of their life separated from their loved ones and often had attachment and behavioral problems as a result. I recognized that both the adolescent girls in residential treatment and the dogs in shelters needed social interaction, attention, connection, love, physical affection, goals, and a sense of purpose. I envisioned bringing them together and seeing them work on these goals for mutual benefit, and to have fun and make a connection.

This realization led me to apply to graduate school to make this vision a reality and do animal-assisted psychotherapy. I also got my own dog, Sasha, who became my therapy dog and my guide for doing this work. She was an integral part of my personal and professional journey and was an inspiration for doing animal-assisted psychotherapy and starting AATPC. Despite numerous traumas and tragedies in her life, Sasha was intuitive, gentle, loving, patient, accepting, and affectionate, but she was also brave, playful, and determined. Her

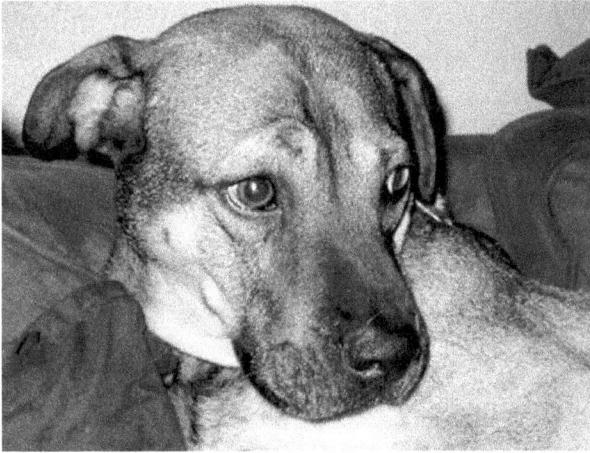

Ellen's therapy dog, Sasha.

adversity, spirit, and soothing energy helped set the tone of love and strength we wanted for AATPC. She worked with me for many years and then moved with our family from Colorado to Oregon, helping me create a new home and welcome my own children. My bond with her was incredibly powerful and is hard to put into words, but I am grateful every day that we found each other and created this amazing path together.

In the years since we started AATPC, I have learned about and connected with many animals and have seen the powerful impact they have on me, our clients, their families, and our AATPC team. Writing this book has been an honor and a privilege, and I truly hope it inspires and motivates clinicians who want to do this work. While life has removed me geographically from AATPC, I remain passionate about our work and training clinicians in how to integrate animals into their work in safe, ethical, powerful, and fun ways.

ANIMAL ASSISTED THERAPY PROGRAMS OF COLORADO (AATPC): OUR STORY

Ellen and Linda met in 2009 through an animal-assisted therapy interest group and quickly realized we had the same vision: to create a nontraditional counseling setting that integrated our amazing animals, Mazey and Sasha. We started with a single office and quickly added another clinician with two therapy dogs, an intern, an additional office, and a playroom/training center. Linda also adopted the first dog in her life, Rupert.

From the beginning, our goal was to provide services to people who otherwise would not have access to them. This meant finding a property close enough to the city that people could easily get there, and as a result, each of our properties has been close to public transportation and in urban or suburban areas.

Within two years of the AATPC's creation, we moved to our first one-acre residential property, named Barking C.A.A.T. Ranch, our Center for Animal-Assisted Therapy. We got our first baby farm animals, pygmy goats. Next came two miniature horses and a quarter horse, from owners who could no longer take care of them. Thus began our legacy of rescuing or rehoming animals who were promised a permanent home and sanctuary with us. As of this writing, we have rescued a total of 5 horses, 2 donkeys, 2 alpacas, 7 goats, 12 cats, 3 rabbits, 8 guinea pigs, 12 rats, 5 chickens, and 2 ferrets. We have also added butterflies and other invertebrates to our family. Many clinicians work with their own trained and certified therapy dogs, and we have had nearly 20 dogs over the past 13 years. Most of our rescued animals have worked with clients, but those who are less interested still have a loving home with us.

Though we began as a small business, a designated LLC, we became a nonprofit 501(c)(3) organization in 2013 to expand our low-fee program to meet the needs of our community. Our nonprofit status also allowed us to seek more donations and grants, which enabled us to hire several clinical staff and expand our programs even further. Because of this growth, we needed more physical space, so in 2018, we moved to our current 3 ½-acre ranch in Arvada, Colorado, only four miles from downtown Denver. Several grants have allowed us to expand and improve this new space, hire more clinicians and an on-site ranch/animal care manager, expand our training program, and rescue more animals.

As of 2024, about 80% of AATPC's clients are low income and pay little or no fees for counseling. We now have nine professional counselors representing different specialty areas as well as up to five master's level interns at any given time. Combined, our staff and interns see over 250 clients per week, of all ages and diagnoses. Linda, Ellen, and our clinical director provide supervision and training to staff, interns, and certificate students. We have trained over 40 counselors through our intern program and taught several hundred individuals through our online certification program.

We believe that AATPC is now one of the largest organizations in the world providing outpatient animal-assisted counseling and psychotherapy to clients of

AATPC's equine herd.

all ages, mental health issues, and financial status. Our clients complete questionnaires at intake, periodically through treatment, and at termination, to help determine the effectiveness of AACP and our programs. As AACP becomes more evidence-based, we hope to add to the research while maintaining the creativity of individual clinicians. Our long-term goal for AATPC is to continue to provide animal-assisted counseling and psychotherapy to all who need our services, regardless of their ability to pay. We have expanded our training to being a hands-on, year-round training center for professionals who would like to learn more about integrating animals into their work. We also hope to expand our certificate program in animal-assisted psychotherapy to more countries around the world.

INTENDED AUDIENCE

This book is written for professionals and students in mental health, counseling, social work, or psychology who want to work with animals and clients in safe, ethical, and effective ways. We want to help these individuals find innovative and creative ways to incorporate animals into their clinical work. We have learned through our own practice that clinical work with animals can be as powerful and unique as our imagination. We hope the ideas in this book will stimulate and inspire your own thoughts and creativity about working with your animal so that together, you can make unique contributions to this field.

BENEFITS OF ANIMAL-ASSISTED WORK

Numerous books and articles have been written about the human-animal bond and the benefits of interventions with animals. Rather than duplicate those efforts, the following is a brief summary of the benefits of animal-assisted work.

Animals have been shown to reduce physiological and psychological stress levels in blood pressure and heart rate, decrease cortisol levels, and increase oxytocin levels. Nancy Parish-Plass wrote a comprehensive article detailing the many ways that animals impact the neurobiology of clients with trauma (Parish-Plass, 2021), including animals' calming effect on clients, which in turns helps clients engage in the therapeutic process. Reducing arousal and having an animal as a motivating factor may also lead to increased attention and alertness for children (Hart, 2006; Kruger & Serpell, 2006). Animals can also help clients feel more comfortable in sessions, as they stimulate conversation and take the focus away from the client. They are a safe and neutral topic for discussion, especially if the client is not yet prepared for intimate disclosures. The clinician can discuss the animals, their history, or talk about the client's own pets.

Clients may also project their own issue onto the animal; for instance, a new client might say "Sasha looks really uncomfortable about meeting me." Though this statement may be true, it may also be an insight into the client's own feelings about being in therapy and can inform the clinician about how to move forward therapeutically. Moreover, a clinician who includes an animal in a therapeutic session is often seen as less threatening, more empathic, more trustworthy, friendlier, and happier, which may help clients feel more comfortable in session (Kruger & Serpell, 2006). Allowing clients to feel more comfortable and having an animal present to facilitate rapport building may enhance and expedite therapy, making sessions more efficient and cost-effective.

Animals are nonjudgmental and can provide unconditional, positive regard to clients, especially those individuals who may be used to criticism, judgment, or ridicule. An animal's affection and reliability in therapy may help clients understand and develop empathy, which can lead to feelings of social and emotional support, self-esteem, and a sense of trust. By working with an animal and fostering empathy, clients, especially children, can also develop patience, self-control, autonomy, and a sense of industry (Chandler, 2017). Animals can also help people learn about appropriate social interactions, as they provide immediate, honest feedback about pleasant and unpleasant interactions (Kruger & Serpell, 2006). For clients who have experienced trauma, animals can be especially powerful in therapeutic work. Beetz and Schöfmann-Crawford (2019) do an excellent job reviewing the myriad ways that animals can impact trauma work, such as animals' ability to create "optimal preconditions for learning" (Beetz & Schöfmann-Crawford, 2019, p. 106).

In group or family sessions, an animal can act as a neutral presence that diffuses tension and allows the family to feel calm enough to discuss difficult topics. The clinician can also design fun interventions with the animal, using problem-solving and cooperation, while focusing on pertinent family issues without direct confrontations. Animals can also serve as a gauge for the mood in the room and help family members realize how their body language, tone of voice, or other behaviors affect those around them. For instance, we often work with families who struggle to communicate effectively. Perhaps one parent often yells and one parent often speaks softly. We can incorporate the animal into session and teach the family how to give an animal command using a strong, assertive voice. We may then discuss with the family how this assertive voice worked in giving commands as compared to either yelling or speaking softly. This lesson can then be expanded into how to communicate more effectively as a family.

Overall, animal partners in therapy sessions can increase rapport and trust, decrease anxiety, improve motivation, and make therapy less stressful, more enjoyable, more efficient, cost-effective, and more fun. AACP can be utilized with numerous treatment focuses, including social, emotional, cognitive, and behavioral concerns, as well as trauma, abuse, neglect, resistance, self-esteem, anxiety, depression, anger, developmental delays, and improving family dynamics (Van-Fleet & Faa-Thompson, 2017). For these reasons, AACP is a powerful adjunct to other therapeutic interventions.

Psychotherapy assumes that clients will discuss and have insight about their issues, but any experienced clinician knows that many clients are not able to do this. Children and teenagers, clients who have experienced trauma, and resistant clients are generally not able or are reluctant to verbalize their thoughts and feelings. AACP offers a way for these individuals to communicate and to express themselves. One of the most profound elements of AACP is that thoughts, feelings, and behavior are simultaneously addressed in animal-assisted interventions. This work is experiential, because we are not just talking "about" issues or hearing a client's self-report about how they act/react, but we are witnessing and addressing these issues in the moment with clients. Clinicians can see how clients handle success, failure, frustration, joy, anger, and other significant situations. Throughout this process, the animals help maintain the client's motivation and commitment. Clients can project onto the animals ("Cody is really scared right now") or interpret an animal's behavior in a certain way ("Milo hates being touched"), and we can use these comments to inform our work with the client. In the moment, we get to see what the client notices about the animals, and then how they interpret and handle it. These observations give clinicians valuable information about clients that we may not otherwise have obtained. Clients can participate in a process with an animal and receive the benefit, without having to understand or explain it.

A good example of the nonverbal impact of AACP is a 12-year-old girl we worked with who came from a very chaotic family background and as a result had attachment issues. Her clinician recognized that she wanted to give this client a hug, but that ethically, it was not appropriate. Instead, during a session, the client walked to our large horse, Cody, and draped her arms around his back in a type of hug. The client had found a way to get this physical need for affection met through an animal. She had learned how to nurture, touch, ground herself, and calm her emotions.

Working with animals is also good for us, the clinicians. In a field of high burnout and secondary trauma, the animals help us stay grounded and provide necessary stress relief when we need it most. Our relationships with the animals help sustain us every day, especially when we work with the many challenging clients who find their way to us. We can take breaks with the animals, go for walks, play with a dog, hug a horse, or laugh with a goat. We can also look to the animals during session, petting them with a client during difficult disclosures or uncomfortable moments. This stress relief allows us to be more present, playful, creative, joyful, and genuine when working with our clients.

Finally, AACP can make therapy fun. In a field known for bringing up painful emotions and tears, we have found that psychotherapy can be effective even when accomplished through fun activities. The interventions discussed in this book allow us to focus on developing an enjoyable relationship between the client, animals, and clinician, while also meeting therapeutic goals. The animals provide the perfect opportunity for clinicians to invite clients to be present, playful, silly, childlike, real, and authentic, but also to help them learn new ways to think, act, and feel. This joy and learning provide a foundation for change at a deep level. For children, this experience feels genuine, while for teens and adults, it is an opportunity to awaken elements of themselves that have been suppressed but can now spark new ways of interacting with the world.

Animal-assisted counseling and psychotherapy can be beneficial to individuals of all ages, including children, adolescents, adults, and the elderly. We have worked with clients as young as 18 months, elderly patients with dementia, and every age and developmental level in between. The animals benefit each population in unique ways, and the match of an individual animal with the client is an important relationship and factor in therapy.

HOW TO USE THIS BOOK

We have broken this book into four parts, with several chapters in each part. The first part covers many of the basic, foundational issues of AACP, including how to get started and what is required of a clinician's animal(s). We also look at the important legal and ethical concerns that are unique to this field. Part 2 reviews how different animal species can be integrated into therapy and the unique and interesting ways they can help clients. Part 3 looks more specifically at how AACP can be applied with different age groups of clients. We discuss various aspects of animal-assisted counseling and psychotherapy, and explore the power of this specialty with various client groups and types of animals. The chapters in Parts 2 and 3 are organized so that they can be read independently, depending on the readers' own animals and client population. Finally, in Part 4, we provide a list of treatment goals and interventions that we have developed over the years, including the types of animals and the client populations that can be included in those interventions.

Each chapter explores ways that different animals can assist in counseling work with different groups of clients and various presenting issues. We believe that any list of interventions is only useful when you also understand the specific context. This book is meant to give you a place to start, some ideas, and a launchpad for your own creativity.

There are perhaps hundreds of interventions that are not listed in this book because they are developed in the moment by a clinician who noted the client's treatment issue, the animals' behavior, and how that unique dynamic provided an opportunity for learning, growth, and change. We discuss this in the chapter called "Catching the Moment" in Part 3. This concept of creating an intervention in the moment is relatively advanced, but is the key to allowing your therapy animal to truly be your co-clinician as they spontaneously communicate about their perspective. It is the creativity, uniqueness, and beauty of these spontaneous interventions that provide the richness and power of this field.

Working with animals allows you to reimagine your work with clients and provides infinite possibilities in the ways you can help. The field of animal-assisted counseling and psychotherapy provides you with the opportunity to be creative, passionate, mindful, and excited. We encourage you to contribute to this great field in an ethical, intentional way and hope this work helps you to feel renewed and excited about AACP.

An aside: An apology for those of you who are sensitive to anthropomorphizing, but we do it. We anthropomorphize because our clients use that language and it helps us relate the animal's experience to their own. Moreover, we believe that animals do have thoughts and feelings, even if they are different from our own. However, we only have the language used for humans' thoughts and feelings. We acknowledge that an animal's "happy" may be different than a human's "happy," just as each individual person's experience of happy is unique. We leave any further debate about anthropomorphizing to the ethologists. In all examples, identifying information about clients has been changed in order to protect their privacy and all photos use actors, not clients.

We look forward to hearing your stories and your successes with clients and animals!

REFERENCES

Beetz, A. M., & Schöfmann-Crawford, I. (2019). Clinical objectives for animal-assisted interventions: Physiological and psychological targets in trauma-informed practice. In P. Tedeschi & M. Jenkins (Eds.), *Transforming trauma: Resilience and healing through our connection with animals* (pp. 15–54). Purdue University Press.

Chandler, C. K. (2017). *Animal-assisted therapy in counseling* (3rd ed.). Routledge.

Hart, L. A. (2006). Community context and psychosocial benefits of animal companionship. In A. H. Fine (Ed.), *Handbook on animal-assisted therapy: Theoretical foundations and guidelines for practice* (pp. 73–94). Academic Press. https://doi.org/10.1016/B978-012369484-3/50006-2

Johnson Binder, A., Parish-Plass, N., Kirby, M., Winkle, M., Plesa, D., Enders-Slegers, M. J., Fowler, J.-A., Hey, L., Howell, T., Kaufman, M., Kienast, M., Kinoshita, M., Ngai, D., & Wijnen, B. (2024). Recommendations for uniform terminology in animal-assisted services (AAS). *Human-Animal Interactions*, *12*(1). https://doi.org/10.1079/hai.2024.0003

Kruger, K. A., & Serpell, J. A. (2006). Animal-assisted interventions in mental health: Definitions and theoretical foundations. In A. H. Fine (Ed.), *Handbook on animal-assisted therapy: Theoretical foundations and guidelines for practice* (pp. 21–38). Academic Press.

Lien, A. T. (2017). Working like a dog: Legal considerations for therapy dogs. *The Therapist*, September/October.

Parish-Plass, N. (2021). Animal-assisted psychotherapy for developmental trauma through the lens of interpersonal neurobiology of trauma: Creating connection with self and others. *Journal of Psychotherapy Integration*, *31*(3), 302–325. https://doi.org/10.1037/int0000253

Stewart, L. A. (2014). *Competencies in animal assisted therapy in counseling: A qualitative investigation of the knowledge, skills and attitudes required of competent animal-assisted therapy practitioners*. Dissertation, Georgia State University. https://scholarworks.gsu.edu/cps_diss/100

Stewart, L. A., Chang, C. Y., Parker, L. K., & Grubbs, N. (2016). *Animal-assisted therapy in counseling competencies*. Alexandria, VA: American Counseling Association, Animal-Assisted Therapy in Mental Health Interest Network.

VanFleet, R., & Faa-Thompson, T. (2017). *Animal-assisted play therapy*. Professional Resource Press.

PART 1

GETTING IT RIGHT
FROM THE START

"The animal does not question life. It lives. Its very reason for living is life; it enjoys and relishes life."

— *RAY BRADBURY*

Before getting into the details of providing AACP, there are certain foundational elements that must be considered and discussed. We suggest reading this section in its entirety, as it provides information that is frequently relevant and could have a large impact on your practice, animals, and clients.

In Chapter 1, we explore the numerous terms used in the animal-assisted field, as there are many confusing terms and acronyms. We explain our use of the term *animal-assisted counseling and psychotherapy* (AACP) and discuss its difference from other animal-assisted activities. In Chapter 2, we explore the many important legal and ethical issues that are unique to AACP. The protection and safety of our animals, clients, and profession is of utmost importance. This chapter will outline the areas that every clinician should consider before they begin this complicated work.

Many animals will not be appropriate as a therapy partner. It takes special skills and temperament, and most importantly, desire. In Chapter 3, we explore how to acquire a therapy animal and prepare them to be a therapy partner. Training is a large part of qualifying an animal to become a therapy partner, and training the animal can also be a clinical intervention. It is important to understand how to train your potential therapy animal and the reasons behind using positive, force-free training methods.

1

SO MANY ACRONYMS . . . CLARIFYING THE TERMINOLOGY

Animals have a long history as unofficial helpers in health care, from the Greeks in the 1600s to Florence Nightingale in the 1800s. In more recent history, Boris Levinson used the term "pet-oriented child therapy" to describe the benefits he found when including a dog in his work with children with mental health problems (Levinson & Mallon, 1997). Since then, numerous terms have been developed to describe how animals are included in health care work with humans. However, as the inclusion of animals in various settings has expanded, so too has confusion about the variety of terms used to describe the different types of animal-assisted work. We define the terms that we use throughout this book for clarity in reading, but also because terminology is important if we hope to legitimize the field. First, we look at the various types of animal helpers and then describe different types of interactions with animals.

ANIMAL HELPERS

We focus on three types of animals that assist humans: service animals, emotional support animals, and therapy animals. Though these labels and terms are often interchanged, the role of each animal helper is quite distinct.

SERVICE ANIMALS

Service animals are animals that are "individually trained to do work or perform tasks for a person with a disability" ("ADA Requirements: Service Animals," 2020). The work the animal does is directly related to one individual's needs, and the animal has been specifically trained to assist that person. Service animals are typically dogs and are usually chosen when they are very young. They go through hundreds of hours of training and are highly skilled. These animals may help guide those with visual impairments, signal those with hearing impairments, alert and protect a person having a seizure, or help those with other challenges. Recently, psychiatric service dogs have also been partnered with individuals with post-traumatic stress disorder and other mental health diagnoses. Service animals are covered under the Americans with Disabilities Act (ADA) and are allowed in public areas.

Most service animals are dogs that are specifically bred to fill this role; however, some organizations do adopt dogs and train them to become service animals. In Colorado, Freedom Service Dogs is one such organization. Occasionally, a private trainer will train a person's personal dog to become a service animal, but because service animals require such specific skills, this is not always successful.

EMOTIONAL SUPPORT ANIMALS

Emotional support animals are companion animals that provide a benefit to their owner, such as alleviating symptoms of anxiety or depression. They are often mistakenly called therapy animals, companion animals, or therapy pets. The animal must be a person's personal pet, and there is no required training or evaluation for emotional support animals, nor are they required to be able to perform any specific tasks. The human needs a letter from a doctor or medical professional stating that the pet qualifies as an emotional support animal. Many individuals can apply for and receive those letters online, without a professional having met the human or the animal. Clients may reach out to mental health clinicians about writing a letter for their animal, and this is a tricky topic with many factors to consider. It is beyond the scope of this chapter to examine the decision to write these letters and the ramifications for doing so.

Emotional support animals are covered under the Federal Fair Housing Act and are intended to help individuals requesting their companion animals for housing needs. Laws regarding emotional support animals are regularly changing, so it is a good idea to check with your locality for the most current laws.

THERAPY ANIMALS

Therapy animals are the animals that we work with daily. Our therapy animals work in partnership with a clinician to help other people, specifically, clients or patients. We use the term *therapy animal*, but our animals have been trained and evaluated, when possible, to work in a mental health setting, with a mental health professional. Our animals generally do not go into other settings to work or volunteer, though we have brought some of our animals to various events. Therapy animals should be trained to work in a clinical setting, but they are not nearly as carefully or rigorously trained as a service dog, and they are not trained to help only one individual. Though they are often certified with an individual clinician, they are expected to work with a variety of clients, whereas service animals are expected to perform tasks only for their specific owner. Therapy animals do not have the same status or protection as service animals and are not covered under ADA.

The confusion with the term *therapy animal* is twofold. First, many organizations use the term *therapy animal* to describe the animals in their volunteer teams, and second, the animal and their handler's training and certification process is geared toward volunteer visiting animal programs that provide animal-assisted support, not therapy. The owner/handler does not need any particular background to volunteer. These organizations may certify a mental health professional and their animal, but their training and certification is not specifically aimed toward a mental health population or the kinds of situations and environments that mental health clinicians face. For example, an organization may certify a mental health clinician and their dog who hope to work in a clinical mental health center, and also certify a lawyer and her dog to volunteer in a mental health setting, such as a group home. The certification organization has the same test for both teams and uses the same term of "therapy animal" for both professional and volunteer activities, even though the needs and jobs of the animals are different. Moreover, organizations that certify volunteer-animal teams will not provide insurance to a clinician if they are working in a professional setting.

Therapy animals are generally certified by an outside organization that evaluates the animal and the handler as a team and declares that they are safe to work with people in a specific environment. These evaluations look at the animal's temperament, training, and response to certain commands and situations, including stressful events. They also review the handler's ability to connect with, manage, and calm their animal, and the bond between the handler and the animal. Most often these programs evaluate dogs, but some do evaluate cats, horses, and small animals. Examples of these organizations are Pet Partners, Therapy Dogs Inc., Therapy Dogs International, and the Human-Animal Bond in Colorado (HABIC). For therapy animals that are not able to be certified by an outside organization, such as goats, llamas, alpacas, or rats, it is vital that you get to know them well, understand their temperament, and if appropriate, work with a trainer to learn how to safely manage their behavior. All our "nontraditional" therapy animals were temperament tested, socialized, and worked with staff for many hours before they began to work with clients. We consult with animal behaviorists, trainers, and veterinarians about any behavior or training questions we have.

TYPES OF ANIMAL-ASSISTED SERVICES (FORMERLY ANIMAL-ASSISTED INTERVENTIONS)

Because this is a developing field, the terminology is still changing to distinguish different types of animal-assisted activities. The term *animal-assisted services* (AAS) was recently proposed as the overarching term for all activities that include a human and animal, and are conducted for the benefit of humans (Johnson Binder et al., 2024). Within this group are three categories: animal-assisted education (AAE), animal-assisted support programs (AASP), and the group that describes our profession, animal-assisted treatment (AATx). Below, we briefly explain the terms and acronyms that are used in the field and explain our rationale for using the term AACP in this book.

ANIMAL-ASSISTED EDUCATION

Animal-assisted education (AAE) includes animals as part of an educational or psychoeducational process, without a focus on mental health or self-improvement: "The nature of AAE goals may be academic, social-emotional, cognitive, vocational, and/or organizational development and may focus on emotional regulation, coping strategies, prosocial skills, and/or empathy development" (Johnson Binder et al., 2024, p. 6). For example, a horse would be included in a biology lesson about equine skeletons, or a dog may be included in science lesson about wolves. Reading programs in schools or libraries, where individuals read to dogs, are a type of AAE. Individuals who are interested in being humane animal educators would be included in this definition. AAE is usually provided by an educator or paraprofessional who has been trained in animal-assisted education.

ANIMAL-ASSISTED SUPPORT PROGRAMS (FORMERLY ANIMAL-ASSISTED ACTIVITIES)

An animal-assisted support program (AASP) is an event or program that involves an animal for motivational, educational, and/or therapeutic reasons and is usually guided by a volunteer. Johnson Binder et al. (2024), suggested the term *animal-assisted support programs* to "refer to the mediated, guided or facilitated animal-assisted processes, where humans are benefiting from the integration of animals into the process led by a human provider, practitioner or professional" (p. 22). AASPs can occur in a variety of environments, such as schools, hospitals, and nursing homes, and are provided by individuals who are trained to provide AASP but are generally volunteers or paraprofessionals.

AASPs do not have a specific treatment goal, visit events are generally unstructured, and the provider is not required to take notes. The provider should have taken a training course and completed an evaluation with their therapy animal, but they are not required to have any professional information about the setting or population with whom they are working. Generally, AASP interactions are casual and spontaneous. An example of an AASP is a volunteer visiting program at a hospital, and the AASP handler could be a librarian, doctor, lawyer, or any individual working with their pet partner. Organizations such as Pet Partners and Therapy Dogs Inc. focus on training and certifying animal teams for AASP.

ANIMAL-ASSISTED TREATMENT
(FORMERLY ANIMAL-ASSISTED THERAPY)

Animal-assisted treatment (AATx) replaces the confusing term *animal-assisted therapy* (AAT). AATx differs from animal-assisted support programs (AASPs) in several ways. AATx is a goal-directed, documented intervention that includes an animal and is delivered by a health or human service professional in their area of expertise. AATx is a formal therapeutic process, and because it is goal-directed and documented, detailed notes about the specific treatment goals and objectives must be kept for each client. The new term for this category was developed "in order to be more inclusive of professions that employ treatments by mental and physical health professionals that are not necessarily therapy, but are part of the scope of their profession" (Johnson Binder et al., 2024, p. 27).

Animal-assisted treatment can be conducted by a variety of professionals, including mental health professionals, but also occupational therapists, physical therapists, speech/language pathologists, or medical professionals, as long as they are involving animals in their area of expertise. This means that to conduct AATx in a mental health setting, a clinician must be a mental health professional, such as a licensed professional counselor (LPC), psychologist, or social worker, working with a mental health client. A physical therapist working with a client on gross motor skills and incorporating her dog to practice throwing motions is doing AATx; a physical therapist doing social volunteering at a hospital with her dog is not doing AATx—she is part of an AASP.

ANIMAL-ASSISTED THERAPY IN COUNSELING

The term *animal-assisted therapy in counseling* (AAT-C) was proposed in 2016 when the American Counseling Association (ACA) published the first set of competencies for counselors who were integrating animals into their counseling practice (Stewart, 2014; Stewart et al., 2016). ACA chose to use the term *animal-assisted therapy in counseling* because it differentiated the work professionals did from volunteers. The ACA guidelines provide clear qualifications and ethical guidelines for providers of AAT-C.

ANIMAL-ASSISTED PSYCHOTHERAPY

The term *animal-assisted psychotherapy* (AAP) takes animal-assisted therapy and counseling one step farther and specifies that we are doing clinical mental health work or psychotherapy with the assistance of trained therapy animals. This term helps clarify that the work we are doing is different from that of visiting animal programs. This term also emphasizes the fact that we are trained mental health professionals and have the capacity to provide counseling and more in-depth psychotherapy with clients (Parish-Plass, 2013).

Generally, AAP is an adjunct to traditional therapies, meaning that a clinician incorporates AAP in addition to a more standard theoretical orientation, such as cognitive behavioral therapy or play therapy. AAP can be incorporated with most theoretical orientations, with clients of all ages, groups, families, or couples, and sessions can be directive or nondirective.

ANIMAL-ASSISTED COUNSELING AND PSYCHOTHERAPY (AACP)

Animal-assisted counseling and psychotherapy (AACP) is a term we started to use specifically for this book. The purpose of combining these terms is to recognize that interventions for both counseling or psychotherapy may look similar, and one clinician may be doing counseling or psychotherapy, depending on the client, the goals, and the phase of treatment. This term allows us to be as inclusive as possible of the clinicians who provide clinical work with clients with the assistance of animals. It also recognizes that animals can assist in work that is on a conscious or unconscious level and can be integrated easily into practices such as cognitive behavioral therapy or object relations therapy.

PROVIDER-SPECIFIC TERMS

As part of their recommendations, Johnson Binder et al. (2024) provided more descriptive terms for the humans conducting an animal-assisted service. If you are reading this book, it is likely that you are (or are becoming) an *animal-assisted treatment professional* (AATx-P). Other terms for providers as defined by the work group include *animal-assisted treatment paraprofessional* (AATx-PP) and *animal-assisted volunteer*. The volunteers could be included in any of the three categories above, but with the designation of V. Thus, the terms and acronyms would be: animal-assisted education volunteer (AAE-V), animal-assisted support program volunteer (AASP-V) or animal-assisted treatment volunteer (AATx-V).

COUNSELING VS. PSYCHOTHERAPY: DETERMINING THE APPROACH

If the terminology above is not complex enough, we want to introduce the distinctions between counseling and psychotherapy as it relates to AACP. In most publications, including research papers, the terms *counseling* and *psychotherapy* are used synonymously and interchangeably. However, others argue that they are two related but distinct forms of treatment. Animals can assist in both counseling and psychotherapeutic goals and processes, which you will see as you delve further into this book. Because there is often an overlap with when and how counseling and psychotherapy are used with clients, we will not distinguish each example as one or the other, but we do want to clarify those distinctions here.

Counseling and psychotherapy have many structural similarities. Both approaches start with establishing a positive, trusting therapeutic relationship. In the middle phase of treatment, both counseling and psychotherapy address client issues that are associated with current or former life problems. Counselors and psychotherapists may use one or more theoretical approach to organize treatment and meet the client's goals.

The primary difference between counseling and psychotherapy begins in the middle phase of treatment and addresses the client's ability to access and utilize information needed for change. In general, the process of counseling involves engaging the client's understanding and awareness of conflicts that are within their conscious mind. The client can explain those conflicts for the clinician through discussion of their present life. The clinician can help with the awareness of important features of the client's story and then help the client to make changes to certain aspects of their life. For example, the clinician may help the client to think in new ways or behave differently (Lammers, 2022).

In psychotherapy, the middle phase of treatment also focuses on the issues that the clients bring to session. However, psychotherapy is indicated when the client's conscious awareness and understanding of the problem does not precipitate behavior change. These clients may be stuck in patterns of behavior that have been rooted in much earlier relationships or trauma, and therefore their treatment will necessitate an approach that can reach into the unconscious for insight to occur. In both counseling and psychotherapy, the last phase includes using the information gained in the middle section of therapy to make concrete, behavioral changes that will create a more satisfactory life.

In this section we briefly explore some of the key concepts in counseling and in psychotherapy that are relevant to AACP. Please note that we are merely skimming the surface of this topic. For a deeper exploration of each topic, we recommend Nancy Parish-Plass's book, *Animal-Assisted Psychotherapy* (2013), and Cynthia Chandler's book, *Animal-Assisted Therapy in Counseling* (2017).

COUNSELING

The American Counseling Association (ACA) defines counseling as "a collaborative effort between the counselor and client . . . counselors help clients identify goals and potential solutions to problems which cause emotional turmoil; seek to improve communication and coping skills; strengthen self-esteem; and promote behavior change and optimal mental health" ("What Is Professional Counseling?," n.d.). Many issues can be resolved in counseling, and most graduate clinical mental health programs in the United States provide training in counseling. These training programs include a focus on relational skills that promote a trusting working relationship with the client and facilitate change for the client in some way. Students are taught the basics of many common theoretical approaches, although some programs provide more focus on one or more theoretical orientation. These skills help clinicians and clients build a trusting relationship and enable clients to be open to various problem-solving options.

Counselors use skills such as rapport building, questioning, silence, attending, active listening, reframing, reflecting, and focusing (*The Skill of Challenging in Counselling*, 2019). Literature notes, "Counseling is a professional relationship that empowers diverse individuals, families, and groups to accomplish mental health, wellness, education, and career goals" ("20/20: Consensus Definition of Counseling," 2010). Ultimately, the goal of counseling is symptom relief so that client can return to a higher level of functioning. Common challenges addressed in counseling include communication skills, grief and loss, divorce or changes in family status, and adjustment to life changes, such as relocation or beginning a new job or transitioning to a new school. Counseling goals may include skill-building, assertiveness, self-regulation, and social skills, all of which can lead to positive changes. Counseling is generally short term, and at completion, the client will feel symptom relief or have made changes that have improved their life.

Problems addressed in counseling take place in the present and involve conscious, cognitive processes and/or behavior. Counseling can be effective for issues such as an adjustment disorder as the client is consciously struggling with a specific life change (Geng, 2023). Clients in counseling are working on clearly defined treatment goals and are focusing on *how* to think or behave in a new, more effective ways. An excellent resource to learn more about the depth of counseling skills can be found in Brew and Kottler (2017).

Counseling with the assistance of animals may include the animal to help calm the client or reduce their anxiety about therapy so that they are more open and comfortable to share their concerns. Counseling sessions may intentionally involve the animal in a certain intervention that allows the client to practice a new skill or behavior. For example, Mary has a difficult time setting limits with her grown child who lives with her. The goal of one counseling session may be to learn and practice assertiveness skills while working with a stubborn goat. The clinician gives Mary a large red ball and instructs her to use the ball, as needed, to create space between herself and Lily, the overly friendly goat. The clinician is aware that when Mary enters the goat paddock, Lily may try to headbutt her in greeting, and while this is not a safety concern, it does require that Mary set a strong physical boundary. Mary can also practice using her voice to tell Lily how she feels about this greeting. Over time, Mary may help with Lily's training and reinforce the command "stay," which is being taught to mitigate Lily's behavior. These interventions and discussions are done overtly and on a conscious level with Mary. During the sessions, as Mary is practicing these new assertive behaviors, the clinician may address the similarities to her situation at home with her adult son. They may discuss how the ball is a metaphor for setting limits at home and how she can bring these lessons and skills into her interactions with her son.

This intervention and therapeutic goal of assertiveness can also be incorporated into psychotherapy, though it may look a bit different, as you will see in the following section.

PSYCHOTHERAPY

Boris Levinson was one of the first practitioners and promoters of psychodynamic psychotherapy with animals (Levinson & Mallon, 1997). He compared the dynamics of "pet psychotherapy" to a child's natural maturational process, evolving through different psychodynamic stages as the child's relationship with the animal develops. Nancy Parish-Plass's approach to psychotherapy "is based upon the belief that emotional difficulties and pathologies likely originate from problematic relationships in the past, and therefore the client must use relationships in the here and now in order to change" (2013, p. xxi).

In this book, we use the term *psychotherapy* as is consistent with Levinson and Parish-Plass, with a primary goal of uncovering unconscious processes, patterns, and beliefs rooted in early childhood that are causing disruptive emotions and behaviors. Psychotherapy asks "why" before "how." The goal of psychotherapy is to (1) bring these processes, patterns, and beliefs to light (consciousness) so that (2) the client has awareness and understanding (insight), (3) they have an emotional catharsis, and (4) they learn and practice skills that allow them to move forward in a more functional manner (Gabbard, 2017). Instead of moving directly toward solving a problem, psychotherapy takes time to explore the roots of the problem, often related to early memories embedded in the unconscious mind, and then allows the client to experience the memory or awareness in an emotional and visceral way. Through this insight, the client should be able to address the issue at its root and make more lasting change. By enabling emotional catharsis, the client can complete the grieving process necessary to move forward in a new way.

Animal-assisted psychotherapy incorporates numerous concepts of traditional psychotherapy, such as therapeutic neutrality, developing transference relationships, the use of projection as a tool to the unconscious, exploring resistance, exploring the transference relationship, actively addressing and repairing ruptures in the therapeutic relationship, interpreting behavior as it relates to the clients' unconscious issues, and catharsis or emotional processing of the insight or awareness of the interpretations (Buckley, 1986; Roth, 1987). As in counseling, psychotherapy will encourage new thoughts, feelings, and behaviors as a means to move forward productively (Roth, 1987). These are complex topics and we address only a few of them as they relate to animal-assisted psychotherapy.

Psychotherapy is indicated for clients who have patterns of disruptive behavior, whether in relationships, self-soothing, attachment, addiction, chronic depression, or anxiety. Often the issues that we address are related to abuse, trauma, or neglect. While we can work on the presenting symptoms or behaviors, the deeper issues will likely return if the root cause is not healed. Psychotherapy actively uses the therapeutic relationship to help clients develop through stages in a healthy way so that those aspects of development that were interrupted are now built. The therapist and their animal(s) becomes the "good enough" caregiver, a term coined by Winnicott in the 1950s (Buckley, 1986, p. 149; Winnicott, 1986, p. 231).

A client who could benefit from psychotherapy may have had tumultuous or traumatic experiences as a young child, which created unconscious patterns of thinking or feeling. These individuals may never have created positive attachments to caregivers and would benefit from psychotherapy rather than counseling, because they need to uncover and address those deeply rooted issues before lasting change can happen (Parish-Plass, 2008).

In the example with Mary used above, psychotherapy would likely start much the same way as counseling. But in the middle stage of psychotherapy, going into the pen with Lily might be precipitated by asking Mary what if feels like to have various types of interactions with Lily. The clinician may ask Mary to delve into memories that remind her of the similarities between herself and Lily, and then explore the feelings associated with those memories. In this situation, the clinician is attempting to find the ruptures in Mary's early relationships that have led to her inability to set boundaries. Through various sessions with different animals, the clinician may notice a pattern of interactions and offer an interpretation, such as, "I've noticed that with each of the larger animals, you've said you felt 'small' and 'insignificant.' I wonder if this feeling started when your older brother would kick you, and your mother didn't believe you when you told her. I would imagine you would have felt powerless and small and insignificant. It hardly mattered to stick up for yourself." The client and clinician can then process how this memory has impacted Mary's relationship and interactions with the animals, and then how it may have impacted her relationship with her son. Through the emotional release associated with the memory, the client is working through her early challenges and moving to a place where she can choose new behaviors.

WHY THE DISTINCTION IS IMPORTANT

We believe that there is an ethical and practical reason for determining whether a clinician is providing counseling or psychotherapy. The two approaches can be quite different, which will have an impact on the client's time, finances, and emotional life. Ultimately, it is the client who must determine the type of therapy they want and need. A client may have a deep-seated unconscious pattern of destructive relationships and the clinician may recommend psychotherapy. However, the client may only want relief from their current symptoms or may have limited resources for mental health treatment, so they may not be prepared for the depth work of psychotherapy. There are also situations where clients do not have the intellectual or emotional resources to participate in psychotherapy, as it can be an intense cognitive and emotional process. Psychotherapy requires the ability to connect memories to feelings and to behavior and to emotionally process deep memories and experiences. In these cases, the clinician will need to work with the client to decide how treatment should unfold.

Very young children may not have the capacity for the insight required for psychotherapy; however, they can still benefit from the psychotherapeutic process through play, which allows expression of both conscious and unconscious issues through the medium and metaphor of play. Providing an age-appropriate form of play therapy with the assistance of animals may be a valid approach for clients who lack the cognitive ability for insight.

REFERENCES

20/20: Consensus definition of counseling. (2010). ACA Conference, Pittsburgh, PA.

ADA requirements: Service animals. (2020). https://www.ada.gov/resources/service-animals-2010-requirements/#:~:text=A%20service%20animal%20is%20a,public%20are%20allowed%20to%20go

Brew, L. M., & Kottler, J. A. (2017). *Applied helping skills: Transforming lives* (2nd ed.). Sage.

Buckley, P. (Ed.). (1986). *Essential papers on object relations.* NYU Press.

Chandler, C. K. (2017). *Animal-assisted therapy in counseling* (3rd ed.). Routledge.

Geng, C. (2023). *Psychotherapy vs. counseling therapy: What is the difference?* https://www.medicalnewstoday.com/articles/psychotherapy-vs-therapy

Johnson Binder, A., Parish-Plass, N., Kirby, M., Winkle, M., Plesa, D., Enders-Slegers, M. J., Fowler, J.-A., Hey, L., Howell, T., Kaufman, M., Kienast, M., Kinoshita, M., Ngai, D., & Wijnen, B. (2024). Recommendations for uniform terminology

in animal-assisted services (AAS). *Human-Animal Interactions, 12*(1). https://doi
.org/10.1079/hai.2024.0003

Lammers, J. (2022). Therapy vs. counseling: Is there a difference? Which is right for
you? *Ohio State Health & Discovery.* https://health.osu.edu/health/mental-health
/therapy-vs-counseling-is-there-a-difference

Levinson, B. M., & Mallon, G. P. (1997). *Pet-oriented child psychotherapy.* Charles C Thomas
Publisher.

Parish-Plass, N. (2013). *Animal-assisted psychotherapy: Theory, issues, and practice.* Purdue
University Press.

The skill of challenging in counselling. (2019). https://counsellingtutor.com/the-skill
-of-challenge

Stewart, L. A. (2014). *Competencies in animal-assisted therapy in counseling: A qualitative investigation of the knowledge, skills and attitudes required of competent
animal-assisted therapy practitioners.* https://scholarworks.gsu.edu/cgi/viewcontent
.cgi?article=1107&context=cps_diss

Stewart, L. A., Chang, C. Y., Parker, L. K., & Grubbs, N. (2016). Animal-assisted therapy
in counseling competencies. *Animal-Assisted Therapy in Mental Health Interest Network.*

What is professional counseling? (n.d.). https://www.counseling.org/aca-community
/learn-about-counseling/what-is-counseling#:~:text=Counseling%20is%20a%20
collaborative%20effort,change%20and%20optimal%20mental%20health.

Winnicott, D. W. (1986). The theory of the parent-infant relationship. In P. Buckley (Ed.),
Essential papers on object relations (pp. 233–253). NYU Press.

2

MY GOAT THINKS TOES ARE JELLYBEANS . . . AND OTHER LEGAL AND ETHICAL ISSUES UNIQUE TO AACP

"It's not enough to love animals; we must actively protect and preserve them. It's our duty and responsibility as custodians of this planet."

—*DAPHNE SHELDRICK*

This chapter covers the necessary elements of running an AACP practice. Adding animals to your work adds specific legal and ethical risks and decisions to your clinical practice. Significant consideration is required to prevent harm to your client, your animal, or you. It is important to recognize if you are willing and able to make the commitment to doing this work safely and ethically, and if you have the necessary information to make that decision. Making a true contribution to the field of AACP takes training and practice, which takes time. These recommendations are based on our many years of experience but should not be considered legal or ethical advice. Please consult a professional organization or an attorney about your own program's needs.

LEGAL ISSUES

Legal issues in AACP pertain to laws and regulations in your city, county, state, and under your professional license. They are the "musts" that if done incorrectly, put you at risk for legal action. Inappropriate or incorrect actions could lead to a civil lawsuit, criminal charges, or the loss of your license. Additionally, if you work at an organization, your supervisors and/or board of directors could also be held liable for your actions.

Legal liability becomes more complex when you introduce an animal to your practice. You are introducing a live being that does not speak your language, may have its own agenda during sessions, and could potentially do harm, both physically and emotionally, if not handled correctly. Adding an animal also introduces elements of spontaneity that while often therapeutic, can also be damaging. It is essential to be aware of the potential risks for each animal you work with, prevent risks as much as possible, and inform clients of these potential risks.

CLINICAL COMPETENCE

Each state and/or country defines and manages mental health licensing and clinical competence differently. However, there is a common standard that dictates that clinicians only use modalities in which they are trained and supervised; in other words, in which they are clinically competent. This applies to AACP as a specific modality as well. Clinical competence can be achieved in a variety of ways, including school coursework, graduate school programs, postgraduate training, and self-study. Clinical competence also usually indicates that the clinician has received supervision in that particular area.

It is important to note that there are not yet legal requirements to practice AACP. However, in 2013, Stewart, Chang, Parker, and Grubbs identified nine core competencies in animal-assisted therapy for counseling (AAT-C) for the American Counseling Association (Stewart et al., 2013). There are no classroom hour or credit requirements, but the recommended competencies are clear and include the following: AAT-C training, assessment, and supervision; in-depth animal knowledge; integrated ethics; general counseling competence; intentionality; specialty area incorporates skills and abilities; responsibility to animals; AAT-C advocacy; and professional values. Please see the complete article for further explanation of these competencies.

CLINICIAN TRAINING AND EXPERIENCE

Clinical competence in your profession may require supervision and evaluation, so it is important to carefully choose your training to ensure that it meets professional requirements and best practice standards. It is very important to obtain sufficient training in AACP to protect you legally and to ensure that your approach is ethically sound and clinically appropriate. Too often, clinicians bring animals into session without understanding the potential risks to the client or animals. As with other clinical specialties, such as eye movement desensitization and reprocessing (EMDR) or dialectical behavior therapy (DBT), AACP is a specialty that has its own inherent risks. A clinician should not attempt to practice EMDR or DBT with a client after a brief two-hour seminar; similarly, they should not bring an animal to sessions after a short introduction on the topic.

We started our certificate program in AACP because we saw a need and interest for good clinical training for those wanting to do in-depth psychotherapy with clients. There are other training programs around the United States and internationally, but we have found that many are quite general; for example, they may be focused on volunteer visiting teams and are not specific to bringing animals into the clinical counseling setting. If your client or insurance company asks about the training that qualifies you to practice AACP, it is important that you have a strong training foundation and can describe it confidently. A leading cause for legal action against clinicians is the practice of an intervention for which they are not adequately trained.

Clinicians who practice the specialty of AACP without the proper training and without adhering to best practices can be held legally and/or ethically liable for harm caused to a client. An example of a worst-case scenario happened in California in 2017, when a clinician included a dog in her practice and the dog bit and injured a client. The clinician had not been trained in AAT or AACP and was found to be practicing out of the scope of her license and competence; she subsequently lost her license to practice (Tran-Lien, 2017).

CLIENT WELFARE

When practicing AACP, both the animal and the client are relatively unpredictable components of therapy. Their interactions, the setting, weather, sounds, smells, and other aspects of the treatment situation are variables that can affect the dynamics in sessions. Even with our best efforts to anticipate and manage these factors, we must be aware of and prepared for unexpected situations.

Moreover, animals cannot communicate with words when they are feeling stressed, afraid, angry, or exhausted; instead, they use nonverbal behaviors, body language, and sometimes vocalizations. It is essential that you learn those cues not only for each species of animal you work with, but also for the individual animal(s) that you may be working with. For instance, dogs communicate with *calming signals* (Rugass, 2006) or stress signs. While there are general nonverbal cues all dogs give, each unique dog will demonstrate certain signs more than others or show different signs depending on the circumstance. Most animals will provide some nonverbal cues or sounds, akin to *whispering* to us. Nonetheless, you will never hear your cat say, "Please move away or I'm going to scratch you!" As animals become more stressed, they may *speak* up and demonstrate their request more forcefully with more obvious and numerous cues or vocalizations. If we do not pay attention to these cues, our animal may feel the need to *shout* at the client, which may come in the form of scratches, bites, kicks, or other body language that is often deemed "aggressive." This behavior is our animals' attempt to stop an interaction. Clients are always at risk of harm from these actions, but even more so if we as clinicians do not notice the animals' cues. It is your responsibility to know your animals' preferences, stress cues, and communication styles and act accordingly.

Some minor injuries may happen when an animal is being playful or "frisky," as with Linda's therapy dog Rupert or our goat Dahlia. Rupert is a big dog and can knock over a small child with just his wagging tail, whereas Dahlia thinks that small children want to play like goat kids and headbutt. Dahlia also likes to bite little painted toes; we think she believes they are treats. Ellen's dog Sasha once scratched a client during a training session because she was so excited about offering her paw for a treat during a training session. These are all examples of friendly animals interacting as animals and unintentionally causing harm. However, these actions can still frighten, injure, or negatively impact a client if not managed and handled appropriately.

Furthermore, if threatened or feeling unsafe, animals can act out more intentionally. For example, if our goat Duncan felt threatened, he would headbutt an animal or a person; our miniature horse Misty can be sensitive and will turn her head to nip if she does not like how someone is approaching her. Being prepared for these situations and able to respond appropriately are essential aspects of your legal and ethical responsibilities as an AAP practitioner.

At our facility, all interns, clinicians, staff members, and volunteers are taught to safely interact with each animal at the ranch. Our interns and clinicians partner with our ranch animals or their own trained therapy animals, and before they work with clients, all are required to spend time with each animal to learn the animal's preferences, likes and dislikes, understand the animal's body language and stress signs, and earn the animal's trust.

All clients learn how to safely engage with each animal before they are allowed to interact with that animal. If we have specific concerns about the client's ability to safely engage with the animal, we may discuss and practice safe behavior with pictures, books, toys, puppets, and stuffed animals until we feel ready to introduce them to live animals. One advantage of having different animals is this flexibility, because the client can demonstrate safe behavior with a dog or miniature horse before they hold our rats or work with the guinea pigs.

Despite all these precautions and preventive measures, it is still possible that a client could be physically, psychologically, or emotionally damaged through interaction with your animal. Unfortunately, we have had that situation happen; a client was working with her clinician to feed our horse, Cody, when he accidentally knocked her into the paddock gate in haste to get to his dinner. The client was physically unharmed, but it was three months before she would return to the arena when Cody was present. She worked with her clinician to process the moment and her resulting emotions. We certainly learned from this situation and recognized that our horses are most excited during feeding time and therefore more likely to act unpredictably. As a result, we have trained our clinicians to understand that if clients are involved in feeding, the clinician must be extra vigilant and take specific measures to keep the client safe, such as always being first to approach the horse, carrying the food, and/or staying between the client and the horse. We also no longer allow clients to hand feed the horses.

This example demonstrates the importance of intentional steps to try to prevent animals from causing harm. Simple measures are helpful, such as keeping claws trimmed, giving treats only in safe ways, and having client rules such as, "No animal can be picked up by a client." You can also use proactive training measures, such as teaching animals how to sit to say hello, to wait at a door, not to jump or to jump only on command. Animals can also be taught how to use their mouths more safely. As part of his training, Linda often played with Rupert's teeth and tongue. By having a hand in and around his mouth, Rupert learned how to be gentle with his powerful jaws. However, even with this training and Linda's trust in Rupert, one cannot assume that Rupert would never bite someone. He is still a dog, and unexpected situations could elicit a bite. He could also bite accidentally during play. We do not want to give our clients an assurance of complete safety that we cannot guarantee. Though we cannot promise how our animals will act, our responsibility is to lessen the chance that any harmful interactions will occur.

CULTURAL CONSIDERATIONS AND CLIENT COMFORT

We must acknowledge that some clients may not want or benefit from AACP. Some individuals are not comfortable with animals, do not like all animals or specific ones, or do not want to include animals in their therapy. Some people have phobias of animals or of specific species or breeds as the result of a bad experience. There are also cultural, religious, socioeconomic, regional, and other differences in how specific animals are viewed, treated, understood, and accepted. In some parts of the country and the world, many of the animals discussed in this book would not be ideal therapy animals. For example, some groups see dogs as part of the family, others see them as protectors or helpers, and others view them as unclean or unlucky. In many areas, rats signify uncleanliness. Culture is deeper than just country-of-origin; there are subcultures all around the world that may or may not be identifiable but that may have an impact on a person's desire or ability to work with an animal. For example, we had an experience with this early in our work, when a woman called us on behalf of her elderly father who was depressed and wanted therapy with animals. However, she wanted to confirm that we did not work with any German shepherd dogs, because her father was a Holocaust survivor and had a deeply rooted fear of this breed due to his past experiences. Many people find it unpleasant that we have rats as therapy animals. It may be unethical to push our positive views of animals on our clients, but we can offer them the choice to see these animals differently.

A useful model to ensure clinicians have cultural sensitivity was developed by Jegatheesan (2015) and includes elements such as identifying the clinician's own level of cultural knowledge, assumptions, and thought processes about client culture; the clinician's ability to gain the relevant knowledge about the specific client's sociocultural background, rather than making broad cultural generalizations; and developing the skills to sensitively practice the work and to work with the client to determine a treatment plan that is both comfortable with the client and effective. We recommend that when working with diverse clients, clinicians research and explore the client's comfort level with different animals.

Before introducing AACP to any prospective client, it is important to ask the client how they feel about having an animal present. Clients need to have ample opportunity to work with you without an animal present if that is their preference. It is advisable to discuss this issue prior to the first visit, when making the initial appointment with the client. Even if the client gives verbal permission for the animal to be present at the first session, we often suggest that the intake session occurs without an animal. This option allows for a more comprehensive discussion about AACP, a chance to gauge the client's interest and comfort with animals, and time to complete any necessary paperwork before putting the client or animal at risk. However, depending upon the office environment, having an initial animal-free session can be challenging, so this is a factor to consider. For example, if a counselor at a large community mental health center has her dog at the office for a certain day, but one client in the middle of the day does not want the dog in the therapy room, the clinician has to find an alternative spot for her dog during this session. In this example, the front office staff may agree to watch her dog; however, without this option, both client and animal may be in an uncomfortable position.

When talking with clients about their comfort with your animal, it helps to describe the animal and their usual interactions with clients. Each of our animals has their photo and biography on our website. We encourage clients to look at this page so they can learn a little about our animals before coming to the office. This step can also provide an early indication about their level of interest in AACP and the animals. This information can then guide you in decisions regarding whether and how to integrate the animal into your work. Some clients will be tolerant of the animal but will have little interest in interacting with them. In that case, if your animal can unobtrusively stay in the room with the client, the animal may still have a potentially soothing effect on the client. Many clients will want to immediately engage in an activity with the animal. However, we generally think it is better to give both the client and animal some time to get to know each other before engaging in any hands-on interventions.

CLIENT HEALTH ISSUES AND ZOONOSES

Zoonoses are harmful germs such as bacterium, fungus, parasites, or viruses that can be transmitted from animal to human or vice versa. These illnesses can range from mild to severe and some can even cause death. There are over 200 zoonotic illnesses, but most are rare and some, such as rabies, can be prevented with vaccination and other methods. Animals and humans can also share illnesses via insects or worms, such as scabies (sarcoptic mange), flea bites, ticks, and roundworms. A common example of a zoonosis is the bacteria toxoplasmosis found in cat feces and transmitted by touching a cat with feces on the fur or from cleaning a litter box. This illness can be devastating for pregnant women and they should not be around any cat feces. Other common or well-known zoonoses include tinus (ringworm), which can be transmitted by dogs, cats, horses, and goats, and salmonella, which can be transmitted by reptiles and poultry. Humans can also carry infections that they can pass on to animals, such as strep throat. This transmission is called *reverse zoonosis*.

Because animals often carry germs or bacteria that can be transmitted through the skin or saliva, it is important to know the common zoonoses or shared illnesses that are relevant for your animal(s). Depending on your treatment setting, you may be working with clients who have medical issues that could put them at greater risk of harm from interacting with animals. Young children, the elderly, and pregnant women can be at higher risk of contracting or getting seriously ill from various infections. Other medically compromised groups include those with compromised immune systems, such as clients with blood disorders, HIV/AIDS, chemotherapy patients, and people who have had organ transplants. Thin skin (as is common in the elderly) and open sores (which can occur because of illness, drug addiction, or other reasons) can also be more problematic and increase the risk that an animal could scratch the client and/or transmit germs. It is important to choose which clients may or may not be appropriate for certain animals, based on the client's ability to remain safe from potential harm. For instance, we work with many young children who may put their hands in their mouths, so we are very careful when allowing them to work with our chickens.

In addition to zoonoses, issues of cleanliness and allergies need to be considered when conducting AACP. Your animal should be kept clean with regular bathing and grooming, including nail trimming and teeth brushing. Having animal wipes or a damp cloth to wipe off your animal can be helpful. It is also important to keep your animal's nails trimmed to prevent scratches. Brushing your animal's teeth is important for their oral hygiene and can also help prevent bad breath. Conversations about hygiene, bathing, brushing teeth and fur, and trimming nails can also be a very useful activity for clients who are learning about self-care or struggling with hygiene.

Your office should be kept clean and as free of hair and dander as possible. We keep cleaning supplies around the office, such as dusting cloths, antiseptic wipes, and vacuums, and we also have a regular cleaning service for deeper cleans. We have outdoor supplies to clean up when the dogs go to the bathroom and have regular checks in case anything was missed. We have hand sanitizer in every room and multiple hand washing stations around the facility, and we require clients and staff to wash hands between animal interactions and after sessions.

To prevent zoonosis or illness via insects/worms, your animal should get regular checkups with a veterinarian, be kept up to date with shots and vaccinations, and you should have a letter from your veterinarian clearing your animal for therapy service. Most certification organizations will also require this letter certifying the animal's health. It is imperative that you know your animal well and carefully monitor them for change in appearance, behavior, or more obvious signs of illness such as rashes, vomiting, or diarrhea. Never work with your animal when they appear ill. Sick clients should not come into the office, for everyone's health and well-being.

CONSENT, RISKS, AND RULES

Working with animals is an inherently unpredictable addition to therapy, even with its many benefits. Clinicians should discuss potential risks and include these on a disclosure and consent form that each client (and/or client guardian) reviews and signs before beginning treatment. The consent form should also include rules/policies about client interactions with your animal(s) and any treatment setting considerations. Your form should be reviewed by an attorney, and you should keep a signed copy on file.

Because our treatment setting is a small urban farm/ranch, we have many hazards and have adapted our consent form as our property, animals, and therapeutic techniques have evolved. Many of our policies were added after experience; for example, we have added rules about closed-toed shoes for safety with the horses and goats; not climbing on the trees or fences; and walking rather than running when with animals. It is unlikely that you will be able to anticipate the numerous situations that can arise once you include many variables into the therapeutic process. It may be necessary to update your form several times as you learn more about the specific risks at your office. You may open yourself to more risk with more animals, larger and complex spaces, varied interventions, and complicated clients.

We recommend that your consent form be as inclusive as possible, but we are also aware that this a traditionally American litigious view and it may not be appropriate for all clinicians. Additionally, a signed consent does not necessarily protect you from a lawsuit but does show due diligence on your part in explaining the potential risks to clients and documenting their acceptance of those risks.

LIABILITY

Professional liability insurance or malpractice insurance provides coverage for clinicians who may get sued by a client. In most states in the United States, any client can sue any clinician for any reason, even with a signed consent form. If an animal were to cause a client harm as part of an AACP session, one might assume that the insurance company would cover the injuries and provide legal assistance. However, insurance policies usually state that their company is only required to insure you for practices that are within your scope of training and experience.

AACP is considered a specialty field, so if a clinician does not have specific training in AACP, they increase the risk of being denied support from their insurance if a client makes a claim of harm due to working with an animal. This harm may be claimed due to minor injuries, development of an animal phobia, increased mental health symptoms due to animal interactions, clinician negligence, or other types of harm. If you have received training that meets your profession's competencies, documented that you shared the rules/risks with the client, and your insurance company has agreed to insure you with full knowledge of your work, then you have a greater chance of support from your insurer.

ETHICAL ISSUES

There are many books written on ethical mental health practices and this book will not cover all these issues. This section highlights the unique AACP ethical issues that require special emphasis. Because AACP is a new and expanding specialty, it is imperative that we make extra effort to define and maintain ethical practice.

Whereas legal issues are the "musts," the ethical issues are the "shoulds" of AACP. There is a great deal of overlap of legal and ethical issues, though ethical issues are rarely clear cut and there may not be one right answer. One way to think of this is that every legal issue has an ethical element. In other words, a clinician may have a legal situation (such as a therapy dog biting a client), but there is also the ethical *management* of that issue (how the clinician handles the client getting bitten). When there is an ethical breach, a clinician can still be sued, lose their license, or lose their ability to practice. Therefore, it is best to be aware of and attempt to avoid any of these concerns before engaging in AACP.

ANIMAL WELFARE

Some of our agency's most important ethical guidelines address the critical issue of animal welfare and happiness. Clinicians should monitor the animal's nonverbal communication and recognize when the animal needs a break. Every animal should be able to make the choice to be in a session (or not), and they have the right to leave or change their mind at any time. Every office has a quiet, private space for animals so that they can take a break from the session, or we can leave the room or relocate the animal if necessary. We only allow clients to pick up and hold certain animals, and only then if a staff member is assisting and the client is sitting down. Many animals cannot be picked up due to safety considerations. For example, our rabbits are never picked up, because there is a very specific way to pick up rabbits safely and our rabbits do not like to be held. However, the rabbits can choose to jump on a client's lap if they feel comfortable doing so. For some clients, such as those working on being calm, staying still, or developing trust with others, the rabbit jumping on their lap can be a therapeutic milestone.

Clinicians should always monitor their animal's behavioral cues and overall well-being, including signs of stress, anxiety, or discomfort. For instance, if you are working with a dog, it is important to know canine calming signals, such as head turning, sniffing, avoiding eye contact, moving slowly, freezing, lying down, rolling over, shaking off, or raising hackles. In addition, you should know which signs your dog demonstrates most often and the meaning of each cue. It is also important to be aware of signs of more significant distress or illness, such as panting, pacing, changes in appetite, sweaty paws, trembling, whining, destructive behavior, avoiding clients, and any other significant change in behavior. These behaviors may indicate that your animal is stressed or unhappy about their role in sessions or about working in general—a situation that would require that you re-evaluate your animal's role as a therapy partner.

It is also important to consider how often your animal can work, both how many days per week and how many hours per day. There is mixed information regarding how much therapy animals should work, depending on which agency/organization you follow and on animal type and breed, age, environment, and clientele. Regardless, it is essential not to overwork your animal, as that could cause chronic stress. One study documented an instance of a black Labrador retriever in a school setting who developed Cushing's syndrome, which may have been the result of being overworked and overstressed (Heimlich, 2001). Your animal's ability to work will likely require constant monitoring and adjustment. For instance, Linda's cat Norman used to go to work with her almost every day. However, when Linda moved to Colorado and their commute included a windy mountain road, Norman became carsick and no longer wanted to go to work. For his health, he was retired. In contrast, Linda found that Rupert loved riding in the car, being with Linda, playing with the other animals, and interacting with clients. Even at his current age of 13, when Rupert is asked if he wants to "go to work," he will run to the door, excited and ready to leave. However, due to his age and physical changes, Rupert is now semiretired, and accommodations have been made about how much and in what ways he is involved with clients; for example, clients are asked only to play ball in five-minute increments, for a total of 15 minutes each day, due to his arthritis.

In the early days of our work, Ellen's dog Sasha would work several days per week and was excited to come to work, but Ellen also noticed that sessions made her tired. Sasha would often retire to her quiet space throughout sessions or sleep after a session. Ellen scheduled a medical exam, to include a check on Sasha's energy level and weight, during which the vet theorized that Sasha was likely older than the rescue organization had reported. This realization made Ellen reconsider how often Sasha could work and began to reduce her hours. Sasha remained excited to go to work until her retirement, even if she was not involved in every session and was simply resting near Ellen.

SAFETY

Keeping both clients and animals safe is an important legal and ethical issue, and some situations will be riskier than others. Clients can more easily harm smaller animals, such as guinea pigs and rabbits, whereas larger animals can more easily harm clients, even unintentionally. We are very thoughtful about how we pair clients and animals, particularly because we work with a diverse client base that includes young children, individuals with trauma responses, clients with behavioral and impulsivity issues, and clients who have previously harmed animals. We want both our animals and clients to feel safe and have a positive experience during interactions. We may have clients start work with animal representations, such as stuffed animals, puppets, figurines, and photos, especially those individuals who are more unpredictable or who have a history of animal harm. Once these clients have demonstrated that they can make safe choices, use gentle touch, and respect the animal's autonomy, they can progress to observing animals, and then finally to working with our "steadier" animals like dogs and goats. Clients may also be able to earn a chance to work with a particular animal by accomplishing certain steps in their treatment or meeting specific goals.

Not all clients like rat kisses.

UNDESIRED ANIMAL BEHAVIOR

Certainly, some animal behaviors can lead to client injury. Minor injuries such as scratches are the most common, but other animal behaviors can be undesirable, such as licking, jumping, stepping on clients, nibbling exposed skin, playing rough, and knocking into clients. We encourage clients to play and physically interact with our animals, but there are certain behaviors that are inherently unenjoyable or dangerous, even if the intent is innocent. For instance, displays of affection or grooming such as licks and kisses may be unwanted. For this reason, Linda taught Rupert to bump his nose on her nose instead of licking her or others. As it is harder to train cats or rats not to lick and groom, we alert clients to that possibility when they are working with those animals. Smaller animals, such as rats and guinea pigs, may also relieve themselves when being held—either because they are very comfortable or anxious. We warn clients about that possibility and use a blanket or towel on their laps for animal comfort and as a protective barrier.

Some animal behavior can be both undesired and potentially harmful to clients. The clinician's job is to be aware of, curtail, or train alternatives to these behaviors. Our goats like to wrestle and headbutt each other, but occasionally they also want to do this with humans. We are transforming the headbutting behavior of our large goat Lily into a therapeutic task for both Lily and the client by teaching her to "stay" and to push against a yoga ball instead of people.

Animals' sexual behavior can also be an issue, as animals go through phases of maturity and sexuality, and under different circumstances, they would be seeking a mate. Animals do not have hesitation or embarrassment about performing mating behaviors in front of clients. This can either present a problem or an opportunity, depending on your perspective and how you handle it with clients. If we become uncomfortable and awkward, then it becomes clear this is a "bad" or taboo situation. However, if we can be prepared for a calm discussion with clients and address the situation without judgment or discomfort, we may find that it leads to a therapeutic discussion. We have been surprised by how many clients took our goats' mating behavior as an invitation to discuss their own sexual issues or dilemmas. We have included the possibility of seeing animal sexual behavior in our disclosure statement, so that clients and caregivers/guardians are aware of the issue, and we can have a conversation if needed.

ANIMAL CERTIFICATION

We recommend getting your animal certified whenever possible, because it provides an external evaluation of the animal's skills and the relationship between you and your animal, which enables you to work safely as a team. Becoming certified demonstrates your level of expertise and competency in working with the animal. Certification not only tests specific skills, but also puts you and your animal in mildly stressful situations to evaluate how you deal with those situations as a team. Each certifying organization has different expectations and standards, including rules about the animal's age and the length of your ownership.

Most animals that get certified are dogs, and we believe that therapy dogs should be trained and certified. There are some organizations, such as Pet Partners, that will certify other animals as well. However, most certifying organizations are geared toward volunteer opportunities with therapy animals, such as taking an animal into settings such as hospitals, schools, libraries, or hospices.

This work is quite different from the work you do with your animal in AACP. Therefore, most certification exams will ask your animal to demonstrate behaviors that might not be necessary or helpful in your counseling setting. For example, they may require your animal to be on-leash or contained (for example, a cat in a basket). We prefer that animals be unencumbered during counseling sessions, to allow for natural, spontaneous interactions and to empower the animal to choose whether and how to interact.

There are a few organizations geared toward clinicians and their dogs (Professional Therapy Dogs of Colorado is one example). Their examination process is more relevant to the work we do in a clinical setting, and we hope to see more of these organizations as time goes on.

MATCHING CLIENTS AND ANIMALS

At AATPC, we have numerous clinicians with unique specialties and interests and various types of animals. This diversity allows us to match each client's clinical needs with the most appropriate clinician and to choose the most suitable animal, depending on the client's preference and clinical treatment. Several years ago, our therapy dogs were the most requested animals to work with, but now all our animals are equally in demand, from our rats and guinea pigs to our horses and donkeys. Some clients may begin their work feeling unsure or fearful of certain animals, but eventually decide they would like to overcome these fears. We then work together clinically to build the capacity to partner with those animals.

Matching clients and animals is a more complex process than merely responding to a client's preference. We may choose an individual animal based on a client's treatment goals; for instance, our stubborn and independent goat, Lily, may work with a client who is practicing patience and frustration tolerance. When Ellen worked with a child with ADHD, Sasha was a great match, because she was calm and focused and could help a child regulate. The client could pet Sasha while practicing mindfulness and centering. However, young Rupert was not always a good fit for these clients, because while he could match the client's energy, he also became distracting and overstimulating for them. Sometimes, the client could help Rupert calm down and focus, and thus practice and utilize those skills themselves. The decision about which animal to include and which is best suited for a session depends on the client, their goals, their presentation at each session, the clinician's abilities, the benefit to the animal, and countless other variables.

The factors affecting the match of client and animal can change from week to week. Having a variety of animal species and individual animals allows us to work with an animal that can help the client meet certain treatment goals. These goals may change over time, as could the client's ability or desire to work with certain animals. Often, clients will "graduate" to working with more challenging animals who can help them learn new skills, healthier ways to interact with others, and how to create and maintain positive relationships. We feel lucky that we can offer work with different animals to best meet our clients' therapeutic goals. However, we do recognize that our situation is unique and not all clinicians will have the ability or opportunity to work with multiple animals. If you have one animal to work with, you may modify the interventions you do with each client, matching them carefully to the client and their issues, or you may choose not to do AACP with certain clients.

DUAL ROLES

Because this book focuses on mental health professionals conducting AACP, your role in sessions becomes more complicated. You are not only the clinician responsible for the welfare of your client, but you are also the handler responsible for your animal's well-being. The balance between the welfare of your client and that of your animal is a very complex issue. We do occasionally have to manage animal behaviors that are a risk to clients, such as a cranky horse trying to nip or a feisty goat attempting to play (Chassman Craddock, 2024a, 2024b). We have also had several situations where we had to stop a client's behavior that could have harmed our animal, such as a child throwing toys or becoming physically aggressive. These behaviors may have been allowed as therapeutic expression in other settings, but we cannot allow them around the animals because of the safety risk to our animals. We do not allow clients to act aggressively or demonstrate negative emotions at the animals. Clients may be frustrated or irritated if the animals do not listen, but they cannot act out against the animals. If clients are too upset to regulate, they are moved away from the animal. We do have therapy rooms and areas where clients can act out physically and express themselves in more aggressive ways, but those areas are away from our animals.

We are our animals' advocates: their voice and protectors. It is an ethical decision in the moment about when you intervene with a client's behavior. We never allow clients to engage with our animals in ways that knowingly make the animals uncomfortable or puts anyone in unsafe situations. That said, even with the most careful supervision, events can occur that an animal will not enjoy, such as an awkward pet or a loud noise. In the moment, it is an ethical decision to decide when and how to intervene and when to let the moment pass.

For example, working with a client who shouts out of excitement and briefly startles the animal would be handled differently than a client who yells at an animal out of anger. A client may play chase or tag with an active therapy dog during session as a fun game, but in the next session, tries to chase a different dog who does not like to chase and feels stressed. As clinicians, we need to be aware and respond. Does the client notice and understand this difference and stop their behavior, or do they need some quick intervention and guidance to understand that this dog is unhappy with the game? One client may try to pet a cat in a clumsy way without knowing it is uncomfortable to the cat, while another client may try to irritate the cat with an awkward pet; we need to use our clinical judgement and knowledge of the client and the situation to decide how to respond in a way that is therapeutically appropriate and helpful. What this response looks like will depend on the client, the animal, the behavior, the clinician's comfort, and other day-to-day elements. If you are going to work with your animal, be prepared to encounter and answer these questions regularly.

TERMINATING WITH CLIENTS

When clients finish their therapeutic work with us, it is essential to allow them the opportunity to say goodbye to the animals with whom they have worked. Clients have developed important relationships with the animals, and modeling healthy endings is an important part of the treatment process. Our animals have also likely bonded with the clients, so they need the opportunity to say goodbye as well.

When clients are finishing therapy, we may provide them with a photo of their favorite animal and have the animal "write" them a letter on the back. The animal might thank them for taking them on walks, helping to calm them down when they felt nervous, or share a special memory. This type of personalized transitional object is a reminder of the significance of the mutual relationship that the client and animal built over time. Sometimes a clinician will also give a small token to the client, such as a stuffed animal, picture frame, or painted paw print. We may also share photos of the clients and a special therapy animal. Because our approach is relationship-centered, teaching the clients that relationships continue, even if there is no more contact, is an important lesson. The client has made a permanent imprint on the animal, as much as we hope the animal has made on the client.

ANIMALS RETIRING

Therapy is not a permanent business for any animal. There will come a point when they let us know they are ready to retire. Ellen's dog Sasha made it clear that she was ready to work less when she spent less time with clients and went to the door earlier in the session, asking to be let out (which she always was). Regardless of the clients that the animals work with, it is hard work for them. Just as this work is hard and emotionally draining for us, it can also have that impact on our animals.

Retirement may often be related to an animal's age, but not always. We must allow the animals to make the choice if and when they are ready to slow down or stop. Our rat Ethel retired at about two years old, but not because she stopped liking clients. While she loved playing with clients, the busy ranch setting was too hectic for her and she had begun to overgroom, which was a sign of stress. We made the decision to let her retire at Linda's home where she lived for 18 more happy months. She had done remarkable work with many clients, and she earned those months of leisure. Had she been kept at the ranch, even in retirement, we doubt she would have enjoyed so many more months of her life.

Preparing clients for the retirement of animals is never easy. Clients will need time to say goodbye to their cherished friend and may not understand or fully grasp the reasons the animal is leaving. Providing ample time for the client and animal to be together and say goodbye is helpful and therapeutically essential. Allowing the client to realize the clinician's and animal's struggle about retirement can be therapeutic. We can help the client to understand the reasons for retirement and that they are in the best interest of the animal. We can also have discussions about the healthy, relaxed life that the animal will have in retirement. Clients can write goodbye letters and send well-wishes to the animal so that they can feel they have had a chance to have a good ending. If clinicians feel comfortable sharing, they may also provide updates to clients or share pictures of the animal in retirement at later sessions.

SAYING A FINAL GOODBYE

Death is an inevitable part of life. We have had more final goodbyes than we like to think about. Linda's first AATPC cat, Mazey, died at just 14 months, only a few months after AATPC first opened. Linda also had to say goodbye to her original therapy cat, Norman, in 2014, when he was about 18 years old. Ellen's therapy dog, Sasha, passed away in 2017, and it was heartbreaking for Ellen. Due to the shorter nature of their lives, we have had many sad farewells to our smaller animals, such as guinea pigs and rats. In the last few years, our miniature horse, Stormy, our senior horse, Cody, and our pygmy goats, Duncan and Dahlia, have passed away, all due to age-related health issues. As an organization, we had planned as much as we could for these eventual goodbyes, with as much care for their comfort and well-being as we could, while also minimizing potential trauma to clients. These animals helped form the culture and history of our organization, and they will always be in our hearts and minds.

While losing our animals is painful and devastating to us as clinicians and family, it is also very difficult for our clients. Some have never experienced the loss of a loved one, while others may have experienced a loss, but were not given the opportunity to openly grieve or to process the loss. Balancing our own grief while providing space for our clients to grieve for the beloved animal is difficult. How much of our own grief and feeling can or should we share? When our hearts are breaking, how do we let our clients experience the loss in the way they need to? There are no easy answers to these questions. What we have found is that some level of self-disclosure and genuineness is appropriate and helpful for both the clinician and client. This level will change depending on the clinician, the client, and the circumstances of the death. By sharing our sadness and allowing the client the opportunity to say goodbye, we can all process and heal. We can honor our animals by allowing others to express their appreciation and love for them, and give them a way to have an ending that is meaningful to them.

For each animal goodbye, we have had an open memorial for clients, volunteers, staff, and others who felt the need or desire to say a more formal goodbye.

Our sweet Rosie, who passed away during publication of this book.

We have done our best to honor these animals and the gift they gave to us and our clients. We hope that we are providing an example of how to say goodbye with respect, reverence, and grace, while also acknowledging the difficult feelings. Many of our new offices are named after these legacy animals, and we have a beautiful memorial rose garden to remember their gifts to us.

REFERENCES

Chassman Craddock, L. (2023). The clinician's role in managing safety during animal assisted psychotherapy. *Animal Behaviour & Welfare Cases*. https://www.cabidigital library.org/doi/abs/10.1079/abwcases.2023.0019

Jegatheesan, B. (2015). Influence of cultural and religious factors on attitudes towards animals. In A. H. Fine (Ed.), *Handbook on animal-assisted therapy: Theoretical foundations and guidelines for practice*. Elselvier.

Rugass, T. (2006). *On talking terms with dogs: Calming signals* (2nd ed.). Dog Wise.

Stewart, L. A., Chang, C. Y., & Rice, R. (2013). Emergent theory and model of practice in animal-assisted therapy in counseling. *Journal of Creativity in Mental Health*, *8*(4), 329–348.

Tran-Lien, A. (2017). Working like a dog: Legal considerations for "therapy dogs." *The Therapist* (September/October 2017).

3

CAN WE BE PARTNERS? ACQUIRING AND TRAINING THERAPY ANIMALS

"If having a soul means being able to feel love and loyalty and gratitude, then animals are better off than a lot of humans."

—*JAMES HERRIOT*

S ome of the most frequent discussions we have with clinicians hoping to practice AACP are about obtaining and training a potential therapy animal. Because many types of individual animals can be tremendous therapy partners—and each animal requires a different type and intensity of training—there is not a clear set of guidelines about this process. That said, we do have some recommendations based on our experiences and beliefs. The following chapter addresses those topics as comprehensively as we are able.

OBTAINING YOUR THERAPY ANIMAL

There is no guaranteed way to find a therapy animal. It is always lovely when you realize that a current pet would make a great therapy partner. The authors both recognized something special in our pets and were inspired to work with them. However, often clinicians will believe in the power of animals and the human-animal bond, but they do not yet have an animal that is appropriate for therapy work. In fact, most animals will not be good therapy partners, as it is a special animal who has the right combination of temperament, skill, and desire.

The best therapy animal partners, first and foremost, are your family members. You have the bond necessary to understand, love, and trust each other. You have chosen them, raised them, and demonstrated a consistent level of love and commitment. Your animal needs to trust that they are safe, even as you put them in new, changing, and sometimes stressful situations. You both must trust and understand that you can navigate these challenges together. Most certification organizations will not certify animals under one year of age, and they must be in your care for a minimum of 6 to 12 months. This allows you to develop this strong bond and to communicate with each other in a wide range of circumstances.

There is always the potential that your animal decides they do not like being a therapy animal, but they will remain a member of your family. We tell all our students and staff that you must be willing and excited to have this animal in your life, whether or not they become your therapy animal. It can be difficult to put your hopes and dreams on a single animal and then to honestly acknowledge that your animal does not want or is not suited to do therapy work. We want to avoid having animals who are stressed, unhappy, and do not feel respected and heard by their owners. If you go into this looking for a family member to share your life with, and you can also work with them, that is a gift.

We recommend that whenever possible, clinicians adopt animals from shelters or rescue organizations. This helps an animal in need, one who has likely experienced difficulties or losses in their lives, and it gives context to your animals' personality and behavior. Our animals' stories are one of the most helpful aspects of AACP, because clients can connect with and find parallels with the animals' lives. Clients may feel that the animal understands them or sees them in a different way than others, because they have experienced similar events. Adopting or rescuing also helps our clients to see that we do not expect perfection and that we are willing to see past challenges to give someone another chance.

Many clinicians want to obtain purebred animals, and there may be purebred animals at shelters as well. We have worked with clinicians who adopted purebred but "imperfect" animals—those deemed unacceptable to the breeder and their typical clientele. One clinician got a Pomeranian with a heart murmur and alopecia, another got a Welsh corgi with one droopy ear. Though purebred, these animals were essentially rescued because they were unwanted and would likely have been euthanized or given to a shelter. These stories of rejection by their previous owners helped the clients relate to dogs who felt they did not fit in, were not accepted by their families, or felt physically different than those around them.

If you choose to purchase a specific breed of animal for certain qualities or traits, remember that your individual dog may not choose to do therapy work or it may not be a good fit, regardless of breed or bloodline. Clients may also have a more difficult time connecting to a purebred animal. The animal may not have a history that the client can relate to, or the client may wonder if you will accept their imperfections. For better or worse, our clients make assumptions based on the interactions they witness and the stories they know, so having an animal with a rich, complex background can provide a great deal of therapeutic material.

ANIMAL AGE

There are many advantages to adopting a puppy or a kitten: you get to raise, socialize, and train them in preparation for the work you hope they will do someday. You can establish a strong bond with your animal without worrying about their history or challenging experiences/behaviors that you may need to untrain. You are also able to see the young animal's personality and try to provide opportunities to allow them to be friendly and open to therapy work. However, young animals do not always grow into the animals we expect. As babies, animals may be more willing to tolerate certain experiences and then later determine that they do not like these same experiences. Just like children, young animals' personalities and desires change, and it takes time for them to develop and make choices for themselves. While it can be disappointing if you have built a practice around your animal and they decide they do not want to participate, this is also totally acceptable, as we emphasize the need to give each animal the choice to do therapy work. Linda learned this with her cat, Samantha, who was a social and engaging kitten but grew into a more solitary, aloof cat. She loved therapy work as a kitten and then decided it was not for her; Linda accepted this, and Samantha became a happy house cat.

When you adopt a grown animal, you are bringing in an animal that has had experiences that shaped its personality and potentially created some challenging behaviors. You will likely need to spend time socializing and training this animal to feel safe and comfortable with you before you can determine if they want to work as a therapy animal. Often, rescued animals adjust well to being part of your family and working with you, but there will be times that their past experiences do not mesh well with our professional goals. We have found that often the work we do with our adult animals to help them overcome their earlier experiences prepares them (and us) to be great therapy partners.

There are multiple organizations that work with shelter animals and train them to be good pets; these rescues know their animals very well and can suggest an animal that meets your family and professional needs. Colorado Cell Dogs is an organization that helps rehabilitate dogs by pairing them with prisoners who have been taught how to be dog trainers. Linda's dog, Rupert, was adopted from Freedom Service Dogs, an organization that takes shelter dogs and trains them to be service dogs. Though Rupert did not qualify as a service dog due to social anxiety, he did have the temperament and basic training to be a wonderful therapy dog. Furthermore, clients can relate to Rupert's experiences with anxiety; we can reframe his story to show that Rupert did not fail but instead found a path that better suited his needs, abilities, and preferences.

Regardless of how you decide to obtain your animal, they are a part of your family first, and your therapy partner second. Choosing an animal that fits into your family's lifestyle, budget, and comfort is more important than finding an animal well-suited for your work. If you do hope to work with your animal, look for one who is social, trainable, and comfortable with the population with whom you work. Ellen's dog, Sasha, was comfortable around all people, but she preferred to work with calmer clients. Some animals may be more anxious around loud noises and unpredictable behavior; other animals may be wary of individuals of a certain gender or stature. A horse rescued from an abusive home may have ingrained fears about hats, for instance, whereas a goat may see hats as something to grab and nibble. It is a special cat that can tolerate an excitable child, but some dogs love it.

Give your animal time to be part of your family and expose them to different environments and types of people before attempting to incorporate them into your work. If, and when, you do integrate them into your work, start slowly so that they can adjust to the new demands and expectations being placed upon them. Be alert for signs of stress, anxiety, boredom, illness, and any other indications that they prefer not to be at work. And most important, allow them to choose every day if they want to go to work with you.

PET VS. BORROWED

You may know an animal you think would be an ideal therapy animal, but it lives with your parent, neighbor, or friend. As discussed above, the ideal partnership is with an animal that you own, have a deep connection with, and is considered family. This loyalty and bond cannot be replaced. Working with someone else's animal means you do not know the animal as well—their quirks, behavioral cues, and preferences—but also that you may not be aware of events in their daily life that may impact their ability to work. Your neighbor's dog may have encountered a rough stranger on a walk and be skittish for the week, but if you were not present for that encounter, you may not know why he is suddenly unfriendly with clients.

It is also common practice for horse stables to lend out horses to work in equine therapy sessions. Not knowing the horse can be particularly dangerous, since horses are large, sensitive, and sometimes unpredictable. But if you take the time to get to know particular horses and they learn to trust you, this may be an option to integrate animals that you are not able to own independently.

AATPC has resident animals who live at the ranch and are essentially owned by the nonprofit. Ellen and Linda think of all the animals as part of their family, and for years, we were the primary caregivers. We now have a ranch manager to monitor and care for the animals; however, each intern, staff member, and volunteer begins their work at AATPC by spending time with the animals and developing a mutually trusting relationship with them.

WILD VS. DOMESTIC

There are many wonderful animals in the world that could make tremendous therapy animals, but in all likelihood, they do not want to—nor should they be—therapy animals. Dolphin-assisted therapy has been presented as an exciting new option, with claims of success particularly with individuals on the autism spectrum. Not only have the results on its effectiveness been repeatedly challenged (Marino, 2021), but many clinicians, including us, question the ethics of asking wild animals to work for humans without choice.

Linda's dream is to adopt a baby tiger and Ellen's is to adopt a baby elephant! However, we know these are just dreams, and that tigers and elephants are wild animals and have not been adapted to live around humans, let alone work with them. Wild animals' happiness depends on the ability to remain wild, not being expected to conform to the living environment we may create for them. The animals in AATPC's family include dogs, cats, horses, donkeys, alpacas, goats, rabbits, rats, guinea pigs, ferrets, chickens, insects, a snake, and a lizard. Some are owned by the ranch and some by individual clinicians. We have turned down opportunities to be given hedgehogs and sugar gliders (which are becoming increasingly popular as pets) because we are not convinced that these semi-domesticated animals would be comfortable with the demands of being around a wide variety of humans during much of the day and week.

There are numerous issues around including non-domesticated animals in therapy. For starters: do they want to be around people, how do we know if they do, and do we know enough about their nonverbal communication to understand what they need? Plus, being around people is likely to be inherently more stressful for them as they have not evolved for human relationships. There also will be different medical issues in keeping non-domesticated animals, so you must be aware of those issues and have a vet who is familiar with that species. There are some animal rescues that allow observation and perhaps some interaction with wildlife/non-domestic animals when they are unable to be fully rehabilitated to return to the wild; however, that does not fully address the safety and stress issues for the animal and clients.

THERAPY DOGS

As with any animal, there is no one right way to find a therapy dog, and even dogs bred from other therapy dogs are not guaranteed to be successful therapy dogs themselves. Generally, we suggest that clinicians look at shelters and rescue organizations for prospective dogs to work with, because, as mentioned above, animals that are rescued have a history and experiences that may resonate with clients.

It is important to remember that even if you choose a prospective puppy from a litter with therapy lines, or a hypoallergenic breed that is typically good with people, each individual dog may not be suited to do therapy work or may not work well with your clientele. You may have a playful puppy but work in a small office with calm adults who do not want an energetic dog who becomes an unwanted distraction, rather than a therapeutic asset. A calm, snuggly dog may be too boring for some active clients or be too attached to their owner to engage with clients. Since their personalities change as they grow, even observing the dog in a social situation is not a guarantee of how they will respond to working with clients who are experiencing strong emotions and behaviors. This is important to remember because you are adding a family member, even if they choose not to work as a therapy dog.

It is also important to match your dog with your setting; some dogs will do well in a quieter office setting but feel stressed in a more active, busy setting. For instance, schools can be a chaotic, noisy environment that some dogs love but that is incredibly stressful for others. Our ranch environment is highly complex and therefore potentially stressful, as there are a lot of people and animals coming and going all day. Moreover, a therapy dog may not always be involved in a session and therefore be away from their owner, so they also need to tolerate that separation. We have had several great therapy dogs that were too stressed in our environment but were able to work well in a calmer setting. For these reasons, finding "a good therapy dog" for your situation is a complex and multifaceted question that will depend on countless factors, and sometimes you do not know if it is the right fit until you try.

THERAPY CATS

Choosing a therapy cat is tricky because cats are ever-changing, complex creatures. We recommend that you get a cat because you love them as your pet, and then if you notice that they enjoy socializing and riding in the car with you, then allow them the opportunity to explore being a therapy cat. If you introduce them to your clients and your office environment and they enjoy the work, then perhaps you may have found a good partner.

If you have a kitten that you are hoping will want to come to work with you, socialize them early: take them in the car, let people of all ages interact with and pet them, take them to new locations, and give them a diversity of experiences. This will give you good information about your cat's interest in leaving home and interacting with others, and will help your cat to be more sociable and adaptable for your work in the future. Having had several great therapy cats, as well as several cats who determined they did not want to work, Linda has learned a lot about therapy cats. Two important lessons are: (1) cat personalities can change dramatically over time; and (2) it only takes one negative experience to impact a cat and alter its behavior for a long time, so ensure their environment is a safe one. One dog chasing them in a certain location may frighten them enough to not want to return to that location.

To find a cat, you can work with a local shelter, rescue, or foster agency that has their adoptable cats in someone's home. The foster parent may have a great deal of information about the cat's history and preferences. If you are looking for particular qualities in a cat, this option may prove the most fruitful since they will know the cat well.

SMALL ANIMALS: RATS, RABBITS, GUINEA PIGS, FERRETS, REPTILES, INSECTS, AND MORE

Small animals, like rats, rabbits, and guinea pigs, tend to be more cautious and shyer, especially when meeting new people, so it may take longer for you to determine if they are a good fit as a therapy animal. With almost all our small animals, we spend several weeks getting to know them, their likes and dislikes, nonverbal cues, and how comfortable they are at the ranch before we integrate them into sessions. It is not until we learn as much as possible and the animals feel comfortable with us, that we begin to bring them into therapy sessions and let clients work with them. In general, getting small animals when they are young is helpful, because you can handle and socialize them immediately. You can help them feel comfortable and safe when being played with or held.

We have been gifted small animals by individuals who could not care for them anymore, and we also purposely have adopted small animals. Our first pair of rats was given to us by an experienced clinician who had worked with them for some time, so they were eager and well suited to working with clients. Our next rats were all adopted from shelters, rescued from pet stores, or relinquished by former owners. Many pet stores will have rats for adoption; you can also look for rats that have been bred for reptile food, which is how we rescued several of our girls. There are several different species of domestic rats that are available for adoption. We have had standard rats and Dumbo rats, which are slightly bigger with large, round ears.

If you are looking for small animals to adopt, try to meet several animals and look to see who comes to your hand and shows curiosity and interest in meeting you and being held. You want an animal that appears social and friendly and is not stressed by interaction the with a human. If you are choosing among a group of rats, we have found that the ones who "popcorn," making a squeaky noise and bobbing up and down, are usually the more secure, friendly, interactive rats. You cannot predict their personality once they grow older or come home with you, but there are some traits that are more favorable for a therapy animal, such as that initial confidence and friendliness.

Our guinea pigs and rabbits were obtained from local shelters. We received bonus guinea pigs when one of our adopted piggies was pregnant and surprised us with three babies. We do not breed our animals, but this was an exciting accident that completed our guinea pig family. We have worked with several breeds of guinea pigs, including American guinea pigs and hairless guinea pigs, also called skinny pigs. Adopting hairless guinea pigs provides a difference that clients immediately notice, and they often use projection about how the pigs must feel. The skinny pigs are remarkably soft, and it is always surprising how many clients gravitate toward them. As with other small animals, look for a friendly and curious pig.

Our first rabbit, Maggie, was left at our ranch by a family who could not take care of her, and she was very shy and reserved. Because rabbits often want to live in pairs, we realized Maggie might be lonely, so we reached out to our local House Rabbit Society and put Maggie through the rabbit version of speed dating. We brought Maggie to the shelter and met dozens of male rabbits, choosing several we thought would make a good partner for Maggie but who would also be comfortable around humans as a therapy rabbit. Maggie was then introduced to each rabbit and spent several hours with each one as we watched their interactions. The final choice was Maggie's; she picked a large black rabbit named K.C. She was initially intimidated by his size, but K.C. was very patient, allowing Maggie to approach, run away, and approach again, for hours until they finally touched their noses to say hello. Over the next several days, Maggie and K.C. spent time together at the shelter while we got daily updates about their progress. Maggie chose well, and K.C. was a loving and respectful partner and a friendly and gentle therapy rabbit. Maggie and K.C. have since both died of old age, but paintings of them decorate our rabbit room and look over our current therapy rabbits.

If you have a space where the rabbit can freely roam and will not be harmed by other animals, such as dogs and cats, we recommend contacting your local House Rabbit Society. Rabbits are often abandoned, especially after Easter when they grow larger and the novelty has worn off for the humans. Rabbits enjoy living in pairs so if there are two rabbits that enjoy each other's company and are comfortable with humans, it can be great to have opportunities to observe their relationship dynamics. Just be sure they are the same gender or spayed/neutered, otherwise you may have baby rabbits to manage.

Our current ferrets were rehomed to us after their owner could not give them the time and attention they needed. There are ferret rescues around the country that can help you choose a pair of ferrets that might work well with your clients. Ferrets' gregarious nature makes them a fun animal to work with, but not all ferrets enjoy being handled by humans and may bite. Make sure you have met the ferret, interacted with them, and they seem comfortable engaging with you. Ferrets are active and like to run around and explore, so they can be good for clients who like active sessions. As ferrets age, they may slow down, which can provide more snuggle time. Ferrets are social, so getting at least two ferrets is important. They can also live in larger groups if you have the time, energy, and space for a whole family of ferrets.

Though we do not have reptiles living at our ranch, we do have several colleagues, interns, staff members, and students in our certificate program who work with reptiles such as bearded dragons, snakes, and turtles. They have shared that these animals love interacting with humans and are familiar with their stress signs. Because we have not worked extensively with this group of animals, it is not in our scope of expertise to say much about how to acquire a good therapy reptile; however, local shelters and reptile rescues should have knowledge about the personality and preferences of the particular animals. Overall, as with any therapy animal, you want a reptile who seems comfortable around humans and enjoys social interaction.

The newest type of animals at our ranch are insects. We have a millipede, several horn worms, and Madagascar cockroaches, all purchased from a reputable entomologist. We want to ensure that our insects are treated with respect and are not taken from their wild homes; that said, we have found injured insects in our garden and helped them to recuperate with the plan to return them to their natural environment. For example, a clinician and client found a praying mantis with a broken leg that likely would have perished if left outside. During their session, they thoughtfully and carefully created a suitable temporary environment for the mantis so they could observe and feed it; they were able to release it when it appeared stronger. Not only was this a humane act, but it was a powerful therapeutic interaction and process for the client, as they were able to witness another creature in need, identify and help meet those needs, and watch as the creature healed as a result.

HORSES AND OTHER EQUINES

All of our horses have been adopted from horse rescues or have been given to us by owners who could no longer care for them. Our miniature horses came as a pair from a trusted friend who no longer had space for them, and our first full size horse, Cody, came to us after his horse companion died and as a result he had begun to show health issues. When our veterinarian evaluated Cody, he appeared sound and enjoyed interacting with us. It was an adjustment for him and for the miniature horses when he joined the ranch, and it took some time for them to establish a friendship and hierarchy. This is an important consideration if you have a horse or a herd already; you will need to determine how a new member will fit in and how the herd will respond.

As mentioned earlier, we generally recommend that you include your own horse or equine, rather than occasionally working with someone else's animal, so that you know their history, personality, quirks, preferences, and daily experiences. There are many horse rescues that know their horses well and can advise you of a horse that is a good fit for your space and client population. We also recommend that you have a veterinarian evaluate the horse you are considering, as there are many horse health issues that can become problematic and costly. As with other animals, you also need to accept this horse as part of your forever family, because there are no guarantees that they will want or be able to work with you. Horses' lifespan and cost of care are often a major considerations for owning them, so make sure that you can care for your horse for the duration of their life and that you are prepared to pay the bills for vets, farriers, teeth cleaning, hay, supplements, and any other costs your horse might accrue.

Like all our animals, we allow the horses to opt out of sessions, by walking away or refusing to engage with the client. Our horses also let us know when it is time to retire with their behavior and other physical cues. Our miniature horse, Misty, is now in semi-retirement, which means that she is still with the herd but will not be asked to work with a client, though she may join a session if she chooses.

FARM ANIMALS: ALPACAS, GOATS, CHICKENS, AND OTHERS

There are numerous farm animals that can be wonderful therapy animals. We have been lucky to work with alpacas, several types of goats, and chickens; we have colleagues who work with pigs, cows, and sheep. Our standard advice applies here: get an animal you are willing to have as part of your family, that you are either familiar with or are willing to learn about, and that you can provide with the space, care, and longevity they require. We quickly discovered that pygmy goats and Nubian goats had different skills and needs; the pygmy goats could sneak through small fence openings as babies and jumped onto everything, whereas the Nubian goats could knock over a fence or a client. Ensure that you know the differences in animal breeds and how this impacts their needs and behaviors.

Many farm animals are social and need companionship. Often this means having two of the same type of animal, but there are times when cross-species friendship can also meet those needs. Our pygmy goat, Duncan, and our full-size horse, Cody, were great friends and liked to eat together, but they also both enjoyed spending time with their own species.

There are rescue organizations that have farm animals, and these may be a good place to start your search; there are also usually species-specific rescues for farm animals. There may be breeders who have animals that will not sell for a variety of reasons, and you may be able to provide a good home for them. We loved getting our goats as babies and they feel like family, but we have also created strong bonds with our rescued adult animals.

SOCIALIZATION AND TRAINING

Ideally, therapy animals should be well socialized and exposed to a variety of settings, circumstances, animals, and people of different ages, genders, and cultures, so that they are comfortable with the ever-changing environment of a therapy setting. If possible, exposing animals when they are young is very beneficial. Before the animal starts working with clients, it is essential to give the animal time to feel safe in the clinical setting. This allows you to see how your animal reacts in the setting and if it is a good fit for them. During sessions, watching for the animal's continued comfort and choice to engage with clients is essential.

There are many different approaches to training animals. We strongly believe that animals should be trained with positive-based, force-free methods. Even if other methods seem effective, they are detrimental to your animal's safety, well-being, and relationship with you. In addition, your client is watching and learning from you and your treatment of your animal. If clients see you pulling on a choke chain, yelling, or intimidating your animal into compliance, their sense of safety and trust in you may be compromised. Clients may question whether you will accept their mistakes and wonder how you will support them during tough times. Positive training and engagement with your animal also models the impact of positive motivators and interactions on behavior. Firsthand observation of the positive change in behavior without yelling or punishment can be very powerful to clients and family members. If a task cannot be done using a positive training technique, it may not be worth training or may be beyond your animal's abilities. For instance, if your dog refuses to drop a ball during fetch despite positive training methods, this may not be an activity to do with clients. Or, if your goat refuses to learn how to jump onto a tree stump, perhaps you can find a different trick to teach them. Therapy animals need to be able to tolerate and behave safely when exposed to the sometimes-stressful conditions that occur in therapy, such as loud voices, unpredictable behavior, and emotional outbursts. You must be able to notice if your animal is stressed and respond appropriately, and this ability to notice and respond is based on a trusting relationship, which begins with positive training.

Training an animal requires that you have a motivating reward for your animal—often food, but it also can be a toy or the sound of a clicker, if they are clicker trained. A verbal reward, such as "good girl!" or "yes!" is also helpful and can act as a marker of the correct behavior. We use a combination of verbal cues, treats, toys, and clicker training with our animals. We recommend having both a verbal and a hand signal for commands, as a hand signal allows you to silently give a request to your animal without interrupting clients and allows nonverbal clients to train your animal. For many animals, the verbal and hand cues, paired with a treat or verbal praise, is sufficient for training. Since most skills are complex behaviors, you can start with reinforcing increasing approximations of the desired behavior and giving a reward each time they are closer to performing the behavior you desire. For example, if you are training "shake" or "paw," each time the animal moves their foot, you may say "yes!" and give a treat. Eventually, you can give a verbal or hand signal for the desired behavior and only reward them once they have completed the full task. With clicker training, you need a specific clicker device as well as treats. The "click" is paired with a treat, so that the animal learns that the click marks the requested behavior, and eventually, the click becomes a reward in itself. We have done clicker training with dogs, cats, horses,

Our good friend Shlomit, training our goat, Lily.

goats, and chickens, and it is a wonderful way to train, but does require a bit more equipment and the ability to multitask.

Training therapy animals can also be an important and powerful intervention for clients. We encourage the client's participation in training the animals, as it provides many useful learning opportunities. As you will see in the upcoming chapters, training can be done with most therapy animals. We use both clicker training and simple positive reinforcement techniques. Clicker training is nice because it teaches the client a new skill that requires some coordination and mastery. We usually start with the client using the clicker to mark the behavior and the clinician giving the treat. As the client becomes more adept at training, they can do both behaviors. There are many wonderful books on training animals using clickers and other positive forms of reinforcement.

TRAINING DOGS TO ASSIST IN THERAPY

One of the first steps in working with a future therapy dog is socialization. This means getting them out into the world and allowing them to feel comfortable in different settings, with various ground textures, noises, lighting, surroundings, and many other variables. Therapy dogs also need to be comfortable meeting new and unique people—big, small, loud, active, slow, and the countless other ways that people vary. Bring your dog to venues and locations such as outdoor restaurants and shops, pet stores, farmers markets, stores like Home Depot, dog parks, and anywhere else they are welcome and can interact with friendly people. Invite people to say hi to your dog; having treats with you and giving other people treats to share with your dog teaches your dog that they are rewarded by being in new places and interacting with people, which encourages them to be social and friendly.

In addition to socialization, dogs generally require training prior to working as a therapy dog. Each therapy dog may need to possess different skill sets depending on their work environment and clientele. A dog in an office setting may need to learn how to ride an elevator; a dog in a school may need to learn how to tolerate the bell and chaotic nature of the hallway; and a dog in a ranch setting will need to be trained to safely interact with various animals. To teach these skills, we recommend only force-free trainers. We are adamant about working with trainers who do not use forceful, shameful, fear-based, or dominance-based training methods. Additionally, we will not work with a trainer who uses a metal choke or prong collar or "corrects" a dog with a yank at the throat. Though it is beyond the scope of this book, the dominance method of dog hierarchy and training has been shown to be not only misinformed, but harmful to the dog and the relationship with the owner (Bradshaw, 2012).

Force-free training methods may take slightly longer to teach skills, but they do work with consistency and practice. If the dog cannot learn a certain skill, it is worth evaluating if it is necessary and/or if it is somehow uncomfortable or stressful for the dog. For instance, at one of our intensive workshops, participants were trying to teach Rupert a new trick called "sit pretty" or "bear," where a dog sits back on its back legs, its torso upright and front feet held up. Rupert is a smart dog and a tremendous learner, but he refused to perform this skill and we quickly realized that it was uncomfortable for him to sit in that position due to his size and joint issues. If a trainer had used force and yanked him into position, he may have been able to perform the skill, but at a cost to his own health, well-being, and trust in his trainer and owner. Moreover, because training dogs is a powerful intervention with our clients, we want to model techniques that show respect and convey our trust and love toward the animal. We also want our clients to feel safe with us and our animals, and seeing us force our animals to behave in a certain manner could impact the client's sense of safety with us (McConnell, 2003).

Our therapy dogs need to be reliable and predictable, so we know that they will respond if we use a voice command or hand signal to interrupt a potentially dangerous behavior. Clinicians also need to know that their animal can tolerate the quickly changing environments and emotions they will be exposed to in therapy sessions. However, it is essential to note that the training for a therapy dog is vastly different from that of a service dog, and we have different expectations of our animals. We do not want or need our dogs to be as "perfectly" trained as service dogs for numerous reasons. Most of all, we want our dogs to be dogs. Including them in therapy sessions should not take away from their "dogness," and that is what makes animal-assisted work so powerful. Clients connect to the animals and their stories, even more so when the animals engage in a behavior that the clients can relate to and understand. The dog's personality quirks, challenging behaviors, and antics add levity to sessions and allow clients to relate. Clients can also help the animal manage and solve challenging behaviors. When we accept and embrace our animals' flaws, clients recognize that we will accept their own human imperfections. Our animals' behaviors allow you to see what the client notices, how they interpret the world and others' behavior, and then how they respond. These situations can become hugely teachable and therapeutic moments.

SOCIALIZING CATS TO ASSIST IN THERAPY

Cats also can be socialized and trained to be therapy animals, though they may learn fewer specific tricks than dogs. Cats primarily need socialization, so exposing cats to a wide range of people will help you to learn if they have the temperament and interest to be a therapy cat. As with dogs, introducing them to friends who offer treats can help cats be excited to meet and engage with people. Cats can learn behaviors or skills that translate well to the therapy setting. Some basic cat skills include coming when called, scratching a designated area or cat tree, politely asking to be picked up, and staying off counters with food. As with dogs, it is important to use positive training methods, and clients can participate in training your cat to learn fun new skills.

As mentioned previously, if you adopt a kitten with the intent of training and/ or socializing it to become a therapy cat, remember that a cat's personality can change dramatically and that no amount of training or socialization will change temperament or personality.

SOCIALIZING SMALL ANIMALS, REPTILES, AND INSECTS TO ASSIST IN THERAPY

Small animal species have different capacities and interest in learning new skills. While each of these animals can be trained to do various activities, we primarily focus on socializing our small animals. We ask staff and volunteers to begin slowly with gentle interactions and handling, and gradually to introduce the animals to new objects and toys. Over time, we take them into larger spaces and may eventually let them run free in these spaces, such as an enclosed office. Most small animals establish a hierarchy when meeting new members of their species, so you may also need to do gradual introductions and exposure to new animals you adopt. It can take months before animals can live together unsupervised, and we have discovered that some of our animals do better apart; we have a guinea pig who prefers to live with our rabbits and have had to use separate enclosures for some of our rats.

Small animals can bite when stressed or even when playing, so we make sure to handle and play with our small animals regularly before clients are able to hold them; however, we do always warn clients that they may be bitten or scratched because these are still animals. Training small animals can be complicated and depends on the species and individual animal; while rats are very smart and can be trained for a variety of tasks, we have found that our rabbits have very little interest in learning tricks and are less food-motivated. By using a clicker and treats, we have trained our rats to come when called, run through a maze, and do several other tricks.

Many small animals can be trained to use a litter box or designated bathroom space in their enclosure, which is very helpful and sanitary. Our rats, ferrets, and rabbits have small litter boxes in their enclosures. You can use special litter, hay, or unscented clay cat litter in a low box in the corner of an office or enclosure.

We are beginning to work with reptiles and insects, so our knowledge here is less extensive but expanding daily. Reptiles and insects generally do not need special training. However, many reptiles and insects can be "trained" to do a variety of behaviors that provide stimulation and excitement for the insect, as well as providing an amazing, novel opportunity for your clients. Our resident insect expert clinician is training our cockroaches to navigate a maze. Working with insects is a learning opportunity for clinicians as well as clients. As long as you have a willingness to partner and consult with experts or local entomologists, and research the insects you are interested in working with, you can find many creative ways to engage and learn (Bauer, 2023a, 2023b).

TRAINING HORSES AND OTHER EQUINES TO ASSIST IN THERAPY

There is an enormous industry for horse training, and we certainly are not experts in that field. We recommend that you have experience with horses or reach out to an experienced, force-free trainer if you hope to work with equines. We have consulted and worked with several horse trainers and have witnessed some surprising and concerning behavior. Make sure the trainer you find uses positive methods to work with the horse and is not set on dominating, intimidating, or "breaking" your horse. That will adversely impact your horse, their behavior, and their relationship with you.

We do only groundwork with our horses, so they do not need to be trained to be ridden by clients. Our horses do need to be trained to be haltered and walked with a lead rope, which is good for clients' sessions, but is also necessary for safety when moving horses. Some of our horses have also been taught to lunge, where a person holds them on a long lead and encourages them to move in a circle. This is an activity that certain clients can do with our horses. Our horses also need to be able to stand still and be safe when we clean their feet. Other than these skills, we do not expect, nor do we necessarily want, our equines to be trained like other horses to perform on cue. Sometimes our equines' stubbornness and unwilling-ness to follow directions is exactly the therapeutic moment that a client needs. To us, having a reliable, safe, and happy animal is most important.

SOCIALIZING FARM ANIMALS TO ASSIST IN THERAPY

Farm animals will vary widely in their ability and interest in training, but all need to be socialized to enjoy working with clients. We raised our pygmy goats from babies, which fostered a strong connection and ample time for training from a young age. As babies, we taught them to feel comfortable wearing a har-ness and going for walks or hikes, which gave them good exercise and brought smiles to the people we met. They also became comfortable riding in Linda's car. In general, goats are very smart and highly food-motivated. They can be trained to come when called, perform tricks such as jumping onto an object or standing on hind legs, or even pull a cart if they desire. We allow our clients to train our goats, and they have taught them to dance, wave, jump up, jump down, and go around a circle of logs or tires. Each of our goats has different skills and a differ-ent level of interest in being trained, so what and how you teach them will de-pend on the individual goat.

We have discovered that our alpacas are much shyer, and even with a lot of love and attention, we have one alpaca who is still hesitant about human contact. We adopted them as one-year-olds and gave them months to adapt to our ranch before we worked with them, but most of our work even now is observing and building relationships slowly. Our alpacas' unique personalities provide a won-derful opportunity to explore how relationships develop differently.

Our chickens were raised from chicks, love being around people, and some like to be held. We have been able to clicker train them, and several have even com-pleted an obstacle course during our 3-day training courses. Our colleagues who work with cows, sheep, and pigs have shared that those animals are also incred-ibly social and have unique personalities. If you choose to work with farm ani-mals, we recommend spending significant time with them, just sitting outside with them whenever possible. Expose them to new people and unique items like hula hoops and balls for stimulation and fun, but also to habituate them to new objects. Recognize how your animal does with people—if they seek out contact or shy away—and then observe how they behave when they are around humans. All of this knowledge will inform you about whether they are interested in work-ing as a therapy animal.

Our goats, Wednesday and Enid.

REFERENCES

Bauer, T. (2023a). Invertebrates in therapy. https://www.animalassistedtherapyprograms
.org/post/invertebrates-in-therapy

Bauer, T. (2023b). Working with arthropods in therapy. [Unpublished paper.]

Bradshaw, J. (2012). *Dog sense: How the new science of dog behavior can make you a better friend to your pet*. Basic Books.

Marino, L. (2021). Third time's the charm or three strikes you're out? An updated review of the efficacy of dolphin-assisted therapy for autism and developmental disabilities. *Journal of clinical psychology*, 77. https://doi.org/10.1002/jclp.23110

McConnell, P. (2003). *The other end of the leash: Why we do what we do around dogs*. Ballantine Books.

PART 2

FROM BARKS TO NEIGHS: DIFFERENT ANIMALS AND DIFFERENT OUTCOMES

"You cannot share your life in a meaningful way with any animals such as a dog, cat, rabbit, bird, rat, pig, horse and so many more and not know that we are not the only sentient and sapient beings on the planet."

—JANE GOODALL

Many clinicians, especially those new to AACP, work with only one animal or one species of animal. If that is your situation, we still encourage you to read this section in its entirety to explore the numerous ways that various animals can be integrated into your work and provide new opportunities for your clients. Different animals can play powerful roles in treatment, depending on the goals you are working on with your client (Luksaite et al., 2022).

We may believe that a certain animal will be a great therapy partner for a client, but we cannot predict if that animal wants to work with that client, or if that client feels like working with that animal on any given day. We may choose a cat to help a client with emotional regulation; however, our cat may have very different ideas. The animal's response to our client may not be what we anticipated and could therefore complicate or derail our session plan. For instance, perhaps our cat decides he does not want to interact with the client that day, so they cannot practice certain interventions, or perhaps the cat decides all he wants to do is sit on the client's lap, also preventing the desired interventions.

ANIMAL DISTINCTIONS

One animal distinction we find useful to discuss with clients is that of predator and prey animals. In general, animals that are predators are hunters and carnivores, such as dogs and cats. Having evolved from wolves and wild cats, they are meat eaters and in the wild would have to hunt for their food. These animals have forward-facing eyes, so that they can see in front of them when they chase. Even the most well-behaved dog or cat will likely demonstrate the chase instinct when they see a small animal running, such as a squirrel or rabbit. They quickly sense movement when they are looking forward and can react quickly to obtain their food. It is interesting to note that predator animals often cannot see food that is directly in front and below their gaze. For example, though they can likely smell the treat, cats cannot see treats that are held in front of their mouth, because their eye position prevents them from seeing at that level.

In contrast, prey animals are generally herbivores and do not hunt for food; rather, they are food sources for predators. Prey animals have eyes on the sides of their heads so that they can see much of the world around them and stay alert to danger, using their peripheral vision to see predators. Rabbits, horses, and goats are all examples of prey animals. Some of our animals, such as ferrets and rats, are both predators and prey; their face structure resembles that of a predator (forward-facing eyes and narrow snout), but they are also hunted by larger animals.

We work with both predators and prey animals and find that clients often identify with or relate to one type more than another. For example, a child who experiences bullying may relate to our rabbits and want to hide when they meet new people. A more energetic or aggressive child may feel like running and chasing during sessions, next to one of our dogs.

Having discussions with clients about evolutionary adaptations, such as the fact that cats' long tails evolved to help their balance in trees, can be powerful therapeutic tools and help clients identify traits about themselves that may have been adapted as part of their historic origin. For example, dark skin evolved and is adapted for hot climates, because more pigment means greater resilience from the sun. Looking at physical traits in this way can help remove some of the ingrained stigma and perceived judgement that comes with some cultural and class prejudices. Reframing can be useful in examining physical traits a client dislikes or rejects in themselves; in an adaptive context, that very trait may have been advantageous. Just as in animals, our traits can be seen as functional, not "beautiful" or "ugly." You will never see the winner of the "ugliest dog award" shying away from attention out of embarrassment.

PHASES OF TREATMENT

The counseling process can be broken into three phases: beginning, middle, and end. There are different goals for each of the three phases and various animals can play a more prominent role in each of those phases. If you only have one animal, they can still be helpful in each phase as you modify interventions. We have found that a diversity of animals allows us to better tailor treatment goals for each phase.

BEGINNING PHASE

The general goal for the beginning phase of treatment is to help establish a therapeutic relationship with the client and to help the client feel safe and motivated to engage in treatment. It is also when the clinician assesses the client's needs and starts to develop a treatment plan. We have found that dogs are often excellent animal assistants in the beginning phase of therapy. Because dogs are generally accepting, nonjudgmental, and friendly, they can help the client feel more comfortable and relaxed. Coming into therapy can be stressful and anxiety-provoking for many individuals, particularly those who have had negative experiences with therapy in the past or are reluctant or resistant to treatment, such as teenagers or court-referred clients. Dogs are uniquely beneficial in the initial phase of treatment because they are predictably friendly and welcoming. Our therapy dogs are playful and energetic, but also can be calm and physically supportive. We want to provide a positive initial therapy experience, and dogs are wonderful at being both a calming and joyful presence. A friendly greeting from a dog may decrease the client's physiological anxiety level, allowing them to be more willing and able to engage in the session. Moreover, having a dog that is excited to see and play with them and provide physical affection helps clients to feel accepted and valued. Clients may also then get the sense that this treatment will be different from what they had expected or previously experienced; it could even be fun.

Therapy dogs provide a wide range of activities for clients, such as playing fetch, going for a walk, or simply sitting together. The purpose of these interventions in the initial stage of treatment is to help the client feel more accepting of the therapeutic environment, to feel connected to the animal and clinician, and to start developing a relationship with the animal and clinician. Our focus is on allowing the client to enter the therapeutic process at their own pace through developing a relationship with the dog. By deemphasizing the relationship with the clinician, clients may feel less pressure to participate and "get better," and therefore be willing to continue attending sessions.

Dogs also are helpful in this early phase of treatment because many clients have experience with dogs. This familiarity may provide a sense of stability, comfort, and form an association with other positive experiences they have had with dogs. Additionally, dogs have evolved with humans; they are attuned to our emotions and behaviors and want to be in relationship with us. This is why so many therapy animals are dogs. However, there is a downside to this evolutionary connection; dogs are often so friendly and forgiving that they are sometimes less able to help challenge clients in later phases of treatment.

Though we often choose to work with dogs initially, we do usually introduce our new clients to all our ranch animals in early treatment. We want clients to meet the variety of animals and to understand that there is the option to work with most of them, given treatment and safety considerations. If there is an animal the client really wants to work with, and the clinician feels this would be safe and positive, we will try to accommodate them. Watching the client's interaction with a variety of animals also can help with our assessment and with establishing treatment goals. However, we generally do not begin therapy work with an animal that is shy or takes a significant time to create a relationship with, such as a rabbit. This can be frustrating for the client and does not enhance the rapport and trust needed in the initial treatment phase.

MIDDLE PHASE

Once a strong therapeutic relationship, including trust and rapport, has been established with the animal and clinician, the bulk of the therapeutic "work" is done in the middle phase. In this phase, the clinician starts to gently challenge the client's behaviors that are not functional or useful. Clinicians will develop a treatment plan and work toward treatment goals by developing specific interventions.

The middle part of treatment is where having a variety of animals to work with can be particularly helpful. While dogs' exuberance and acceptance are wonderful when initiating clients into therapy, their tolerance of various undesirable behavior from people may be unhelpful during later phases of therapy, and clients may not get the necessary feedback that can come from the animals. For example, when a client pretends to throw a toy and then laughs when the dog tries to chase it, the dog will wait patiently until it is thrown and then eagerly and happily continue to play with the client. In contrast, a cat or a goat would lose interest and leave the setting if the client was teasing or not giving the expected or desired behavior.

If our therapeutic goal is to help a client see and change behaviors and ways of interacting that cause others to avoid them, we can compare two ways of confrontation. In traditional therapy a clinician might say, "I wonder why your friend Joe hasn't called you back over the past two weeks? Could you have done something that made him unhappy or uncomfortable being with you?" Instead, we can use the animal's reaction to gently confront the client about behaviors that cause the animal, and likely other humans, to be uncomfortable: "Hmm. I noticed when you pretended to throw the toy at Sigmund, he turned his body away from you and went to the door. I wonder what he is telling us?" This in vivo response to a client's behavior provides the client a way to examine their own actions. Moreover, the animal's response provides a more neutral and gentle confrontation than a direct comment or question from the therapist. A variety of animals may create different interactional scenarios, thus allowing the client to see how they affect others, and then to provide a judgement-free opportunity to practice new behaviors.

This process operates on several principles:

1. the client is motivated to develop a trusting relationship with the animal so that the animal will interact with them;

2. focusing on the animal's need for safety removes the judgement of the clients' behavior;

3. through indirect confrontation, the client can experience the thoughts, feelings, and physiological changes occurring in the body without as much need for defensiveness;

4. helping the client to stay open to the animal's feedback then opens pathways of insight and learning, and provides the motivation to change their behavior;

5. providing a therapeutic experience that engages behavior, thoughts, feelings, and physiology prepares the client to learn a new way of being with the animal that is more expeditious; and

6. when the client engages in prosocial interactions with the animal, the behavior, thoughts, feelings, and physiology of the client are externally and intrinsically rewarded.

TERMINATION PHASE

The end or termination of treatment is about gaining closure with the thera-peutic relationship, reflecting on and generalizing skills developed to the world outside therapy, and planning for further implementation of the client's learn-ing from therapy. It is time to say goodbye to the clinician and to the animals that clients have connected with, and also to provide clients with a positive ex-perience of goodbyes.

Ultimately, we want the client to have internalized what they have learned through working with the animals. Whether that means making a cat purr or be-ing able to pet an alpaca, it is important that the client start to internalize that re-ward so that they can see and feel the benefit in making another being feel good. Through various ways of interacting and forming relationships with the animals, clients have learned to engage in behaviors that make a relationship strong. They have experienced, in a holistic way, what it can feel like to receive and give sup-port. The client also has seen themselves in different ways and has overcome var-ious obstacles. The process of having been in a relationship with an animal over time, and through a variety of situations, has hopefully created an internal tem-plate for the client about how other relationships can develop and grow.

The termination phase of therapy allows the client's relationship with the an-imals to deepen, but also prepares them to say goodbye. We help clients inter-nalize their relationship with the animal and recognize that trust, warmth, ac-ceptance, challenges, and other therapeutic experiences are important for their ongoing functioning. We are intentional about encouraging clients to hold onto and internalize those relational feelings and experiences they had with the ani-mals so that they can access them at other points and places in their life.

We find that clients often have a more difficult time saying goodbye to the animals than to the humans they have worked with during treatment. We accept and honor the bond the clients have with the animals and understand that these bonds make this therapeutic process so transformative. In this phase of therapy, we often provide some kind of transitional object, such as a photo, artwork, or letter from a client's favorite animal. Some of the termination rituals we have done include photos of a client and animal, decorated picture frames, painted paw prints, written notes from the animals about their favorite memory with the client, and small stuffed animals resembling the client's favorite therapy animal. Linda gave a small stuffed cat to an adult client who left a domestic violence rela-tionship. This client kept this toy in her purse for years, saying it reminded her of the strength she had found in herself through her work with Norman. Clients of all ages appreciate these tangible reminders of therapy. They are lasting reminders of the hard work they did in therapy, the importance of their contribution to the animal's life, and a reminder of how the animal changed their life.

In the following chapters in this section, we explore how different species of animals can assist clients in treatment. We examine what makes the animals uniquely suited for AACP, characteristics you may want to look for in a good therapy animal of each species, what challenges that species may have as a therapy animal, and what sort of housing requirements and logistics are relevant for these animals. We also provide a therapeutic example of integrating that animal species with a client.

INTEGRATING AACP AND YOUR THEORETICAL APPROACH

This is an expansive topic, well beyond the scope of this book; however, we want to clarify that AACP is used in conjunction with the theoretical approach or approaches in which the clinician is trained. In other words, we are mental health clinicians first, and then we are incorporating the medium of AACP to assist in our work. Our clinicians work from a wide variety of approaches, including psychodynamic, cognitive behavioral, narrative, solutions-focused, systems, somatic, gestalt, and many more. For more information, Laura Bruneau and Amy Johnson have explored how many different theories can be integrated with AACP (Bruneau & Johnson, 2011).

REFERENCES

Bruneau, L., & Johnson, A. (2011). *Fido and Freud meet: Integrating animal-assisted interventions with counseling theory.* American Counseling Association Conference, New Orleans, LA.

Luksaite, J., Zokaityte, E., Starkute, V., Sidlauskiene, S., Zokaityte, G., & Bartkiene, E. (2022). Personalized strategy for animal-assisted therapy for individuals based on the emotions induced by the images of different animal species and breeds. *Animals (Basel)*, *12*(5). https://doi.org/10.3390/ani12050597

4

(WO)MAN'S BEST FRIEND: DOGS AS THERAPY ANIMALS

"The great pleasure of a dog is that you may make a fool of yourself with him and not only will he not scold you, but he will make a fool of himself too."

—SAMUEL BUTLER

Dogs are one of the most widely accepted therapy animals, and many people hold positive beliefs about dogs. Dogs generally are eager to engage with people and are friendly and playful. Dogs have adapted to live with humans; they have developed a powerful ability to read humans and their needs, often responding to nonverbal communication and body language. They are attuned to the subtle emotional cues of humans and are usually responsive to clients' behaviors and signals that human professionals may miss. Dogs can be trained to be safely around most people and animals, and are generally more easily accepted into shared spaces like schools, offices, and mental health centers. For all these reasons, dogs are the most common animal partner in AACP.

UNIQUE CONTRIBUTIONS OF DOGS IN THERAPY

All dogs are different with regard to temperament, personality, skills, and challenges. There are aspects of each dog that make them special. While we may have our own ideas about what makes our dog special, clients may see different traits, as the dogs develop unique relationships with them. Some clients may prefer a young, playful dog to run around outside with and train, while others may want a calm, cuddly dog who wants to sit with them on the couch. Some therapy dogs may be able to do both these tasks; for instance, they may be playful and energetic at the beginning of a session and be more willing to be calm and settled after some short playtime.

As mentioned earlier, dogs are a great animal for clients in the initial stage of therapy. In general, dogs portray the qualities necessary for a successful therapeutic relationship: they are unconditionally accepting, congruent and genuine, and naturally empathic (Hare & Tomasello, 2005). As pack animals, dogs long to be part of your pack or family. They generally will accept your clients into the pack and treat them with care, which is a powerful gift. Therefore, dogs are especially helpful for clients who may be resistant to the idea of therapy, or who have had negative experiences with therapy in the past. Clients who are mandated to be in treatment can also be motivated by the friendship the dog creates with them.

Research has found that clinicians who work with a dog are perceived as more friendly, accepting, and genuine (Schneider & Harley, 2015). For clients with complex issues who need a longer-term therapy, creating an environment that feels safe and comfortable will be critical before moving into deep emotional work. Having an animal involved will help the client to move more quickly into issues they may not have dealt with before. It also helps to break any stereotypes people may have about clinicians and what happens in therapy. Starting the therapeutic process in a unique way, different from expectations, allows the client to be open to change.

We have found that observing how a client sees a dog and interprets their behavior gives us a tremendous amount of information about the client's worldview and how they see others. In addition, watching the dog's interaction and responses to the human client gives us a wealth of information, especially in terms of relationship dynamics. We can learn not only how the client views and interacts with the world, but also how they form relationships and what they do with these relationships moving forward. The ability to work within relationships is the most powerful work we do; the *process of relating* and the emerging and changing relationship the client has with a dog provides us with countless opportunities to encourage insight and produce change.

CHARACTERISTICS OF A GOOD THERAPY DOG

Generally, dogs are accepting and good-natured. A good therapy dog will enjoy meeting new people and being around a range of different ages, genders, and types of people. They will desire physical contact, playtime, and quiet companionship, and are able to tolerate minor inconveniences such as unpredictable behavior and clumsy petting. The best therapy dogs we have seen are

Rupert is a great example of a therapy dog who loves to play hard but also can provide comfort when needed.

capable of being both fast and slow; they can play with gusto and be active with clients, but they can also settle down and snuggle on the couch to provide needed comfort.

Dogs are such wonderful therapy animals because of this diversity of behavior and ability to adapt to the needs of those around them, though some dogs are more perceptive than others. One of our therapy dogs, Coral, was especially sensitive to the emotional needs of clients. She was playful one minute but then able to sense when a client was in distress and would come and offer a cuddle. Rupert is a wonderful therapy dog as well since he enjoys rambunctious activity and also knows how to "go to work" by jumping on the couch and snuggling with the client when they need extra emotional support.

Many breeds can make good therapy animals. Depending on the population you work with, it is helpful to consider if a particular breed may be more effective or difficult. For example, dogs bred to herd animals, such as heelers or border collies, may want to herd small children. Retrievers have an innate need to chase and therefore may be harder to train to avoid small therapy animals. Huskies are very energetic dogs and beautiful to pet and cuddle, but they can be quite vocal and need a great deal of exercise. Of course, these are generalizations, and an individual dog of that breed may have different characteristics. An individual dog from any breed could make a good therapy dog, as each individual dog will have its own unique behaviors. Most of our dogs are mixed breeds that have come through the shelter system. A dog that has experienced a positive change in their life circumstances because of living with you may be an especially loyal and affectionate partner.

Therapy dogs are generally smart, motivated by treats or toys, and enjoy the learning process. Therapy dogs need to be able to meet a set of criteria to pass a certification test, so having a dog that can learn tricks and skills is also important. Generally, in order pass a certification test and to make a strong contribution in therapy, a therapy dog needs to know the following skills: come, sit, down, stay, leave it, drop it, and place or bed. They will also need to be able to tolerate loud noises, clumsy petting, and being left in a room without their owner.

Being able to reliably respond to these cues is important for any therapy dog because it not only helps ensure the safety of the dog and client, but it also helps a client feel successful when they are able to give a cue that the dog follows. Moreover, we often have clients train our dogs as part of a therapeutic intervention, so the dog's ability to learn provides a foundation for additional skills that a clinician or client would want to teach a dog. Our clinicians often do not train their dogs in many complex skills so that clients can be the ones to teach them. Training a therapy animal has a multitude of benefits for the client, including problem solving, patience, frustration tolerance, empathy, communication, social skills, and feelings of success and accomplishment.

Being a therapy dog is hard work, so the dog needs to have the desire to do the job. They need to be adaptable to the clinician's working environment, including physical space, background noises, other animals, or humans. For instance, we have multiple cats and small animals in the building, so a dog that wants to chase other animals is not a good fit for our organization. Knowing your setting and how your dog will react to it is critical to creating a successful therapeutic environment for your clients and your animal.

CHALLENGES WITH DOGS AS THERAPY ANIMALS

Although dogs are accepted by many cultural groups, they also can be rejected or viewed unfavorably. In some parts of the world, and in various cultures, dogs are seen as unclean or not suitable to be inside. They may be perceived as threatening or aggressive, kept outdoors, or left to roam freely. We routinely see individuals who are fearful of dogs in general, or fearful of specific breeds, colors, or sizes.

Dogs can have a strong preference for certain people, especially their owner. One of the most common behaviors we see among new therapy dogs working at our ranch is the dog's anxious attachment to their owner. If the clinician decides to work with another animal and the dog is not in session with them, these dogs may whine, bark, and become stressed, which is hard on the dog, the owner, and others present in the office. This issue is one that the clinician can work on early, so that the dog has a secure place in the office when they cannot be included or do not want to join a session. Some of our dogs are crate-trained and enjoy their quiet space. Others have their own beds in the general staff space where they can enjoy the attention of other staff members. However, we have had several trained and certified therapy dogs who were never comfortable with this separation from their owner, so their owners ultimately decided they were not a good fit for working at our facility.

Additionally, if a dog is highly attached to the clinician/owner and is not interested in interacting or engaging with the client, it can be hurtful for a client who may be longing for the dog's attention. If this happens occasionally, the attention of the dog can be useful in determining the client's behavior that may be causing the dog to retreat. It can lead to a powerful therapeutic discussion for the client, with the clinician encouraging the client to notice the dog's behavior, how they interpret or explain that behavior, and then how they manage their own reaction or response. However, if the dog routinely chooses to engage only with the clinician and not with clients, the therapy dog may not be a good fit for that setting, population, or for therapy work in general.

If a therapy dog is going to be working in a setting where there will be other dogs or animals present, the therapy dog must be safe and comfortable around those animals. As predators, many dogs naturally want to hunt and chase, especially smaller animals such as cats or rabbits. They also may want to play and interact with other dogs working nearby. If a therapy dog is reactive to other animals or dogs, they may be able to be trained to be in that setting safely, but it can take a lot of work. In addition, even if they are trained to be in that setting, it may still be stressful for the dog, so it is a balance and requires knowing your dog well and what they can tolerate while still enjoying work as a therapy dog. Rupert has learned "leave it" when it comes to our rabbits and ferrets at the ranch, but being in their rooms when they are running around is too stressful. He has to work too hard to restrain his innate tendency to chase, so Rupert has made his own choice to stay out of their rooms and not have to deal with the constant temptation.

Dogs need frequent bathroom breaks and their owners are responsible for picking up after their dogs regularly. Depending on where you are working, you will want to establish a routine so that your dog has time to get exercise and relieve themselves throughout the day. This can also be a good time for you to stretch your legs and get some fresh air. Figuring out how to schedule clients so that you have time to exercise your dog and give them a break can be challenging. Many clinicians work a full 8- to 10-hour day with back-to-back clients, and this is not a fair or reasonable schedule for a dog. Creating a schedule that meets your client and income needs, as well as your dog's needs for rest and exercise, can be a complicated logistical problem.

Clients may not want to work with a dog, so the clinician will need to find an option for the dog during these times. Options may include bringing the dog home, bringing it to a daycare, having a nearby office or colleague who will be with the dog, or putting the dog in a safe spot or crate in the office. Clinicians can also schedule non-dog office days, which could be longer client days that allow them to work with clients who do not want AACP. Then, clinicians can schedule shorter days or days with longer breaks between clients when the dog is present.

Sometimes clinicians will take their dogs on walks with clients, and while that is good exercise and outside time for your dog, it does not count as a break since your dog is still working. It is also never the client's job to pick up after your dog. Clinicians should always practice responsible dog ownership by quickly cleaning up after them and disposing of dog waste properly (then washing your hands when you return). Watching you pick up after the dog can be a therapeutic interaction with clients who find poop unpleasant or who struggle with bodily functions. All animals poop, and modeling a matter-of-fact way to handle this natural act can help clients learn to discuss and accept it as part of life.

HOUSING AND LOGISTICS FOR DOGS

How people provide housing for a dog in the United States has changed a great deal over the past few decades. In many parts of the US, it is common for dogs to be treated like family members and have access to most of the inside and outside of the home. Dogs may sleep in a crate, in the bedroom with their owner, or even on the bed. However, different individuals, cultures, and countries have different ideas about where a dog belongs. Many dogs are not treated as family and, as such, are provided fewer comforts and are more likely to sleep outside in a doghouse or kennel. This book is not about making judgments about different animal welfare choices, though we certainly have our own beliefs about how dogs should be treated. That said, when considering housing for a therapy dog, one issue to consider is how your clients will identify with the ways you treat your dog. There is a strong chance that they will make assumptions about how you will care for them based on your treatment of your dog.

Generally, therapy dogs will travel with you to work, so they should enjoy being in the car. Once at work, there needs to be a comfortable place for the dog to stay while working with clients, but also a safe/quiet space when the dog chooses not to be with the client. In a single office setting, the dog's safe space may need to be under or behind a piece of furniture or in a kennel, if they have been kennel-trained and view it as a happy place. For example, a clinician has a dog bed in her office and if the dog chooses to lay on its bed, that indicates the dog is taking a break from working in the session. In accordance, clients are asked not to interact with the dog until it gets off its bed. The clinician can teach the client about impulse control, boundaries, and respecting others' limits during this time and talk about the dog, but not interact with the dog. If it is possible for the dog to leave the therapy room or area and go somewhere else to take a break, that is ideal. In our facility, the dogs can leave an office and go to the other areas of the ranch building if they need a break. Our dogs may stare at the office door or bark if we have not noticed; they are asking, "Can I please leave now?" Our answer is always "yes" because we respect their needs and desires and will never make them work if they are not interested.

Dogs need time and space to move around, get their energy out, and relieve themselves. Even if they are happy working in an office, it is important to let them be dogs. When he was a younger dog, Rupert needed to stop at the dog park and play before he came into the office; otherwise, he could not settle down enough to be a focused therapy dog. He needed his dog time before he could attend to our clients. Other dogs may need a long walk in the morning or between sessions or may need frequent breaks throughout the day. If a dog is in an office all day, they may also need a long walk or playtime at the end of the day to decompress. If you have a larger facility where they can have plenty of dog and outside time, your therapy dog may be able to work longer than a dog who would be inside an office all day.

All animals need breaks, and no animal can work for hours on end. Observing your dog for signs of fatigue, boredom, disinterest, or stress is an indicator that they are done working. After monitoring the dog for a couple of weeks and reading their cues, most clinicians will be able to determine how many hours or how many sessions they can comfortably work. Rupert, and therefore Linda, had a three-session limit before needing a break. If the session involved playing fetch, Rupert would be engaged in the session for longer and could be more attentive during the quieter talking times. Ellen's dog, Sasha, could work for about three sessions in a row at the start of her career, but by the end she would work for one session and then need a break, which meant Ellen had to adjust her schedule accordingly, alerting clients about Sasha's absence or working with other animals. It is important to learn the needs and limitations of your own dog.

Dogs need to be brushed, bathed, and have their nails trimmed and teeth brushed. Many of these activities can be done with clients. These interesting, functional, and fun interventions can model caretaking and good hygiene, and can lead to powerful discussions about empathy, patience, kindness, and gentleness, among others (McConnell, 2003).

AN EXAMPLE OF
AN INTERVENTION WITH A DOG

Lee was a 35-year-old trans female who came to therapy for extreme social anxiety. She had been coming for several sessions and was most comfortable working with the dogs. The clinician's dog, Mable, joined the session and instantly went to Lee and lay on her feet. The clinician asked if Lee would like to join Mable on the floor. After moving to the floor, Mable shifted position so her paw was touching Lee's leg. The clinician asked Lee to spend a few minutes quietly spending time with Mable. After about 10 minutes, the clinician asked Lee to put on paper what it felt like to be next to Mable, and especially what it felt like to have Mable touching her. Lee asked, "Do I need to draw Mable or myself?" The clinician responded, "You can if you want, or you can just draw something abstract. It's completely up to you. See if you can just feel your way through it." Lee proceeded to choose vibrant colors and drew abstractly in two spots on the page, and in the middle they merged. She then drew hearts all over, then teardrops. The clinician asked if Lee would like to share about her drawing, but Lee said, "No. But I want to take this home because it reminds me that I do connect with others, and sometimes they connect with me. If I can just be with them and not worry about what they're thinking, I think I'll be OK around other people." Though Lee did not want to process her drawing during that session, her comment provided valuable information to the clinician about Lee's inner monologue and how to guide future sessions.

REFERENCES

Hare, B., & Tomasello, M. (2005). Human-like social skills in dogs? *Trends in Cognitive Sciences, 9*(9). https://doi.org/10.1016/j.tics.2005.07.003

McConnell, P. (2003). *The other end of the leash: Why we do what we do around dogs.* Ballantine Books.

Schneider, M. S., & Harley, L. P. (2015). How dogs influence the evaluation of psychotherapists. *Anthrozoös, 19*(2). https://doi.org/10.2752/089279306785593784

5

FURRY MIRRORS: CATS AS THERAPY ANIMALS

"A cat has absolute emotional honesty: human beings, for one reason or another, may hide their feelings, but a cat does not."

—ERNEST HEMINGWAY

There is something very special about the feeling of a cat loving you; it can feel quite different from having a dog's love. Cats are often particular about who they befriend, and it can take longer to earn a cat's trust. Cats may be more discriminating in their affection if they are not treated in their preferred way. Linda often says that you should feel "privileged" to have a cat's love; she compares it to the Egyptian view of cats as royalty and having to work your way into their favor.

UNIQUE CONTRIBUTIONS OF CATS AS THERAPY ANIMALS

There is less research into the therapeutic benefits of cats and some contradictory evidence as to whether interactions with cats are stress-reducing (Tomaszewska et al., 2017) or have an excitatory effect on the nervous system (Nagasawa et al., 2023). People often assume that because cats are more restrictive with their affection, they will not make good therapy animals. However, their conditional affection and strong preferences actually make them powerful therapy partners. Cats are self-protective; being small, they have learned to be vigilant about their safety and will tolerate much less discomfort than dogs will. A good therapy cat will tolerate a small amount of irritation but as soon as they perceive any chance of being harmed, they will move away. Because cats mirror the conditional relational dynamics of humans, the client may see their own relational problems reflected through the cat's response to them. For example, if a client is nervous about meeting new people, their behavior may elicit a nervous response from the therapy cat. These genuine and sometimes uncomfortable interactions provide fertile ground to recognize and explore clients' issues.

Cats are nonverbally expressive. Although cats do not smile with their mouths, they do seem to smile with their eyes. Cats also purr, which usually indicates that the cat is feeling happy and is enjoying the moment. This purr provides immediate feedback to clients about how their behavior is positively impacting another being. The cat's purr can also calm the client's nervous system (Bradshaw, 2014). Cats may knead an area when they are getting comfortable, called "smurgling," another tangible piece of evidence that a cat is feeling safe with a client. These nonverbal behaviors offer positive feedback to clients that they are causing the cats contentment.

Several of our therapy cats were initially adopted to be barn cats. We wanted to provide them a safe home but they were frightened of human contact. These cats showed signs of post-traumatic stress disorder (PTSD), demonstrated by widening pupils, bristling fur, and pulling their ears back. Clients were intrigued by and drawn to these cats and would sit quietly in the barn during sessions, patiently waiting for the cats to come out of hiding and interact on their own terms. We allowed this because the cats made their own choices about interacting, and we would always leave the space if the cats showed signs of unhappiness. Several barn cats would come out of hiding to observe and over time would cautiously interact with clients. This gentle patience, persistence, and love from clients allowed these hesitant cats to trust humans and eventually to enjoy human contact. It is important to note that these barn cats were not certified therapy cats; they did not have the traditional traits of therapy cats, nor was that their role, and we had no expectations of them to engage with clients. But they were still able to provide a therapeutic benefit to clients, who practiced patience, stillness, understanding, empathy, gentleness, and other skills as they calmly waited for the cats to feel safe. This experience benefited the clients but also the barn cats, allowing them to feel safer with humans. It is worth noting again that if the cats seemed unhappy or stressed with humans in their space, showing overt cues of distress, we would end this activity and move the session to a different location.

One of these barn cats, Clementine, became so comfortable with humans that she moved to the office setting and would sleep in a bed next to Linda's desk. She would purr when clients pet her; however, she would sometimes still show mild signs of nervousness, such as dilated pupils. This desire for affection but persistent anxiety showed clients that it is acceptable and common to have mixed feelings about certain situations and to set boundaries when needed. It also showed clients that PTSD and its related symptoms are normal and can be worked on and improved over time.

Another good example of a therapy cat providing boundaries was Linda's cat, Norman. Linda worked with Norman in a group home for adolescents who had experienced neglect and abuse and subsequently had severe behavioral issues. Norman was very sweet and accepting but required certain behaviors to feel comfortable and to relax with individual clients. He showed clients that you had to start slowly, with gentle, friendly interactions. Over time, clients learned to accommodate another being's limits and boundaries, respect those limits, and then create a deeper connection within the safe boundaries. Norman helped demonstrate how healthy relationships develop and that trust and a deeper sense of intimacy could develop between individuals over time.

CHARACTERISTICS OF A GOOD THERAPY CAT

The most important quality for a good therapy cat is that they want to be a therapy cat. Even if they are discriminating in their affection, therapy cats need to be comfortable around people and meeting new clients on a regular basis. They should be friendly enough to allow some interaction with your clients, whatever their ages and needs. This skill may be the biggest challenge, because cats can be very particular; many are more skittish around loud or fast-moving humans, such as young children.

A therapy cat also needs to be comfortable in your therapy setting, whether that is a small office, a large mental health center, or a ranch setting. Often, cats will need to travel from your home to the office, so they need to be comfortable in various environments and traveling to the office. They also need to feel safe and happy in your office setting. Cats can be territorial, but if they are socialized to be curious about and enjoy new environments, they may be more relaxed in the office.

It is helpful if your therapy cat clearly communicates their feelings using behavior that clients can observe and understand. As mentioned above, cats may accept some discomfort but will leave if it is too much, which allows the client to clearly understand what is acceptable for this cat. This interaction teaches clients about differences in individuals, windows of tolerance, accepting limits, and reading, interpreting, and understanding body language. It also allows clients to

A client playing guitar for Hagrid.

practice behaviors that make others feel good and provides concrete evidence of this when they earn the cat's elusive purr.

One study by Tomaszewska et al. (2017) suggests that certain breeds of cats may be better suited as therapy cats, but we have found that any domestic cat can be a wonderful therapy animal, if they have the proper qualities and desires. We have worked with a wide range of therapy cats, each with their own distinct personality, which makes them a fantastic therapy partner. For example, Fred is very vocal and loves walking around the ranch on a leash, while Hagrid is quiet, sweet, and likes people to bring him soft toys to snuggle. Lune is a feisty but curious boy who sets clear limits with a swipe of his paw. Our three-legged cat, Sigmund, had a front leg amputated as a kitten but is as athletic as any other cat and serves as an inspiration to many clients who feel disabled by their own limitations. Sigmund is also our hugger and office greeter—he can often be found stretched across the chest of a waiting parent, both quietly resting. Blue is a big, fluffy cuddlebug who seeks out clients and will nap on their laps, but only if they are calm. Finally, Marble is a very sweet but sensitive girl and takes the most time to warm up and feel safe with clients, but once you receive her love, it is like no other reward.

We have three cats with feline immunodeficiency virus (FIV+). Cats with this illness are difficult to adopt out of shelters since they cannot live with non-FIV+ cats, so we adopted a whole brood and provided them with their own room and "catio." While they do have more health issues, these cats are very engaging. There are no health risks to humans, and clients with chronic health problems or those who feel isolated from others can relate to their stories.

CHALLENGES OF WORKING WITH CATS

Cats are finicky creatures. They have clear preferences, likes, and dislikes, and have no hesitation in letting them be known. Therapy cats, even though they are social and adaptable, will still have preferences about situations and people, which may change over time. Cats also have sharp claws, and we strongly advise against declawing them, as it is akin to chopping off the top portion of your finger. These claws can scratch clients and damage furniture, so we recommend having a warning about this in your disclosure forms. Cat allergies are also common, so ensuring that clients are not allergic to cats and cleaning your office thoroughly between clients is important.

Some clients may not work well with cats, for several reasons. Excitable, exuberant children and teens may be too overwhelming for more sensitive cats. Clients who have experienced rejection may struggle with the contingent nature of cats' affection, and it may not be therapeutically beneficial at many points in treatment. For instance, Linda had a teenage client who was incredibly intelligent but was also socially isolated and resisted new friendships because she "didn't like people." She loved cats and enjoyed working with Mazey and Norman, who were both very friendly and accepting, but after Mazey's death and Norman's retirement, Linda's new therapy kitten-in-training, Samantha, decided she did not want to snuggle and began to sit under a chair in sessions. This behavior elicited painful feelings of rejection for the client, and she would quickly give up trying to engage Samantha, further reinforcing her negative self-image. It became clear that the client did not have sufficient ego strength to understand Samantha's behavior as anything but rejection, no matter how Linda tried to reframe it. In this case, the cat's natural behavior was not therapeutically useful for this client.

HOUSING AND LOGISTICS

Typically, therapy cats are your own personal pet that you bring to and from your office. Having a regular routine where your cat knows how to get into the cat carrier before going to work can help with the transition. This can also help prevent car sickness. You will need to have basic cat supplies at your office, such as a litter box, fresh water, food, a brush, a bed, and toys. It is also very important for your cat to have a safe spot where they can hide or rest and where clients cannot bother them. Cats often like to sit in high spaces (like a leopard in the tree) so they can see everything around them and pounce as necessary, so having spots for them to climb and explore is important. Cats are independent animals and most often do not require another cat as company; in fact, many cats are reluctant to share their space and owner with another cat.

Over the years, we have adopted many cats that now live at the ranch. We have three indoor cats in our main office, as well as a separate space with a large catio for our FIV+ cats. Each of these cats came through a local shelter and each is friendly, unique, and responds to clients in different ways. These cats are a definite favorite for clients of all ages.

INTERVENTIONS WITH CATS

One of the primary ways cats can assist in therapy is to be a responsive mirror to the energy and temperature in the room. Most cats feel comfortable in a room with humans who are presenting within a specific range of behaviors and energy

Lune (on his leash) exercising his wild side.

levels. Many cats are wary of loud noises and quick or unpredictable movements. If a client wants to engage with the cat, or even just keep them comfortable in the room, the client will need to be aware of their energy level and how it is impacting the cat, and then modify their energy if necessary. The cat's behavior can provide feedback and reinforcement about the client's behavior. For example, if a rambunctious client calms down and sits still, the cat may relax, sit with the client, and start purring. Including cats with couples and families can provide a visible measure of the tension in the room; couples can set a goal to have a difficult conversation while observing the cat and speaking in a way that enables the cat to continue to feel safe and comfortable. Many clients are also calmed by watching a sleeping cat, and when done with intention, this can be a valuable therapeutic intervention.

Several of our therapy cats enjoy walking around the farm on a leash. This is a different experience from walking a dog since the cat is driving the direction and time. Clients will need to let go of control and expectation, and instead observe and respond to the cat's needs. We also have a wall with mounted jumps and tunnels that clients can train the cats to navigate or simply observe the cats as they maneuver the obstacles. There are many different types of cat toys, and each cat has different preferences. However, it is also fun to let the client create a fun cat toy using nearby items, such as a stick, string, or feather. These kinds of toys are important for the cats to exert their natural prey drive and expend energy.

REFERENCES

Bradshaw, J. (2014). *Cat sense: How the new feline science can make you a better friend to your pet.* Basic Books.

Nagasawa, T., Kimura, Y., Masuda, K., & Uchiyama, H. (2023). Effects of interactions with cats in domestic environment on the psychological and physiological state of their owners: Associations among cortisol, oxytocin, heart rate variability, and emotions. *Animals, 13,* 1–16. https://doi.org/10.3390/ani13132116

Tomaszewska, K., Bomert, I., & Wilkiewicz-Wawro, E. (2017). Feline-assisted therapy: Integrating contact with cats into treatment plans. *Polish Annals of Medicine, 24*(2), 283–286.

6

LITTLE FRIENDS: INTEGRATING SMALL THERAPY ANIMALS

"The animal does not question life. It lives. Its very reason for living is life; it enjoys and relishes life."

—RAY BRADBURY

There are many species of animals that can assist in therapy. Many small, domesticated animals enjoy contact with humans and have unique behaviors that can teach relational skills, reach areas of the client's unconscious, and help clients practice empathy. A recent study of the literature by Macauley and Chur-Hansen (2022) found that "non-conventional companion animals may benefit their guardians by providing social support through acting as attachment figures, facilitating social opportunities and daily routines, fulfilling cognitive needs, and recreating restorative capacities of mindfully observing natural landscapes" (p. 1). Their findings support the idea that humans can connect with and benefit from relationships with small animals.

We believe that the only appropriate small animals to add to a therapy practice are ones that have been domesticated to the extent that they enjoy human contact. The small animals at our ranch include rats, rabbits, guinea pigs, and ferrets; we also have a staff member who works with her own bearded dragon. Each of these animals was adopted from a shelter or rehomed to us. It is essential to find an animal that enjoys interaction with clients and can be integrated safely into your practice. As with other animals, this will depend on the individual animal, and not all domesticated small animals will want to be therapy animals. This animal will be a member of your family, and they deserve a forever home with you, regardless of if they choose to be a therapy animal, so it is important to choose an animal that fits with your family's lifestyle and budget. Some animals require a great deal of caretaking or have a very long lifespan. All will require specialized veterinary care, which can be expensive, and many veterinarians are not trained to treat "exotic animals," so it can be difficult to find a good local veterinarian.

A major consideration for small animals is their size, which can be both a positive feature and a potential challenge. While smaller animals can easily be transported from home to work or live in a small enclosure, their size also makes them more fragile. This means they need careful handling, which can be difficult for some clients, as this requires a more nuanced level of care and attention. Because small animals are often more unusual and less understood, clients may desire to create a special connection with these animals.

Some small animals, such as rabbits, are prey animals, but some are both prey and predators, such as ferrets and rats. Being a prey animal means they may be more cautious, protective, and take more time to develop a relationship. These qualities help make these animals uniquely powerful therapy animals because they are relationship-builders. They require similar understanding, empathy, patience, and responsiveness that many human relationships necessitate. Working with these little animals provides client the opportunity to practice new skills and ways of behaving and to develop healthy relationships. We can ask the client what safety means for each animal, how the animal communicates its feelings and needs, and how the animal expresses its desires for contact with that human. Clients must wait patiently for the animal to approach them, which puts the relationship on a more equal footing. The client and animal must demonstrate consent and nonverbally negotiate what level of contact feels safe at any given moment.

Even if the animal does not choose to interact with the client, the clinician can help reframe the animal's behavior so that it does not feel like a rejection to the client. The clinician can observe specific client behaviors or ways of engagement that create less safety for the animal, which can then lead to a discussion about how the animal is exhibiting a dislike of a certain behavior, not a dislike of the client as a person. The client can then choose to modify their behavior and interaction in order to elicit a different response from the animal. The clinician can provide coaching, or the client can use trial and error, but hopefully the client will learn what it takes for the animal to feel safe and connect with to the client. That connection is a powerful reward.

An amazing thing about these interactions is that the client is learning skills that they need when relating with humans. For instance, they are learning to take relationships slowly, talk softly, share the space, be reciprocal, show interest in the other, find out what the other likes, and listen carefully. We can help clients generalize this learning and apply their new skills to interactions with people. If a client can make friends with a skittish rabbit, they may also be able to make human friends.

CHALLENGES OF SMALL THERAPY ANIMALS

One downside of working with small animals is their size, which makes them more vulnerable to injury or accident. They can be easily hurt if mishandled, which is clearly dangerous for the animal, but also can be harmful to a client's emotional well-being and treatment. We are very careful about which clients can hold our small animals and under what conditions. Many rats and guinea pigs will not remain still to be picked up, so clients may feel hurt or rejected when they want to cuddle and the animal runs away. That said, our clients are not allowed to pick up any animals themselves, so clinicians will pick up the small animal and then gently transfer the animal to a sitting client. We do not pick up our rabbits at all, unless medically required, because when picked up, rabbits can kick their back feet so hard they injure their backs.

Small animals love to climb and go into small, dark places, such as under couches or inside heating vents, so finding a safe place for them to freely engage with clients can be a tricky balance. Ferrets, rats, and some reptiles are escape artists and can quickly break free and hide if you are not paying attention. We have a therapy room without hiding places or escape routes, so we let the rats, rabbits, and guinea pigs roam freely, and clients have fun putting up props and building structures and mazes for them. Many small animals such as rats and ferrets are nocturnal, so they may often be sleeping during the day. However, we have found that our small therapy animals are excited to wake up and engage with clients for an out-of-cage adventure.

Small animals can bite quite hard, especially if someone smells like food. It is important to know under what conditions your animal might bite and to do some prevention. For instance, some animals may be tired at the end of a workday and become agitated more quickly. To help mitigate bites, we spend several months getting to know each of our small animals—their temperaments, quirks, and preferences—before we allow them to work with clients. We also require clients to wash their hands before handling the small animals.

Due to the stigma associated with their breed, rats can be a more challenging animal for clients to accept and want to handle. Certain cultural, ethnic, or geographical groups will have different beliefs about rats depending on their experiences with them, perhaps only being familiar with city rats associated with filth and disease. However, domestic rats have been bred to select for gentle traits and are usually friendly and clean. It may take more time to desensitize a client or the client may opt out of working with the rats entirely. We accept this situation with any animal; clients are never required to work with any animal. Nonetheless, we may gently encourage certain clients to push themselves out of their comfort zone and work with rats or another animal about whom they are hesitant or ambivalent.

Additionally, some humans can be allergic to small mammal fur, saliva, dander, feces, or urine. Many rats can be potty-trained so they will not urinate on people, but even if there are traces of urine on their feet and it comes into contact with skin, people can have a reaction. We recommend that clients wear long sleeves or put some fabric between their skin and the rat. Male and female rats each have unique challenges. Adult male rats tend to have a large scrotum, which make some clients uncomfortable. Female rats are prone to mammary tumors, which are not always fatal but can grow large and interfere with the rats' movement and quality of life. We generally choose to work with female rats and get them spayed, which helps avoid the tumors and extend their lifespan.

Reptiles have several distinct characteristics that can make them more complicated to include in therapy. Reptiles (and amphibians) may carry salmonella on their skin, which can be very dangerous to a human who does not thoroughly wash their hands after handing them. In addition, reptiles are carnivorous; snakes eat rodents and other reptiles eat insects. Reptiles must be fed live or frozen rodents and insects, which can be difficult for staff to supply and can be traumatizing for some clients to witness. We do not have resident reptiles at our facility, but we do have clinicians who bring their reptiles into the office to work with specific clients; however, the reptiles are fed at home, and clients are given a detailed explanation about the hygiene risks.

The final and perhaps largest problem with small animals is their short lifespan. We have said goodbye to several rats, guinea pigs, and rabbits, and these goodbyes were difficult for both staff and clients. We do always try to make these challenging situations into teachable moments and discuss grief, loss, and how to process losing someone you love, but it is never easy. Several clients have been able to see the benefits of a positive goodbye and having a ritual or memento to remember a loved one.

HOUSING AND LOGISTICS FOR SMALL ANIMALS

Even small animals need a sizable enclosure with room to explore, exercise, and rest. If the enclosure is small, animals will need time away outside of it to explore and play. We like to give our guinea pigs, rabbits, and ferrets large rooms in which they freely roam and have a large, three-story enclosure for our rats that we re-arrange regularly. These animals also need safe, hidden spaces within their living quarters to hide and rest. Small animals tend to like and need hiding spaces and soft, snuggly areas where they can curl inside for much of the day. Studies have found that small animals, such as guinea pigs, can become stressed and display an increase in freezing behaviors and decrease in eating if they do not have access to hiding shelters during animal-assisted interventions. Having several kinds of shelters in their home allows them to retreat as needed and control their own level of stress (Gut et al., 2018; Wirth et al., 2020). Rooms with vents in the floor or low wall heaters can be hazardous. Electrical cords cannot be left in reach of any small animal as they can be chewed and pose a lethal danger to the animals and their humans. We have found that for our animals, having tiled floors with lots of soft blankets and hiding spaces is the best combination of safe, cozy, and sanitary.

Small animals should have a lot of toys and enrichment items in their en-closure, including wood or hard items to chew on and keep their teeth at a safe length. Our ferrets love to have small toys to drag around, and they also love to play in water. Small animals need a consistent supply of food and water; we have more than one water bottle in the enclosure at all times, several dry food bowls for them to free feed, and also give each species appropriate fresh food such as vegetables, cheese, and meat every morning and evening, both to give them ex-tra nutrients and because we love them.

A major consideration with small animals is cleanliness, as small animal en-closures contain their excrement and may smell unpleasant. Ferrets can have a strong scent, but this can be mitigated by being spayed or neutered and having their scent glands removed. Small animals such as rats, rabbits, and ferrets can be potty-trained to defecate in a certain area, so having an area with a small litter box can be convenient and easy to clean. Guinea pigs generally poop all over the enclosure, so keeping it clean is more difficult. Having a thorough cleaning rou-tine helps keep the animals healthy and reduces any unpleasant odors.

Small mammals are social and prefer to live in pairs or small groups. When one individual dies, it can be difficult for the remaining animal to accept a new partner, but with patience it can be accomplished. Reptiles tend to be more solitary. If you are sharing your office space with other animals, such as dogs or cats, it is essential to make sure your small animals are safe from them. Do not house your ferrets or your snake with your rats, as that is a dangerous combination for the rats. Overall, be mindful of what animals may be present in your space and how they will interact and impact one another.

Reptiles have different housing needs depending on the species. They are generally kept in a wide or tall terrarium, depending on the kind of mobility they require. Some reptiles can grow quite large and should have a natural and comfortable environment. There are also temperature, humidity, and solar requirements to consider, which again will vary depending on your animal. If you hope to work with a reptile, make sure to do your due diligence and learn about the species and its unique housing, feeding, and health needs.

SMALL ANIMALS: CHARACTERISTICS AND UNIQUE THERAPEUTIC CONTRIBUTIONS

There are obviously vast differences between species of small animals, but many can make excellent therapy animals. In this section, we examine many of the common small animals that can be included in therapy and how they can uniquely benefit sessions.

RATS

Rats have distinct personalities; whereas some are gregarious and outgoing, others are quiet and shy. We have had some rats who love being held and learning tricks and other rats who are more timid and take time to trust people. Rats are quite smart and can be taught to come when called and perform tricks, such as dancing or running through mazes. Some rats enjoy the enclosed exercise balls that allow them to roll around and explore a large space. Rats can be very affectionate and will snuggle with people and groom someone they trust.

When determining if a rat is a good fit for therapy, you can observe how it behaves when it hears or sees you coming. If a rat comes to greet you at the door of its enclosure, they are demonstrating a desire for human connection and engagement. When you are holding or playing with a rat, pay attention to whether it comes back to you for play, snuggles with you, or seems to prefer hiding under the couch or being independent.

As rats get older, they often prefer to cuddle rather than play and may want to curl up in a blanket on a client's lap and rest. We have found that gently petting a rat's nose and up over the eyes helps the rat relax and go to sleep; this activity has the added benefit of calming down our clients as well. Clients must practice being still, calm, mindful, and moving carefully; they are also using gentle fine motor skills and paying close attention to how the rat responds to them.

Our rats elicit the most varied responses from clients, from elation to shock to disgust. These strong reactions and even prejudice about rats is part of what makes them good therapy animals. These responses give clinicians ample opportunity to discuss what clients assume or believe about rats, and often we can connect this to their experiences with humans in their lives. Clients may feel misunderstood or as though people make assumptions about them based on how

A client building a "Rat City."

they look; they can relate to how rats may be stereotyped or labeled negatively. We can also work on acceptance and trying new, challenging behaviors, such as holding a rat, which is a tremendous example of acceptance. It also is a good example of how once you get to know someone, it can be easier to relate to, care for, and even love them. Recent research has shown that rats are capable of empathy (Bartal et al., 2011; Cox & Reichel, 2020), which challenges clients' beliefs about the capabilities of others. If rats can feel empathy, perhaps our clients can learn empathy as well.

Rats are incredibly playful and may even laugh. Jaak Panksepp (1999) conducted a study that documented that rats emit a high-pitched vocalization when tickled, akin to a laugh (Panksepp & Burgdorf, 1999). The rats continued to return to the hand that was tickling them, demonstrating that they were enjoying the interaction. (There are some fun videos you can watch on YouTube of rats getting tickled to give you and your clients some inspiration.) Clients can practice petting and tickling the rats and observe their behavior. We also can talk about the importance of play and the joy it elicits, which is something many of our clients are missing in their lives. Clients can make mazes and structures with toys, ramps, and tubes for the rats to play in and explore. Clients can help rearrange the rats' home, which allows for caring, empathy, and creativity. This activity may also enable the clinician to discover what the client values; for instance, one client may create a lot of space for the rat to run and be active, while another ensures the rats have a place to hide. This can inform the clinician about what is important to the client and perhaps what they may need in their own lives. Rats also like to sit on shoulders, under long hair, in hoodies, or inside long sleeves. These are powerful ways to connect with a gentle creature and get some unique sensory input.

GUINEA PIGS

Guinea pigs are herd animals with a strong hierarchy. As they became domesticated, they became more comfortable and less reactive with humans (Bays, 2006). Generally, guinea pigs are active, vocal, and expressive. Some guinea pigs may be more active and others more relaxed, and it is nice to have guinea pigs with each quality to help with different goals in therapy. Young guinea pigs tend to be more playful and interactive, but as they age, they may slow down and appreciate a cuddly blanket in a client's lap. Like most small animals, guinea pigs have short lifespans, usually less than five years, so you may want to adopt a young one.

We have had six long-haired guinea pigs, who are soft and more traditionally cute, and two hairless "skinny" pigs, who are more unusual looking and elicit a wide range of responses from clients. Some clients think they look silly or scary, some think they are adorable. Clients may feel sorry for them, empathize with them, or want to protect them. Clients often feel a desire to care for the skinny pigs, Rosie and Gloria. These unique animals bring out a nurturing side in many clients, who like to rub oil on their dry ears and feet or knit them sweaters. We also have had clients from our addiction groups with complicated pasts who snuggle Rosie and Gloria, demonstrating gentler, caregiving elements of their personalities.

Our skinny pig Rosie was albino, pink, hairless, and had one red eye. She also had a delightful white mohawk and tiny goatee. While her appearance was surprising, she was incredibly social, friendly, gentle, and snuggly. This seeming contrast between her appearance and her temperament allowed many clients to bond with her; it also stimulated discussion about how appearances do not necessarily reflect anything about someone's personality or inherent worth.

Guinea pigs can easily startle, so they may run to a safe spot when they see a person, but with patience, they will come out of hiding and engage. Many guinea pigs enjoy being held, which is a good characteristic for a therapy guinea pig since clients usually want to hold them. One of our pigs, Snickers, has never liked being held, but will interact with clients when they sit quietly in the enclosure. Several of our other guinea pigs, including our two hairless pigs, love to interact and be held by clients. When being cuddled, guinea pigs will make sweet noises and may even purr. Happy piggies will "popcorn," jumping up and down, and "wheek," a distinctive sound that demonstrates happy or excited feelings.

As with other prey animals, clients need to practice sitting still, being quiet, and keeping a calm body to allow the guinea pig to feel comfortable enough to emerge from hiding. Clients can create mazes and play areas for the guinea pigs or help to rearrange their enclosure, deciding what they think the pigs need most. Learning what entices a particular guinea pig to come out of hiding and run through a cardboard town is a fun way for clients to practice care and empathy. Guinea pigs have been called the "small great clinician for autistic children" due to their ability to increase the quality and quantity of social behaviors in children with autism (Talarovičová et al., 2010). Clients with autism may relate to the sensitive nature of guinea pigs and their need to take extra time to feel comfortable in certain situations.

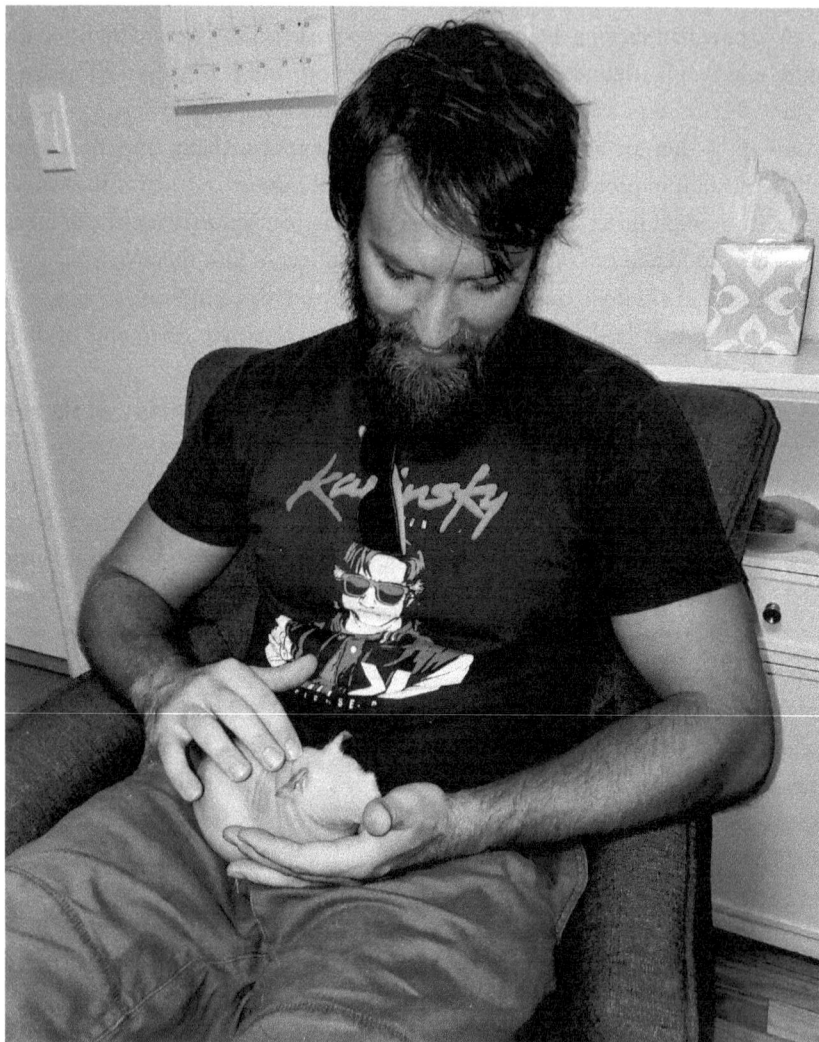

Rosie was a favorite for all kinds of clients.

Due to their small size, guinea pigs are easy to transport. This means clinicians may be able to bring them into the office on certain days or for certain clients, as long as there is a safe space in the office for them. If guinea pigs are socialized early and learn to be comfortable in multiple environments, they can add flexibility to your practice. We found that Rosie, was too stressed to travel, while another pig, Rollo, delighted in meeting new people. He even represented our agency on several television programs.

RABBITS

Rabbits are relatively small and fragile, yet not as fragile as rats or guinea pigs. They are prey animals that prefer quiet, calm environments. Our rabbit room is probably the most meditative of all our therapy spaces. Rabbits will tolerate only a small amount of stress in the room before they hide and refuse to emerge. Rabbits are great teachers and are excellent at reacting to the energy of the room. They require an energy and mindset very different from our other animals, quietly demanding respect and patience. Clients must practice being slow, quiet, and gentle if they want to interact with the rabbits, and they quickly discover that they need to use a soft voice and sit calmly in order to help the rabbits feel safe. Maintaining this behavior for a session is amazing practice at self-awareness, empathy, and self-regulation.

Some therapy rabbits are affectionate and will sit on a client's lap, while others may be more aloof and sit near a client only after a relationship has been established. Rabbits are incredibly soft and show contentment in their ears, eyes, tail, and whole body when being pet appropriately. To watch a rabbit relax under your touch is very rewarding; our rabbit Maggie would spread out her legs and lay flat on the ground when she felt safe and happy. Rabbits are highly social and prefer to live in pairs, often with a mate. Our rabbits' relationship with each other is a model of patience, interdependence, and autonomy. They are kind and gentle, groom each other, share their food, and sleep together; however, they can also be independent and play with their own toys or interact individually with clients.

Rescuing a rabbit can be a powerful story of connection, trust, and respect. We adopted Maggie because she was neglected and left outside during a cold Colorado winter. Maggie had not been socialized, and due to her trauma and fear, at first she would attempt to bite humans. After an adjustment period, we allowed staff to interact with Maggie in order to help her feel safe and secure in her new home. Eventually, Maggie learned that humans could not only be trusted, but would give her affection, love, and treats. We provided Maggie with a large room and toys, and she bonded with a small stuffed tiger and would play hide and seek with clients.

Several years later, we adopted a pregnant guinea pig and her male baby, Rollo, needed to be separated from the female guinea pigs. We temporarily moved his enclosure into the rabbit room and he sought out Maggie, purring when he found her. He bonded with Maggie and she mothered him for the rest of her life; this three-week-old guinea pig had found the love and connection he needed. Rollo, Maggie, and her mate, K.C., bonded and created a unique blended family. Their story of neglect, love, and resilience allowed clients to connect with them in a special way.

FERRETS

Ferrets are less common as therapy animals and ferrets are not allowed in certain geographical areas, so make sure to research your community's policies and laws. Ferrets that are available to be adopted as pets have been bred to be domesticated and accept contact with humans (Bays, 2006). Ferrets are predators, which generally means they are confident and less apt to hide from humans. As with other small animals, some ferrets are more outgoing than others, but as long as they seem comfortable and will play with humans, they may be a good candidate as a therapy ferret. They can tolerate being handled and engaging with active clients. Socializing ferrets before introducing them to clients is important, and then closely monitoring ferrets' initial contact with clients helps ensure they are consenting to and enjoying human interaction.

Ferrets are fun, active animals and can be playful, exuberant, and silly. Clients may enjoy creating structures, playhouses, ball pits, or water zones for the ferrets. A fun activity with ferrets is to dangle different toys in front of them and see which ones they try to grab or chase as they engage in agile ferret acrobatics. Ferrets also like to hide toys, so clients may enjoy hunting for the various toys the ferrets have hidden around their room. Ferrets play with complete abandon, which is a wonderful model of enjoying the moment.

Ferrets are social, playful, and love to snuggle.

REPTILES

Reptiles are a recent addition to our practice because we were cautious about the risk of salmonella. However, once we developed sanitary practices to mitigate this risk and hired a clinician who had her own reptile, we embraced the idea. Not all reptiles will be interested in being a therapy partner, but bearded dragons, geckos, and certain breeds of snakes, such as corn snakes and ball pythons, have been domesticated to the extent that they enjoy contact with humans. For example, "Bearded dragons are highly social, friendly, animated, curious, docile, and gentle animals that are easy to tame and are very responsive to their owners" (*Owning Bearded Dragons*, 2023). Reptiles have preferences and personalities, so they will need proper socialization and exposure to the therapy environment. A good therapy reptile will be one that initiates and enjoys contact with humans, can be easily moved, and can remain safe when held. Snakes, for example, "were first [included] as 'animal-therapy' in London to help people struggling with depression and anxiety. Now, there are many who find emotional support with the likes of lizards, geckos and iguanas. For obvious reasons, these reptiles have also helped people overcome their fears and increase their confidence, as well as enhance concentration and raise mood" (Phys.org, 2023).

Clients may feel confident, brave, and powerful as they form a bond with a reptile. For those clients who are squeamish around reptiles, it is a good opportunity for them to challenge themselves, test their beliefs and stereotypes, and get out of their comfort zone. Reptiles are quite unique, as they look and feel different from typical therapy animals. They are also interesting to observe; many reptiles move slowly and can create a quiet, sedate atmosphere that can help with anxiety. Their unique tactile qualities provide many opportunities to practice mindfulness. Snakes, such as boas, can give a client a deep squeeze that may feel comforting or meet sensory needs.

INTERVENTIONS WITH SMALL ANIMALS

Small animals, especially our rats, love to run inside of enclosed spaces. They will happily run up your client's arm under their sweater, across their back, and down the other arm, which can provide some interesting sensory input to clients. Rats, guinea pigs, and ferrets can explore a structure, obstacle course, or maze made by your client, or play hide-and-seek. Once these small animals have met their exercise and play needs, they may cuddle up and go to sleep on a client's lap, usually inside a blanket so they feel protected. This is a good opportunity to discuss our own varied needs, how to recognize when we need something, and how to meet those needs. It is also a fun way to give the animal exercise and affection.

Most of our small animals have a large space or even an entire room full of toys, including small balls, stuffed animals, tunnels, items to chew, and small pools. The animals love to play with their toys in a variety of ways. Rabbits can be taught to jump on a chair or other lower piece of furniture. Rats, ferrets, and even bearded dragons can be walked on a leash and come when called. They can be given baths or groomed with a damp towel. Many small animals are unusual to look at and can simply be observed while the client and clinician wonder out loud what they might be contemplating. Clients can be asked to mimic the animal's movement or to stay still for as long as the animal.

A primary focus with small animals is empathy, calmness, and finding ways to create enjoyment for the animal. One of the most useful and powerful interventions with the rabbits is to match the energy in the room and to practice calm, quiet stillness. A teenage client with an eating disorder laid on her back with the lettuce on her stomach, and as she settled her body and calmed her anxiety about food, the rabbit jumped on her stomach to eat her dinner. Clients learn that by making the animals feel happy and safe, they feel good too.

REFERENCES

Bartal, I. B.-A., Decety, J., & Mason, P. (2011). *Empathy and pro-social behavior in rats* (Vol. 334). American Association for the Advancement of Science. https://doi.org/10.1126/science.1210789

Bays, T. B. (2006). Guinea pig behavior. In T. B. Bays, T. Lightfoot, & J. Mayer (Eds.), *Exotic pet behavior: birds, reptiles, and small mammals*. Elselvier Health Sciences.

Cox, S. S., & Reichel, C. M. (2020). Rats display empathic behavior independent of the opportunity for social interaction. *Neuropsychopharmacology, 45*(7), 1097–1104. https://doi.org/10.1038/s41386-019-0572-8

Gut, W., Crump, L., Zinsstag, J., Hattendorf, J., & Hediger, K. (2018). The effect of human interaction on guinea pig behavior in animal-assisted therapy. *Journal of Veterinary Behavior* (25), 56–64.

Macauley, L., & Chur-Hansen, A. (2022). Human health benefits of non-conventional companion animals: A narrative review. *Animals, 13*(1), 1–24. https://doi.org/10.3390/ani13010028

Owning Bearded Dragons. (2023). VCA animal hospital. https://vcahospitals.com /know-your-pet/bearded-dragons-owning

Panksepp, J., & Burgdorf, J. (1999). Ultrasonic chirping in young rodents. In S. Hameroff, A. Kaszniak, & D. Chalmers (Eds.), *Toward a science of consciousness III: The third Tucson discussions and debates*. Institute of Technology.

Phys.org. (2023). Snakes as therapy animals: Reptiles help heal in Brazil. https://phys.org /news/2023-06-snakes-therapy-animals-reptiles-brazil.html

Wirth, S., Gebhardt-Henrich, S. G., Riemer, S., Hattendorf, J., Zinsstag, J., & Hediger, K. (2020). The influence of human interaction on guinea pigs: Behavioral and thermographic changes during animal-assisted therapy. *Physiological Behavior, 225,* 113076. https://doi.org/10.1016/j.physbeh.2020.113076

7

GENTLE GIANTS OR PSYCHIC GENIUSES: EQUINES AS THERAPY ANIMALS

"I have seen things so beautiful they have brought tears to my eyes. Yet none of them can match the gracefulness and beauty of a horse running free."

—*UNKNOWN*

Equine therapy is one of the oldest and most researched forms of AACP, and while the research focuses primarily on horses, equines also include donkeys and mules (Kovács et al., 2020; Lee et al., 2016). There are many specific training programs that teach equine-assisted psychotherapy (EAP) work, including Gestalt Equine Psychotherapy (Gestalt Equine Institute), Equine Assisted Growth and Learning (EAGALA), and Professional Association of Therapeutic Horsemanship (PATH). These programs use various approaches to equine therapy, each with different strengths, weaknesses, and benefits for populations and presenting issues. Many organizations also include equine-assisted learning, riding therapy, and/or hippotherapy, which incorporates the movement of an equine to help with physical, occupational, or speech therapy goals. Many of these programs include two professionals in each session—a mental health specialist and an equine specialist. At our facility, we prefer to have just one clinician in each session; that clinician is familiar with the equines and feels comfortable working with these animals and the client at the same time. We do only groundwork at AATPC, which means clients do not ride the animals, but they may feed, groom, halter, and walk them.

CHARACTERISTICS AND UNIQUE THERAPEUTIC CONTRIBUTIONS OF EQUINES

Being aware of equines' natural inclinations helps to understand how they may respond in certain situations and to appreciate the significance of their reactions. Equines are prey animals that traditionally live in a herd with a specific leader. They look to the leader for guidance about how to respond to situations, but the entire herd works cooperatively to protect each other. For example, it is rare to see all horses sleeping at the same time; more often at least one horse will remain awake and alert for predators. Equines have adapted incredibly sensitive ways of listening to and interpreting their environment because their survival depends upon noticing subtle cues. They notice changes in their environment, the weather, wind patterns, sounds, and pressure. Because of this sensitivity, they may not be comfortable working on certain days when the weather is changing or when their environment has been altered.

Domesticated equines are used to being around humans, and a good therapy equine will be quite comfortable with a range of clients. It is important to work with equines who like being around people and enjoy being touched and groomed. This does not mean they always want to be with humans or be groomed, but they should enjoy it most of the time. It is helpful to have an equine that is patient and affectionate, but also gently stubborn. Because equines are so sensitive to their environment, they often pick up on subtle cues or changes in clients and will respond accordingly. Some of the most powerful therapeutic moments we have had are when our equines resist the client's requests. These powerful equine responses speak volumes about what is going on for the client and how it is impacting their relationship with the animal. Equines will not respond simply because you ask them, as a well-trained dog might. They are genuine and honest in their responses, and we cannot force them to follow our directions. This behavior allows clinicians to gently explore with the client what might be triggering the equine's response and often leads to therapeutic insight and honesty.

Equines come in varying sizes, from small, miniature horses to mid-size donkeys to large quarter horses, so having a diverse selection of equines can be quite useful, though may be logistically challenging. Smaller equines, such as miniature horses, can be a good starting point for young clients or those who feel apprehensive about working with a very large animal. Small equines can still be dangerous, but their smaller size lessens any potential harm. However, being small does not mean they are well behaved. Our miniature horse, Batman, is incredibly agreeable, reliable, and gentle, whereas our other mini, Misty, is quite feisty and can be a bit moody. However, when she is feeling feisty, the risk to clients is much lower given her smaller stature. Similarly, our full-size horses are a study in personality contrasts. Tunka is steady, patient, and tolerant, so she is wonderful to work with on a harness and lead rope. She is a good full-size horse for more anxious or labile clients, because she is calm and listens well. In contrast, Hawkeye, our youngest and largest horse, still acts like a defiant teenager at times and is mischievous and playful. He requires our clinicians be comfortable, confident, and attuned to the subtle cues that he is going to act out.

Donkeys are the most affectionate, perceptive, and mellow of our equines, and the most interested in interacting with clients who need emotional support.

Receiving comfort from Millie, our donkey.

Our donkeys, gentle Millie and lovable Daisy, are mid-size and a great beginning equine for clients. They will almost always come to say hello and stand still for a hug or a good cry with a client. They are generally sweet, mellow, and eager for gentle affection, but can be incredibly stubborn and vocal as well.

Clients enjoy working with each equine type and individual for different reasons. Having three breeds and sizes of equines provides diversity and unique experiences. Any size of equine can demonstrate risky behavior, such as kicking or biting, so it is essential to understand which scenarios and behaviors are stressful to each animal, constantly monitor each interaction, and know how to respond quickly and safely.

The novelty of working with an equine can be a new, positive experience. It feels like a privilege for such a large animal to give you attention and work with you. Many of our clients have no experience with horses and are intimidated by their size and strength. The sense of pride and accomplishment that comes from successfully walking one of the horses is incredibly powerful for many clients, especially those who feel timid or overlooked in their daily lives. For our youngest and smallest clients, to be able to walk a full-size horse or donkey is a wonder. Moreover, caregivers can see these children in a new light and watch them accomplish something significant and beautiful. Caregivers and family members may also gain a new sense of respect and awe for their child, especially if the caregiver tries the same task unsuccessfully. This activity allows children and family members/guardians to see each other in new ways, offer respect and admiration, and support and teach each other.

One of the major strengths of equines is their ability to quickly recognize and respond to congruence, truth, and honesty. They notice and react to ambivalence or incongruence. The equine acts as a mirror, reflecting the client's true, often hidden, feelings back to them. Clients also seem to project more onto the equines than the other animals; they may reflect their own energy or emotions onto a horse when they are not comfortable sharing. Clients may notice relational dynamics within the herd and interpret behaviors or view equines as different personalities in their own lives. Perhaps it is due to their size or the herd dynamics that often mimic those of human families. These factors allow clients to interpret the equine's behavior in a way that reflects their inner monologue, relationship dynamics, or other therapeutic issues and allows for powerful insight. AACP with equines is very flexible and complex work, often allowing the clients and equines to engage in unstructured ways, while the clinician observes and helps the client interpret the interactions.

Hawkeye is our feisty teenage horse.

A good example of these relational dynamics comes in working with our quarter horse, Hawkeye. Being a mischievous teenage horse, he may do the opposite of what a clinician or client is asking him to do. He provides a great metaphor for parents or caregivers of adolescents who are struggling with control and independence. To work successfully with Hawkeye, clients need to demonstrate confidence and congruence, while also giving and expecting respect. Caregivers and children can practice these behaviors with Hawkeye, see the tangible results in behavior, and translate their actions into changes with family members.

Our first horses were miniature horses, Misty and Stormy. They were rehomed to us and though siblings, had opposite personalities. Stormy was patient, silly, and easygoing. He was happy to interact with all clients and was so mellow that he was routinely painted with horse paint as a clinical activity. Clients could express themselves in nonverbal, unique, powerful ways as he grazed and nudged them with his soft nose. In contrast, Misty is feisty, high-spirited, and willful, though loving, and requires that people be attentive, intentional, and focused when they are with her. Though small, Misty demands respect and often bosses around the larger equines. She is a great example to clients about making your needs known, being clear about your desires, and that size does not matter. We include Misty in sessions with only certain clients who can maintain strong boundaries and be assertive. Though Misty is now elderly and semiretired, she is still sassy and makes her preferences well known when we are in the arena.

Cody was our first full-size horse, given to us after his horse partner passed away and he struggled with depression. He was a wonderful therapy horse; he was sweet, calm, and enjoyed being around people. He patiently allowed people to lean on him and cry, whisper secrets in his ears, and braid his tail. Perhaps given his own experiences with loss and grief, he understood what clients needed. However, Cody also could be very stubborn and would not willingly walk on a halter and lead rope for every client. Clients learned that they needed to demonstrate that they were a leader who Cody could trust. For most of our clients, this meant that they needed to change their beliefs about themselves and modify their physical presentation so that they could consistently and congruently demonstrate their intent to have Cody walk. If their assertiveness or intention waned, Cody would stop in his tracks. Cody was amazing at challenging incongruence, and faulty and distorted thinking, and he did it without saying a word.

We have been lucky to work with many horses throughout the years. AATPC currently has two miniature horses, two quarter horses, and two donkeys, all from rescues or rehomed with us from families who could no longer keep them. Each of our equines has a very different personality, and they are invaluable in challenging and offering benefits to our clients and staff in many ways.

HOUSING, LOGISTICS, AND CHALLENGES WITH EQUINES AS THERAPY ANIMALS

Equines are incredibly complex creatures with unique social, physical, and medical needs. Equines not only require a lot of space, but they are also social creatures who have evolved to live in a herd. They will need to live with other equines, or at least a companion animal such as a goat. You will need enough space for these animals to live comfortably together. Equines have evolved to walk and feed all day, so they will need a lot of space to move around, field graze if possible, and have constant access to food and water. If temperatures go below freezing, you may need a system to get water into their pasture year-round. At our facility, we had to build a special underground system because the hoses and water troughs froze during cold Colorado winters.

Equines require a great amount of hay. Each equine has different nutritional needs, so it is critical to find the proper type and amount of hay for each. Whereas our larger equines need a tremendous amount of food, our miniature horses eat much less, and despite their huge appetites, they can quickly become overweight, which can lead to severe health issues. To help our equines eat the appropriate amount throughout the day, we have tried a variety of slow feeders. Eventually, we found round slow feeders that are safe and effective and act as wonderful toys at the end of the day when they are empty. All of our equines also receive daily supplements, and the larger horses eat beet pulp in the evening.

Equines are uniquely sensitive to their environment, so they will need to have a safe, covered paddock space to retire if it is windy, stormy, or very cold. They need secure fencing, appropriate ground cover, and fresh grass. Their fencing should be safe with secure gates; our horses actually learned how to open certain gates, so we now use a complicated latch and hook system. Equines attract flies, which bite humans as well. We have fly spray for the horses and insect repellent for the humans, but bites can still occur. Horse manure can attract flies and can bother some individuals. The manure should be removed from client spaces and the areas kept as clean as possible. Regularly cleaning equine stalls, paddocks, arenas, pastures, and working areas is essential. Disposing of manure can be a challenge, as equines create a lot of waste, so you will need a system to compost or dispose of the manure. Not all trash companies will accept manure, and it can take a while to compost large amounts of manure, so this is not a small issue.

Equines have complex health and medical needs, and each equine will have individual needs. Generally, equines require an intense amount of medical monitoring and specialized veterinary care. They should be monitored daily by someone familiar with equines, as their health needs can change quickly. While many equine vets will travel to you, some may not, or some procedures can only be completed at an equine hospital. That means you must have access to emergency transportation, a horse trailer, and have trained your equine to reliably enter the trailer. Equines routinely need vaccinations, teeth floating (cleaning), hoof trimming or shoeing, weight monitoring, and careful feeding. Equines often can have dental issues, gut issues, or problems with their feet. Although equines are large, they are also surprisingly fragile and prone to injury. They can easily get hurt by sharp fencing or sticks, stumbling in holes, or nips or kicks from their friends. Many equines will require specialized food, medicine, or supplements, which can be difficult to administer. Serious equine ailments, such as colic, can occur quickly and be deadly. Other issues, such as Cushing's disease, may be hard to detect until it is a serious issue. Our horse Cody struggled with age-related Cushing's disease that affected his feet and ability to walk.

Due to their size, equines can injure humans, intentionally or unintentionally. They can step on their feet, kick, bite, nip, or knock into a person with their body. Even if done with love, these behaviors can injure or frighten a person. An angry, impatient, frustrated, excited, or frightened equine can do a lot of damage very quickly. For example, our equines get very excited around feeding time and may move rapidly, though happily, toward the person with the food, which can be scary or cause harm if the person is not paying attention. Equines may spook from an unexpected noise, sight, or smell, and may lash out without awareness of what is around them. Even with training, awareness, and confidence, injuries can still happen. However, knowing about equine communication and each individual equine's needs, triggers, and signs of stress and anxiety can help mitigate risk. Equines have a tremendous amount to offer clients in terms of growth and therapeutic benefit, but they are also a challenging and expensive animal to keep healthy.

Some individual clinicians may not have their own equines and may choose to rent or borrow an equine or herd to include in sessions. This can be beneficial for clients for the reasons previously mentioned; however, please be certain that you know those animals well and that they know and respond to you. Even if there is a separate equine manager/handler, the clinician should understand the equine's communication, preferences, needs. If you do not know a particular equine, you could be putting everyone in a risky situation, and injury and lawsuits can happen when we are not adequately prepared.

AN EXAMPLE OF
AN EQUINE-ASSISTED INTERVENTION

Pete, a 28-year-old client, was struggling to remain sober from opioids after being discharged from a six-month program. In the beginning of the therapy process, Pete developed a trusting relationship with our donkey, Millie. Pete came to session a few days after a relapse feeling distraught and afraid. The clinician brought Pete into the paddock with Millie and her herd. In tears, Pete talked about his self-hatred and shame for being unable to stay sober. Millie approached Pete and stood face-to-face with him, just looking into his eyes. She then stood still as Pete hugged her. After several minutes of crying in Millie's mane, he looked up to see that the rest of the herd had encircled him. "What do you think is happening?" the clinician asked quietly. After several quiet moments, Pete stated that the horses and donkeys had come to support him when he needed it most. The clinician asked him to quietly take in the concern, care, and strength the herd was sharing with him. Pete was able to feel that they had accepted him into the herd. Pete and his clinician quietly explored how he could integrate the feeling of the herd's collective strength as a support in his sobriety.

REFERENCES

Equine Assisted Growth and Learning (EAGALA). https://www.eagala.org

Gestalt Equine Institute. http://www.gestaltequineinstitute.com

Kovács, G., van Dijke, A., & Enders-Slegers, M.-J. (2020). Psychodynamic based equine-assisted psychotherapy in adults with intertwined personality problems and traumatization: A systematic review. *International Journal of Environmental Research and Public Health, 17*(16). https://doi.org/10.3390/ijerph17165661

Lee, P.-T., Dakin, E., & Mclure, M. (2016). Narrative synthesis of equine-assisted psychotherapy literature: Current knowledge and future research directions. *Health & Social Care in the Community, 24*(3), 225–246. https://doi.org/10.1111/hsc.12201

Professional Association of Therapeutic Horsemanship (PATH). https://pathintl.org

8

IS THAT A CAMEL OR A LLAMA? FARM ANIMALS IN THERAPY

"An animal's eyes have the power to speak a great language."

—*MARTIN BUBER*

There are many nontraditional but lovable and friendly animals who can be amazing therapy partners. In addition to our cats, dogs, small animals, and equines, we also work with several types of goats, alpacas, and chickens. We have colleagues and friends who work with pigs, sheep, cows, and ducks, and there may be other farm animals that can be wonderful therapy partners. If you have a large enough space, a safe and nurturing environment, knowledge, willingness to be flexible, and lots of love and attention, you can work with a variety of farm animals. As always, it will depend on the individual animal whether they choose to work with you and your clients.

Farm animals provide novel experiences for most clients, with new sights, sounds, smells, and interactions. Many of our clients have never seen farm animals before, so simply seeing and observing the animals is a powerful experience, let alone being able to engage with and train them. In addition, our work with farm animals is done primarily outside, which brings added benefits of being outside and in nature. This type of work also brings unpredictable elements such as weather, other animals, insects, and other unexpected challenges that we can help clients navigate.

Below are examples of farm animals that can be therapy partners. It is beyond the scope of this book to describe the full extent of all these animals' needs, but we briefly address some of the qualities, characteristics, benefits, and challenges of working with each. At the end of the chapter, we share several interventions with farm animals that have been useful with clients.

GOATS

We have found that people often have strong reactions to goats; they either think they are adorable and funny, or they have stories about goats being mean-spirited or aggressive. In our experience, goats are terrific. We adopted our pygmy goats, Duncan and Dahlia, as babies and spent months socializing and training them. We later added two adult Nubian goats and two young Nigerian dwarf goats to our herd when we moved to a larger space. The goats' size, behavior, and personalities are different as a breed and as individuals.

Despite their often mischievous nature, goats are also friendly, curious, silly, smart, and loyal. We think they are worthy of adoration and make terrific therapy animals. As babies, Duncan and Dahlia loved to follow us around the ranch, get tummy rubs, ride in Linda's car, go on hikes, play with anything that moved, taste test everything, and test our fencing for ways to escape. Several of our goats have been clicker trained and enjoy learning new skills, doing obstacle courses, and going for walks on leashes. Goats display a tremendous mix of characteristics that many clients and caregivers can relate to and understand. Sometimes they are loving and affectionate, while a minute later they may headbutt a friend and walk away. This mix of characteristics helps show clients and family members that no one is all good or bad; we all have the potential to push limits and cause chaos, but also to be silly and loving.

LLAMAS AND ALPACAS

Llamas and alpacas are part of the camelid family but are very different animals. Llamas are generally larger and have a longer snout; they tend to be confident, brave, and a little sassy. Alpacas are smaller with a rounder nose and are usually gentle and shy but can be curious and friendly as well. Both llamas and alpacas can provide protection for smaller farm animals, alerting for predators and acting out aggressively if threatened. The lifespan for both is about 15 to 20 years, with proper care and attention.

We adopted our alpacas, Kronk and Kuzco, from a herd that was living in unsuitable conditions. Though raised in the same environment, they have very different temperaments. Kronk is brave and loves to interact with clients and go for walks on his lead, while Kuzco is more timid and takes much longer to feel comfortable with new people. Both love rolling in scratchy grass, running through water, and

Kronk and Kuzco sharing a bite.

playing in their kiddie pool. When our alpacas run, their necks and legs seem to go in all different directions, which is a delightful sight that can bring joy and laughter to clients and clinicians. Our alpacas also love carrots and may even take a carrot out of your mouth if you hold quite still, an exercise in patience and calmness. They have very thick, curly hair, but neither love being brushed. Grooming the alpacas can therefore be a powerful but challenging therapeutic activity, as clients gain their trust, work to harness them, and patiently work through the tangled hair.

CHICKENS AND DUCKS

Farm birds such as chickens and ducks also can make wonderful therapy animals, particularly if they are raised, handled, and socialized from a young age. Our chickens were adopted as baby chicks, and we handled them frequently so they became comfortable with humans and enjoy a variety of interactions. They love people and run toward us when we come out to their pasture. They will come as a group when called and run around the pasture with clients. Their group interactions are complex, dynamic, and fascinating to observe with clients. Several of

Playing follow-the-leader.

our chickens enjoy being held and cuddled, which is an exciting and novel experience for many clients. Their soft feathers and unique textures also provide an interesting sensory experience. Chickens are smart, can be clicker trained, and have unique personalities. They also can provide you with fresh eggs, a rewarding activity for many clients.

We recently met therapy ducks in Australia where a colleague had a flock of ducks and chickens. Ducks are quite vocal and share their opinions loudly, so they can be a good model for using your voice and not being shy. They love treats such as frozen peas and will noisily dive into the pond to find them. You can ask clients to choose a duck and interpret what they are saying, which allows for projection, metaphor, and often laughter. Ducks are typically not viewed as being intelligent or having distinct personalities, so helping clients see these animals in a new light is powerful.

PIGS

Pigs are smart, affectionate, social, and clean animals. They can be trained similarly to a dog and can be housebroken. Pigs are very affectionate and enjoy the company of humans and other animals. The temperament, size, and lifespan of a pig will depend on its breed and the individual pig, but many pigs are sweet, playful, and curious. We have colleagues who have worked with full-size pigs, potbellied pigs, and miniature pigs. We have not worked with pigs and so cannot speak to how to socialize or train them, but we do believe that they can be effective therapy partners. It is important to choose a pig that you can provide with enough space, stimulation, and love, and that you learn about your pig's breed and special needs.

COWS AND SHEEP

Sheep and cows are typically docile, calm creatures who enjoy contact with humans if they are socialized early. Both species require a large amount of space to graze and food to eat, but if you have the option, they can be a wonderful addition to therapy. We know individuals who work with miniature cows and full-size sheep and have shared with us how unique and special each animal is. Working with sheep and cows gives clients a new experience and allows them to reframe how they view certain animals. As with pigs, we have not worked with them directly so our knowledge is limited; however, when done with education, understanding, and flexibility, we feel they could be a useful addition to therapy.

CHARACTERISTICS AND UNIQUE THERAPEUTIC BENEFITS OF FARM ANIMALS

Farm animals are generally unique, intelligent, friendly, and can make wonderful therapy partners who challenge clients and open their eyes to many new interactions. As with most therapy partners, you will want to find animals that are friendly, curious, social, and interested in being around humans. This does not mean they always want to engage in sessions, but that they are open to being with people and are not stressed by these interactions. A good therapy farm animal also needs to be safe around people. Many farm animals are quite large, and they can all bite, even in play. In addition, certain animal behavior can be dangerous, even when playful, such as goat headbutting, so it is important to ensure that your animal is safe and that their behavior can be managed.

A major element of therapy work with farm animals is their novelty and creating new experiences for clients. We are not only exposing clients to new animals and connections, but also helping them to see animals in a new way. For example, pigs are not just dirty, smelly creatures that become consumable. They are smart, clever, love to solve puzzles, and enjoy belly rubs. Chickens have personalities and complex social dynamics. These reframes and new viewpoints may eventually encourage clients to see other situations, people, and experiences in their lives in new ways.

Furthermore, we are showing clients that therapy can be much different than they expected. Therapy can be silly and fun because honestly, many of our farm animals are ridiculous. They may look silly, act funny, and make undignified noises or smells. It is nearly impossible to work with our farm animals without smiling or laughing. Clients who are struggling with trauma, anxiety, depression, grief, relational issues, or other challenges may lack an ability to feel joy. If we can give them an experience where they can access this joy again, we can remind them that some joy is still present and perhaps help them find it in their daily lives too. Simply watching the goats play together or the alpacas lope around the pasture may allow the client to experience life in their body again. Many clients have been so entrenched in their problems that they have forgotten how to be alive, but observing the animals and experiencing laughter can enable them to feel levity and social connection again. This also demonstrates that therapy can be fun and involve laughter while still being effective.

Farm animals typically live in herds, which allows for many social dynamics and opportunity for projection, interpretation, and relational discussions. Watching the animals' interactions can stimulate conversations about relationships, friendships, and family dynamics. Because our herd includes alpacas and three types of goats, we also can discuss how families may not look alike or come from the same background but can still support each other. Clients may notice traits in different animals that remind them of family members, or they may see parallels in how the animals act with their own families.

We can discuss the role each animal has in the herd and how it can shift depending on circumstances. Our shy alpaca, Kuzco, likes to chase our goat Lily around the pasture. While he is generally timid and sweet, this is his opportunity to be in the lead and take charge. These types of behaviors allow us to talk to clients about how animals may show different behavior at times, for various reasons, and with varying consequences, and then connect that to human behavior. Another example is when we adopted our young, mini-Nigerian goats, and Dahlia began to headbutt them, a behavior she had not previously displayed. Clients were able to view this behavior and discuss their understanding of it. Whereas we understood that Dahlia was trying to establish her role in the herd, clients had varied interpretations of her behavior, and their thoughts gave clinicians insight into what the client saw, experienced, or felt in the world.

Farm animals can be wonderful at teaching about boundaries and holding firm, because animals can be quite pushy at times. Our Nubian goat, Lily, is still working on being polite and sometimes tries to headbutt people. We are careful about who we allow to work with Lily, and prior to their work, we ensure the client can stand strong in the face of a large goat. Clients learn that it is not only acceptable, but necessary, to hold their own space and boundaries with another being. Our alpaca, Kuzco, is an excellent teacher about boundaries in a much different way; because he is shy and sensitive, clients need to recognize his nonverbal communication and respect the boundaries he is setting. They cannot force a connection with him and so must learn how to build a relationship at a slower pace.

While our farm animals are all friendly, their different temperaments and quirks allow clients to relate to them on different levels. As mentioned above, our mischievous Lily and sensitive Kuzco help teach about boundaries. Our pygmy goat, Dahlia, is lovable and friendly with everyone, so she is helpful for those clients who need love, affection, and laughter. However, Dahlia can be quite resistant when you try to take her on a walk, so clients must work with her stubborn behavior and use creativity and empathy to motivate her to take even a single step. Clients, and sometimes their family members, recognize that pushing or pulling will often meet with more resistance, whereas flexible thinking, problem-solving, and kindness get you farther.

Teaching or training the farm animals is an unusual and powerful experience that is often much different than training a dog or cat. Farm animals can be incredibly stubborn but are also quite clever, so clients must find interesting and novel ways to teach them. Clients have trained our chickens to come when called, go through an obstacle course, and even play kickball with a ping-pong ball. We have created snow tunnels during the winter and encouraged the goats to go through them. As you might imagine, these training sessions involved a lot of problem-solving, creativity, and laughter.

A client helping Dahlia through a snow cave.

There are many other benefits to the unique aspects and elements of working with farm animals. Much of AACP work is done with clients' interpretations of the animals and projection of their thoughts onto the animals. For example, when we shear our alpacas every summer, it allows clients to see them in a much different physical way. The alpacas look much more delicate, vulnerable, or even silly, depending on who is working with them. The alpaca wool is also incredibly soft, and feeling or holding it can be a powerful sensory experience. Farm animals such as pigs often have negative connotations associated with them ("You're such a pig!"), so clients may relate to this experience and feel misjudged or underestimated by those in their lives. They can also learn that stereotypes are not always true and can learn that there is a lot more than meets the eye when it comes to animals, humans, and situations in life.

HOUSING, LOGISTICS, AND CHALLENGES WITH THERAPY FARM ANIMALS

Because most farm animals are prey animals and grazers, they should have a lot of space to roam during the day, but also a safe, secure place for nighttime and for rainy, cold, or stormy days. This space not only gives them a warm and dry escape, but also keeps them safe from predators at night. Even in our suburban neighborhood, coyotes and foxes are prevalent; therefore, we put our farm animals to bed in their enclosures at dusk. Our alpacas and goats each have their own fully enclosed shed, and our chickens are put to bed in their coop. They get some appropriate treats to coax them in for the night, as well as hay or feed and water in their space. Clients can often help put the animals to bed, which is fun and allows for practice with caregiving, empathy, and patience. In the winter, these enclosures have heat lamps and water heaters, so the animals are warm and their water does not freeze. This covered area should also have absorbent ground cover, such as pine shavings, that can be changed regularly. This keeps their feet dry and prevents health issues such as hoof rot.

Farm animals come with a unique set of needs and considerations, depending on the species and individual animal. Animal size, behavior, odor, and cleanliness are some of the primary issues to address. Male goats who have not been castrated can be notably fragrant and can also be fairly aggressive. Female goats will go into heat, which can provoke even a wethered (castrated) goat to act more aggressively to get their attention. Llamas and alpacas need to be sheared every year, and all the animals need their feet and hooves monitored and trimmed regularly. Farm animals also come with many unpleasant odors, which some clients may not enjoy. These animals relieve themselves in their pastures and enclosures, so it is important to try and keep those spaces as unsoiled as possible with daily cleaning. While horse and alpaca manure are relatively easy to clean, cow and pig feces can be much messier. Birds such as chickens can also carry salmonella on their feathers, so it is important to ensure that clients do not touch their faces and do wash hands carefully after working with the chickens.

Farm animals have different health needs than other domestic animals, and most traditional veterinarians are not trained to work with them. It is important to have a veterinarian that is knowledgeable about each animal and who is willing to travel to you for emergencies. We do not breed any of our animals, but we do collect the chicken eggs and use the alpaca hair after their annual shearing. If you do plan to milk or breed an animal, this requires a tremendous amount of medical attention and puts additional stress on the animal. It is important to think about these issues before you obtain any new animals. Finally, it is essential that someone on the staff can monitor the animal's behavior and watch for signs of health issues.

Many farm animals are new to clients and may be larger and bulkier than clients expect. Their behavior also can be surprising or intimidating if you are not familiar with them. Llamas, pigs, and large goats are heavy and can step on or knock into clients, startling or scaring them. Some clients may come into sessions with preconceived ideas about certain animals and think they are mean, ugly, or dangerous. There are also cultural and religious issues to consider, and some clients may not be willing to work with certain animals, which is always acceptable. Because most farm animals are not specifically trained or certified as therapy animals, it is important that the clinician knows the animals well, especially when it comes to signs of stress or anxiety. Even playful behavior can be dangerous or scary to clients.

SAMPLE INTERVENTIONS WITH FARM ANIMALS

One of the unexpected and wonderful aspects of AACP is that clients' work with the animals can be frustrating, and we may actually encourage those situations when therapeutically appropriate. For instance, we may ask clients to walk a goat or harness an alpaca; both are activities that can be fun but also can elicit an animals' stubbornness. Often, the animal's natural tendencies or resistance to the client's plan may mirror how life or other humans can be frustrating or defiant. These situations provide moments for you, as a clinician, to observe how the client truly handles these situations, rather than relying on their self-reports of how they manage difficult situations. Clients may project onto the animal or the situation how they act or feel in their daily lives, which gives us valuable clinical information and allows us to help them handle tough situations in new ways. Clinicians can encourage clients to find alternative ways to their usual methods and coach them through the challenge if necessary. We may be able to say: "Take a minute, breathe, slow down your thinking, and focus on the solution," "What might the animal be thinking right now? What could we do differently to help them feel safe coming with us?," or "Is there something that may help the situation that we need?" In this single encounter, you are giving the client the opportunity to practice important skills to manage frustration and to reach a solution that feels positive to both parties. We think that this approach is much more effective and fun than simply sitting in the office, talking about what the client did or could do, and hoping they remember this discussion during their next frustrating situation.

Most farm animals can be walked, groomed, pet, and even bathed. Clients can feel the various areas of the animals, the unique textures, and patterns of fur, and see if the animal responds differently depending on where or how they pet the animal. Watching and listening to an animal eat can provide a beautiful mindfulness opportunity. Many farm animals, such as cows, sheep, alpacas, and goats, are ruminants, which means they digest their food multiple times. They have multichambered stomachs, so will regurgitate food and chew it multiple times to fully digest the material. This can be a powerful parallel to the thought process that many clients experience, if they struggle with anxiety, depression, trauma, perfectionist traits, or other cognitive stressors. We can discuss how ruminating on thoughts or reprocessing ideas can be helpful, in some circumstances, whereas overthinking or dwelling on certain thoughts may be counterproductive.

There are countless interventions that can be done with farm animals and adapted to each species and individual animal. If your herd has combinations of animals with different physical characteristics, as ours do, you can discuss blended and found families and observe how all types of animals can meet their social and caregiving needs in different ways. You also can observe and discuss group dynamics, relationship styles, and how to work with others who may be very different than you. Clients can choose a farm animal that they most identify with and explain why; additionally, they can choose animals for significant individuals in their life and explain how the relational dynamics are similar or different to what they are observing with the animals. Grounding and mindfulness work can be done with calm farm animals. Clients can touch, pet, or even hold an animal and focus on their five senses or a mantra as they do so. Clients can observe and interact with farm animals when they are in varying emotional states and discuss how different it feels to be around that energy.

9

BEAUTY AND THE BEAST: INSECTS, GARDENING, AND NATURE

"If all mankind were to disappear, the world would regenerate back to the rich state of equilibrium that existed ten thousand years ago. If insects were to vanish, the environment would collapse into chaos."

—E. O. WILSON

One element of the beauty and power of AACP is the ability to work outside and absorb the benefits of being in nature. There is a growing body of research that supports the benefits of nature for people. In their meta-analysis of 49 studies that included over 3,000 participants, researchers (Gaekwad et al., 2022) found that exposure to nature had a medium to large effect on increasing a person's positive affect and decreasing negative affect. E. O. Wilson developed the biophilia hypothesis (Kellert & Wilson, 1993; Gaekwad et al., 2022), which emphasizes humans' inherent need for a connection to nature. We have found that even if an animal is not involved in a session, simply being outside and engaging with nature can be beneficial to clients.

Some of the most recent additions to our ranch include a garden, a greenhouse, and insects. We are just beginning to discover the beauty within the world of insects. One of our clinical staff is passionate about insects and has introduced cockroaches, millipedes, hornworms, and painted lady butterflies to our family of therapy animals. We have learned that insects have unique personalities and skills, and as the insect clinician says, "If you can care about a cockroach, you can care about anything." Humans of all ages can benefit from connecting with insects, seeing them in a new way, and learning to respect the world in which they live and thrive (Bauer, 2023).

For the purposes of this chapter, the term "nature" will refer to cultivated green spaces such as gardens and parks; wild green spaces such as forests or trails;

and the wild animals and insects that live in these spaces. We will use the term "ecotherapy" to refer to doing therapy in these settings or with these wild creatures (Wolsko & Hoyt, 2012). In rural and urban areas, nature is all around us, and bringing elements of nature into session can help clients of all ages.

CHARACTERISTICS AND UNIQUE CONTRIBUTIONS OF ECOTHERAPY AND THERAPY INSECTS

There is growing research into the mental health benefits of being in nature, tending gardens, and even simply being outside (Gaekwad et al., 2022; Kellert & Wilson, 1993; Ulrich, 1984; Young-Soon Jun et al., 2016). Allowing clients to be outside and engage in nature may be a new experience for them, particularly those individuals who live in urban areas. Many people spend the majority of their days inside, often engaging with screens and technology, and we want to reintroduce clients to nature. Because we strongly believe in the healing power of nature, we encourage clients to be outside with us, sitting at the river, walking around the property, or digging in the garden. To be outside while it snows, to play in the rain, and to watch the effect of weather on the animals, birds, and insects creates a different kind of mood and atmosphere with clients. Each intentional interaction with nature also can demonstrate to clients that there may be a quick, easy, and effective way to change their mood. Additionally, we can discuss how they can enhance their mental health outside of session by going for a walk, growing flowers in pots on their deck, or participating in a local community garden. While we recognize that nature and being outside will not usually solve a client's issues, we feel it is one step in helping them find possible alternative solutions and experiencing life in a new way.

Our ranch is intentionally close to Denver, a large urban area of Colorado, so that we can provide our urban clients with access to nature, gardens, animals, and insects, which they might not otherwise experience. We have several large green spaces, a creek, and a variety of native plants and trees. We also have a rose garden (our animal memorial), organic vegetable garden, and organic greenhouse where we grow food and flowers for our animals, staff, and clients. Clients love to help in the garden, and there are many ways that they help. Early in spring, they can plant seeds, cultivate the plants, and watch their growth. Throughout the growing season, clients can help maintain the garden by culling small plants and weeding. Being able to focus on the garden, see the physical changes from hard work, and experience a sense of satisfaction can be incredibly powerful. Eventually, clients can see and taste the tangible fruits of their labor. This ability to create something and then share it with others can enrich the giver and receiver. Moreover, doing these activities side-by-side with clients is an excellent way to help them feel less pressure to verbally engage and can eventually increase their comfort and willingness to share.

Nature is a wonderful place to practice mindfulness or meditation. Clients can focus on their senses, feel the changing air, touch the earth, and observe the world around them. We may ask clients to simply sit outside, take note of their five senses, and share with us what they hear, see, smell, feel, and taste. We might also ask clients to lay on the ground and embrace the support of the earth below them. Other activities may challenge clients to go outside their comfort zones, such as walking barefoot on the earth, rolling around in the grass like the horses or goats, and smelling or hugging trees. Clients may resist or feel silly at first, but often these interventions lead to powerful insights and laughter.

There are numerous metaphors we can include when working with nature. For example, when gardening, we can discuss how we need a certain number of seeds or plants, and that even though more may seem better, there can be too much of a good thing. Too many seeds or seedlings do not allow the plants to grow into their capacity and may lead to more plants dying. However, too few seeds and we run the risk of not having enough plants. We might be able to relate this to health struggles—too much or too little food and our bodies cannot function properly—or social dynamics—too much social time leaves us without time to replenish ourselves, but too little social interaction leaves us lonely.

Another metaphor exists with how we care for our garden and what a garden requires. We can discuss how every living being has certain physical needs, both plants and humans, and what those needs are. Plants need to be handled gently and may even grow better when we talk or sing to them. We can relate this to caring for others, meeting their needs, and being gentle in how we handle our relationships and ourselves. Finally, we can share with clients that we fertilize our plants with manure that comes from our animals. This can lead to conversations about the interconnectedness of plants, animals, and humans, and how we rely on each other to grow and thrive. It may also be a powerful metaphor for how good things can come out of seemingly bad or unpleasant situations.

Many humans think of insects as pests or nuisances. However, insects play a vital role in the natural world, and when you really examine an individual insect or an insect species, you may find it is living a life of purpose: "Insects comprise

A child in awe of the garden.

over 80% of terrestrial species on Earth, and include bees, ants, butterflies, grass-hoppers, and beetles, among many others. Insects drive the production of essential seeds, fruits, and vegetables via pollination, and are necessary decomposers of organic matter" ("Why We Need Insects," 2023). Allowing clients to observe insects closely and discuss how these tiny creatures benefit the world around us can be a powerful reframe and new way for clients to view certain creatures. This simple activity also can help clients realize the power in even very tiny things— tiny creatures, tiny actions, and tiny changes. Children might realize that even though they are small, they can do big, important things. Clients of all ages may realize that small acts of kindness or gentleness can make a big difference to others; or, in contrast, that a small act of anger or defiance can strongly impact those around them.

Researchers have studied the impact of caring for insects and mental health and found that it has a positive influence (Young-Soon Jun et al., 2016). In a review of the literature, Macauley and Chur-Hansen (2022) explored how humans could benefit from interactions with numerous species of animals, including birds such as parrots and chickens, reptiles such as tortoises and snakes, and amphibians, fish, and crickets. Their analysis found seven main categories of research (1) companionship and attachment, (2) social facilitators, (3) purpose and routine, (4) connectedness with nature, (5) decoration and aesthetics, (6) physiological benefits, and (7) commercial media describing benefits of nonconventional companion animals (Macauley & Chur-Hansen, 2022). Ingram et al. (2021) integrated arthropods into educational programming in order to increase social and emotional learning while teaching STEM (science, technology, engineering, and math). They found that students' beliefs about arthropods changed from negative to positive with exposure (Ingram et al., 2021). An innovative study by Park (2022) gave senior citizens an oriental garden cricket to care for, feed, and observe. The study found that caring for this tiny creature improved the seniors' mobility and sleep patterns (Park et al., 2022).

Working with insects in therapy may involve observing them in nature or in the garden, or it may mean having certain species in an enclosure. Insects are small, easily portable, and inexpensive or free when found in nature; while we never remove insects from their natural habitat, we may help rehabilitate those we have found outside. Clients can create a habitat for an insect outside or help rescue a bug that has fallen in a water trough. Some insects may be safe to hold, and some seem to enjoy interaction with humans. Children may be drawn to insects and are often braver than adults when interacting with bugs.

Insects have unusual appearances and behavior that is quite different from other animal species. Much of the work we do with insects involves observation. We can observe and discuss what a particular species has to teach us. For instance, caterpillars provide excellent metaphors for transformation and change, as they go from a perceived ugly pest to an important and beautiful butterfly. Just as with

A brave client holds a hornworm.

watching a plant grow, we can talk about how change can take time and feel un-comfortable but may ultimately lead to beauty.

If you want to work with insects, you do not have to be an expert. You simply need to have a curiosity about arthropods and an excitement for learning and shar-ing knowledge. It is also important to have a willingness to be creative, flexible, play-ful, and perhaps a little uncomfortable. When working with insects, it is helpful to be ready to lead your clients to their version of success, whether that means holding a bug or simply getting close enough to look at it carefully. You may need to find your voice as an insect advocate and reframe or redirect the way that clients want to interact with these little creatures. Some clients may not be willing to work with insects, which is always acceptable, but you may need to reinforce the need to be respectful of the insects and natural spaces around them during sessions. We can try to encourage this behavior outside of sessions, but it is a careful line to encourage humane treatment without pushing your beliefs on a client (about any animal), and we certainly cannot guarantee or reinforce the behavior outside of sessions.

Interventions involving nature, gardening, and insects offer a holistic experience where clients can observe and create lasting impact in their environment. When we plant flowers that attract bees, we can see how the bees come to the garden and then pollinate our vegetables. Clients can help rescue a ladybug and experience the power in doing good for the natural world. Taking this time to recognize and appreciate the diversity, interconnectedness, and interdependence of species may be important themes for clients who feel disconnected or different from others. We can help clients recognize and feel a relationship with the plants, animals, insects, and humans around them. Clients may also be able to see that growth takes time and patience but will eventually come.

CHALLENGES WITH ECOTHERAPY AND INSECTS

The primary challenge for many clinicians is access to nature; many do not have access to green space or a garden in their therapy practice. However, there are ways to integrate nature in sessions, even if it takes some creative thinking. You can take walks with your clients, sit outside on a bench, or meet clients in a park to do therapy while on a hike. There are several considerations when doing work outside, including comfort, safety, and confidentiality. When outside with clients, there may be some elements of discomfort, so clients should be aware of that possibility, and you can help remind them to take the necessary precautions, such as wearing comfortable shoes, sun and eye protection, and weather-appropriate clothing such as long sleeve shirts and pants to prevent bites or scratches. If outside of your therapy setting, it is also important to discuss the risks to confidentiality and how clients would like to handle situations where other people may be present. For instance, if on a hike in a public park, you and the client should have a plan if you encounter someone that you or they know.

If being outside with clients presents too many hurdles or is not feasible for your situation, there are also a number of ways to bring nature into your office space. Plants, flowers, and potted fruits and vegetables can be in an office setting; even fake plants can bring greenery into your space if you do not have a green thumb. Pictures of nature, windows for natural light, sound machines playing nature sounds, and small water features can bring in additional elements of nature. You can also find rocks, clay and other types of soil, sticks, leaves, and other natural elements and integrate them into sessions through mindfulness, sensory work, artwork, and other creative ways.

A major consideration when working with insects is that many people do not like or are afraid of insects. Adults may be squeamish or dislike certain insects, whereas children or teenagers often have a natural curiosity about bugs or unusual creatures. You may be able to help a reluctant client by showing them a unique view of an insect. For example, Linda was not excited to work with cockroaches, but she watched a video of a session as a clinician and client tried to determine the best high-value treat for a cockroach to learn a maze. The video included a close-up of the cockroach's tiny face as it ate and clearly enjoyed a tiny fish flake. Watching this video helped Linda to see this insect in a new way. Having clients watch videos or look at pictures of insects is often a good way to get them prepared to work with the live animal.

Perhaps the biggest concern when working with insects is their well-being. Unfortunately, we have not found any books that describe the insects' stress signals, those behaviors that indicate whether they like or do not like something. We need to use our best judgement about what types of interactions are appropriate and which would be stressful for an insect. Some insects seem to enjoy human touch, but most likely should just be observed. Our invertebrate therapist spent many hours with her different insects to learn what each bug's consent looks like. We also need to consider the insects' living environment and create a home that most resembles their natural habitat if we are going to keep them in captivity. It is also important to research each insect and learn as much as possible about them before introducing clients to them.

HOUSING AND LOGISTICS WITH THERAPY INSECTS

Since most insects will be observed in their natural environment, they will already have appropriate food and shelter, so you may only need to ensure that their habitat is protected. Insects in captivity require different kinds of care, so it is essential to research the insects' needs before bringing them home, such as necessary social, environmental, food, and water needs. Some insects feed on other insects, so you will need to determine how to obtain their food and how to process with clients about this situation. Additionally, insects such as caterpillars will change over time, which means their environmental and food needs will likely change. Many insects prefer to live in groups or colonies, so having multiple insects may also be important for their well-being. Some arthropods, like cockroaches, move a great deal and will need an enclosure with larger space. Some habitats may be small enough to travel from home to office as needed, but this will also depend on the habitat and your office space.

SAMPLES OF INTERVENTIONS WITH NATURE AND INSECTS

Nature is an integrated system and each change impacts the surrounding environment and creatures. For example, the painted lady butterfly starts out as a caterpillar and then becomes a chrysalis clinging to a leaf. We cannot see the changes and growth within the chrysalis, but a tremendous amount is happening within this nurturing environment. With clients, we can discuss how humans often need to ponder change before taking action, so while we may not see a difference, change can still be happening within us or others.

When the butterfly is ready, it slowly moves out of its temporary home, shaking out its wings and eventually flying to a new home. Recently, we released a set of butterflies, each one taking its time to fly from the temporary environment into the open sky. The last butterfly remaining seemed to have sticky wings and it took its time before it left. A client and clinician observing this process discussed anxiety about change as they watched it struggle. They wondered if this last butterfly would be able to fly off and survive or if it would remain in the enclosure, relying on humans to care for it. They talked about the different options, the benefits and challenges of each situation, and why the butterfly might be struggling. However, eventually this last butterfly did fly away and landed on a nearby rosebush, then took off again toward the trees. This butterfly's experience was a living metaphor for many situations and led to powerful therapeutic discussions about the need to grow and change, how that process can be stressful and scary, may take multiple small steps, and that the entire process takes bravery and strength. Watching a butterfly's process allows clients to see the struggle for growth in a tangible way and to open avenues for discussion that simply talking about hypothetical situations does not. Having the memory, emotion, and visualization of that transformation can remain in the working memory of a client and provide an ongoing model about how change occurs.

AN EXAMPLE OF
INSECT-ASSISTED THERAPY

A clinician and her 13-year-old client were working with hornworms, and the clinician had taken several worms from their large enclosure and put them in an open container for observation. The client decided to move the hornworms back to their large enclosure, and as she held one, she began to yell "move" to get the worm into the enclosure. Not surprisingly, the hornworm did not act in response to this command. The clinician helped the client recognize the anxiety and frustration she was feeling about the insects being out of their enclosure and ignoring her demands. The clinician was able to witness the client's quick escalation and frustration and process it with her in the moment. The client had previously told her clinician that she was "pretty patient" when frustrated, so this situation also allowed the clinician to have a different view of the client's responses and behaviors. Together, the client and clinician put the client's feelings into words and practiced calming skills. This experiential, hands-on moment with the smallest of creatures led to a powerful therapeutic moment.

REFERENCES

Bauer, T. (2023). *Working with arthropods in therapy*. [Unpublished paper.]

Gaekwad, J. S., Sal Moslehian, A., Roös, P. B., & Walker, A. (2022). A meta-analysis of emotional evidence for the biophilia hypothesis and implications for biophilic design. *Frontiers in Psychology*, *13*(27). https://doi.org/10.3389/fpsyg.2022.750245

Ingram, E., Reddick, K., Honaker, J. M., & Pearson, G. A. (2021). Making space for social and emotional learning in science education. *Frontiers in Education*, *6*. https://doi.org/10.3389/feduc.2021.712720

Kellert, S. R., & Wilson, E. O. (1993). *The biophilia hypothesis*. Island Press.

Macauley, L., & Chur-Hansen, A. (2022). Human health benefits of non-conventional companion animals: A narrative review. *Animals*, *13*(1), 1–24. https://doi.org/10.3390/ani13010028

Park, J.-Y., Ko, H.-J., Song, J.-E., Ji, S.-M., & Kim, S.-Y. (2022). Pet insects may improve physical performance and sleep in community-dwelling frail elderly people with chronic diseases: A single-arm interventional pilot study. *Clinical Interventions in Aging*, *Volume 17*, 1919–1929. https://doi.org/10.2147/cia.s387603

Ulrich, R. S. (1984). View through a window may influence recovery from surgery. *Science*, *224*(4647), 420–421. https://doi.org/10.1126/science.6143402

Why we need insects. (2023). *Penn State Huck Institutes of the Life Sciences.* https://www
.huck.psu.edu/institutes-and-centers/insect-biodiversity-center/why-we-need-insects

Wolsko, C., & Hoyt, K. (2012). Employing the restorative capacity of nature: Pathways
to practicing ecotherapy among mental health professionals. *Ecopsychology, 4*(March),
10–24. https://www.liebertpub.com/doi/abs/10.1089/eco.2012.0002

Young-Soon Jun, Sung-Min Bae, Tae-Young Shin, Seung-Hee Lee, Won-Seok Gwak,
Yong-Oh Ahn, I., n-Hui Kim, S., ee-Nae Lee, Dong-Jun Kim, Tae-Ho Kim, & Woo,
S.-D. (2016). Effects of an insect-mediated mental healthcare program for mentally dis-
ordered children. *Entomological Research, 46*(1). https://doi.org/10.1111/1748-5967.12149

PART 3

I'M TOO OLD TO PLAY: WORKING WITH ANIMALS AND DIFFERENT AGE GROUPS

"An alpaca is basically a clown in a furry costume."

—JOHN GREEN

Clients come to therapy with different motivations, experiences, abilities, and needs. Determining the appropriate animals and interventions for each client will depend upon all these factors. Since age plays a role in each of these elements, in this section we break down client populations into children, teens, and adults. In chapter 10, we discuss interventions that can be utilized with all clients regardless of age. In the following chapters, we look at some of the most commonly used interventions for each age group. Most of the interventions we discuss can be modified depending on the animal you choose. At the end of each section, we give examples of how the interventions are implemented with clients with differing issues and/or diagnoses.

10

ACCIDENTAL PLAY: ANIMAL INTERVENTIONS FOR CLIENTS OF ALL AGES

"We are never more fully alive, more completely ourselves, or more deeply engrossed in anything than when we are playing."

—CHARLES SCHAEFER

A nimal-assisted counseling and psychotherapy is appropriate for clients of all ages. We sometimes call our interventions *accidental* play because we see all our clients, including adults, enjoying their time with the animals and often being playful and silly. Therapy is frequently difficult, especially when our clients have experienced trauma, loss, illness, addiction, or countless other difficult life circumstances. When clients play, they are fully engaged; their body, mind, emotion, thoughts, and physiology are all activated so that learning can take place on multiple levels. This process is especially helpful for clients who are overthinkers, tend to rationalize, or have done only talk therapy, as it creates change throughout the entire body, rather than just in the mind. The client's whole self is involved in making change happen as they engage with the animals in new and challenging ways. If our ultimate goal for clients is to have happier, more productive lives, this involves making changes, not just talking about changes. This holistic and experiential approach is part of the beauty and power of AACP.

Animals provide physiological benefits with their presence, which opens up pathways for learning that might otherwise be blocked (Olmert, 2010). For individuals who are seasoned therapy clients or resistant to treatment, there is an added benefit, as they do not know what to expect from this type of counseling experience and therefore cannot as easily defend against efforts toward improvement. We sometimes call this a *sideways approach to therapy*, since the client is being impacted by an intervention without anticipating it (Chassman Craddock, 2022).

Animal-assisted interventions can be introduced to clients in a variety of ways, depending on their age, presenting issue, your setting, and the animal(s) you have. Some options include the following strategies:

- The clinician can start a session with a preplanned intervention with a specific animal, based on the client's treatment goal.
- The clinician can ask the client which animal they would like to work with and then create an intervention that meets a specific therapeutic goal.
- The client can ask to work with a specific animal and be allowed to freely interact without direction or a specific planned intervention. This is more often done with teenagers or adults.
- The client is sharing about an issue, and in the moment, the clinician thinks of a way to involve an animal that will help with that particular issue or goal. The client and clinician integrate the animal and the client is able to move from thinking to doing.
- The client may be talking about an issue and the clinician notices an animal behavior that could provide helpful input about this topic. The clinician directs the client's attention to the animal and the behavior, and then incorporates it into the relevant issue. For more details on this approach, see chapter 15, "Catching the Moment."

Most of our AACP sessions start in an office. Many of our offices have animals living in them, though our play therapy rooms do not. This allows children to be as loud and active as they need while not stressing the animals. During the session, if appropriate, we may bring an animal into an office or move the session to a space with an animal, such as outside. Clients often spend the last few minutes of a session with an animal of their choice, if the animal is available. This serves partly as a positive ending to session, but also helps regulate clients before leaving.

With teens and adults, we may ask the client to "help us help the animal," "try an experiment," or "try something new." These gentle challenges move the client from talking about their problems to being engaged and creating relationships with the animals. The amount of time we spend talking about client issues versus working with the animals depends on the client and how much they need to use their cognition and verbalization of issues to process and move forward. Even clients who expect to do primarily "talk therapy" while petting an animal will benefit from a clinician who can say, "Hey, let's go outside and try something! I have an idea of how we can work on this in a different way."

There are countless animal-related interventions, so creating a complete list is impossible. This chapter focuses on interventions that can be done with clients of various ages and with different animals. Many of these interventions require having a therapy animal to work with, but not all do; some can be done with animal toys, representations, media, or analogies. The interventions listed in this chapter are some of our favorites, because they are versatile, address many different treatment goals, and work for a wide variety of clients.

There are multiple impactful elements within the overall AACP therapeutic process, regardless of the specific intervention. These elements include projection and interpretation, processing, and action toward change. We go into detail about each below and then move into describing specific interventions.

PROJECTION AND INTERPRETATION

Both projection and interpretation are aspects of psychotherapy. Projection is a natural process that occurs when the therapeutic environment is neutral and uninterpreted. The goal is to allow the client to simply observe the animal and its behavior, including any interactions with other animals, the environment, and the humans present, and to describe what they think the behavior means. Clinicians, especially those beginning to practice AACP, are often tempted to comment on, explain, or interpret the animal's behavior for the client, especially if the clinician knows the animal well. Clinicians often want to offer facts or information to the client that explains the behavior, but this can impede the client's work. Unless there is a safety concern, it is useful to hold these thoughts so that the client can make their own interpretations.

It is important for the clinician to know the client well enough to understand the meaning behind the projection; in other words, to be able to connect the interpretation to the client's story. For instance, is the client seeing elements in the animal(s) they wish were aspects of themselves or are they seeing negative aspects in the animal(s) that represent similar parts of themselves? There is a lot of good clinical information to be gained from listening to the client's interpretation of animal behavior. We can learn about assumptions about the animal and what the animal's look or behavior means; how the client handles negative information; how they view the world around them; and how they process and react to various events. We hear many types of projections about the animals, such as, "She's sad because her mom couldn't take care of her," or

"He's angry because he's trapped in a cage, and no one will let him out," or "He misses his real family." These comments say a lot about what the client has experienced, what they notice, and how they are feeling, which then informs the clinician how to move forward.

AN EXAMPLE OF PROJECTION

When Linda's therapy dog, Rupert, was young and still in training, he was in a session with Susan, a young adult with suicidal and self-harming tendencies. Rupert started to bark at something outside, and he has a big bark that can be quite startling. Linda asked Susan what she thought was going on for Rupert, and they looked out the window to discover that Rupert was barking at another therapy dog outside. Linda then asked Susan what she thought Rupert was thinking and feeling at seeing the dog. The client's response was both enlightening and profound: she said that Rupert was excited because he wished he could be that dog running free, but also anxious and scared because the dog was alone without anyone to take care of him. It does not matter if Susan was correct in her interpretation of Rupert's response. The important part was that the comment gave the clinician a profound insight into Susan's conflicting emotions. She had projected her own longings and fears onto Rupert; she wanted autonomy from her family but was also afraid when on her own. Her statement gave the clinician valuable insight and helped to inform and guide their therapeutic process. Linda and Susan then discussed how Susan could help Rupert handle his conflicting feelings and what she might say to him. Rupert's genuine "dog" response during this session is a great example of how our therapy animals' imperfections are integrated into sessions and are often helpful. There is a tremendous amount of value in these genuine and animal-led experiences; these situations are when much of the insight, growth, and change happens for clients.

PROCESSING

Projection and the resulting interpretation, personalization, and behavior allows the clinician to see the contextual importance of the client's interpretation. They can then work together to explore the issue further, recognize recurring issues for the client, and find opportunities to challenge the client's assumptions or actions. How the clinician processes with the client will largely be directed by the clinician's therapeutic approach. For example, if using a psychodynamic approach, the clinician may follow-up with a question such as, "I wonder what happened to make them act that way?" A cognitive behavioral clinician may ask, "Do you see any negative assumptions or distortions in what you just said?" Regardless of therapeutic orientation, the reflective process allows clinicians to assist with the client's issues that may not yet be conscious and lead them to insight. Talking or playing as a follow-up intervention can enable the client to focus on helping the animal, while simultaneously practicing new ways of thinking, behaving, and feeling to help themselves.

An important clinical decision is whether to overtly connect this discussion to the client's own experience. For many clients, keeping the discussion focused on the animal can help bypass resistance to looking at the issue in themselves. Connecting it directly to the client can cause a client's defenses to flare, and the discussion may be shut down. For example, making a comment such as, "Is that similar to how you behave when you are frustrated?" may result in defensiveness and denial, rather than an open discussion. Sometimes, a client may spontaneously make the connection between what they see in the animal(s) and their own issues. For instance, a client may say, "Wow, Lily gets so feisty when she wants attention and doesn't know how to get attention nicely. It reminds me of when I hit my sister!" But if the clinician had drawn that connection, the client may have denied the similarities. Some clients may be ready for gentle connections between the animals and themselves, such as, "Hmm. I wonder if people ever respond that way." Other clients may be open to directly relating the animal's behavior to their own, but this is a delicate process. Knowing when to make these overt connections and when to continue to work in the metaphorical space will vary, and over time, you will find what works best for you and each of your clients.

ACTION TOWARD CHANGE

A major element of AACP is taking action toward change and growth. After projection, interpretation, and processing has occurred, the clinician can choose an intervention that allows the client to move forward toward resolution or change. For example, if the client identifies that two horses are behaving like his parents, the clinician can ask the client what they would like to say to the horses and what it feels like to observe this interaction. The client could be asked to change the situation in a way that would help to resolve the conflict. For example, the client might suggest that the horses need a break from each other or that they need to do something fun together. The clinician can then ask the client to help the horses with this task, encouraging the client to use their agency in the present situation, allowing them to try different solutions, and enabling them to take that next step toward change. In many situations, clients do not have control over others; for example, a child cannot usually change parental behavior or interactions. But by giving the client a chance to act out their desired situation with the animals, they can practice problem solving, acceptance, resilience, and even walking away.

OBSERVING ANIMALS

Clients of any age can benefit from observing the animals. There are several levels of intervention that start with observation and move to awareness and then change. The first level of intervention is simply watching the animals and feeling how the experience is impactful. These are special moments to share and may not need any words. The clinician may quietly comment on their own internal reaction, such as, "Oh, that felt beautiful," without expectation of the client. These are often the moments when clients with extreme depression have their first reminder or experience of joy.

When there are multiple animals, either of the same or different species, we can watch the animals interact naturally with each other. Because these animals have formed relationships with each other and react to the environment around them, it can be fun and instructive to watch them. They communicate with each other and with humans, mostly nonverbally, and the animals are quite adept at reading each other's signals. They are often quite joyful and playful with each other, which opens up new emotional avenues for many clients. Children may even want to imitate the animals, perhaps by galloping around and making happy sounds. Our goats frequently play, either chasing each other or "goat-wrestling," where they stand on their hind legs and dance toward each other. They look ridiculous playing together, and clients can see how spontaneous and unrestrained play can be.

Projection is always involved in observation since the client is using their own lens to interpret what they observe, which may be affected by unresolved issues in the client's past or present. Using these client projections and interpretations, the clinician can reflect on animal behavior, observe specific themes, and create

A young child processing and working through her fear.

parallel stories. Next, the client can process the content from these interpretations and create a way to move toward change.

There are occasions when working with a live animal is not available, safe, or appropriate. Observation can be done wherever there are live animals: a dog park, zoo, beach, park, or pet store. You can also watch animal videos or look at pictures if leaving the office is not an option.

OBSERVING SPECIFIC THEMES

We can choose which animals to include in a session or guide the session based on a client's goals and the animal's behaviors or issues. For instance, if our goal is to help a client with nonverbal communication, we can observe and then discuss how the animals communicate, which can help the client to think about the ways they communicate. In this intervention, the clinician may point out specific behaviors and ask the client to watch and reflect on what they see. We often teach clients about dog calming signals and then observe the dogs, asking the client to watch for these behavioral cues. Or we may watch a goat standing calmly, chewing her cud, and talk about what it must be like to feel so relaxed and calm. We can point out conflicts between animals, how the animals show dominance, or try to feel bigger.

If an animal has been ill, observing the animal receive its treatment, or struggles with an ailment, can also provide an opportunity to build empathy. When this is paired with action, the client can become involved in helping the animal feel better.

PARALLEL STORIES AND FORECASTING

Parallel stories is a strategy when we explain the animal's history to the client or describe a situation that has occurred with the animal. Often, we will introduce a part of the animal's story at a time when it would make a useful parallel to what the client is experiencing or discussing in that moment. We may ask the client what they think or feel about the animal's experience or if they have any thoughts on how to help the animal. These stories give the client the opportunity to look at their issues indirectly, through another character, which makes it less anxiety-provoking to think about, feel, and work through.

We generally share the animal's story, or relevant aspects, with the client at appropriate therapeutic moments. Very often we find that the issues our client is dealing with are similar to a situation the animal has experienced. For example, we work with a lot of children and teenagers who have experience with social services and the foster care system, so they can relate to our rescue animals who have lived in multiple homes and had many caregivers. We have adult clients who do not have familial support systems, so they can connect to our animals who have created a family or made a "found" family with other species. We can highlight parts of the animal's story for a reluctant client, because it often helps them to open up about their own experience. We can ask the client how they believe the animal felt during that experience. We may also ask how they think the animal has learned to deal with that experience and how it may continue to impact them.

At times, we may directly connect the animal's story to the client's experience, though for some clients, they may be resistant to this direct connection. In this situation, the advantage to including a live animal is that we are sharing true stories, and since the client is developing a positive relationship with that animal, they also build empathy for the animal. This empathy then allows the client to feel closer to the animal and therefore closer to the situation. When clients are connected to the animals, they are then highly motivated to help the animals, so they work hard thinking and talking about solutions. These solutions can be applied to their own lives, over time.

Forecasting is also a form of the client's projection, but is a more spontaneous connection from the animal's behavior to something the client may be thinking or feeling. Forecasting involves asking the client to watch the animal's behavior and interpret or forecast what they believe the animal is thinking or feeling. As we have shared, most of our therapy animals have been adopted from local animal shelters or rescued from a difficult situation, so each of our animals has a complex history or story. Moreover, our therapy animals are not perfect and have minor difficult or mischievous behaviors, often similar to our clients' behaviors. When we point these behaviors out, clients can relate to how the animals have developed those behaviors as ways of coping with difficult situations. The clinician and client can help the animal work through its emotions or behaviors and learn a better way of coping. Parallel stories and forecasting allow the client to identify with the animal's experience and through the process, make sense of their own experience.

AN EXAMPLE OF
FORECASTING WITH PARALLEL STORIES

Ellen's therapy dog, Sasha, had experienced abuse and neglect, so she had some anxiety around other dogs and male humans when she was adopted. Ellen worked for many years to help Sasha overcome her anxiety and trauma responses before Sasha became a therapy dog. During sessions, some minor residual anxious responses would occur, such as freezing briefly when she saw another dog on a walk, which allowed us to observe, discuss, and process this behavior and what it meant. Even though Sasha was in a safe home and had healed in many ways, her past still impacted her at times, and this could help clients recognize how they are affected by their own experiences. Sasha was incredibly loving and gentle, and clients with abuse and trauma histories could relate to her experiences; they often made art or wrote stories about what happened to Sasha, how it affected her, and how she had healed.

ANIMAL PHOTOGRAPHS, ART, AND STORIES

We often create photo albums for our animals, which include pictures of them as young animals or of their previous homes, with their favorite toy, in their bed, engaging in enjoyable activities, favorite animal friends, important moments in their lives, and other interesting or fun events. Going through this album can be a good way for clients to get a sense of the animal and see them in a multidimensional way. Looking at these special pictures and discussing the animal's story also facilitates a client's ability to see the animal as a unique personality worth caring for, but also as a being they can relate to and connect to their own stories. Even simple topics like favorite foods and activities can help the client gently enter the therapeutic relationship with both the clinician and the animal.

It is important to consider how much personal information you include in a photo album and what you are willing to share with your clients. If the animal is your personal pet, the photos may include images of your home, family members, vacations, and other personal images or events. Sharing these images is an important boundary consideration, and you should share only as much as you are comfortable. This comfort level may change depending on the client, their presenting issues, and their boundaries. We often use albums where photos can be easily removed, if we want to share only certain photos or aspects of the animal's history with some clients. Asking the client to bring in a photo album of their pet or family is a great way to open conversation about who is in their life.

When an animal has had a difficult or traumatic time before being adopted, it is the clinician's decision about how much information to share, when to share, and with which clients. This can be a powerful introduction to talking about events that have happened in the animal's life, which helps develop empathy. The clinician can go further with the intervention to invite the client to help the animal with the trauma in some way. Perhaps that means being especially gentle, telling the animal they are loved, or slowly moving to create a safe relationship with them. Clients can identify with aspects of the animal's stories and may feel a special connection based on shared experiences.

We can use time in session for the client to take photos of the animals or of other parts of nature that have meaning for them. Clients can bring their own camera or you can supply a simple digital or Polaroid camera. Taking photos of animals engaging in a variety of behaviors and play can provide talking points for sessions. A simple instruction to take photos of the animals doing something "interesting," "fun," or "curious" can be a good starting suggestion and also tells you how the client understands and interprets those terms. Between sessions, clients can take photos of their own animals or ones they see, and then bring these photos to session to discuss. Going to locations like pet stores or zoos can prompt a discussion about feelings and empathy; you can ask questions such as, "What do you think it would be like to live in that small cage?" or "How do you think the animals feel, living away from their natural habitat?" You can also ask a client to take a picture of an animal who has a certain emotion or seems to feel the same way that the client does.

Art therapy can be integrated with AACP; clients can create, draw, paint, or create collages of a therapy animal engaged in various activities or exhibiting various feelings. Clients can draw pictures of nature or animals, illustrate stories, or create collages about fictional or real events. You can bring art supplies outside into nature or bring natural elements into your office, such as leaves, sticks, grass, and rocks. Whether the art has an animal involved can be up to the clinician and client. The art is simply a medium to process emotions, and including the animal may enhance the meaning of the art for the client. Clients can then write stories to accompany these pictures, providing a context for the picture or creating a narrative for the image. Clinicians can guide the story, providing a prompt or idea, such as, "Write a story about what happened just before this picture" or "Pretend the animals are a family and tell their story." Clients also can create the narrative independently and choose how to focus their writing and art. Either way, the pictures and stories provide an opportunity to address issues experientially. The clinician may decide whether it is helpful to process the content verbally or simply to allow the client to benefit from the experience and metaphor.

AN EXAMPLE OF
SHARING AN ANIMAL STORY

Jose was an eight-year-old boy who was being bullied at school. He loved Rosie, our one-eyed, albino, hairless guinea pig. During one session, he wanted to write a story about Rosie and created a book called "Rosie the Superhero!" He drew the pictures and the clinician wrote the words he dictated. In his story, Rosie was there to support Jose; when he needed help at school, she came to his rescue, wearing a superhero cape. At the end of the book, Jose felt stronger inside because Rosie showed him how to stand up to the bullies. Jose was able to keep the book in his room at home as a reminder of the strength he could borrow from her when he needed it.

GETTING CONSENT, GREETING ANIMALS, AND RESPECTING BOUNDARIES

Our intake questionnaire asks about the client's history with animals, anxieties or fears around animals, and any experience with animal abuse. For those clients who may have a history of abusing animals or who are anxious about live animals, we often begin working with animal representations, photographs, or stories. We are then very careful to ensure the client understands our rules before engaging with any animals.

Clients need to gain the animal's consent and practice safe greetings and respectful boundaries when interacting with therapy animals. This is perhaps one of the most unique ways that animals can help our clients, by teaching them, in a natural and gentle way, about how to get consent, how to greet others, and how to interact socially while also respecting boundaries. Clients learn that each animal must give consent to participate in any session, which means that we never force an animal to be involved with us, and the animal can leave a session at any time. Before beginning any animal-assisted activity, it is important for the clinician to model asking for consent from the animal to be included in a session; later, the client will also need to ask for consent in a similar fashion. This consent will be different for each animal, so the client may need to learn what nonverbal cues indicate the particular animal wants to engage or does not want to engage. This also means that the clinician must explain and demonstrate how to allow the animal to withdraw if it wants to leave.

If the animal consents to being involved in the session, it is important for the client to know how to properly greet each animal. With most of our animals, we teach clients that the animal will smell their hand first as a greeting, before trying to pet them. Most animals use smell when greeting each other, so this allows our animals to feel comfortable and clients to start interacting gradually. With larger animals, such as equines and alpacas, it is important to teach clients how to approach and walk around the animal safely. We want to make sure clients are as safe as possible when in the enclosure with the large animals. With children we sometimes talk about "quiet feet."

Taking time to explain how to approach and say "hello" to each animal gives clients the chance to think about the animal and take their perspective, which helps cultivate empathy and consideration for others' feelings. When needed, we can have clients practice greeting and holding a stuffed animal. Just as we focus on the animal's comfort, our discussion also can invite clients to share their preferences and desires for being approached and touched; this helps build rapport and trust and lets clients know we care about their feelings and preferences. This is an especially important clinical task for clients who have experienced sexual or physical abuse, attachment issues, or other boundary issues.

All ongoing interactions with the animals are opportunities for the client to learn and practice recognizing and respecting boundaries. A critical part of our job as clinicians is to help clients observe how the animal communicates their boundaries and preferences and to ensure the client respects them. Each animal species will demonstrate boundaries in different ways. We need to help clients read the animals' comfort levels through their behavior. A client who can recognize and respect the animal's boundaries can experiment with various types of safe touch and observe how the animal responds. They can be directed to watch for signs that the animal is comfortable, happy, uncomfortable, or stressed, and pay attention to how the animal rewards them when the client does something the animal likes. If a client continues to engage in a behavior even when the animal is clearly uncomfortable, this gives you a lot of information about their ability to read and/or respect nonverbal cues. It also allows for further discussions about boundaries, limits, and how each of us sets our own and respects others' limits. We do interject when a client continues to engage in behavior that makes the animal uncomfortable, as the animal's safety is a top priority.

If a client is highly egocentric (as are most children and teenagers), an intervention may focus on having the client imagine they are the animal and how they might feel, which helps build empathy. Some clients may struggle with this, especially if they have experienced a great deal of abuse or trauma and have shut off their own feelings of discomfort. It might be necessary or useful to slow down and have the client work with a stuffed animal. It also may be an indication that they need help to experience themselves in their own bodies. Using a grounding exercise may be a safe way for the client to experience the positive feeling of contact and gradually introduce them back to their own body. We address grounding in more detail later in this chapter.

With every animal-involved intervention, there is an opportunity to model and practice new ways of interacting that may make the animals more comfortable and ultimately deepen the client's relationship with the animal. We want to help clients to recognize boundaries and also challenge their ways of interacting so that their relationship with the animal can continue to grow.

Dogs tend to be more flexible with boundaries and are generally accepting of touch; however, if a dog is too tolerant, or is subtle about their displeasure, clients may not learn about appropriate boundaries. In contrast, cats tend to have defined boundaries and communicate very clearly, so they may be a good fit for clients who push boundaries. Small animals and equines usually have a smaller window of tolerance. It is your job as clinician to both encourage your client to be creative, but also keep their interactions within a minimal level of stress for your animal.

One of the largest challenges we face is when a client wants to work with an animal, but the animal is showing signs of stress or does not want to engage with a client. Because we allow animals to choose when and how to interact with clients, the animal may behave in ways that hurt the client's feelings or frustrates them. There are other times when the human starts to engage in behavior that creates stress or discomfort for the animal or even risks harming the animal. Before getting to a harmful point, the clinician can suggest the client try a different way of interacting. If this still does not work, the clinician may need to stop an intervention. Practicing statements that can gently but firmly interrupt potentially dangerous behavior is helpful so you are prepared if it happens. If a client's behavior escalates quickly, we may need to remove the animal for its protection.

AN EXAMPLE OF
GREETING AND RESPECTING BOUNDARIES

After practicing with a stuffed rat for several sessions, six-year-old Katie was allowed to hold Cinnamon, a young rat. After a few moments, Katie lifted Cinnamon over her head because she wanted "to fly her around." There was not much time to think about the most therapeutic way to ask Katie to safely put Cinnamon down, so the clinician quickly said, "I'll take Cinnamon!" To spare Cinnamon any additional stress, the clinician needed to respond quickly, set a firm boundary, and ensure the animal was safe. Once Cinnamon was safely back in her enclosure, the clinician was able to process with Katie and discuss how Cinnamon may have felt being held up so high. Had this clinician not processed with Katie after taking Cinnamon, there could have been a breach in their relationship.

Situations like these can be difficult, but an animal's welfare must come first. The breach in the clinician's relationship with Katie was quickly addressed and repaired, an essential aspect of good therapy. This clinician was able to help Katie empathize with Cinnamon and understand the need for the abrupt interruption. For clients who have experienced abuse, this also models appropriate care and concern. Other statements we might make to regulate increasingly worrisome client behavior include: "What do you think the animal is feeling right now? How would you feel if you were a little animal being held very high? What could you do that might make them feel safer?" Gently helping a client to understand how an animal might feel in different circumstances can be an important therapeutic goal (Chassman Craddock, 2024).

CREATING AN ENVIRONMENT

Clients can help set up living areas, play areas, or special environments for many therapy animals. It is helpful to do this after a space has been cleaned; for example, after a room has been deep cleaned or an enclosure has been scrubbed. Clients can be given a lot of liberty to choose how to design the animals' environment, but the clinician may give certain reminders, such as noting that the home needs to be safe, comfortable, and fun. Then clients can choose how to set up the space in a way that they think the animal will enjoy and feel safe. It is helpful to have water, animal toys, soft bedding items, food, treats, and other fun items available for the client to choose. When a client is asked to make the animal happy or comfortable, they need to try to think like that animal, which involves empathy, imagination, and creativity.

We have found this intervention useful especially for clients who are in transitory living situations, or who have recently been impacted by changes at home and may need to navigate new living situations, such as two homes. It also is helpful for clients with social anxiety, as it can help them consider items that bring comfort and safety and what those elements are for themselves. This activity also gives the clinician valuable insight into what the client values and how they interpret certain criteria, like "safe" or "fun."

AFFECTIONATE TOUCH AND RECIPROCITY

Touching an animal is one of the most natural and powerful interventions in AACP. When an animal is nearby, many people feel inclined to touch or pet it. There is something that humans crave about touching an animal. Each animal species and individual animal is unique with the type of touch they enjoy and how they show this enjoyment. Most of our animals approach clients, come out of their enclosures, or walk to the fence when they see clients coming, which shows that they are interested in the humans and are seeking affectionate touch. The experience of physical affection is different with each animal and even with various parts of the animal. But for most people, especially those who have requested AACP, petting or being near an animal is an inherently pleasant, soothing activity.

Petting and affectionate touch can be a spontaneous intervention, where there is no direction given by the clinician, or it can be directed and more structured. When the client is discussing a difficult subject, having a nearby animal to simply touch can be reassuring and calming. Most of our therapy dogs will lean on or put their head on clients, sit next to them on the couch, offer a paw, sit on their feet, or snuggle with them on the floor. This affection and physical touch often give the client needed reassurance.

This physical affection is a mutually beneficial activity, which may be a rare experience for some clients. Physical contact such as petting has been demonstrated to help calm humans and animals and can release dopamine in both parties (Odendaal, 2000). This calming and pleasurable effect can help relax clients and allow them to feel more comfortable in sessions and discussing difficult issues. Clients also can recognize that their actions can bring joy to others, and they in turn can feel pleasure from that interaction.

Many animals are not comfortable with hugs and will demonstrate signs of stress if hugged, because hugs are not a typical animal behavior. Hugs also can be dangerous to small animals, because clients may be unaware of how tightly they are holding an animal. Dogs and cats may prefer to lay next to a client on the floor or sit next to them on a couch. Some animals are very physically affectionate and want to be held and snuggled, while others prefer a brief pat, and many will have different preferences based on the day or moment. Larger animals like equines may tolerate or enjoy full body contact, but it will usually depend on the client and the equine's mood, as well as the relationship the client has with the equine. All that is to say, know your animal and how they like to be touched, and then help guide the client to find this understanding as well. You do not need to tell your client exactly what to do, but you can help them observe and understand what the animal is communicating and help the client connect their actions and the animal's response. Often, an animal will move itself into a physical position that allows the client to pet them in just the right spot. The human just needs to pay attention and the animal will guide them. You can note how the animal shows appreciation, with facial expressions, body or tail movements, or vocalizations. Even if the client is not able to read this relatively subtle language, the clinician can ask the client to notice or observe what the animal is doing and what they think that behavior means. Some clients may need more specific guidance on how to pet an animal: which direction, what pressure, how often, or where on the body. Other clients may have some knowledge about animal touch, but it is your job to always observe these physical interactions and then intervene if you notice the animal becoming stressed or unhappy.

As long as the client is touching the animal in a way that is not hurtful or dangerous to the animal, it may be good to let them experiment and to dialogue about what they notice in the animal's reactions. A simple question like, "When you pet the rabbit like that, what do you notice?" This teaches them that awareness of others is important in relationships. It also allows you to see what the client can notice, how they interpret what they see, and how they process this information.

Linda's cat, Norman, was a natural at communicating what he liked and what he did not like; he was never mean and gave clients many chances to modify their behavior. Norman had a loud purr and would give nose kisses when he was happy. But if his feelings were ignored, he would move away. This is quite reflective of how humans engage with each other; we often give people several chances, but if they do not listen, we may give up trying.

A more directive way of including animal touch may happen if the clinician is attempting to teach the client a skill, such as anxiety or stress reduction. Giving a simple direction such as "find the softest part of the dog" can become a quiet activity that allows the client's mind to move away from their discomfort (anxiety, depression, pain, etc.) and focus instead on something pleasant. The direction also can focus on doing something positive for the animal, such as "see what makes the cat purr." This helps clients practice mindfulness and stay focused on the present moment.

Discussing safe and appropriate areas to touch an animal can be helpful for clients who have been sexualized or struggle with sexuality, as it provides opportunity to talk about the animal's "private areas." During all these discussions, you can keep the conversation about the animals on a metaphorical level or you can make the connection to the client's life. For instance, you might say, "So, you noticed Sasha moved away when you touched her that way." You can leave it there, or you can follow up with a general question, such as, "I wonder if she didn't like what happened?" Or you can go farther and connect it to the client's presenting issue, saying something such as, "Has someone ever touched you in a way you did not like?" Whether you make this connection overt or keep it metaphorical is a question of clinical judgement and will depend on multiple factors.

Many clients come to therapy because of behaviors that do not facilitate positive human relationships. These clients may have experienced abuse or neglect, trauma, struggle with social skills, or have mental health diagnoses that impact their ability to connect with others. With AACP, we can teach these clients how to engage in reciprocal ways, observe others, respond, and modify their behaviors, which are skills required in all types of relationships. Clients can learn empathy, social skills, and how to have mutually beneficial relationships by simply petting an animal. Initially, they may be adamant about petting an animal because they want to, regardless of the animal's desires, or they may be reluctant to receive affection from others, including an animal. Regardless of the reason or the behavior, these relational approaches do not have a balance of reciprocity. Because animals are open and direct with their communication, especially when compared to humans, clients can observe what others need or want. They can practice observational and relational skills with the animal and learn to respond in a way that will increase the likelihood of an ongoing relationship with the animal. This engagement teaches reciprocity, a critical aspect of attachment work and healthy relationships. Clients can learn a great deal in their relationships with the animals, which can translate into improved relationships with others in their lives.

CALMING AND GROUNDING

We see many clients with anxiety, hyperactivity, dysregulation, and even mania. These clients often need skills to help calm down their bodies, not only for their own well-being, but also to help others feel comfortable with them and to help them function in all areas of life. We have several therapy animals with mild anxiety or hyperactivity, which helps clients connect to them and build skills together. Calming an animal can be done with any animal that is excited or overly enthusiastic, and each animal may require different actions and behaviors to calm down. Clients need to use problem-solving to decide how to calm the animal down. They may need some trial-and-error to practice some techniques, determine if they worked, then perhaps try something else. During this process, clients are skill-building, problem-solving, engaging in flexible thinking, and observing body language. Additionally, they are calming themselves down at the same time. Focusing on the calming behaviors and attending to the animal's energy level helps clients control their own behavior and energy.

Grounding is similar to calming but is a bit more physically focused on the client. It is very helpful for those clients who dissociate, become disorganized, or are dysregulated. For clients who have severe anxiety, manic or psychotic episodes, or behavioral issues, knowing how to quickly get back to homeostasis is an essential skill. It can help clients not just feel better, but keep themselves and those around them safe. Grounding involves getting your physical body involved, most importantly the stomach/core area. This front, middle area of your body can be an area of power or a place of vulnerability, and we focus on it as we do grounding exercises.

A good analogy to share with clients is the porcupine or hedgehog, whose soft tummy is their only true vulnerable spot when they are curled up in defensive mode. Many other animals, including humans, tend to cover up their stomach/core when upset or reveal it when they feel safe. For example, humans often cross their arms or hold a purse or item over their stomach when uncomfortable or nervous. Animals, such as dogs, will curl up tightly when upset but will lay back and show their belly when feeling safe. When grounding, we try to help that vulnerable, central core region feel safely protected.

An animal the size of a cat is perfect for grounding exercises, but a small dog, rabbit, or even a stuffed animal, pillow, or backpack can be included. A live animal has the benefit of contributing warmth and calming energy, but the animal does need to be willing and able to be held against the client or sit on the client's lap. For a basic grounding exercise, the client simply holds the animal firmly against their core and focuses on the pressure against their body. This exercise is also a way to practice mindfulness, and you can include deep breaths, counting, visualization, or other interventions that help them feel calm. The soft presence and pressure on the client's core can help to calm them quickly.

Belly breathing is similar to grounding, but clients lie on their back and have an item or small animal on their stomach. The client focuses on slow, deep breaths, and tries to make their stomach go up and down visibly with each breath. This activity requires that clients slow their breathing, focus, and use their breath to calm themselves. It has the added benefit of a visual cue with the rising and falling stomach, and if a live animal is involved, it can also lead to fun and laughter as the animal moves up and down. Of course, the animal needs to be comfortable during this intervention and going for a ride.

Grounding and belly breathing are activities that you can teach clients during sessions and then implement at home. Clients can work with their own pet or find something else to feel the pressure against their core. Children, teenagers, and even some adults may want to pick a special stuffed animal or pillow that they use just for this activity. It can be an item that holds special significance, which can help with attachment and regulation. Clinicians also can give clients a small token of their work together, such as a stuffed animal, to function as a grounding and transitional object. This can be especially helpful and impactful when a client is terminating therapy, as it can remind them of their therapeutic progress and special relationship with the therapy animal.

AN EXAMPLE OF
GROUNDING

When Rupert was a young dog, he was described as "exuberant," a polite term for his energy and enthusiasm. Every time four-year-old Joan came to the ranch, she bounced around the waiting room, talking to everyone present. She tried to grab the cats, and her mother could not settle her down. Rupert's excitable nature worked well for clients like Joan who needed help regulating, because Rupert needed that help too. Bouncing Joan made Rupert want to bounce right alongside her. After noting this energy balance, Joan's clinician would take the opportunity to say, "Gosh, Rupert is too excited right now to focus on what we're asking him to do. Can you help him calm his body down?" or "Yikes! What do

you think Rupert needs to calm down?" They learned that Rupert quickly benefited from a few firm strokes from his neck to his tail. If Joan could not practice this behavior on her own, the clinician could say, "Hmm, let's try this!" and
demonstrate the deep stroking down his back, having Joan continue the behavior until Rupert was calm. As she stroked Rupert, Joan also calmed her own
body and became more regulated, thereby ready to engage in sessions.

PLAYING GAMES

There are many games to play with animals and people, though some animals are
more playful than others. Linda's dog, Rupert, would break his leg to catch a ball
or Frisbee, while Ellen's dog, Sasha, loved to chew on bones but had no interest
in fetch. Our goat, Lily, loves to headbutt a large rubber ball, and our little goats
love to jump onto any nearby object. The play should be fun not only for the client, but also for the animal. Remember, consent.

One basic but fun game to play with therapy animals, particularly dogs, is
fetch. This simple game involves throwing an object, such as a ball, Frisbee, or
stick, and the animal runs to get it, retrieves it, and returns the item to the thrower.
Many dogs will instinctively perform the retrieving element of this game, but
often need to be taught how to "drop it" or "hand" the item back. This is an important aspect of fetch, in part because animals could nip humans if they are not
willing to give up the item easily. Fetch also provides an opportunity for clients
to be outside, active, and focused on an external activity, yet one that still allows
them to talk to the clinician. Fetch allows client to have fun while also practicing social skills, prosocial behaviors, reciprocity, turn taking, and patience. Clinicians can help the client to observe and discuss the animal's behavior, especially
if the behavior is relevant to the client. Fetch also teaches about cause and effect,
which is beneficial for young clients or those with attachment issues.

Playing fetch with dogs is a lesson in so many aspects of life. For instance,
when Rupert was young, he was very competitive and could be quite intense and
determined when playing fetch. He was large and strong, so would unintentionally knock over other dogs or humans to get the ball and would even grab toys
away from other dogs. This was not polite dog behavior, but it mirrored many
of our clients' struggle with appropriate social interactions. Watching Rupert's
intense focus on fetch, to the detriment of others around him, often stimulated
conversations about wanting something so badly that you disregard the feelings,

desires, and needs of those around you. Rupert struggled to stop playing fetch, even when he was exhausted or injured, which paralleled many clients' addictive behaviors, which initially felt good but ultimately caused them harm in many ways. Rupert's intense focus on fetch could be harmful to his own body, and could also be too overwhelming for those around him, causing dogs or humans to avoid playing with him. As he got older, Rupert had to reduce his time playing, which was a struggle for him (and the humans around him). Clients could observe how Rupert's mind wanted to play, but his body was unable, which relates to many client issues of conflict, feeling torn, and difficult decisions. We could also discuss how sometimes others set limits for us, which can feel unpleasant or frustrating, but may be in our best interest.

Many animals love to bite, tug, and pull on a rope or string toys, which can be a fun activity, but should be considered thoughtfully since there is a risk of a client being inadvertently nipped by an excited animal or being pulled over by a large, strong animal. We have found that using a long rope with a plastic handle on one end and big knots at the other end allows for a safer distance between the client and the animals' mouth. Clients and the animal can take turns pulling each other around or shaking the toy together, which is a tremendous way to release pent up energy in the body. Some smaller clients can even hold onto a toy and be pulled around gently by a large dog. This activity is a fun way to get clients to relax, loosen up, laugh, and experience a silly pleasure.

There are several ways to play with cats, but they are a bit more particular about when and how they play. Cat toys, often long sticks with string or toys at the end, often activate the cats' drive to attack prey. Clients may want to wave the toys around dramatically, which can be scary to the cat. Instead, clients need to find a way to wave the toy that is enticing to the cat but also safe and enjoyable. There needs to be a balance where the cat is challenged to catch the toy but not so frustrated that it gives up. This requires problem-solving, observation of body language, creativity, and empathy, as clients determine what the cat enjoys and what it needs to succeed. Encouraging the client to observe the animal's reactions and behaviors, rather than telling them what to do, is helpful so that the client learns to observe behaviors and understand how they impact others. In addition, cats can be quite silly as they leap around trying to catch the toy, which can elicit joy and laughter for clients.

The traditional game of hide-and-seek is an excellent intervention which is fun, active, uses problem-solving, and can help build attachment. For clients with attachment issues, this game helps them experience the excitement of finding someone special, and more importantly, the excitement of being found. Adding an animal into the game makes it an even sillier, more unique experience. There are several ways to play hide-and-seek with clients and animals. Clients can hide and have an animal look for them—this often works best with dogs, as they are motivated to find humans and can use their powerful sense of smell. The clinician and dog also can hide, and the client can look for them, but this can sometimes be anxiety-provoking for the client. Additionally, clients can hide treats around the office or outdoors and animals can look for them. This is a wonderful game to play with the chickens and small animals like rats, ferrets, and rabbits. It is a creative, fun game and allows the animal to be engaged and be rewarded for their participation. The animal and human are both delighted and excited to have been found, find someone, or get a treat.

Other games that can be played with animals are kickball or soccer, with an animal retrieving the ball. You can also play board games while the animal observes and the clinician can narrate how the animal appears to be viewing the game. Clients can be creative and problem solve as we encourage them to decide how to include an animal. Overall, playing with an animal, regardless of the game, provides endless opportunities for observation, learning, self-reflection, and therapeutic discussions. Watching the client play with the animal or even watching two animals play together allows for discussion about reading and interpreting nonverbal communication, the animals' thoughts, and feelings, and developing empathy for the animals' experience. We also can discuss how animals handle challenging issues, how they tolerate frustration, whether they keep trying, and how they regulate their behavior if they face obstacles. For example, if Rupert cannot find the ball after it was thrown, we can observe his behavior and discuss if he keeps looking, shows stress cues, asks the humans for help, or gives up. Moreover, we can discuss how animals communicate to each other that they are playing and what happens if one animal gets overstimulated, frustrated, or takes the game too far. Finally, clinicians can direct the client's attention to the animals' self-awareness and self-care—whether the animals take a break when they are tired or if they need support or guidance to rest.

One important note is that while playing with an animal can be fun and therapeutic, it can also be a way for clients to avoid doing hard therapeutic work. This was the case with an adult client who would choose to play fetch with Rupert for his entire session, only talking to Rupert about the ball. His clinician recognized that for this client, play was his way to avoid talking about his presenting issues, so sessions were then structured with play at the end, after therapeutic work had been completed. Play became a motivator for the client to do introspection and the harder therapeutic work, and then both he and Rupert were delighted to have a release of energy at the end of the hour.

AN EXAMPLE OF
PLAYING FETCH

Gayle was a teenage girl who was incredibly focused on being popular and winning school competitions, which was creating difficult social dynamics. During a session playing fetch with Rupert, she noticed Rupert's focus on winning the ball as he knocked the other therapy dog out of the way. She and the clinician discussed how the other therapy dog likely felt during this inter-action and how it might impact the dogs' relationship. Gayle told Rupert that he needed to "work on being less intense" and let the other dog "share the good feelings" of getting the ball. She told him that it felt good to have friends too, and sometimes letting them feel good was more important than winning. We do not always connect these metaphorical discussions to the client's issues, but in this case, the clinician asked Gayle if she was similar to Rupert. After some thought, she noted, "Yes, I'm a very intense person and sometimes other kids don't get me." This led to an insightful discussion about how she might mod-ify some of her behaviors to help her peers feel more comfortable around her, and allow her to create some meaningful social relationships.

WALKING AN ANIMAL

While most of the therapy dogs in our program have already been taught to walk politely on a leash, there are some, like Linda's dog, Rupert, who still like to pull. A calm, easy to manage dog is probably the best way to start so the client feels competent. Walking sessions usually take place in the neighborhood around the ranch, but we also walk many animals around the property, such as cats, goats, and equines. We have a safe, relatively quiet area to take clients and animals on a walk, and going into the neighborhood or to a park can provide some "stretch-ing" for a client with anxiety and other issues. By focusing their attention on the animal, they can often push themselves more than without the animal. The ani-mal provides a buffer between the client and people they may encounter on the walk, but also acts as a "social lubricant," encouraging connection, because strangers may want to pet or talk about the animal, giving the client an opportunity to practice spontaneous social interaction.

Though most people think of dogs when we talk about walking therapy, many types of animals can be walked. One of the most fun and challenging interventions is walking a goat. They are difficult to harness because they are so playful and want to run, and then they are often quite stubborn once on the lead. Clients must practice problem-solving, patience, frustration tolerance, and empathy when trying to take a goat on a walk. We have several cats who love to go for walks outside and will sit by the door, ready for their harness when given the chance. We can also walk some of our smaller animals, such as rabbits, rats, and guinea pigs, if they are comfortable with being outside and wearing a harness. The small animal is allowed to take the lead and the humans follow.

Walking a novel animal, such as a goat or cat, can help a client to build a sense of mastery and accomplishment and add to a burgeoning positive self-concept. Providing new and fun activities where clients can feel a sense of ownership, confidence, and success can help develop a new positive sense of self. For example, not many children or adults have or can walk a goat, or have never seen one on a walk, so imagine the awe, joy, and laughter that situation elicits in others. As a result, clients can feel a sense of uniqueness, self-worth, confidence that they are the catalysts for creating joy in others. It is really inspiring for the client to see how powerful they are in the world, especially with the animals that are more reluctant to be led. Clients may be eager to share their experience with those they meet or with family and friends, thus enhancing social connections.

Working with larger animals on a lead, such as alpacas, donkeys, or horses, provides benefits and skill-building in a new way. For instance, our quarter horse, Hawkeye, can be quite determined and stubborn when asked to walk on a lead. He will stand still, and the client needs to demonstrate confidence and leadership qualities before he takes a step. Hawkeye does not mind if the client is a 50-pound child or a 200-pound man; if the person does not display leadership through self-assurance and intention, then Hawkeye will plant his feet and not budge. We have had staff members who are unable to get Hawkeye to walk, but a five-year-old child was able to effortlessly lead him around the paddock. How the individual approaches and engages with the horse makes the difference. Thus, this activity is great for people of all ages who may be indecisive, incongruent, fearful, narcissistic, victimized, anxious, or full of self-doubt. The client does not just need to act differently, they need to *be* different. If clients want to accomplish this goal to walk a horse, they can find and experience their best self through this type of activity. When clients find this self, feel it, and see the positive impact it has in their life, they are much more likely to repeat these new behaviors. This is a great example of the power of AACP; there is not a "right" way to successfully walk Hawkeye or our goats. Clients must experiment by exploring, challenging, and practicing different aspects of themselves. When they find the right combination, they are instantly rewarded with an animal ready to accompany them on a journey.

AN EXAMPLE OF
WALKING AN ANIMAL

In the middle phase of Cyndi's treatment for bulimia, her clinician suggested they take pygmy goat Dahlia on a walk in the neighborhood. It was a beautiful day and her clinician knew there were likely to be others out and about with their own animals. The clinician gave Dahlia's harness to Cyndi who fumbled with it for several minutes, while trying to hold a squirmy goat. Cyndi finally asked the clinician to hold Dahlia while she put on the harness. With this help, Cyndi was able to put the halter on and headed for the gate, holding Dahlia's lead, but Dahlia did not move. Though a pygmy goat, Dahlia is strong, especially when she is refusing to move. Cyndi tried to gently pull Dahlia, then pulled a bit harder, to no avail. Cyndi gave the clinician a look that showed all the frustration she was feeling. "What can I do to help?" the clinician asked, and Cyndi burst out in frustration, "What do I need to do to get her to move?" The clinician responded, "OK. Let's take a few minutes to figure this out. If you were Dahlia, what would help you want to go on a walk?"

They discussed what would motivate Cyndi to leave her own comfort zone. What motivates her? What does it feel like when someone pulls or pushes her to do something new? In the meantime, Dahlia had wandered over to graze on a bush. Cyndi gathered some leaves from the bush and squatted down to Dahlia's level. "Let's go for a walk Dahlia," she said in a clear, firm voice. When Cyndi stood up, Dahlia looked at her, looked at the leaves in Cyndi's hand, and walked toward her. Giving Dahlia some leaves, Cyndi tried again to pull her, but Dahlia wouldn't budge. "Forget it!" said Cyndi, with a high level of frustration and irritation. The clinician suggested they sit down and take a break for a few minutes.

In this example, the goal was not necessarily to get Dahlia on a walk, but to help Cyndi find a way through her frustration and sense of failure when she could not control a situation. The clinician also wanted Cyndi to see that getting what she wants and needs is not always about force and control. The clinician wanted Cyndi to empathize with Dahlia and to understand what Dahlia needed in order to be led. It took several sessions of trial-and-error before Cyndi could be calm enough to project her intention of a walk to Dahlia. At that point, Cyndi was able to calmly get Dahlia's attention, project her intention to walk, then start walking confidently, with Dahlia willingly joining her.

TRAINING AN ANIMAL

Earlier in the book, we discussed the importance of teaching skills to therapy animals that allow them to be safe and manageable when working with clients. We keep our therapy animals' training relatively simple so that clients can train more complex tricks during sessions. Each animal species and individual animal has a different capacity to learn and respond, and some are certainly more challenging to train than others; however, it is the process of training that is therapeutic, even if the training is never successful. The activity itself is powerful, teaches and utilizes many skills, and tells the clinician a lot about the client.

Training an animal involves multiple steps and skills and can address a variety of therapeutic goals. Levels of training can be modified and adjusted based on the client's interest and abilities. Training an animal involves a lot of empathy, as clients need to understand what the animal is capable of and comfortable with, and then set goals based on those unique characteristics. Clients also need to think about what is rewarding to that animal. Clients cultivate empathy as they work with the animal, read their nonverbal cues, notice and understand the animal's needs, and then respond appropriately. Training also involves a tremendous amount of patience and frustration tolerance, as clients and animals get distracted or frustrated as they struggle to master the chosen skill. Clients need to focus on staying calm and regulated, as an animal will usually become distracted by someone who is agitated or dysregulated. Many clients struggle with being passive or too aggressive in their communication styles, and animals do not respond well to either. Clients must find and practice using their strong, assertive voice, and are then rewarded in a concrete way when they see the results of their successful training.

When clients train our therapy animals, the client usually chooses the skill and the teaching method, which involves goal-setting, forward-thinking, and problem-solving. Clients need to implement their plan, which involves focus, patience, staying on track, giving and following directions, and clear communication. They will need to make necessary modifications and use problem-solving skills, based on how the animal responds. Clients are also multitasking throughout this process, as they give verbal commands and hand signals, notice behaviors, and offer rewards. If they are using a clicker, clients are integrating even more skills and tasks, which can be both rewarding and frustrating. Since training includes so many goals, it is very helpful for clients needing to develop greater executive functioning.

Learning the animal's capacity and boundaries is essential for training, so clients need to learn how to read and interpret body language and make decisions based on that information. Clients must look for nonverbal cues to monitor how the animal is faring; for example, whether the animal simply needs a break from training or if this particular skill is unrealistic, and how to tell the difference. It is unlikely we will teach a chicken to "shake," but they can be trained to go through an obstacle course. Many animals have a short attention span for training, so clinicians can bring attention to cues that it is time to take a break, for either the animal or client, and discuss how to be flexible with expectations or goals.

Throughout training, clients must also be rewarding the animal for their actions and behavior, which means they are paying close attention to the animal and providing feedback. They are focusing on the positive and providing praise and encouragement for the animal. This helps clients learn to focus more on positive behaviors. Clients may be able to absorb some of this praise and success, and clinicians can provide encouragement and support for the client as well, focusing on their effort and the process, rather than the outcome. We want to notice, "Wow, you are working so hard with Lily today," rather than, "You got Lily to do the trick," because it is not the outcome that is most important. Often, clients are not able to successfully train an animal a particular trick they wanted the animal to learn. Accepting "failure" or when to move to a different goal is a critical life skill. Sometimes we must adjust expectations and accept that we cannot accomplish everything we try. Despite the outcome, clients can still feel success and pride in their work with the animal, their ability to treat the animal respectfully, have fun, and strengthen their relationship with the animal. In addition, training is helpful enrichment for the animals, so they enjoy it and clients can feel encouraged by bringing joy to the animals.

Whenever you work with a therapy animal, it is essential that your training method is not forceful. Using aversive or forceful training may teach the animal; however, these training methods run counter to the very basis of AACP, which is about developing positive relationships. Forceful methods cause animals stress and discomfort and convey your willingness to control and cause fear or pain to your animal. Your relationship with your animal models how you will treat your client and can impact your client's ability to trust you and feel safe in the therapeutic setting. If a client sees you punishing your animal for a misstep, they may wonder how you will respond to them when they make a mistake. Modeling patience, tolerance, kindness, flexibility, and persistence is critical when training an animal.

The process of training, especially the challenging moments, can lead to insightful therapeutic discussions. We can process with the client about what went well with the training, what was a struggle, and why the animal responded in certain ways. The focus of these discussions can differ, depending on your client, their age, presenting issues, and therapeutic goals. For example, with a younger client who struggles to focus, the discussion may center on how well the animal paid attention, what distracted the animal, and how we can set up training next time to help the animal pay attention and have more success. We may talk about how other animals nearby were distracting and how the animal got too focused on the treats to learn well, so next time we should go to a quieter location and use different treats. In contrast, with an adult client who is working on self-concept and challenging internalizing failure, we may instead focus on what was going on for the animal that day that impacted its ability to learn, separate from the client. We can discuss how it is close to dinnertime and the animal never learns well when she is hungry, so no matter what the client did, the animal's issues were the impeding element. We can help clients to recognize there are multiple factors in every situation and some of them are out of our control.

AN EXAMPLE OF
TRAINING AN ANIMAL

Arney was a 38-year-old client who wanted to work on his self-esteem and improve his relationships. He was very interested in the alpacas and asked to train Kuzco to walk on a lead. Kuzco is our shyest farm animal, so this was going to be a feat. The clinician first talked about expectations and Arney realized that it would take many weeks of sessions to get Kuzco to stand still and accept the lead. Even so, Arney wanted to try because he felt a real kinship with Kuzco. Arney felt if he could train Kuzco to step out of his comfort zone, it would show him the way as well.

It took many weeks of calmly approaching Kuzco without a lead and sitting quietly in front of Kuzco before Arney could even touch Kuzco's nose. Eventually, Arney and the clinician used a two-person clicker method, where Arney used the clicker to mark a desired behavior by Kuzco in the process toward standing still for the lead, and the clinician gave a treat to Kuzco after each click.

Arney found the training sessions gratifying and could see how he was helping Kuzco feel more comfortable with humans. This made Arney feel proud of himself, and he shared that he had told his coworkers about Kuzco, and they thought it was amazing that Arney was able to train an alpaca. This was a huge therapeutic step in itself, as Arney had struggled to approach or make conversation with his coworkers, so he felt proud of his ability to converse with them. He was developing a level of confidence and seeing that he could build relationships, even if the process was slow.

OBSTACLE OR AGILITY COURSES

An extension of training, but a bit more complex and requiring more physical space and props, are obstacle courses, agility work, and mazes. We do these with almost all our animals, including walking horses around cones and stepping over poles, rats running through Lego mazes, goats jumping into wheelbarrows, and chickens running through tunnels. Creating and executing these courses give clients and animals a fun way to get mental stimulation, creativity, and exercise. As with training skills, the courses should be realistic and fun for the animal, while also challenging but not too hard or stressful. Obstacle courses address many of the same therapeutic goals as training, including empathy, frustration tolerance, patience, problem-solving, creativity, reading and responding to nonverbal cues, adjusting expectations, giving and receiving praise and encouragement, and being assertive. Clients also use gross and fine motor skills as they move around with larger animals or create small mazes for smaller animals.

For our larger animals, we have a traditional animal obstacle course, which includes a tunnel, poles (to wind through while walking or running), a seesaw, a pause pad (to stand still on), and a small jump. We also use hula hoops for animals to walk or jump through, logs, old tires or wheelbarrows, step stools to climb, tunnels to go through, cones to create gates, and many other items around the ranch. Creating these courses allows clients to be creative in what they find and use for the obstacles and encourages them to move their bodies and use empathy to gauge what an animal could accomplish. Often, clients will demonstrate the obstacle course for or with the animal, which not only gets the client moving and active, but is usually quite silly and leads to a lot of joy and laughter.

For smaller animals, such as cats, guinea pigs, rats, and ferrets, clients can develop a maze or obstacle course with boxes, tubes, blocks, Lego, or any items in a playroom. Clients can create tunnels, jumps, turns, slides, various levels, and rewards at different parts of the maze. This activity involves a lot of creativity and fine motor skills, which is an added benefit for many young clients. This is also a good activity if you do not have the space for larger animals or if the weather does not allow for extended time outside.

A client teaching Fred how to go through the vertical obstacle course.

Another simple version of creating an obstacle course is a four-square game. You can do this inside or outside, with any animal. Draw or mark four square areas on the ground, each associated with a predetermined task or trick, and instruct the client to guide the animal into each square. For instance, squares might be marked "sit," "speak," "shake," and "down." Depending on the age and skill level of the client, you can write or draw in the square or ask them to remember each skill. This requires the client to practice memory skills, as well as patience, sequencing, and many of the other skills learned as part of skill training. It is also fun and stimulating for the animals.

In sibling, couple, or family sessions, clients can work together to teach a trick or complete an obstacle. This requires additional therapeutic skills, such as communication, cooperative problem-solving, and conflict resolution. We also can ask a younger or less dominant family member to teach a skill to the rest of the family, giving them a unique opportunity to demonstrate mastery over something. Observing our clients doing this activity together gives clinicians the opportunity to witness how the family system functions. We can witness and better understand the dynamics, relationships, alliances, communication styles, and conflict styles. Seeing the family system in action, rather than how they self-report, gives clinicians valuable information about real-time processes and interactions. Then we can work in the moment to address these issues, ask the family to reflect on the process, and help them experiment with different ways of interacting, communicating, and working together.

An important aspect of this type of intervention is to observe how the animal figures out what they are being asked, how the client can encourage the animal and reduce the animal's frustration, talk about when and why the animal might give up, and how to manage that response. For some clients, such as those who struggle with anxiety or perfectionist tendencies, it may be helpful to let the animals take a break and move onto something else. For clients who tend to quit or give up easily, it may be more valuable for them to watch the animal problem solve, learn how to give and receive encouragement, and witness the animal persevere. For clients with attention issues, we may focus on the animal's short learning period, working within the animal's capabilities, and understanding when they are ready to work again. Clients learn to watch the animals for the signs of fatigue or loss of focus, give the animal permission to take a break, or encourage them to keep trying. How clinicians manage these situations and what they focus on will depend on each client's presenting issues and their ability to cope.

During this process, the clinician should be monitoring the client and animal for signs of frustration, anger, fatigue, loss of focus or attention, or any other behavior or emotion that could result in a safety issue. You may need to stop the training activity and introduce another intervention aimed to refocus or calm the client. In times of frustration, you can encourage clients to express their feelings, take deep breaths, pet the animal, or another intervention that might work with this client. When the client is once again focused and calm, it is good to return to the training activity. This reinforces the behavior of acknowledging difficult feelings and behaviors and finding ways to manage and work though them, rather than quitting. Giving the animal verbal praise teaches clients that it feels good to encourage and be kind to others, and that they can simultaneously feel positive and rewarded by the animal's enjoyment in learning with them. It is often helpful to end the training session with lots of praise for the animal and positive affirmation for the client. One of our favorite affirmations for clients during training is, "You can feel proud about that," or a similar comment that teaches the client to acknowledge and embrace their sense of success and pay attention to their internal validation. When clinically appropriate, we may ask the client to reflect on how they felt about the training process and how they managed their emotions and behavior, which helps with self-reflection and verbalizing thoughts and feelings.

AN EXAMPLE OF
AN ANIMAL AGILITY COURSE

Chuck, a 55-year-old grandfather raising his three young grandchildren, loved the cats and identified with their chronic illness (FIV+) as he had liver disease. Our FIV+ cats live in a room with an elevated obstacle course, and the cats can freely jump around on the structures attached to the wall. We had just installed the obstacle course, so the clinician asked Chuck to help the cats feel comfortable with this agility course while giving also them exercise and enrichment. Chuck explored the room for toys and motivators that would encourage the cats to climb onto the course. He selected an ostrich feather and chose to work with our cat, Fred, trying to get Fred to chase the feather. After several tries, Chuck placed dried tuna flakes, a high-value treat, on each step, which got Fred's attention and he jumped to the first two steps. Over several sessions, Chuck tried a variety of ways to motivate each cat, realizing that each cat had a different interest, desire, and motivation to engage. As they worked, Chuck and the clinician discussed whether this activity mirrored anything in

Chuck's own life, which led to a conversation about his grandchildren. Chuck was able to realize that as with the cats, his grandchildren each had different needs, interests, and motivators, and that modifying his approach with each child would help them all feel more successful and positive.

FEEDING AND CARETAKING

One of our clients' favorite activities is helping with animal feeding and bedtime. Each of our animals is "put to bed" in a specific way. The evening routine begins with preparing the nighttime meal, giving the animals food, then putting them in their nighttime enclosures. The smaller animals get a meal of fresh produce at night, and clients enjoy choosing which fruits and vegetables to put in the animals' salad. Clients can chop and prepare the produce and present it in a bowl to the animal; usually, the animal shows excitement and gratitude at this food offering, so the client can feel good about creating that response. The client is able to take the animals' perspective about what they would like to eat but must also take into account what is healthy and safe for each animal. (We have a list of unsafe foods for each species.) The client also can see the cause and effect when the animal is excited about the food; they were the ones to deliver this delight and contributed to the animals' well-being.

Feeding the larger animals is more challenging, as well as potentially dangerous. We have developed specific procedures when feeding our horses and donkeys, since they can step on and injure a person in their frenzy to get to the food. Feeding the larger animals is a very active intervention that may involve coaxing or corralling an animal or two. The goats are notorious for resisting bedtime, so clients are challenged to find ways to get them to cooperate. This is also a good parallel for clients who resist their own bedtime. After the frenzy of activity as animals get to their food, it is calm and peaceful once they are in their stables quietly eating. Clients can enjoy the quiet evening, which can provide a nice opportunity for reflection.

AN EXAMPLE OF
FEEDING THE ANIMALS

Anjan was a 15-year-old client on the autism spectrum who was selectively mute. Anjan's weekly session was at 4:00 p.m., which is when we put our small animals to bed in the darker winter months. Anjan loved the chickens, and putting them to bed allowed him to quietly and calmly approach each chicken, gently pick them up, and carry them to their coop. After a few weeks, he started to quietly call to each chicken by name and then whisper to them as he carried them to bed. Anjan looked forward to this activity each week and started to talk at home about the personalities of each of the chickens. Feeding the chickens helped him gain confidence, a sense of mastery over a unique skill, and a more positive self-concept. It also calmed his body and mind, relaxing him enough to start verbalizing.

GROOMING AND BATHING

Grooming, brushing, or mindfully petting an animal are great ways to affectionately engage with an animal and can be wonderfully relaxing. These activities allow clients to feel helpful and observe the relaxation and enjoyment of the animals. The focus on taking care of another creature helps build empathy and compassion. For example, clients have to pick the correct brush for the animal, groom in the right direction, and do so in a way that is comfortable and hopefully pleasant for the animal. Clinicians can help clients notice how the animal responds to brushing and expresses its pleasure, which can lead to discussions about cause and effect, nonverbal communication, empathy, and how we can impact those around us. If the client brushes the animal in the wrong direction, rather than correcting them, simply ask what they notice about the animal or its reaction. If the animal shows any signs of discomfort, you can bring that to the client's attention or ask the client to try to brush it the other way and see if there is a difference in the animal's reaction. A small comment such as, "That must feel good to see how happy you make Misty!" can go a long way in helping the client build a sense of self and feel the ability to create a positive world around themselves. If there is more than one animal, or the animal is large, both the clinician and client can be grooming, so both are physically occupied while conversing. This ability to chat without sitting still or looking directly at another person can help clients who are uncomfortable with direct conversations or making eye contact.

Grooming a large animal, such as a horse or donkey, takes concentration and thought since there are several different types of tools used, each with a different function. Grooming correctly is less important than simply the act of doing

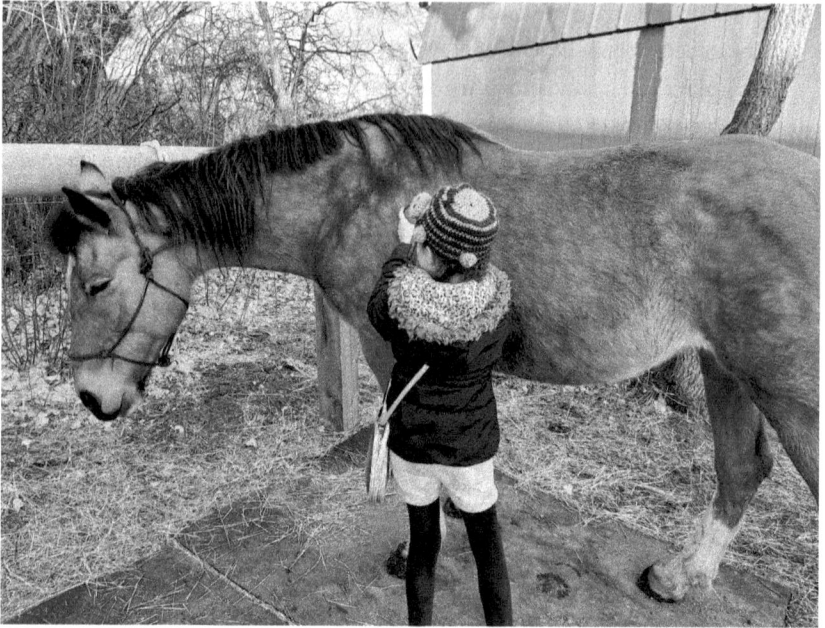

Tunka is a calm, gentle horse. She enjoys being groomed,
which is relaxing for her and clients.

it; the horse really does not care if its mane is combed with a curry comb or soft brush, as long as it is not uncomfortable. Seeing dirt or mud come out of the horse's hair, or the winter coat coming off at the start of summer, can feel rewarding and satisfying to both human and animal. This activity also can demonstrate cause and effect, which is beneficial for clients with attachment issues, autism, and other neurologically based problems.

Other times, grooming may be a way to help the client learn about hygiene and the necessity of cleanliness. For example, some animals may not love being brushed or getting a bath, but it is essential to keep them clean and healthy. For clients who may resist self-care, bathing an animal, such as a goat, is a fun and very engrossing intervention. Feeling the grimy fur of the goat and seeing the dirty water pour down can help a client to feel as though they have accomplished something important. Moreover, goats generally do not love baths, even though they occasionally need them, so clients can focus on firmly holding them while calming and soothing the goats as well. Feeling the soft goat fur and seeing the happy goat after the bath is a good reinforcer for clients, since they may not necessarily appreciate the difference in their own hygiene before or after a bath. It may also remind them that bathing can feel good once it is over. Finally, the client may get wet or dirty themselves, therefore encouraging them to take a shower or bath once they are home.

AN EXAMPLE OF
GROOMING AN ANIMAL

Beth was a 21-year-old college student who suffered from social anxiety disorder. Each session, she and her clinician spent the last 15 minutes grooming the donkeys. Beth worked with one donkey and the clinician groomed the other. As they brushed and groomed the donkeys, the clinician would ask Beth to focus on different aspects of her donkey in order to practice mindfulness and being in the moment. Beth could focus on the donkey's smell, the feel of her mane, the temperature of her breath, or the rhythm of her breathing. As Beth focused on these elements, sometimes she was silent and other times she verbalized her experience. After the intervention they discussed Beth's experience, including her anxiety level, using a 1–10 scale. After the third week of practicing mindfulness with the animals, Beth's anxiety had reduced to a one or two, down from seven or eight. They talked about the reasons behind this decrease and the power Beth had over her thoughts. In each session this strength was highlighted, and Beth was able to use these mindfulness skills in social situations outside the ranch.

FINDING DELIGHT

Having mental or behavioral health issues is daunting. Clients may wonder what causes happiness and how some people seem to wake up happy every day, or whether happiness is something we can learn. Clients may find their focus on the negative events in the past, present, or future. In doing so, they miss the tiny miracles and delights spontaneously happening around them, which could impact them and help create moments of happiness. We think there is no better place to learn about joy and delight than on a beautiful farm with loving animals.

While "finding delight" is associated with mindfulness, we intentionally separated the two interventions, because you do not need to know how to be mindful to catch a moment of delight, and you do not have to be joyful to practice mindfulness. However, to find happiness, you do need to know where to look or how to change your focus. Finding delight means focusing on the moment and what around us that is beautiful, fun, or sparks joy. Gratitude, joy, and delight are fragile and can be easily clouded over by difficulties, routine, and boredom; however, we believe that most, if not all, people have the capacity for joy.

Finding joy in small moments is exemplified by our youngest goats every time they run. They jump, turn, and twist in excitement. This aerial show is a delight to watch if you take a moment to observe. We can help our clients not only see these little moments, but revel in them and allow them to inspire joy.

AN EXAMPLE OF
FINDING DELIGHT

Recently, our staff and a few clients gathered together to release butterflies that clients had raised from larvae to caterpillars to butterflies. It was not a flurry of colorful wings but instead was a slow, delicate process as each butterfly practiced moving their wings for the first time and then took flight into the rose garden. We took those few moments together, out of our hectic days, to notice the blue sky, celebrate the butterflies' launch, and feel pride and camaraderie about what we had accomplished together. It was a delight.

INTERPRETING SPONTANEOUS ANIMAL BEHAVIOR

This intervention is probably the most important and most difficult to learn in AACP, so we have devoted an entire chapter to it. Chapter 15, "Catching the Moment," describes in depth how a clinician can observe an animal's spontaneous behavior and then weave it into the session. It is hard to quantify or describe this process, as it changes depending on your animal, client, setting, and ability to manage the situation. For more detailed information on integrating spontaneous animal behavior into sessions, please read that chapter.

REFERENCES

Chassman Craddock, L. (2022). Sideways interventions. In M. Kirby (Ed.), *Nourished: Horses, animals and nature in counselling, psychotherapy and mental health.* Aware Publishing.

Odendaal, J. S. (2000). Animal-assisted therapy—magic or medicine? *Journal of Psychosomatic Research*, *49*(4), 275–280. https://doi.org/10.1016/s0022-3999(00)00183-5

Olmert, M. D. (2010). *Made for each other: The biology of the human-animal bond.* Da Capo Press.

11

LEARNING THROUGH PLAY: INTERVENTIONS WITH YOUNG HUMANS

"It's the things we play with and the people who help us play that make a great difference in our lives."

—FRED ROGERS

P lay is the language of children. Most clinical work with children is done through play therapy, which is easily integrated with AACP since both children and animals like to play. Play therapy is often the most effective way to engage children who are about 3 to 12 years old. Since "talk therapy" requires introspection, insight, and other advanced cognitive skills, play therapy is more appropriate for most children. There are exceptions for children who have good cognitive and verbal skills and can have thoughtful discussions with a clinician. We also do a fair amount of play with teenagers and adults who are responsive to playful interventions, as addressed in the previous chapter. This chapter focuses on play therapy with children and how animals can enrich that process. Please note that this is not a full description of play therapy. If you would like to learn more about play therapy, there are many texts that focus on the topic in depth. We recommend *Play Therapy: The Art of the Relationship* by Garry Landreth (2023) and *Child-Centered Play Therapy* by Rise VanFleet, Andrea Sywulak, and Cynthia Caparosa Sniscak (2010).

There are two general approaches to play therapy that we will focus on: nondirective play therapy, which is initiated and led by the child, and directive play therapy, where the clinician designs and/or manages the activities. We have found that using a combination of nondirective and directive play therapy works well with our clients. We decide which approach to use depending on the client's unique needs, therapeutic goals, and progression through treatment. The clinician's job is to give meaning to the client's play. Fantasy play is the child's reality, and a change in play usually indicates a change in the brain. When animals are involved, this fantasy play can be richer and more engaging. Children can incorporate the animal into play, and clinicians can create unique play opportunities that are centered around the animal-child interaction.

DEFINING THE CLIENT

Generally, children are referred to therapy by parents, caregivers, social services, or other adults, so often these people inform the clinician about the issues they want addressed in therapy. While the child is the identified client, caregivers often play a role in sessions. At the start of treatment, it is important to determine how a caregiver will be participating in sessions and to what degree, as there are different levels of involvement in therapy. Some caregivers want to be told every detail of each session and others want to leave everything to the clinician's discretion and be uninvolved. Neither of these extreme approaches is beneficial for the client, and it is the clinician's responsibility to find a balance with each family so that child and caregivers are equally invested in the therapeutic commitment. There are several options for involvement: working with only the child in sessions; seeing the child for most sessions but periodically including the caregiver in sessions; conducting sessions with the child with regular check-ins with the caregiver; suggesting ongoing family therapy; or finding another combination of services that best meets the family's needs. Our clinicians usually see the child individually for most sessions and have monthly update meetings with the child's caregivers. Regardless of the structure, it is critical to keep the caregivers involved so that they remain invested in the child's treatment. The clinician also needs to clearly express their recommendations and expectations for treatment regarding who participates in sessions, when, and how often. Moreover, though the child has been identified as the individual who "needs therapy," often the entire family system could benefit from support. Encouraging caregiver involvement also shares the responsibility for change. Therefore, the child is not the only one obligated to modify their behaviors, and both the child and the caregivers are aware of and responsible for implementing change.

Caregivers are often confused about what is done in play therapy, especially when animals are involved. Caregivers may see or hear from their child that sessions involve playing games, doing art, taking a dog for a walk, or creating mazes for a rat, and they struggle to understand how this is considered therapy. It is often difficult for caregivers to understand how play therapy works and how walking a dog could be therapeutic, because it looks and sounds so different than traditional talk therapy. They may want to know what themes are discussed, what goals are being addressed, and whether the client is talking about problems. While a young client likely does not know what "work" is being done during play therapy and cannot convey this to caregivers, the clinician should be able to conceptualize treatment, explain how these playful activities address treatment goals, and regularly convey progress to caregivers. Clinicians need to be able to explain the learning and growth that occurs through play and AACP. Helping caregivers understand the benefits of play therapy with animals makes it more likely they will keep their commitment to therapy and stay involved in the treatment process.

ENGAGEMENT

Getting a child engaged in play therapy and/or AACP is usually not difficult at our facility, as we have the benefit of our amazing animals and well-stocked playrooms. In the intake session, we give the family a tour of our facility and introduce them to our animals. Treatment and therapy are framed in terms of play and fun, and we encourage the child's curiosity about how they will work with the animals in future sessions. We want the children to enjoy and look forward to coming to sessions.

Engaging caregivers can be more challenging, for a variety of reasons. Some caregivers are resistant to the idea that play can be therapeutic and prefer that we talk to their child. As mentioned earlier, some caregivers want to be involved in every session and others want to remain removed from the process, and neither situation is ideal. It is important that the clinician learn about and understand the family or systemic dynamics so that they can successfully support the caregivers' need for involvement. Often, this means discussing the huge role that caregivers play in their child's life and how important they are to their child's well-being and success. We need the caregivers' support for the work we are doing, because they are with their child much more than we are and can support and enhance the work we do in sessions. Clinicians can describe the activities done in sessions, explain how they help meet client goals, and suggest ways that the caregiver can continue these processes at home. For example, clinicians can share that the client is working on awareness of others and empathy as they play with the animals and observe their body language. We can explain how watching the animals' response to certain behaviors allows a client to understand how their behavior impacts those around them and enables a client to recognize other's feelings. Clinicians can ask caregivers to support this process at home and bring attention to the behaviors and feelings of others.

GOAL-SETTING

Caregivers generally bring a child to therapy with specific concerns or presenting problems that they (the caregiver) would like addressed in therapy. Sometimes children understand or acknowledge these issues, but many times they are unaware or do not understand the reasons they are in therapy. Children often demonstrate these issues or challenging behaviors during sessions; yet we have found that clients often behave differently at our facility than they do in other areas of life, like home or school. Because play therapy and time with the animals is fun, and clients get to make choices and feel a sense of control, we often do not see as many challenging behaviors or presenting issues. This can be frustrating to caregivers, because they feel that if we are not witnessing the challenges, we cannot understand or address them. However, this situation can be reframed to show that clients do have the capacity to act differently and that perhaps something in the child's environment needs to change for the client to be successful.

Caregivers generally play an important role in treatment planning and goal-setting. We usually conduct intake sessions with caregivers, as we gather current and historical information about the child. After seeing the child with or without their caregiver, the clinician has enough information to form an initial, general goal for the client. An example of a general goal is that the child will be able to complete their school days without acting out aggressively or their relationship with caregivers will improve. Further goal-setting is done as the clinician observes how the child responds to the animals in varying situations. Watching these interactions often provides the richest information about where the child needs support. For example, we may see that a child is initially rough when petting a dog or expects the clinician to follow them around for 50 minutes as they try to visit every animal. These interactions may indicate challenges around empathy and focus and can inform future goals and interventions.

Once we have a general idea about the goals of therapy, the clinician can decide whether the client would benefit more from unstructured or structured play therapy. As mentioned, most of the play therapy we provide combines both approaches. Some clinicians are trained in a particular approach to working with

A client watching as Sugar, the rabbit, grooms Rollo, the guinea pig.
Rollo grew up thinking Sugar was his mother. Sugar has nurtured
this relationship and they show clients that there are all kinds of families.

children, such as Adlerian therapy, and will need to formulate a treatment plan utilizing those concepts. We have found that the more internal structure the child already possesses, the less direction or structure they require in therapy. For children with severe neglect, trauma, or attachment issues, an approach with a clear focus and direction may be more suitable.

NONDIRECTIVE PLAY THERAPY WITH ANIMALS

Nondirective play therapy provides an environment for the child to create scenarios that represent the areas in their lives that need attention. Clients are given the freedom to explore a space and choose how they want to engage with the items. Usually, the space is a playroom with a variety of toys available to create scenes that represent their issues. If an animal is present, children may include the animal in the play, but there are no specific rules or suggestions since the play is nondirective. This section offers some guidelines for how to enrich this type of play therapy with animals but does not go into depth about how to do nondirective work. If you are interested in conducting or learning about play therapy, finding play therapy-specific training is essential.

During nondirective play therapy, children often replay issues, events, or trauma that they have experienced, sometimes repetitively. The clinician plays a vital role in this activity, as a witness, providing the support and modeling and feedback that would have been appropriate at the time of the initial event or trauma. The clinician will "track" the child's play by making meaningful comments in response to what is happening. During play therapy, children use toys, action figures, sand trays, stuffed animals, and many other items to recreate this play. In AACP, children can integrate the animal into this play in a safe and respectful way. Having an animal available in the playroom during the child's session can encourage the child to find creative ways of engaging the animal; for instance, the animal could be a baby, patient, pet, family member, or friend. The child can use their imagination and be creative about how to involve the animal in play. It is important to consider how your animal is included and how they are involved in the play. Issues to consider include whether the client can put clothes or toys on the animal, .physically move or engage with the animal, or assign the animal a role and act out various scenarios. Each animal will have a different capacity and interest in being involved in the play, and it is your job to know and hold their limits, monitor their welfare, and intervene with modifications as needed.

If the child is not integrating the animal in the play, the clinician can talk to the animal as a way of noticing what the child is doing, much like a narration. The clinician can track the play through comments made to the animal instead of to the child, allowing for a more natural tone. Clients may also feel less pressure or as though the tracking is a less of a commentary or judgement on their behavior. For instance, a clinician might note, "Sasha, did you see how careful Lauren is being when she carries the baby? She is being really considerate of the baby's safety." Keeping your tone light and casual can help the child accept and feel at ease with your commentary.

Clinicians can also give the animal a voice or interpret what the animal is "saying" or "thinking." For example, "S'mores is noticing you stomping your feet and thinks you must have a strong feeling!" Dogs that make spontaneous noises and grumbles are really fun. One of our former therapy dogs, Tucker, was very vocal and would sometimes make audible groans. This provided ample opportunities for the clinician to ask the client what they thought Tucker was saying or to interpret what Tucker was expressing through his noises. Though it was not always evident or clear what Tucker was trying to communicate, the important element was the child's observation, interpretation, and projection.

Play therapy for some children is very intense, and they need space to release this energy and emotion while also being safe and contained. In our facility, we have multiple offices that are playrooms and do not have animals present, so we often start in these rooms with children. If the client requests it or the clinician thinks it is appropriate and helpful, an animal can be intentionally brought into the playroom to include in play. This protects the animals from unexpected outbursts during play that may feel threatening to them. These high-energy, intense, and potentially traumatized children can make an animal feel stressed, so pay careful attention to your animals' cues. At our facility, we are very protective of our animals and remind clients that big feelings are always acceptable but can be scary to animals, so the animal may be removed if a client wants to yell, throw items, or engage in other aggressive play. We also do not allow any aggressive behavior to be directed at the animals and will immediately remove the animal from the session if we suspect it could be an issue. For these safety reasons, nondirective play therapy including animals requires careful attention and consideration for your animal. Not all clients or animals will be a fit for nondirective AACP or may need clear boundaries and guidelines, which makes the work less nondirective. Overall, clinicians need to use their best judgment about the client, situation, and animal to decide what modalities are going to be safe, effective, and fun.

AN EXAMPLE OF
NONDIRECTIVE PLAY THERAPY
WITH ANIMALS

Tom was a five-year old child referred to AATPC for behavior issues in school, impulsivity, and angry outbursts at home after the arrival of his younger brother. In his first few weeks of treatment, Tom chose to play in a room with the cats and kept inviting them to play with him by waving the cat feather toy frantically in the cats' face. Because the cats were able to move away or hide, the clinician allowed this behavior to continue and in fact, each cat moved backward as Tom approached with the toy. Tom would become angry and start to call loudly, "Come on kitty!" and the cats would hide under a chair, which resulted in an angry outburst from Tom. Rather than tell Tom what to do or how to behave, the clinician commented, "You waved that toy and asked Marble to play but she hid! Hmm." The clinician helped Tom to calm down and observe the animal come out of hiding, and then noted, "Now that you are sitting down just holding the toy, Marble is back!" As Tom began to move the toy gently, the clinician said, "Oh, Marble, you really want that toy! It is one of your favorites! You really want to grab it but want to make sure it is safe." Throughout this process, Tom moved the toy slowly and did not acknowledge the clinician's comments but was clearly responding nonverbally and modifying his behaviors.

Over time, as Tom was able to regulate his behaviors with the cats, they became more comfortable with him, and Tom was able to involve them in play. He would create "cat cities" with cardboard blocks, and within those spaces, create "big brother cat-only places" for our male cats. In a soft voice, he would tell our male cat, Siggie, "You need a special place, all your own, where no one can bother you and you can't hear any crying." Tom was working through his frustration and sadness about the changes in his homelife. Working with the cats was a wonderful way for Tom to process his feelings in a nonjudgmental space and without verbalizing his complicated emotions. At the same time, the cats were very clear with Tom about what behaviors they did not like, so he was able to recognize his impact on those around him and practice new behaviors, with a very satisfying, purring reward.

DIRECTIVE PLAY THERAPY WITH ANIMALS

The initial phases of play therapy generally focus on rapport building and helping the client feel safe and comfortable in the therapy space, so often we start with nondirective work. We allow the client to explore the playroom, choose the activities, and guide the play. Over time, however, we often move to more directive play therapy, where the clinician designs and directs the interventions to meet certain goals or needs. Directive play therapy often helps focus on the client's issues and is particularly effective for children who are a bit older and higher functioning, who are acutely dysregulated and easily distracted, or who focus on the animals to avoid doing therapeutic work.

Prior to each session, the clinician will choose and prepare several activities to do during the session. The child can choose which activity they would like to do or which will be first. Since children have shorter attention spans, it is helpful to design the activity to last about 15 minutes and to continue only if the child can manage it. Interventions are designed to address a specific treatment goal. The intervention may be repeated in multiple sessions, depending on how the child responds. Examples of directive play therapy with animals include throwing a ball for a dog; lying next to a specific animal and asking the child to draw a picture of it; creating an obstacle course; rearranging an enclosure; or spending multiple sessions with a shy animal to develop a connection.

Sometimes sessions are a mix of directive and nondirective therapy; we might specifically ask the client to create a maze for the rats, but allow them to direct the process, chose what supplies to use, and how to design and produce the maze. So, while they were given a specific task (directive), the client is then allowed to lead the process and make independent choices (nondirective).

AN EXAMPLE OF MIXED DIRECTIVE AND NONDIRECTIVE PLAY THERAPY WITH ANIMALS

An 11-year-old girl named Maya came to therapy after making a suicide threat. At the time of her intake, Maya was having difficulty making friends at school and was receiving poor grades, despite being identified as gifted by her school. Maya's behavior at home was erratic and sometimes destructive. A year ago, Maya had tried therapy, but after several sessions, Maya had refused to enter the therapy office, so they discontinued treatment. Maya was willing to come to our ranch because she wanted to play with the animals.

Maya began her treatment in our rabbit room, sitting on the floor with her clinician. Maya would quietly describe her feelings of sadness and loneliness as she pet the long, soft ears of our black rabbit, K.C. However, if Maya became agitated, K.C. would quickly hop to the closet, which was his safe spot. This gave her clinician the opportunity to talk about how Maya's change in voice tone and mannerisms impacted K.C. "What just happened with K.C. when your voice got loud?" asked the clinician. Maya said, "He ran away! Great, K.C. hates me just like everyone else." The clinician encouraged Maya to notice how K.C. responded once she calmed down. Maya immediately tried different voice tones to talk to K.C. to see how he reacted. During the next several sessions, the clinician and Maya discussed how rabbits are prey animals, and the clinician was able to reframe K.C.'s reaction as a fear response to Maya's loud voice, not to her as a person. During these discussions, Maya was able to see how her behavior could impact others and make them feel uncomfortable, but had nothing to do with whether or not they liked her as a person.

As Maya became more comfortable in therapy, her clinician suggested that they work with the therapy dog, Rupert. First, the clinician shared Rupert's photo album and his experience of failing as a service dog, due to his social anxiety and certain challenging behaviors. He had moved to five different homes before his forever home with Linda. Maya and her clinician talked about how Rupert must have felt with all of these changes and rejections, and how it impacted his behaviors. For instance, Rupert used to shake every time he got in the car with Linda, and the clinician asked Maya what she thought Rupert's behavior was communicating. Maya projected her own feelings of sadness, fear, rejection, and loneliness onto Rupert, both empathizing with him and relating her own feelings and experiences to his, thus feeling less alone. She gave Rupert a kiss on his nose and told him he was a "sweet boy." Having projected her own issues onto Rupert, she was also able to comfort and regulate herself through comforting him.

In later sessions, Maya and her clinician moved outside to play fetch with Rupert. They discussed how this physical activity was essential to Rupert's physical and mental well-being. They laughed as they watched his joy and eagerness when the word "ball" was spoken, and this allowed Maya to relax and enjoy sessions in a new way. As they played fetch, Maya had to read Rupert's nonverbal cues, which indicated that he needed a break, even when having fun. It was her job to tell him to "take a break" when he needed one. This experience helped Maya to realize how others might need rest and even take some space away from her, even when having fun. She also had some control in choosing when Rupert needed a break and was able to use her voice to give him a direction. Playing fetch with Rupert helped Maya to have fun and be silly, but also to practice new skills in reading body language, relaxing control of others, and giving others space to be with her. This directive work allowed the clinician to structure activities that would push Maya gently out of her comfort zone and practice new ways of behaving and regulating when upset.

A NOTE ABOUT PLAY THERAPY
WITH LARGE ANIMALS

Young children certainly can engage in animal interventions with larger animals, including horses, goats, and llamas. However, we do not explicitly include these activities in the play therapy section because genuine play therapy involves the child's natural behaviors and spontaneous responses. Due to their size and potential to accidentally harm children, we do not engage in unstructured play around our large animals, and we strongly caution other clinicians to be mindful about this as well. Working with the large animals involves interventions that are more carefully constructed and supervised, so these interventions are addressed in later chapters.

REFERENCES

Landreth, G. L. (2023). *Play therapy: The art of the relationship* (4th ed.). Routledge.

VanFleet, R., Sywulak, A. E., & Sniscak, C. C. (2010). *Child-centered play therapy*. Guilford Press.

12

MY ALPACA IS ANGSTY: ANIMAL-ASSISTED INTERVENTIONS WITH TEENS

"When your children are teenagers, it's important to have a dog so that someone in the house is happy to see you."

—NORA EPHRON

Clinicians who work with teenagers know that this population can create a much different experience during counseling and psychotherapy. Clinicians often love or hate working with teens, but most of us agree that animals can make a huge difference when working with adolescents.

In this chapter we discuss some of the elements of working with teenagers and how the animals can assist in that process. We look at how to define the client, how to engage teens, and how to set achievable treatment goals. We also explore how the work in different stages of therapy differs when including an animal. Finally, we describe some of the more common problems our teens bring to therapy and how the animals can assist with those issues.

THE PROGRESSION OF TREATMENT

In this section, we look at some of the important aspects of treatment with teens and how animals can be integrated. There is often confusion within families about who will be doing the work in therapy, therefore, we start the therapeutic process by defining the client. Facilitating teen participation in treatment can be challenging, but incorporating animals can make this process more successful. The "work" of therapy in AACP involves encouraging teens to work and play with animals, and this process may or may not include talk therapy.

DEFINING THE CLIENT

How a clinician approaches therapy with a teenager often depends on who initiated therapy. Ideally, the teen has indicated that they would like support and have agreed to be involved in AACP. In Colorado, teenagers over 15 years old can seek therapeutic support on their own, without caregiver involvement or permission. We have worked with several teens who have researched counseling and come to us independently. However, this is not typical, and caregivers often seek counseling services for their teen for a variety of reasons. It is a more complex situation when the teen was not involved in the decision-making process about therapy.

Regardless of how the teenager came to therapy, the first therapeutic goal is often determining who the client is; in other words, determining who truly needs support. Often, caregivers have their own agenda for what their teen needs to change and will communicate this to the therapist. The caregiver may want to be involved in sessions, dictate what is discussed, and have a lot of input about how therapy is done. We have found this is not usually helpful for anyone involved. It can confuse boundaries and roles, create resistance, and prevent client engagement. Counselors need to set clear limits with caregivers so that the teenager is the client and has the freedom to explore the issues that are most pressing to them.

If caregivers are involved in seeking treatment, an intake meeting with them should include education about the legal and ethical aspects of confidentiality with their teen. The clinician should have a clear policy that they can describe to both the caregiver and the teen that explains under what circumstances the clinician will communicate with the parent. For example, clinicians should describe the ethical limits of confidentiality when it comes to harm to self and others, but also can discuss how they may not disclose other risky behaviors, such as drinking, as that would limit the client's trust in them and ability to share openly. Setting these limits with the caregiver and teen together allows the teen to witness their caregiver agree to these terms, which is a critical step in earning their trust. In addition, having this conversation early and explaining how the clinician will communicate with the caregiver is essential in order to define the teenager as the client. We have found it is helpful to have a brief monthly phone call with caregivers to update them about the teen's general progress and that the teenager should be aware that this communication is happening.

Even if the teen is not interested or motivated to be in therapy, it is crucial for the teen to see that the clinician is involved for the teen's benefit, and not an extension of the caregiver's rules or expectations. The animals can help create a space for the teen and clinician to begin a relationship that revolves around the animals. Once the teen realizes the process does not focus on the caregiver's agenda, they often become open to being involved in sessions. Additionally, clinicians should educate caregivers about the process of AACP and how it is truly therapy and not just playtime with the animals. We have a document that we provide to caregivers who are concerned or have questions about how AACP is beneficial and therapeutic.

ENGAGEMENT

It is essential to engage teenagers in therapy quickly and help them see that counseling can be beneficial. AACP is a wonderful fit for teenagers, because a primary focus for this age is creating relationships, and teenagers can form special relationships with the therapy animals without the scrutiny of peers and adults. They also can focus on their bond with the animals without feeling pressure to relate to the clinician. If you have ever been in your office, facing a teenager who refuses to say anything for a full session, or had a teenager share their deepest secret only when sitting next to you in the car, you have learned that face-to-face communication is rarely the best way to start a relationship with a teenager. It is often easier for teens to have a conversation side-to-side, as you walk a dog or groom a horse, so they do not feel the pressure of direct eye contact and expectations to share. There is the added bonus that these activities are often fun and do not cause the teen to feel like something is wrong with them.

The beginning of treatment with adolescents usually involves casual activities with each of the animals, talking about relatively neutral topics, such as information about the animals and their histories. Often these sessions involve holding, petting, brushing, grooming, and walking an animal. During these seemingly mundane activities, the clinician may communicate with the teen by talking about subjects that are fairly universal, such as school, friends, music, pets, and sports. This process allows the teenager to feel comfortable in the therapeutic environment and with the clinician, and hopefully lowers their resistance to later disclosure.

Over time, clients tend to form a special bond with a certain animal, and we can see how this relationship is unique and important to not only the teen, but the animal as well. It is clear that animals remember and respond to certain people. We can focus and build on this "special" and reciprocal attachment that has developed between the teen and the animal. It is a truly magical process that needs time to evolve and may require a little support from the clinician. Of course, there are times when a teenager does not connect with any of our animals, but that is rare.

GOAL-SETTING

Setting treatment goals with teens can be challenging, because teens often cannot clearly articulate how they need help or may struggle to admit that they want or need help. This goal-setting process may be long, as you allow the teen to share about their life and situations they find challenging. If you have done a good job with the engagement process, the teen should be able to assist you in choosing the areas they would like to focus on in therapy. Together, you can determine a central theme for your work together and develop a treatment plan, though the goals do need to be issues that the teen is invested in addressing.

The primary developmental goals for teenagers include the building of identity, creating relationships, and increasing autonomy. As we learn more about the teen in their environment, it often becomes clear that the presenting problem is related to a delay or rupture in a certain developmental arena. If the teen has previously experienced abuse, neglect, or other trauma, the rupture may have occurred early in their development, and therapeutic work may need to focus on those issues. While it may not be necessary to define the teen's goal in these developmental terms, it is often helpful for the clinician to keep them in mind as you work with the teenager.

Conflicts between caregivers and peers are incredibly common for teenagers, and both are related to the developmental issues mentioned above. New relationships with peers help the teen to develop greater independence and autonomy and also help them to create a new, more mature self-identity. Issues such as substance use, self-harm, and eating disorders can be associated with control and decision-making. For some teens, making choices that they know are upsetting to their caregivers, other adults, and authorities provides the sense of identity and autonomy they are seeking. Substance use is an example of a negative behavior that meets many developmental goals simultaneously, as it can:

- quickly develop peer relationships;
- give teenagers a behavior that is uncontrollable by parents or other authorities;
- offer a clear sense of identity in relation to peers;

- provide an understanding, alternative "family"; and
- supply stress relief, neurochemical release, reinforcement, and overall fun.

Looking at substance use in terms of reality therapy's psychological needs, we see that it meets the needs of belonging, power, freedom, and fun (Glasser, 1999). However, reviewing the above list, we can see that each of those goals can also be accomplished through a relationship with a trusted animal.

Hopefully, the therapeutic goals set with the teenager align with what caregivers or referral sources designated as important. However, often these external adults do not see the full picture and there may be other issues that need to be resolved before the referring behavior can be addressed. When the teenager can see how interventions with the animals can help meeting therapeutic goals, they can then communicate to the adults in their lives what therapy is accomplishing without having to divulge specific, personal issues.

DOING THE WORK

In our experience, the most successful sessions with teenagers combine experiential work with the animals and time spent talking about the teen's daily concerns. The amount of time spent doing active, experiential work or more traditional talk therapy depends on the client, but we do find that teenagers who are reluctant to share or process verbally can learn and process through activities. There are certainly some clients who will prefer to verbally process events and engage in more traditional talk therapy. In these cases, AACP is beneficial because the clinician can integrate the animal throughout the process to help clients work through certain issues or difficult topics.

AN EXAMPLE OF
"DOING THE WORK"

Max was motivated to do talk therapy to process sexual abuse by a former coach. However, Max was only able to skim the surface of his story before he shut down and appeared to dissociate. When this happened, the therapy animal was able to help Max stay focused on the present moment and bring Max back into his body. Max would pet the therapy animal, which allowed for increased regulation, lowered anxiety and blood pressure, and increased oxytocin; all of these physical changes then allowed Max to move forward again sharing his story.

A teenager encouraging Batman to walk.

In one session, Max was talking about the shame he felt about the abuse, but his verbal expressions seemed disconnected from his body. The therapist was able to observe to Max, "It seems like this is hard to talk about . . . are you OK to try an experiment right now?" This moved the session from primarily talking to an experiential intervention, which allowed Max a new way to share and process his disclosure. Here is an example of the dialogue from the session, which took place in our guinea pig room, with our albino, one-eyed hairless guinea pig, Rosie.

Clinician: "Max, take a minute and hold Rosie, pet her back gently, and while you're doing that, look carefully at her. Describe what you see, in detail."

Max: "She's pink and wrinkly and has white fur on her nose. Her feet look funny, like old man feet."

Clinician: "Ha ok. What else do you see?"

Max: "Ok, actually, she's kind of ugly. Her eye looks like it was sewn shut and has a bit of goop coming out of it. It's kind of gross."

Clinician: "Kind of gross. Ok. If you could put yourself in Rosie's shoes for a minute, what would it be like to be her?"

Max (after a few moments of quiet): "I guess I'd feel fine about it. Maybe I'd feel older, since I think she is older, right?"

Clinician: "What about her eye that's sewn shut? What do you think that's like for her?"

Max: "She's a guinea pig. She probably doesn't care."

Clinician: "What would it be like if I told you that you had to tell Rosie that she is ugly and gross and that she should feel terrible about herself!"

Max: "I would never do that!"

Clinician: "Why not? Isn't that what you said about her?"

Max: "Yeah, I guess. But I really like Rosie, and I kind of also think she's cool. I would never want to say something that made her feel bad."

Clinician: "How would you feel if someone else said that to her?"

Max (in a harsh tone): "I'd be angry and tell them to shut up."

Clinician: "Was there someone in your life that made you feel ugly and gross and ashamed of who you are? Wouldn't you be angry at them?"

In this exchange, we see Max getting angry on Rosie's behalf, whereas he could not be angry for himself. The clinician created an intervention that allowed Max to step outside his own experience and confront feelings of shame. The clinician then encouraged Max to put his anger where it truly belonged, not on himself, but on the coach who hurt him. During this process, he was able to hold and gently pet Rosie, which created a physical experience of comfort and care for both Rosie and Max. It kept Max grounded and calm, even while discussing difficult topics, which usually caused him to shut down. This approach allowed the clinician to work with Max on multiple levels, but in a subtle, nonconfrontational way. Though teenagers like Max are able to verbally share their experiences, there are many who prefer not to talk about their issues, or anything at all. However, these clients may still be working on the developmental issue of autonomy and will benefit from experiential interventions.

There are situations where clients or their caregivers do not understand how an intervention is therapeutic; they may struggle to see how teaching a new trick to a dog is a therapeutic intervention, rather than just training the clinician's animal. However, the distinction lies in the different ways the clinician interacts with the client throughout the process and how they focus on the larger goal. For example, we may start with helping a teenage client find an unusual skill to teach the animal, to demonstrate to themselves and those around them that they can develop mastery over difficult things. How the clinician reflects this success and sees the client may be very different from how others in their lives see them, which can be a reflection of potential. The clinician may have the distinction of being the only adult who can accept all of the teen and understand their negative behavior for what it is—the teenager's best attempt to meet their own needs.

By using interventions that focus on developmental issues, we are helping teenagers learn healthier ways of meeting their developmental needs. The animals help these teenage clients discover and meet those needs in new and powerful ways. When teens work with animals, especially novel animals such as goats or rats, they are forced to think about themselves in a different way. As they see themselves succeed when working with an animal, they can create a new image of themselves that does not fit into a former schema, or narrative set up by themselves, parents, school, their culture, or peers. The experience with the animal becomes fused into part of who they are and helps create a new, more positive and functional identity. Once teenagers learn to meet their needs in healthier ways, such as mastering a new skill like training a dog, they will hopefully no longer need their self-destructive behaviors and eventually let them go.

FOUNDATIONAL AREAS FOR TEENS

We would need a separate book to explore treatment for all the diagnoses for teenagers, but we have found several foundational areas for the work we do with teens that are especially appropriate for AACP. These issues include building resilience, developing executive functioning, and helping the teen create a new, healthy identity for themselves.

BUILDING RESILIENCE

It is difficult and frustrating when we work with a teen who wants to do well and is capable of doing better, yet they are trapped in a situation that they cannot escape. We have worked with teenage clients who must rely on caregivers who subject them to abuse, neglect, or other forms of treatment that are detrimental to the teen's well-being. There are families where caregivers are not legally abusive or neglectful, yet they do not provide the kind of support, guidance, structure, or parenting that the teen needs to flourish. In most of these situations, the caregivers have their own struggles and lack the time or energy to provide care, which can be understandable, but also majorly impacts their child.

Sometimes the best way to help a teen in this kind of situation is to create resilience, hope, and a plan. Having a healthy relationship with a supportive adult, including a clinician, can help the teen to see what is possible and that they deserve to be treated differently. The relationship also can provide a platform for the client to launch and develop autonomy in new ways, which may mean that therapy includes helping the teen find resources such as job placement, life skills, and other forms of support so that they can work toward autonomy. If the teen shows an interest and skill in working with animals, the clinician may be able to help find resources to volunteer, such as at a local shelter. This opportunity can help the teen develop translatable job skills and increase their sense of a positive identity.

Additionally, the animals can model resilience during tough times. Cody, our quarter horse, was a model of quiet strength and resilience. He came to us when he was grieving after losing his horse partner and was demonstrating signs of depression such as low energy and lack of appetite. His owner no longer wanted to care for him, due to Cody's affect as well as Cody's chronic feet and knee ailments, which required a lot of care and attention. This type of pain could make some horses unsocial and cranky, but Cody was eager to be near people and found them a source of comfort. He was also delighted to be with our animals and quickly bonded with each of them. In sharing Cody's story, we demonstrate that there can be ways out of difficult situations, even if it means a change in location or support systems. Animal stories like this can show teens that relationships can exist during painful times and that some people can see the best in them, even if others cannot, and will support them as they grow.

Ginsburg and Jablow focused on therapeutic goals with teenagers in their book, *Building Resilience in Children and Teens* (2020). They reference the seven key "Cs": competence, confidence, connection, character, contribution, coping, and control. Each of these goals can be addressed and enhanced with the assistance of animals, so we address them here briefly.

COMPETENCE

Finding and developing skills the teen can accomplish with the animals can help build their confidence and sense of mastery. Teenagers can do small activities to build their confidence, such as feeding or getting water for the animals, and then work toward larger goals, such as harnessing and walking an alpaca or training a goat. We work on creating and building on the client's ability to successfully complete activities and focus on those strengths. Particularly when working with novel animals or on difficult tasks, the experience of accomplishing a unique task can help clients realize that they have more capabilities than they imagined.

CONFIDENCE

Confidence comes when the teen has been able to recognize their accomplishments and believe and accept that they have abilities. We want our teenage clients to understand that they may not always know how to handle situations, but also that they have the confidence to navigate and emerge from challenges. To get to this mental space, clients need to have had experiences where they practiced and demonstrated competence, as mentioned above. We give the clients chances to bond with the animals, understand the animals' challenges, and then help solve these issues. Asking teenagers to be creative, empathic, and solve problems also gives them practice in helping themselves and being empathic with their own challenges. Clients also learn confidence as they see their ability to connect with animals, knowing they are worthy of love, which leads to the next goal.

CONNECTION

Research has shown that even one healthy relationship with a supportive adult can make a difference for a child or teen. Larger support systems, such as school, teams, or religious communities add an extra level of support. Everyone needs people to support them, emotionally and physically, and having a place to go and people to talk to, to cry on, and to get advice from is essential. These people do not need to be family members, and our animals can model diverse connections and how sometimes, the strongest connections are outside one's immediate family.

We have many animals who are closely bonded to and receive support from animals of other species, rather than biological family. For instance, our young guinea pig, Rollo, needed parenting when he had to be separated from his biological family members, so he went to our rabbits for support, connection, and love. Even though they were very different in many ways, Rollo got physical comfort and affection from our rabbits and created a family where he felt safe. Additionally, giving clients a chance to bond and create special relationships with our animals allows them to feel a deep sense of connection with the another being, which is often reciprocated with physical touch and affection.

CHARACTER

Character is one of the components of choosing a good therapy animal, because every animal has its own character, or temperament. The traits that make a good therapy animal are also those that make a resilient teenager: flexibility, acceptance, tolerance, and patience. For teenagers, we might also add honesty and integrity. Having these character traits contributes to the teen's ability to function in changing circumstances and moderate the stress that comes with those changes. By engaging with the animals in a variety of ways, the teen can experiment with their own values and practice becoming the person they hope to be. We also can discuss the traits of our animals, including what makes them good therapy animals and how they are able to manage stress and changing circumstances, and use these parallel stories to connect to the teenager.

CONTRIBUTION

Contribution is about helping others, but ultimately it is about helping oneself to feel worthwhile and valuable. A key element of resilience for a teenager is knowing that they have something to offer to others and to the world. Again, our animals' stories can be a good model or metaphor for this, since the majority of our animals have endured struggle and still found a way to contribute to the lives of others. To us, and to most of our clients, they have meaning. Our three-legged cat, Siggie, is the best hugger we have, because his missing front leg makes it easier for him to snuggle up close. Siggie has turned what many would see as a deficit into an asset, one that allows him to deeply connect with and help others. There are countless ways that teens can contribute with the animals; ultimately, what is important is ensuring the client knows their actions are helping others and that they can feel good about that impact.

COPING

"I get knocked down, but I get up again, you are never going to keep me down"— this line from the song by Chumbawamba summarizes the kind of coping that is necessary for resilience. The first part of the line is equally important, because in life, everyone is going to get knocked down at some point. The first step in coping is to accept this truth and then find a way to keep going, possibly even getting stronger as a result.

Most of our animals have had to overcome challenges from abusive or neglectful past homes, illness, and injury. Some of our animals cope with those difficulties daily, and some have even turned those into strengths, as with Siggie mentioned above. Our cat Smoke had chronic kidney disease, for which he needed daily fluids, administered by IV. He had to be held very still and we allowed some teenage clients to help us with this process. These clients were able to watch Smoke try to move away from humans, but quickly settle in once he was being held, coping with his situation. Smoke tried to avoid something he knew was unpleasant, which was completely natural, but he also knew that once it was happening, he might as well settle in and enjoy the love. This second reaction, the settling and acceptance, is coping, and Smoke was a great model and instigator of discussions about coping with discomfort, illness, pain, and difficult situations.

CONTROL

Having a sense of control over one's fate is an essential aspect of resilience; however, the reality is that no one has control over every aspect of their life. Helping a teen to distinguish what they can control and what they cannot is a helpful exercise. For example, while they cannot change their caregivers yelling at them about school, they can change their study habits. We can help them to see that they have some control over their grades, thus positively impacting their choices for the future.

In contrast, many of our animals have very little control over their lives or their destinies. We act as parents for them, since they can make harmful choices, such as eating dangerous food. For example, we cannot leave food out around therapy dog Rupert, because he will eat it, regardless of what it is and how it could impact him. However, our FIV+ cats do not overeat, so we leave food out for them. There are different rules for these animals, because of their past behavior and choices. Our goats used to try to sneak past our fences, so they were not allowed out of their enclosures, but now they do not, so they are allowed to play supervised in the unfenced areas of the property. Teenage clients can begin to see that our animals do have some control over their daily lives as a result of making "better" choices. These clients hopefully absorb the message that they can have more control over certain aspects of their own lives as well.

We also can give clients jobs that they do each week during their sessions, such as brushing an animal or making a special meal. Not only does this allow the client to feel valued and important, but they develop a bond with the animal, see how their choices benefit the animal, and gain a sense of control over the outcome. Helping teenagers learn what choices they can make to demonstrate and gain more control will help them to build their resilience.

DEVELOPING EXECUTIVE FUNCTIONING

Resilience also requires good executive functioning, which includes cognitive skills such as flexible thinking, memory, and self-control. Executive functioning helps with impulse control and decision-making, moderates feelings and behaviors, and helps teenagers develop new coping skills for the challenges they will face in life. Enhancing executive functioning during AACP might mean engaging the animals in creative play, teaching them tricks, and planning fun activities. Clients need to practice flexible thinking as they figure out how to teach a new skill or build a maze, remember what the animals likes or dislikes, and regulate their own actions and feelings during the activity. Throughout the process, they have to be aware of what is happening not only for themselves, but also for the animal, and respond accordingly.

We recently saw a colleague's therapy dog complete a trick where the clinician put the dog in a "down" position and then put a treat on each of the dog's paws. We watched as the dog worked hard to avoid eating the treat and discussed what was going on for the dog as she successfully resisted her impulse to eat the treats. We discussed whether the dog had executive functioning to help her moderate her behavior; if this was a conscious choice that she was making; and why she waited for permission if she knew she would receive treats eventually. We can use this story, practice a similar skill, or even have the teenage client teach the therapy animal this skill to demonstrate, practice, and discuss self-control and decision-making. This is an excellent intervention for teenage clients who need to build their resilience.

THE BIGGEST QUESTION OF ALL: WHO AM I?

Animals may not have the cognitive capacity to develop a theory of mind, or self-concept, or to think critically about their own choices; instead, they operate almost exclusively from a genuine place. An animal's behavior is generally a direct result of its perceptions, reactions, and emotions. That said, an animal's responses and behavior, and perhaps identity, can change over time. Our cat Clementine grew up in a cat hoarder's home and was essentially feral; she was afraid of humans, and she focused on catching prey or fighting other cats for her food. After we adopted her and she experienced several years of safety, respect, love, and consistency, she became a different cat. She accepted affection from humans and showed no impulse to fight. She seemed quite happy to relax in her special spot next to Linda's desk, get fed regular meals, and accept gentle pats throughout the day. Although Clementine could not have described the change in her identity, she essentially became a different cat.

Sharing our animals' histories, transformations, and details of their change process can be powerful talking points for teenage clients who have little hope for change in their own lives. We can show how a combination of external and environmental changes needed to happen before internal changes could happen. We also can demonstrate how negative external forces, such as friends or parents, can keep a teen stuck in a destructive series of choices and prevent autonomy.

Teenagers are at the cusp of becoming adults who have the potential to contribute to the world around them. We feel a deep responsibility to help our teenage clients develop a positive identity, even if and when it feels frustrating or futile. Positive, strength-based therapy, especially with animals, allows teenage clients to be themselves, while also experimenting with different and hopefully positive behaviors, ideas, and feelings. This practice can move them toward adulthood with a solid sense of autonomy, resilience, and a healthy sense of self.

REFERENCES

Ginsburg, K. R., & Jablow, M. M. (2020). *Building resilience in children and teens: Giving kids roots and wing.* American Academy of Pediatrics.

Glasser, W. (1999). *Choice theory: A new psychology of personal freedom.* Harper Collins.

13

TAKING AN INNER CHILD OUT TO PLAY: THERAPY WITH ADULTS AND ANIMALS

"Play is training for the unexpected."

—MARC BEKOFF

Though we see a lot of children and families, about 25% of our clients are adults, who seek therapy with AATPC because they love animals and often have tried other forms of therapy without success. These adults hope that the inclusion of the animals will help them in a way that traditional talk therapy could not. Yet it is not just our animals that make therapy different. Our therapeutic environment is a crucial aspect of treatment, and we strive to create an environment that is more relaxed, casual, and distinct from a medical model of therapy. Our facility has an intentionally homey, rural feel, even though we are just blocks from a large, busy city. This private, secluded, safe space allows adult clients to feel separate from their daily lives and enables them to enter therapy with an open mind.

Providing a unique and novel therapy experience helps clients who have not done well in traditional forms of therapy or who are subconsciously self-sabotaging. Some of these clients know how to do therapy and what to say or have repeatedly told therapists the same story, yet do not make progress. These clients are uniquely suited for AACP, because with the animals and in a different setting, they do not know what to expect, how to act, or what story to tell. If a client has done therapy multiple times, they come to us because they need something different.

From the outset of therapy, the experience at our facility is different. We stress relationships, both with the clinician and the animals, and we try to move the focus away from rehashing weekly problems. We want make sessions experientially focused, which means more "doing" and less "talking." We remind our clinicians that "less is more" and to allow the animals and the full experience of the session to facilitate change for the client.

It is the clinician's responsibility to structure sessions so that they put the client in new situations requiring new responses. Clinicians should have a general idea or plan for the session, based on the treatment plan, phase of therapy, and current presenting issues. It is rare for a session to go exactly how the clinician anticipated, but it is important to have an idea of what animal(s) will be part of the session, how they will be integrated, and how they will be helpful. We often use the Gestalt approach to ask the client to try an "experiment" with the animal, as this helps introduce new and sometimes uncomfortable behaviors to adults, such as being silly or creative.

In a demonstration that we do in our 3-day training intensive, we ask for a participant to act as a client, and they sit in the equine arena with one of our staff acting as clinician. The animals in the arena are free to wander around and interact as they wish. The clinician encourages the client to talk about an issue. While being attentive and listening, the clinician also watches how the animals move, change, and interact as the conversation progresses. Invariably, one or more of the animals behaves in a way that allows the clinician to bring the client's attention to that behavior. They can ask client what they think that behavior means or what the animal might be thinking. We might comment, "Oh, did you see that? Misty turned around really quickly," or "I wonder what it meant when Misty just turned her back to us." The session quickly moves from the content of what the client is saying to what is happening around in the moment. The session transitions to process: relating with the animal and how that interaction stimulates emotions, memories, or desires of the client. Ideally, this discussion will prompt the client to engage with the animal in a way that is different from how they normally would engage with a human in a similar situation. The clinician can help the client find new ways to approach their presenting issue. It is important to note that the clinician does not interpret what the animal's behavior means, they are simply pointing out the behavior. This allows the client to project and interpret the behavior.

In one example of this intervention, the "client" was talking about having problems with a partner and having the same argument repeatedly. As she talked about argument, the clinician observed Duncan, our male goat, pursuing our female goat, Dahlia, in a playfully aggressive manner. As Duncan was standing on his hind legs and dancing toward Dahlia, preparing to headbutt her, Dahlia simply turned her back to him and walked away. Dahlia's face was sweet and serene, and she did not appear the least bit bothered. While Duncan tried several more times to engage Dahlia in his wrestling game, she kept showing she was not interested. He finally gave up and went to stand with his best friend, our large horse, Cody. The clinician asked the client what they had noticed, and the client described how Dahlia did not engage with Duncan, despite his several attempts. Simply turning away and showing disinterest caused Duncan to stop pursuing her. The clinician said, "Hmm, how interesting . . ." and the client laughed and was able to see the parallel with her own situation, as she would engage and reengage with her partner in arguments that got them nowhere. The client saw a real-life example of how to disengage in a neutral and nonverbal way that could deescalate the situation and was able to make this connection to her own life.

In this chapter, we address many of the presenting issues we see with adult clients and provide examples of how we integrate animals into session. We often address issues in a relatively conscious, mutually intentional way, by providing psychoeducation about the process and how we are working toward a treatment goal, which gives adults a helpful context for the new experiences they are having in therapy. While understanding alone does not necessarily lead to change, it is an important step toward change. The concepts and interventions in this chapter can be applicable to children and teenagers as well as adults, but likely need to be adapted to the appropriate age.

RESISTANCE

One of the most challenging aspects of therapy is client resistance or reluctance to change. Many clients know that they need to do things differently but do not change, for various reasons, deliberate or not. Clients resist changing their behavior for a variety of reasons, and it can be easy to blame other people, circumstances, fate, or bad luck. By adulthood, patterns of resistance may be entrenched and unconscious, and until those patterns can be uncovered and resolved, clients will not be able to make lasting changes.

Animals can be an effective means of addressing resistance since the animal will honestly react to the client's truth and behaviors in an honest way. Animals, especially herd animals such as horses and donkeys, are wonderful at picking up incongruence, which is often how resistance manifests. They react to what the client is doing, not what they are saying. For instance, a client may say, "I'm doing great! My week was fine, no fights with my partner!" Meanwhile, their body is tense and their energy is negative, which the animal senses and reacts to, perhaps by walking away. When the animal reacts to this incongruence, the clinician can ask the client to interpret the animal's behavior. This gentle challenge from the animal, sometimes called a *confrontation*, helps the client face their internal and external discrepancy. Clients may be able to realize that their words and their behavior or body language are contradicting each other. Additionally, because the discrepancy is identified through the animals' behavior, the client has less chance to act defensively toward the clinician.

When the client is confronted by the animal's response to their behavior rather than their words, they typically will enter a state of confusion. This happens because the client's normal way of acting and reacting in relationships is not working, and they do not know how else to respond. At this point, the clinician can skillfully help the client explore other parts of themselves and new ways of behaving and engaging with others. The client can practice these behaviors with the animals, who continue to provide genuine feedback to the client. These interactions challenge the client to look deeper at the underlying issue, feeling, or belief that is perpetuating the resistance. The animals will respond differently once the client is genuine and congruent with their words and behaviors, which can be a positive, tangible reward for the client.

ANXIETY

When working with clients experiencing anxiety, it helps to identify whether the anxiety is related to specific situations or is more generalized. Treating clients with social anxiety or anxiety related to a particular experience is usually different than working with clients whose anxiety is more general, pervasive, and unrelated to specific thoughts or situations. Many specific types of anxiety are triggered by thoughts related to a situation they are currently in (self-observation) or anticipate being in soon (worry). Except in cases of generalized anxiety, it is rare to have an anxious feeling without a precipitating negative thought.

Two goals for treating anxiety are (1) reducing symptoms of anxiety and (2) resolving the root issues of the anxiety. The treatment goal will depend on the client's goals and the length of time available for treatment. While animals can help with both types of anxiety, our focus here will be on the first goal, helping the client learn strategies to reduce anxiety symptoms. We teach clients new skills that help prevent or diminish anxiety symptoms and often begin with a focus on the client's thoughts. We may provide an example of an animal's fear or anxiety, such as a dog's fear of snakes. We could share a story such as this:

> Maple is afraid of snakes because she got bitten last year. But, she is still so excited to go hiking, even though that is when she was bitten. She does not associate hikes with snakes. Sometimes she does react strongly or act afraid of sticks and other objects that look like snakes, but that fear is in the moment, in the present. It does not bother her before we go hiking or after the hike is over.

This example is helpful to clients because it demonstrates how humans, with their advanced brains, can anticipate and worry about the future, or perseverate on the past, which contribute to anxiety. Using psychoeducation, we can find distinctions between human and animal brains and recognize that humans are at a disadvantage. Our advanced brains can anticipate and create scenarios that trigger anxious thoughts, even if nothing bad has happened yet.

Animals can teach the client about living without anxiety, and we can help clients move toward a quieter, less activated brain. Often, it is helpful to teach clients how to refocus their attention from their internal thoughts and worries to an external focus. We can teach clients that rather than changing their thoughts, they can move their thoughts to something else, and animals provide a wonderful external focus for clients' attention.

DEPRESSION

Many of our adult clients come to us for depression or a depressed mood. There are many causes of depression, so it is not always treated the same way. Depression may be exogenous (stemming from external causes or situations) or endogenous (resulting from internal or biological causes), but brain chemistry is changed, regardless of the cause. Creating experiences that allow the client to feel differently and experience happiness and hope can make a huge difference for clients with depression. For some clients, an animal can help break through the cloud of depression and reach them in a way that humans cannot. In a quasi-experimental study using AATPC's collected data from former and current clients, McFalls-Steger, Zattarelli, and Patterson (2024) found that adult clients with depression had a 47% drop in depressive symptoms after approximately six months of animal-assisted psychotherapy. A significant predictor of change in depressive symptoms was the client's positive ratings about the importance of animals in treatment and the client's decision to attend animal-assisted psychotherapy. For a more extensive review on integrating AACP into treatment for adults with depression, please also review McFalls-Steger, Patterson, and Thompson (2022).

Many therapy animals have an innate sense of how to approach and be with a particularly sad client, which allows the client to feel emotionally and physically held. This physical contact and affection is a particularly beneficial aspect of AACP, as physical contact with an animal can provide numerous neurological, physiological, visceral, and emotional experiences. Moreover, many clinicians do not feel it is clinically appropriate to physically engage with a client, so the animal can be a powerful source of tactile comfort. Skilled clinicians can help the client to process this experience with the animal and any new or dormant feelings that arise. They can work together to discover and integrate those parts of themselves that they may have felt were nonexistent or gone forever.

There are so many additional ways that therapy animals can help clients struggling with depression. Here are some examples, but as usual, it is not an exhaustive list.

- The initial and ongoing physical contact with the animal can stimulate oxytocin, which stimulates the region of the brain that wants connection with others.
- The animals' antics and silly behaviors can help clients realize that they still have the capacity for joy.
- The animals can help clients find new ways to move and engage their bodies, be physical, and be in nature.
- Working with the animals to do physical activities, such as going for walks or training, allows clients to try new behaviors and thereby see, think, and feel differently about themselves.
- Seeing themselves in new ways can disrupt clients' former negative thought patterns.
- Focusing on strengths and accomplishments with the animals enables clients to find innate gifts or skills, which they can develop outside of therapy.
- Clients can learn new skills, such as mindfulness, with the animals, which can shift them away from negative thinking.
- The clinician can enlist cognitive behavioral therapy (CBT) strategies and incorporate animals into these interventions both in and out of therapy.
- The clinician also can employ other theoretical interventions (e.g., narrative therapy) that incorporate the animals as a means of seeking change.

MINDFULNESS

Mindfulness can be useful for many mental health issues, and we have found countless ways of demonstrating, teaching, and practicing mindfulness with clients. The animals are wonderful mindfulness teachers. First, they are present in the current single moment, so they are effective role models. Second, animals value us in the moment—the relationship that exists in the here-and-now. While an animal may remember who has been nice or mean to them in the past, their present behavior is only focused on the current moment. The animal is not thinking about how the last client was too silly, the client yesterday was so loud, or what they want to do next session. The animals are simply existing in the here-and-now, with the current client, in the current moment.

A mindfulness intervention is predicated on the idea that humans cannot have more than one intentional thought at a time. If a client's attention is focused on finding the softest spot on the dog, they cannot also think about whether their partner will be home on time. By putting their full attention on a singular thought, in one moment, clients can learn about the control they have over their thoughts. We can build on this control and, in later sessions, focus on how a client can redirect their thoughts. Mindfulness activities are essentially retraining client's mind to move away from internal, anxiety-producing thoughts to external, neutral, or pleasant thoughts. With practice and intention, this process can become more automatic.

Here are some examples of ways that animals can be included in this process and help teach and practice mindfulness with clients:

- Find the softest part on the animal.
- Gently stroke the animal's ear.
- Match your breathing with the animal.
- Use all five senses to learn about the animal.
- Count the animal's whiskers.
- Feel the soft parts between the animal's toes. (Linda's favorite one to do with cats.)
- Listen for the animal's heartbeat.
- Find the animal's favorite place to be scratched.
- Count the butterflies or insects on this bush.
- Pet the cat until they purr.
- Lay on the grass and notice the birds flying overhead. Count them.
- Sit next to an anthill and observe their busy movement.

This is certainly not a complete list, and there are countless ways to practice mindfulness with animals and nature. Each animal and setting will have unique ways to contribute to this process, so be creative.

AN EXAMPLE OF
MINDFULNESS WITH AN ANIMAL

Marjorie was a 52-year-old client with chronic depression who believed she would never get better. At the beginning of each session, her clinician asked her to focus on one aspect of an animal and to be fully present in the experience. In one session, Marjorie focused on the dog's breath and noticed its different smells and temperatures, and how the dog's breath felt on her skin. Rather than judging the dog's breath as good or bad, this intervention provided a rich sensory experience. Marjorie even smiled once, when the dog's breath smelled like bacon, as it reminded her of her childhood dog. This experience allowed her brain to move from its state of depression to a state of curiosity, openness, maybe even joy. This showed Marjorie that she had the capacity to experience and feel more than just her depression. This mindfulness activity also gave Marjorie a new skill, moving her negative, depressive thoughts to neutral or positive ones. Each mindfulness exercise helped retrain her brain to be open to and accept new experiences, and she could practice these skills outside of sessions.

Marjorie was an interesting client because initially she was quite resistant to change. She had already seen several clinicians and had been on medication for many years. She had a firm belief—and commitment—that she would always be depressed. When we explored her resistance, she was able to see how her depression helped hide her fear of experiencing life and trying and failing at new situations. Rather than try to confront this fear directly, we focused on the animals and approached Marjorie "sideways," meaning she did not see the change in her experience coming (Chassman Craddock, 2022). Marjorie knew how to respond to talk therapy, but she did not know how to respond to her feelings and experiences when she was with the animals. In a sense, we convinced her body to feel and experience something positive that she normally would avoid.

In addition to therapy animals, a client's own pets can play an important role in treatment. Daily interactions with a pet and their meaningful and intimate relationship can alter a client's brain chemistry (Olmert, 2010). Having a pet also can be motivation for a client to get out of bed, get outside, and function on a basic level. Feeding, watering, and walking a pet may be a good reminder to the client that they need to care for themselves as well. Finally, some suicidal individuals have reported they did not carry out suicide because of their responsibility to a pet (Douglas, 2023; Love, 2021). Pets can be a protective factor for many adults with depression. Incorporating their animals in sessions or even just discussing them on a regular basis can be a powerful way to encourage clients to participate in the world around them.

POST-TRAUMATIC STRESS DISORDER AND TRAUMA

Many adults who come to our facility struggling with post-traumatic stress disorder (PTSD) have already tried treatment, but they are "talked out" and are feeling ready for an alternative strategy. We may include the animals as a way to help the client share their trauma history; for instance, we can describe our animals' own histories of trauma before they came to live with us. Often, this opens the door to disclosing a client's own experiences. If clients have already shared and processed some of their trauma in previous talk therapy, we may focus on working through the trauma as it manifests in their bodies and subconscious beliefs. Our goal is to allow the body to experience change and embrace a sense of safety.

Trauma is a learning experience; the fact that something becomes trauma means that an incident, or series of incidents, is beyond the person's normal means of coping. The person has no way to manage or make sense of the onslaught of emotions, thoughts, and physical sensations that occur. The mind and body do their best to accommodate by changing things physically, mentally, and neurologically to help the person survive. What remains are a series of maladaptive coping mechanisms that complicate the individual's daily life. Clients feel anxiety and fear in response to circumstances that previously felt safe, because the brain cannot distinguish between the trauma triggers and the benign situations that occur in daily life (Perry, 2001). A common example is the grocery store; this is a chaotic place where there exist many strangers, areas they cannot see, loud noises, strange sounds, bright lights, and other triggering elements. A person with PTSD may experience panic and fear that they are at risk of harm in this location. Because PTSD is an anxiety-related diagnosis, we often start with a focus on this maladaptive anxiety. As clinicians, we may gently encourage the client to be in new situations that allow the body and mind to develop healthy coping strategies for triggering situations.

An important element for many clients with PTSD is educating them about trauma responses and normalizing their experiences. We have several therapy animals who came to us having experienced trauma and who displayed trauma responses. For example, Ellen's dog, Sasha, was scared of newspapers and would drop to the ground if she saw one until Ellen helped gently desensitize her. Our cat, Clementine, was our "PTSD cat." When we adopted her, she had been removed from a cat hoarder's home and was essentially feral. Clementine had some unique skills that were very helpful with clients who were struggling with PTSD, because even after several years in a safe home, she still had residual symptoms of PTSD but loved human interaction. We might ask a client to pet Clementine and observe her reaction. Clementine's eyes would widen and her pupils would enlarge, her ears would go back, her fur bristled a bit, and she appeared just a bit uncomfortable. However, she would not move away and over a few minutes, her eyes would soften, her fur would go down, and her ears would relax. We would also ask clients to observe Clementine's safe space, which was on the top of a high cabinet, next to a large window, and within jumping distance of the basement stairs where she could run and hide. When we shared Clementine's background, clients could readily see how her automatic reaction was like their own. Her fear response was triggered by the type of stimuli that she had learned early in life was unsafe—humans reaching to pet her—even though it was no longer a risk.

Observing and understanding Clementine's reaction to humans helped normalize the PTSD response. This was what Clementine's body did when she encountered her trigger, just as client's bodies respond automatically when they encounter their own triggers. As clients got to know Clementine, they could see that despite her automatic physical reactions, she truly wanted physical affection. Once she knew and trusted a person, she would purr and let them rub her belly. But even as she was enjoying the affection, her ears were alert, and she could only be pet while in her safe spot. This demonstration of ambivalence and mixed reactions is similar to a client with PTSD. The client may want and crave relationships with others, but also feel wary about letting down their guard, trusting others, and working on trigger responses. However, as clients observed Clementine and got to know and understand her, they could see an example of how they could overcome their fears and trust others.

Below are some therapeutic goals in AACP for clients with PTSD. This list focuses on goals where animals uniquely and powerfully contribute to treatment.

PROVIDING TRAUMA-INFORMED CARE

The standard of care for PTSD involves trauma-informed care, which includes safety, choice, collaboration, trustworthiness, and empowerment (Stewart & Bruneau, 2016). We demonstrate these values to our clients through the ways we treat our animals and our clients. We ensure that our animals feel safe throughout sessions, even if that means they need to leave. Our animals always have the choice to participate, and we work with them as partners, demonstrating collaboration and trust rather than coercion. Finally, we value our animals' independence and personalities, embracing their uniqueness and ability to choose their own path with us. We trust our clients to engage independently with the animals and often allow them to choose what activities they want to do. We encourage and empower clients to lead sessions, make decisions, and care for the animals.

CHANGING IRRATIONAL BELIEFS

One of the challenges with PTSD is that the brain does not always differentiate the present from the past. If someone perceives a situation to be threatening, the brain automatically goes into threat mode to cope. One of our goals is to confront that response, by helping the client interpret the situation as it is, rather than how they automatically respond. For example, if a door slams, we want to help them respond with surprise rather than with panic and a fight-or-flight response. One way to do this is to watch the animal's response—whether they react strongly to a certain stimulus or if they are able to stay regulated. If the animal reacts strongly, perhaps the client can help calm the animal down, thereby regulating themselves as well. Alternatively, if the animal stays calm, then the client can take cues from the animal and recognize that there is not any true danger.

Some clients may experience hallucinations or other experiences where they feel they are reliving the trauma. Therapy animals and client's pets can be very helpful when a client starts to go down this path. When the client has a hallucination or some type of misperception, we ask them to observe the animal to see if it is responding to the same stimuli. We worked with one client who saw "shadow people" in her room at night and heard whispers. She then got a puppy, and we encouraged her to check in with her puppy at these times—to note if the puppy was alert, got upset, started barking, or stayed asleep. We discussed how a dog might react if there were truly strangers in the house at night and that the dog could be a good reality check for the client. The client could look to her dog for a check about what was real and what was a function of her mind. She could borrow the animal's sense of reality until the hallucinations passed, and she could rely on the animal's strength and calm during this time.

Another example happened with our miniature horse, Stormy, who was being groomed by an adult male who struggled with distinguishing reality from the stories he created. During one session, he began to tell a story about his bus ride to session, and it quickly became evident that much of the story was fabricated and based on his persecutory beliefs. As the client became more agitated and absorbed with his narrative, Stormy moved over and stepped on the client's foot, which was not painful due to Stormy's size. However, it did serve to break the client out of his illusion and bring him back to reality. He laughed and said, "Stormy just woke me up right there!" and acknowledged that he was being led by his trauma. This kind of challenge to a client's automatic beliefs and responses usually needs to be done many times and in various circumstances until it is solidified, but animals can be powerful assistants for this process.

GROUNDING IN REALITY

Many types of animals can help ground clients when their anxiety is starting to rise. It is best to interrupt anxiety as soon as it is recognized, as it is more difficult to reduce anxiety once it has escalated. We discussed grounding in earlier chapters, but it is an important intervention for clients with PTSD, so it is worth addressing again. Grounding can be done by making physical contact with the animal and putting the focus on the animal. This can be done with a live animal or a stuffed animal, if an animal is not present or does not want to be involved. Clients can simply pet the animal as they sit or lay with them, or hold a smaller animal, such as a cat or guinea pig, against the chest and stomach. It can be quite beneficial if the animal makes notable sounds, such as a purr, or shows behavioral cues of enjoying the contact, such as kneading or snuggling into the client.

Grounding exercises can also be nature-based, spending time outside while noticing and focusing on contact with the external world. For instance, a client can lay flat on their back on the ground, making as much contact with the earth as possible. Feeling the solidity, firmness, temperature, and pressure against their body can help a client pull their thoughts back into reality and feel more present in their body. This is an amazing exercise to do on soft grass or snow, assuming the client is dressed appropriately. Having an animal lay next to the client may be a motivating way to do this activity, as dogs often love to roll in the grass or on the snow and are good role models for how to joyfully be in contact.

Practicing grounding with a content cat.

RETRAINING REACTIONS

One of the most difficult skills for counselors is understanding how to challenge clients appropriately. Clinicians must apply just enough pressure so that a client can rise to a new level of behavior and grow, but without pushing so hard that the client feels afraid and retreats. This is even more critical for clients with PTSD because their reaction and retreat can be devastating. However, because much of therapeutic work involves desensitizing clients to stressors, we must introduce stressors into the therapeutic environment, but in a way that feels safe. It is a complicated balance. Animals are a wonderful inclusion to this process, because the animal can provide stress reduction and levity while the client is working through a difficult situation. The animal's experience also can be a connection or model for the client; for instance, when training an animal, you encourage them to learn a new skill, which can be both stressful and fun, but you also have to know when to stop. The learning and teaching process is both rewarding and difficult. Animals will have a limited capacity to learn before they need a break, and working with clients is quite similar.

REDUCING THE FEAR RESPONSE

There can be a fine line between anxiety and fear. Overall, fear is adaptive, because it is a critical emotional state that warns us to be careful. When most people feel fear, it is a signal to prepare the body for a problem. However, humans often approach situations that do not necessitate fear but have beliefs that irrationally encourage the fear. For instance, if a person is afraid of snakes and enters the desert, they may believe that at any moment they will see a snake, so their fear is fueled or escalates. The body goes into a hyperalert state (anxiety) to prepare for the seemingly appropriate reaction: fight-or-flight. For some clients, especially those who have experienced a great deal of trauma or maltreatment, their fight-or-flight response may not work effectively, and they go into freeze mode. As mentioned above, ideally a clinician will recognize how far to push a client so that they do not enter fight, flight, or freeze mode, or dissociate. If a client has frozen or dissociated, continuing to talk or do anything rational is generally ineffective or even counterproductive. The client's fear has turned into anxiety and is no longer adaptive, but the body has reacted as though it is real, and is in fight, flight, or freeze.

Having an animal present is the ideal way to help a client feel grounded and get back into their body. Simply having a dog nudge them, or petting any animal, can help stimulate the brain to become calmer. Some veterans with PTSD have service dogs that are trained to jump on them or nudge their hand when they sense that their person is in this state of freeze or dissociation, perhaps when having a flashback. Rupert can often sense when a client's stress is getting to an unmanageable place and will nudge the person's hand with his nose. He even does this with Linda and staff members at times. This simple behavior is often enough to stimulate more physical contact, which continue to help deescalate and downregulate the client's emotions.

Fear can be a default response for individuals who have experienced child maltreatment. Having an animal present in sessions can be particularly helpful for clients with this type of fear response, especially since these clients may have more trouble in a therapeutic relationship with another human. The animal can help trigger an oxytocin response, decrease stress hormones, and allow the client to feel open to relating to others. The ongoing presence of the animals can continue to help with this fear. The clinician can integrate specific interventions with the client so that when the fear response is being triggered, they can begin an intervention with the animal to help deescalate. Teaching the clients to scale/rate their fear and checking in periodically can help clients identify when they need to break the cycle before the fear gets debilitating.

Trauma-informed care including animals is a huge topic and area of interest, and we have only scratched the surface. The book *Transforming Trauma* (Tedeschi & Jenkins, 2019) covers this topic in depth and is a great resource for further reading.

AN EXAMPLE OF
WORKING WITH A CLIENT WITH TRAUMA

Julie was a 28-year-old survivor of physical abuse by her mother as a child and a rape in her teens. Julie began by working with Rupert, playing with him and snuggling on the couch. She and her clinician practiced anxiety-reduction techniques with Rupert, such as finding the webbing between his toes and feeling the softness of his ears, and then focusing on these elements. They did scaling to identify the degree of anxiety she felt, and when she got to a certain point of discomfort, she would work with Rupert to complete a mindfulness exercise.

Once Julie felt ready, she and her clinician began to take Rupert for walks around the neighborhood. Our facility is in a safe neighborhood, but there are residential areas without sidewalks, and people, cars, and the occasional barking dog are present. This was a moderately anxiety-provoking situation for Julie, but she knew that she could stop the walk and reach out for Rupert to calm down at any time. During the walk, Julie and her clinician continued the anxiety scaling process as things in the environment changed, and they were able to identify the types of situations that exacerbated her stress and those that reduced stress. They came across a house with a large pig and baby goats in the yard, and Julie was able to identify that seeing the cute animals in the yard lowered her anxiety. She noticed that simply looking at animals from a distance reduced her stress and helped her move forward.

This example shows a type of systematic desensitization that includes the animal as a source of stress-relief. Because it is unlikely that a client will always have an animal in stressful situations, it is important to practice these skills without an animal present. Eventually, the client's body and neural pathways will learn to be more relaxed in the same situations that previously triggered their PTSD responses.

DOMESTIC VIOLENCE

Domestic violence is a violent or aggressive behavior within the home, and it is rarely a one-time situation. Domestic violence is often related to early experiences of abuse, both for the perpetrator and the victim, and exposure to early violence increases the likelihood of intimate partner violence (McMahon et al., 2015). With continued harm, the individual comes to believe that they are inherently a victim, making it far more difficult to interrupt the cycle. In this section, we focus on working with clients who have experienced repeated domestic violence.

An often-overlooked aspect of domestic violence is "The Link" (Ascione & Arkow, 1999), which is the connection between animal abuse and domestic violence. Research shows that if and when someone harms a pet, domestic violence often follows. It is common for perpetrators of abuse to injure, kill, or threaten to harm the family pets in order to control the victim. This tactic often works to keep the victim and other family members in a state of fear and to prevent the victim from leaving. Fortunately, domestic violence shelters are increasingly allowing pets so that people can bring their animals as they leave dangerous situations.

Although leaving the abusive environment is the only way to ensure the safety of the victim, an initial therapeutic goal may focus on encouraging the victim to see themselves in a new light and that they are a different person than their abuser(s) have led them to believe. Other goals may include finding resources to overcome obstacles that prevent the victim from becoming safe and then, eventually, helping the client to leave the situation and find a safe alternative. There are many subtleties to working with victims of domestic violence, and it takes patience and acceptance, even when the victim continues to return to a dangerous situation. This section addresses the therapeutic goals that involve animals, including creating a safety plan that includes children and pets; educating about the cycle of violence; nurturing hope; teaching empowerment; and managing stress.

CREATING A SAFETY PLAN

Almost all domestic violence shelters take children, but few take animals, and about half of all domestic violence victims will not leave the home if they must leave pets behind (Campbell, 2021). Knowing this, more shelters are becoming pet-friendly and some will even house large animals, such as horses. Some animal shelters also have programs that will temporarily hold pets in emergency situations.

As part of a client safety plan, the clinician can help research shelter or other safe escape options and make this information easily accessible. If a shelter cannot accommodate the family pet, clinicians can help brainstorm alternative plans, such as friends or rescue organization. It is useful to call each shelter to ensure they can accommodate the client's specific type(s) of animals. Clinicians also can share stories about rescued animals or animals with traumatic pasts that have overcome their history, found happiness, and thrived. These stories can give clients hope, not only for their pets, but for themselves.

EDUCATING ABOUT THE CYCLE OF VIOLENCE

Education about the cycle of violence can help remove some of the stigma and shame surrounding being a victim. Helping the client identify the unique behaviors, emotions, situations, and triggers about their situation is an important factor in creating safety. Following this education, clinicians can work with therapy animals to demonstrate some important concepts about the cycle of violence. For example, our animals may become frustrated about an external situation and then express their unhappiness or frustration onto another animal. Our horse, Hawkeye, may be annoyed that he was not being taken out to pasture with the donkeys, so he walks over and nips another horse, Misty. Hawkeye was not specifically mad at Misty, and she did nothing wrong nor anything to provoke him, but she received the brunt of his frustration. Talking about this displacement of feelings is helpful; the client can learn how displacement occurs by seeing that the animal who received the frustration did nothing to instigate the aggressive behavior. Instead of taking the blame for the violence, clients can see how numerous—often unseen—forces are to blame.

Related to the above example is another, more complex intervention done with our farm animals. A clinician may remove a horse from the arena and bring them to an area where the other animals cannot see them. The remaining animals often get stressed and run around, kick, and make loud vocalizations.

Dahlia would go to her safe spot on a stump, while Duncan would stand on his hind legs or run around the legs of the other animals. Our mini horses will pace or kick at the gate. The scene looks and sounds very hectic and frantic. The clinician and client can observe this pandemonium and process how a seemingly simple act, such as having a herd member taken away, causes such an overwhelming response. The animals do not know how to handle this situation and often act completely out of character, which can be dangerous. This situation can then be connected to the familial situation, when one seemingly innocuous event can trigger an explosive reaction. During this intervention, no one should be in the arena or pasture with the animals, as it is unsafe. This is an activity to observe from a safe distance.

This exercise shows what can happen when the herd or family is destabilized. You can ask the client to consider situations in their life that are or were destabilizing; perhaps the spouse came home late, dinner was burnt, a child wet the bed, or the dog barked too much. You can then discuss the escalated response and how the various family members played a part. There are several important elements to address in this discussion. First, the event does not have to be major, and the accompanying response often does not match the severity of the event. Second, every individual has a reaction during this situation, even the victim, and identifying their responses without blame is helpful to understand the family system. Finally, the chaotic response time is not the right opportunity to address issues or try to fix them. In our example, if we went into the arena to calm the animals, we may get nipped or kicked, because the animals' behaviors are reactive and unpredictable. Instead, we need to give the animals time to adjust to the "new normal" and calm down. Although this activity is slightly stressful for our animals, it also mirrors real-life situations, when we need to remove an animal from the herd, such as for medical examinations or appointments. The goal is to help the herd learn how to be more flexible and accepting of change, and for clients to witness and learn from this process as well.

Although not all clinicians will have a herd of animals to replicate this intervention, it also can be done with cats, dogs, or smaller animals, as they often exhibit similar displacement behaviors. A common example is when a cat is seemingly jealous of another cat and will displace its hurt feelings by becoming aggressive to humans or other cats. This intervention is a helpful way to observe and discuss how the animals and humans relate to each other in both healthy and unhealthy ways.

NURTURING HOPE

As we have discussed earlier, if a victim has grown up with violence or abuse, an ingrained aspect of their sense of self is that of "victim." We want to give these clients new experiences where they see that they have choices and control. We also want to give them practice in exercising their choices and power. Activities that build confidence and a sense of mastery can assist in this goal. In the beginning, it is important to create activities where they can be successful and feel empowered, but as sessions progress, to make the activities slightly more challenging and frustrating so that the client can grow and gain strength and confidence in their abilities. Here are examples of interventions that can help the client to develop a more positive sense of themselves, which can lead to positive change:

- Teach an animal a trick.
- Walk an animal.
- Develop a special relationship with one animal that will "remember" them each session and happily respond when they return.
- Create a special activity or game with a specific animal that is unique to their relationship, which they can play during each session.
- Encourage the client to bring something special that an animal will love. This should be something that the client does not need to purchase.
- Sit quietly with an animal that "loves" them and ask the client to breathe in the animal's care and strength. This is especially powerful when the client can have close physical contact with the animal by hugging gently or holding them, which allows them to physically feel *how* the animal loves them.

It is also important to encourage discussions about the future when the client, their children, and pets are safe and happy. It is more likely that the client will make positive choices and change when they are acting on behalf of their family members and if the picture of a potential life is clear. Watching animals that are safe and free, such as the therapy animals, can remind the client of what is possible and what their family deserves.

TEACHING EMPOWERMENT

Empowerment is the belief in one's own power and finding the internal strength to make healthy choices and behaviors. A victim's belief in their own power has been systematically depleted by years of abuse and being told they are powerless and worthless. These messages become true if and when the client believes they are true. It is the clinician's job to help the client find the power that remains inside them, even if it is deeply buried. An important element of empowerment is teaching and practicing assertiveness, which includes being both verbally and nonverbally assertive but not aggressive. We often discuss the differences between assertiveness, aggression, and passivity, and may model using different tones of voice and physical behaviors. We can demonstrate how the animals respond differently to each of these presentations. Although we are never aggressive toward our animals, we may use a loud voice and stomp our feet as an example of aggression, and watch how the animal reacts. We can process with clients how the animals respond to each way of being and help the client to work on building their assertive self-confidence skills. Training an animal is another great way to practice tone and volume of voice, stance, and body language, and to process what is effective.

Horses are a great animal to include for empowerment work. Because horses want a leader, they will only work for someone they trust and respect. Walking a horse is not always as simple as it sounds. Misty, our female miniature horse, can be feisty and will kick or try to nip your hand if she does not sense you are in control, because she wants to have the power and control. Our full-size horse, Cody, was stubborn and would simply stand still and refuse to walk. In order to succeed with Cody, a client had to convey their sense of confidence and calm control. Cody could detect a client's confidence by the way they pulled on the lead rope, how they spoke, and how they held their body. Clients needed to both feel and convey self-confidence and intention through their mind, body, and voice before Cody would walk with them. This would often take multiple attempts and even sometimes guidance from the clinician. Once clients did find their inner resource of strength, they needed to repeat and reinforce the behavior over the course of many sessions to truly integrate the feeling into their self-worth. Clients need to truly feel and embrace that part of themselves to generalize that confidence and sense of power to their relationships in the world. If you do not work with horses, you can do this activity with a dog, goat, or any mid-size animal that is comfortable with being walked but who may find ways to be stubborn about it.

To be clear, this intervention is not about controlling others. The body language and strength that clients learn while walking a horse is about finding that pillar of strength inside, projecting it outward, and then communicating it to those around them. It is akin to planting your feet solidly on the ground before someone tries to knock you down; once you are in a power stance, you are more prepared to take on an assault. However, to have power means to have responsibility, so some clients may be afraid of having power. For a client who blames others for their victimization, it may be a struggle for them to accept power, take risks, and then blame themselves if things go wrong. If you see a client resisting owning their power or confidence during these interventions, you will likely have to go deeper into why this feels like a threat, which may necessitate psychotherapy rather than counseling.

MANAGING STRESS

There are countless ways that animals can help manage stress, many of which we have already addressed in this this chapter and previous chapters. Animals can help clients experience joy, laughter, contentment, and remind clients that there is more to life than their presenting issues. Animals also encourage clients to get outside, move their bodies, be physically active, exist in nature, and practice self-care. Doing mindfulness work and grounding with clients can be powerful ways to help clients regulate and reconnect to their internal world.

REFERENCES

Ascione, F. R., & Arkow, P. (1999). *Childhood abuse, domestic violence and animal abuse.* Purdue University Press.

Campbell, A. (2021). *Not without my pet: Understanding the relationship between victims of domestic violence and their pets.* Freiling Publishing.

Chassman Craddock, L. (2022). Sideways interventions. In M. Kirby (Ed.), *Nourished: Horses, animals and nature in counselling, psychotherapy and mental health.* Aware Publishing.

Douglas, V. J., Kwan, M. Y., & Gordon, K. H. (2023). Pet attachment and the interpersonal theory of suicide. *Crisis, 44*(1). https://doi.org/10.1027/0227-5910/a000822

Love, H. A. (2021). Best friends come in all breeds: The role of pets in suicidality. *Anthrozoös, 34*(2), 175–186. https://doi.org/10.1080/08927936.2021.1885144

McFalls-Steger, C., Patterson, D., & Thompson, P. (2022). Effectiveness of animal-assisted interventions (AAIS) in treatment of adults with depressive symptoms: A systematic review. *Human Animal Interaction Bulletin, 12*(2), 46–64.

McFalls-Steger, C., Zottarelli, L., & Patterson, D. (2024). Animal-assisted psychotherapy in treatment of adults with depressive symptoms: A retrospective quasi-experimental study (2024). *Human Animal Interactions*, *12*(1). https://doi.org/10.1079/hai.2024.000

McMahon, K., Hoertel, N., Wall, M. M., Okuda, M., Limosin, F., & Blanco, C. (2015). Childhood maltreatment and risk of intimate partner violence: A national study. *Journal of Psychiatric Research*, *69*, 42–49.

Olmert, M. D. (2010). *Made for each other: The biology of the human-animal bond.* Da Capo Press.

Tedeschi, P., & Jenkins, M. (2019). *Transforming trauma: Resilience and healing through our connections with animals.* Purdue University Press.

14

HANGING WITH THE HERD: ANIMALS ASSISTING WITH COUPLES AND FAMILIES

"Animals don't lie. Animals don't criticize. If animals have moody days, they handle them better than humans do."

—BETTY WHITE

ncluding animals in sessions with more than one client is more complicated than individual therapy yet adds some unique and powerful benefits. As with individual sessions, incorporating an animal into couples or family sessions makes therapy both enjoyable and enlightening. The animals bring a level of lightness and humor that can make serious issues feel more manageable. The animals are a welcome relief to the difficult work clients do, but also provide challenges in a nonconfrontational way.

Couples and family sessions allow individuals to show more of their true selves through the relationships that develop. The animals may respond to the unseen dynamics in the system, pointing the clinician toward issues to address. Furthermore, AACP provides an opportunity for the system to practice change. By creating interventions with the animals, clinicians can challenge the clients to try new ways of communicating, listening, and behaving. Beyond merely understanding the problem, the individual members of the system have an opportunity to try on something new, and with the animals' feedback, to see how well it works. Since the animals' feedback is genuine and honest, noticing and replying to that feedback can feel easier for many clients. It may be more comfortable for a client to be "confronted" by an animal about their unhelpful communication or behaviors. It is gentler to hear "this cat doesn't like you yelling" rather than "your child is scared of you when you yell." It is the clinician's job to help members of the system explore new ways of interacting that create stronger relationships. The animals continue to give feedback, and once the client finds healthier ways of communicating, behaving, and being in the relationship, the animals feel safer and will reward the client by interacting with the client and system.

With more people involved in these sessions, there are more safety considerations for both humans and animals. It takes more vigilance on the part of the clinician to be sure that everyone is safe and that the animals are not becoming overly stressed. Many animals are inherently wary of large or noisy groups of people, especially prey animals such as rabbits. It may be difficult to get certain animals to engage in the session if there are too many people involved. In these circumstances, we can process therapeutically with the humans about what it must feel like to have so many people wanting you, waiting for you, hoping you will do something for them. This can be connected to many human issues and the discussion does not rely on the animal being involved. In other situations, when it is safe, we can encourage the animal to come join the session and watch how the animal handles the chaos. We can watch their body language, nonverbal cues, and stress signs, and integrate these behaviors into therapeutic discussions or activities. However, if it becomes clear that the animal is too stressed, we will remove them from session immediately.

It can be dangerous to have multiple people around certain animals; for example, having several young children with the horses can be chaotic. If an equine feels trapped or scared, there are ways that they will try to escape or mitigate the stress, which can cause injury to a human or another animal, such as kicking, biting, or running quickly. We do not allow our dogs to enter the equine area when clinicians are working, as it is too difficult for clinicians to safely monitor all the people and animals present. It can be beneficial to have more than one clinician working with a family or to include more than one animal, as groups can be overwhelming for a single animal.

Many treatment goals and interventions are similar for couples, families, and other combined sessions. In this section, we focus on some general goals of couples and family therapy, such as understanding the systems they are creating; revealing underlying dynamics of systems; sharing power in relationships; and improving communication. These goals are simply starting points; being creative and noticing how your animals connect to your clients will bring the most change.

CLARIFYING THE SYSTEM

A good place to start with couples or family therapy is with a discussion about everyone's role in the family system. It is helpful to understand where each person sees themselves and others, and if there is agreement between family members. To facilitate this conversation, we often explore the ways that animals create families and how these may differ. We may share that some of our animals are with blood relatives and others are with found family, members of the same or different species that have created a pair or a herd. Often, there is a hierarchy in a herd, so we can ask clients to observe the animals and notice clues or behaviors that indicate the hierarchy. We can talk about what clients noticed, how they interpret behavior and connect it to herd position, and how they think the animals feel about their respective positions. We also can share stories about how the animal families have changed over time with different animals being added or removed, and how that has impacted the system's dynamics, behaviors, and hierarchy. For example, we had a happy accident when our rescued guinea pig, Snickers, gave birth to two babies, as she was pregnant when we adopted her. When Rollo, the male guinea pig was sexually mature, he had to be separated from the females, and we moved him into a room with Maggie and K.C., our rabbits. The rabbits quickly took to parenting the three-week-old Rollo, and he happily purred when cuddled up between his new parents. They became an amazing example of a blended family that met each other's needs.

Connected to the familial roles, we can discuss how forming a group, or family, is adaptive and advantageous; not only does working together help meet basic needs and increase survival, but it also fills the need for affection and connection. We can share how each animal has a role in the family system, which may change over time or day to day, and how the animals negotiate these changes. We can talk about the bonds between the different animals and how some animals have special connections to others, how this shows in behavior, and how those relationships impact the other animals and the herd as a whole. Starting this conversation about our animals and their families allows for a gentle transition as we explore the client's family system.

AN EXAMPLE OF
COUPLES WORK WITH ANIMALS

Charlie and Mitch were a queer couple that came to counseling because they were fighting a lot, a common presenting problem in couples and family therapy. Both partners liked the idea of working with the horses, so their counselor brought the couple to the horse pasture for a session. However, the horses refused to engage with the couple, instead walking away as the couple tried to enter the pasture or get near the horses. This behavior caused the couple to complain and blame each other, taking the horses' "rejection" as a sign that the other partner was causing the horses to stay away. The couple began to bicker, tossing insults and unkind words at each other as the horses moved farther away.

Instead of focusing on *what* the couple were saying to each other, their clinician focused on *how* they were engaging with each other. After stepping away from the pasture, the clinician tried to get the couple to reflect on what happened, but they were unable to make any constructive comments. Their clinician commented that perhaps their tense bodies, angry words, and loud voices were influencing the behavior of horses. The horses were reacting as though the couple were a threat, causing them to feel unsafe and move away to protect themselves. Focusing on the horses' safety allowed the couple to identify the lack of safety in their relationship. This reframe from rejection to safety allowed the couple to step back and see how their behavior was pushing the horses away, just as it was pushing the couple apart. The couple struggled with a pattern of conflict: they would have a disagreement and Mitch would walk away, a fear reaction, leaving Charlie filled with fear of abandonment. Charlie would then react by doing whatever it took to get Mitch to come back. Both partners felt unsafe in the relationship, defeated by their emotions, and resented each other.

In a later session, after these safety issues had been identified in the relationship, the clinician asked each partner to individually approach a horse, without any direction in how to do this, apart from the basic safety precautions we give all clients before working with horses. Though Charlie was eager to try and encouraged Mitch to participate, Mitch scoffed at the intervention and said it was "stupid" but that they felt like they had to try it. Eventually, Mitch verbalized their lack of commitment to the activity but their obligation to participate because Charlie asked them. In a tremendous "aha!" moment, Mitch then connected this feeling to guilt and obligation to stay with Charlie. Eventually, the couple agreed to separate, realizing that a relationship based on guilt and the resulting lack of emotional safety was not healthy.

This outcome may seem like a negative scenario to share in a book about successful therapeutic techniques. But the reality is that with couples, sometimes therapy identifies and/or clarifies true thoughts and feelings, which means a couple may end an unhealthy relationship, which is a positive outcome. In the above example, the animals provided a clear mirror for each individual's true feelings and intentions, before they could admit it to themselves or each other. The horses' genuine reactions to their behavior and the clinician's ability to connect those reactions to the couples' relationship allowed the partners to more quickly come to the realization that the relationship did not have a foundation of safety and that the best path was to separate. The focus on the process of their interactions deepened the therapeutic interactions and helped the clients identify unconscious patterns.

If Mitch and Charlie had decided they wanted to continue the relationship and build safety, a possible future intervention would have been to work together to bring two horses to a given area. This usually involves working together to make a plan, deciding how to approach the horses, and then creating the kind of energy and space that would invite the horse to join them. Because horses prefer being in the herd, the couple would need to adapt their demeanor and energy to welcome the horses and help them feel safe. This exercise could have helped them realize they can work together, be gentle and safe with each other, and recall the positive stages of their relationship.

Cats also make wonderful animals to include in couples and family therapy. One simple intervention is for clients to talk about a difficult topic together while keeping the cat calm and with them—either on a lap, between them, or asleep in the vicinity. Often, difficult topics lead to heated discussions or arguments, so it is likely that the cat will get up and move away from the clients or even ask to leave the room. The cat is mirroring the emotional and energetic temperature in the room. Clinicians can then ask clients to reflect, "What happened for the cat?" This question gives clients an opportunity to see how they react and engage when conflict occurs and the impact it has on those around them. The clinician can see signs of control, passivity, competitiveness or cooperation, and generosity, and gently point out how the demeanor of each person may have impacted the cat's response. In future sessions with difficult conversations, the clinician can include the cat with the same goal, and the hope is that eventually, the clients will be able to communicate in a way that allows the cat to feel safe and present in the session.

Cats also can be helpful in sessions as they often have a preference for one person in a couple or family, and this can lead to powerful insights about how the other individuals respond and whether this situation triggers issues that are already present in the system. The clinician might ask a simple question such as, "What is it like to see Sigmund snuggling with Josie?" Or the clinician could ask Josie to pass Sigmund to her partner and observe what happens, reflecting on each individual's reaction. The clients' responses may reveal issues within the system. As with most of our animal interactions, the animal's behavior sheds light on the dynamics between the individuals. The clinician's job is to notice and bring attention to the behavior, not to directly interpret those dynamics. For example, they can ask the client, "What do you think Sigmund is telling you?" There is no right answer, rather, the projection is the real answer. What the individual notices, how they interpret it, and how it impacts the system give the opportunity to identify persistent beliefs or issues that need to be addressed.

Small animals can also be very powerful for couples and family work. We worked with a family, Sam, Anne, and their two-year-old daughter, Bella. Sam had returned home after being incarcerated, and the primary goal of the therapy was to determine if Anne could trust Sam and continue with the relationship. Both Sam and Anne gave the appearance of being tough and stern; however, both clearly loved their daughter and allowed her to choose their animal partner. Each session, Bella chose Rosie, our one-eyed, albino, hairless guinea pig. During every session, Sam asked to hold Rosie and gently cuddled and petted her the entire session. It was apparent by the way Sam treated Rosie that he had a sweet, loving side to him, even though he did not let Anne or Bella see it often and was instead gruff, short, and impatient with them. After several sessions, the clinician was able to ask Sam about this contradiction. With Rosie providing safety and calm, Sam was able to explore his use of anger as a reaction to the fear of being rejected and let down by others, including his family. In the next session, the family cuddled Rosie together and created a special area for her in her enclosure, where she could go "if she was feeling scared or mad or upset." With Rosie as his guide, Sam was then able to experiment with being as tender with Anne and Bella as he was with Rosie.

POWER DIFFERENTIALS

Many animals that live in groups have a hierarchy, so observing these power differences and behaviors of animals is a unique and nonconfrontational way to start a conversation about power dynamics within a couple or family. Each species will demonstrate power dynamics and shifts in power in different ways. For example, the horses have a clear hierarchy that is often demonstrated during feeding time, as they push each other around to access the food. Observing the horses as they jockey for position can lead to discussions about how members of a couple or family understand and experience positions in their own lives. Often, a goal of couples or family therapy is to increase feelings of safety in the relationship, which means addressing the issues of power and control.

When power dynamics are not clear to the members of a system, animal interventions can highlight the system's patterns. Simply trying to approach, harness, or walk a stubborn horse can demonstrate how a human must step up and feel their own power and control of the situation in order for the horse to follow them. However, if a human tries to control the horse by pulling or pushing the horse around, they will be met with strong resistance. They need to realize both their own power, but also the power and strength of the horse and respect it. This situation can be a metaphor for the system, because even though the human is nominally in charge of this intervention, the human also needs to earn the horse's respect, not simply demand it. The client needs to recognize the horse's own power and respectfully request the horse to join them.

Having a couple or family teach a trick to an animal, like a dog or goat, can demonstrate how a system works together. Clinicians can see how the power dynamics play out in real situations and how individuals respond to each other. We can observe communication and confrontation styles and the resulting emotional and behavioral responses. Clinicians can then encourage clients to practice shifting the power and trying different behaviors in order to achieve a goal. For example, simply asking a dog to put its toys in a toy box will not be very successful. The dog needs to learn a set of steps, given by a human, the cue to do that behavior, and usually get a reward once the task is accomplished. Training the animal involves showing the animal what you are asking and reinforcing the subsequent behavior. We can show clients how positive behavior training is more beneficial than using force, intimidation, or fear. Ultimately, the animal is choosing to work with you and to reply to your requests because they want to, and they get something beneficial in return. We can process how interactions with humans are similar and how humans generally respond well to positive methods of change. We can discuss how interacting in a positive way with a partner or child can be effective and enhance the relationship.

Clinicians can even practice with human-training interventions, which can feel awkward at first but generally lead to positive change and laughter. One individual will work to train one person or several people. We often do this work with a clicker, which helps reduce direct verbal instruction that removes the challenge of the activity. Perhaps the "trainer" wants to teach the human to put toys in the toy box. Without telling their partner what they are trying to train, the trainer uses the clicker to mark the behaviors that lead to the correct sequence of behaviors. This becomes silly very quickly as the human tries a bunch of random behaviors until they do an action relevant to the task. For instance, they turn their body toward the toy box and the trainer gives a click and then a treat. Without talking, the trainee continues to try a variety of behaviors until they finally understand what the trainer is asking. Eventually, the human will get the trick and everyone gets to eat the treats, which they have chosen in advance. This intervention can be a silly way to practice training an animal, but it also allows the clients to experience success and have fun. Even if they are not successful and demonstrate frustration or anger, the clinician can help identify feelings, patterns of behaviors, and work through new ways of responding.

An important element of these interventions is not that each human has equal power, but to find ways to make requests without holding power over someone. These activities also demonstrate that working together and using reinforcement can elicit a more positive response than anger or punishment. People are usually more willing to work *with* someone rather than simply doing what someone says, which is good modeling and practice for relationships.

FACILITATING COMMUNICATION

Communication problems are one of the main reasons we see couples and families in therapy. Teaching communication skills is the first step and can be relatively straightforward. We often start with psychoeducation and homework, which helps the clinician see how the members address the issue, which can signal if there are deeper issues to address. When education about communication does not lead to a change in behavior, this is often an indication of a deeper issue, such as attachment or intimacy problems, as in the earlier example with Charlie and Mitch.

According to Dr. Albert Mehrabian (1980), author of *Silent Messages*, 7% of any message is conveyed through words, 38% through certain vocal elements (tone of voice), and 55% through nonverbal elements (facial expressions, gestures, posture, etc.). The actual percentages suggested by this work have since been disputed, but the research demonstrates that often, nonverbal communication holds far more importance than actual words. Couples and family therapy often focuses on *how* clients are speaking to each other, not just what is being said. When clinicians focus less on the *what* (the actual words) and more on the *how*, they have a far greater reach in stimulating sustaining change for clients. Because animals act as mirrors for underlying meanings and emotions, they can help the clinician notice more subtle messages being conveyed, especially those meanings that are unspoken. The clinician can direct attention to the animal's reactions to focus everyone on *how* the conversation is actually going.

An example of this work happened with Joe and his wife, Cynthia, a couple married 20 years with two children, ages 10 and 12. Joe was unhappy because he felt Cynthia was spending too much money on the children and he felt unappreciated for all his hard work. Therapy was done in the rabbit room with the rabbits freely roaming the room as Joe, Cynthia, and the clinician sat on the floor. As they discussed his feelings and Joe's voice got louder, the rabbits retreated to their individual safe spaces. The clinician asked the couple to take note of what happened with the rabbits, who had just been sitting comfortably on the edges of the room.

The clinician asked Joe to share those same feelings, but in a way that allowed the rabbits to feel safe to reenter the space. With a little coaching from the clinician, Joe was able to share that his feelings were hurt and he felt unappreciated by Cynthia's attention to the kids and not toward him. He was able to keep the tone and tenor of his voice calmer and his body less tense, which reflected his underlying sadness rather than simply anger. This new demeanor allowed Cynthia to respond in a less angry, defensive manner. As the conversation continued about how they could find themselves as a couple again, the rabbits gradually reentered the space, demonstrating that the energy now felt safer. As they talked, Joe and Cynthia each pet one of the rabbits gently. Observing the rabbit's behavior was a way to safely externalize the couple's conflict and demonstrate how their communication style impacted each other and those around them, including their children. In addition, by interpreting the animals' behavior, the feedback was easier to internalize and there was less need to become defensive. In helping the animals feel safe in the room, these clients practiced communication that helped the other humans in the room feel safe as well.

This type of exercise can be done with any animal that is somewhat sensitive to the people and interactions around them. Ellen's dog, Sasha, was a wonderful gauge for the mood and energy in the room, but some dogs will tolerate heated exchanges, so choosing the appropriate animal is important.

EXAMPLES OF INTERVENTIONS SPECIFIC TO COUPLES AND FAMILY THERAPY

The interventions described above can be helpful in family therapy sessions as well, but there is more to manage with more humans present. Having more

than one animal involved in family therapy can be a good way to observe familial dynamics, because herd dynamics can be similar to family dynamics, and
are wonderful for recreating the family system. Families can watch how the animals around them react and then practice new behaviors together. That said,
adding animals also adds more creatures to monitor during the session, so it is
important to only have as many participants as you feel you can manage. Below are several examples of interventions that are uniquely powerful for couples and families.

ANIMAL FAMILY SCULPTING

Popularized by Virginia Satir (Duhl et al., 1973; Satir, 1972), family sculpting involves acting out past events or memories. With the addition of animals, members of the family assign a role to each animal, and together they attempt to put
the animals in a position that demonstrates how they view the family's dynamics.
It can be very informative to see which animal is assigned to each family member and how each of them handles that association. Then the act of moving the
animals, or attempting to move them, reveals a tremendous amount about the
family as well: personalities, interaction styles, emotional responses, power dynamics, and more. As you can imagine, this is a challenging exercise, and it usually elicits both laughter and frustration as the family members try to get the animals to cooperate. Clinicians can highlight the animals' behavior and connect it
to the family's dynamics in a profound way.

A good example of family sculpting occurred with Pete and Angela, who attended therapy with their two teenage children, Adam and Fiona, who had witnessed a kidnapping near their school. At the time of the session, Adam and
Fiona were both involved in testifying against the kidnapper. In one session,
Adam volunteered to go first in the family sculpting and chose our pygmy goat,
Duncan, for himself ("because he is rambunctious like me") and our miniature
horse, Misty, for his younger sister ("because she is pretty and small but is really active"). His father was our full-size horse, Cody ("he's the boss"), and our
other pygmy goat, Dahlia, was his mom ("she seems nervous all the time"). He
moved Cody, the father, some distance away from the other animals, and grouped
Dahlia, Duncan, and Misty together. However, Misty decided she wanted to eat
and walked away, with Duncan following her. Dahlia stood alone momentarily,
and then trotted after Misty and Duncan, looking alternatively between the various groups of animals and humans.

Working together to help chickens through an obstacle course.

Simply watching the animals' behavior and the clients' subsequent responses was very powerful. Both Adam and Angela were quite frustrated at the animals' lack of cooperation, while Pete and Fiona giggled. When the clinician asked what Pete and Fiona were giggling about, Pete said, "This is exactly what it's like at home; Angela is always trying to get the family to do stuff together, but Fiona really wants to go be with her friends. It's like Angela is always trying to keep the kids around her so they are safe, but the kids really want to be on their own. And I'm off on my own reading, or at the computer, trying to stay out of it." Angela confirmed that this dynamic was accurate; she shared that being away from her children made her feel afraid and powerless to protect them after they had already been harmed. These revelations prompted a productive discussion about familial dynamics and feelings. As the animals continued to move around the pasture, the family talked about the balance of protectiveness and autonomy, including ways that the children could be safe but also feel independent.

This exercise was conducted again several months later as the family was getting ready to terminate therapy. Each of the family members was able to laugh at the animals straying from their positions and were able to recognize that families are often static for only a moment. Healthy families can adapt and change when they are aware of the others but can come together when needed.

ROLE CLARIFICATION

Structural family therapy (Minuchin & Fishman, 1981) focuses on the roles and alliances of family members. When families come to therapy with unhealthy dyads or subsystems, the clinician may choose to focus on strengthening healthier alliances and relationships. A common example of this situation is when a single caregiver comes to therapy for one child, the identified patient (IP), often due to behavioral problems. A family clinician may evaluate the entire family and choose to bring in the caregiver and all of the children. We worked with Sima, and her three children, 15-year-old son Abe, and daughters Monica, 10 and Sylvia, 5. The children's father had been absent from the home since Sylvia's birth but saw the children sporadically. He did not provide family support, and Sima had shared with the clinician that he was abusing methamphetamines.

Sima had brought Sylvia to therapy as the IP because of hyperactivity, aggressive behavior toward her older sister and brother, and defiance in her kindergarten class. Observing the dynamics of the family, it quickly became apparent that Sima was looking to Abe for support in dealing with her two younger children. She often spoke to him in a confidential tone while being terse and directive with the two younger children. Abe often scolded the children, trying to get them to sit still, pay attention, and listen to Sima. He seemed to have the authority in the family, making him appear proud, and older than his 15 years. Sima seemed to be calmed by Abe's help with the children, but Abe had been thrust into a parental role, aligned with his mother, and the two younger children were aligned together but against Abe.

The clinician asked the family to pick which farm animals they would like to represent themselves. The two young girls picked our small goats, Wednesday and Enid; Sima picked our goat, Dahlia; and Abe picked Kuzco, our shy, nervous alpaca. The clinician then asked them to describe each of the animals and how they got along with the other animals. This gave several clues as to how they saw their own roles in the family. Abe described Kuzco by sharing, "He is the biggest, but he's a loner. He must make sure all the other animals are OK but he's tired a lot of the time and wishes he could just go run off and play." It appeared that Abe was struggling with his role and lacked time with his friends because of his responsibilities to his sisters.

In subsequent sessions, the family created activities with different dyads and triads of animals and chose how to play with the animals. For example, one week Monica had the two small goats, representing the two younger girls, chase Kuzco, representing Abe. When it was Sima's turn to direct session, she created an activity where all four animals walked around the arena together in a close group. Once each of the family members had a turn choosing how the animals would interact, the clinician suggested some alternative activities that were aimed at developing more appropriate and healthy alliances. For example, she encouraged Kuzco to go into a different paddock with his alpaca partner, Kronk, rather than stay in the arena with the goats. During the next session, the family had to move the small goats into a small enclosure to play while Dahlia and Kuzco rested. These interventions focused on empowering mom (Dahlia) while allowing Abe (Kuzco) to enjoy time with his sisters (the goats) but also have a break and be independent.

The same exercise can be done with puppets or stuffed animals, especially when younger children are involved, if you do not have animals that would make good representatives for the family, or the family is not able to interact safely with the animals. Having the animals represent the family members gives the family a way to experiment with different roles and rules without having to directly confront what may be too threatening. As time goes on, it is important to have a conversation about how the family might make real-life changes to allow for different relationships, as they have done with the animals or puppets.

When an animal in the system is acting in ways that do not support the other animals, this can also be a time to discuss "problem behavior." At one point, we had three female guinea pigs living together: our albino, one-eyed hairless pig, Rosie, our black hairless pig, Gloria, and our long-haired pig, Snickers. There were a few instances where Snickers sought out opportunities to attack Rosie before we permanently separated them. We were not sure the reasons behind this aggression and rejection of Rosie, but we shared with clients about our various attempts to understand the behavior and keep Rosie safe, before we moved them apart. We talked about how each pig might feel, as the victim, aggressor, and witness. This stimulated discussions about family dynamics, roles, behaviors, and how sometimes difficult choices need to be made to keep family members safe. We have worked with several adult clients who made conscious decisions to separate from family members for their own safety, essentially leaving their family herd. This led to discussions about how those hard choices can ultimately be healthy in the long run. We also talked about how Rosie found positive ways to interact with Snickers and Gloria, even after she was living separately; their circumstances had changed but they adapted and found a healthier way to have relationships. Rosie also bonded with several humans and received copious amounts of love and affection in this new arrangement.

HANGING WITH THE HERD

This is a very simple intervention where humans hang out with a herd of animals. This is usually a silent intervention, as humans slowly wander around the animals' space, feel the energy of the herd, and interact spontaneously. People can be on their own or be with other humans, but the important element is to just be. We might suggest that the humans be present in a way that would be most helpful to the herd, however they interpret that suggestion. This activity can be helpful to couples, families, and groups. We have also used this activity with our AATPC team when the need for reconnection arises.

ANIMAL PSYCHODRAMA

This exercise requires a group of animals that can safely be together. It may involve bringing new animals into a relatively small space. We often choose to do this intervention with our larger farm animals, but it can also be done with dogs, cats, or small animals that are accustomed to being together. Each family member chooses an animal and then interprets the animals' behaviors and provides a voice for the animal as they watch the interactions. It can be helpful for the clinician to also represent an animal, so that they can subtly guide the exchange if needed.

During one session, we worked with two alpacas, five goats, and five chickens in a medium-size enclosure. The clinician gave a voice to our alpaca, Kuzco, the mom was our goat, Wally, the dad was pygmy goat, Duncan, the 15-year-old daughter was alpaca, Kronk, and the 17-year-old daughter was our chicken, Chickpea. She was a unique chicken who wore a vest, since at times the other chickens pecked at her feathers. During this session, the alpacas were hanging out in the goat house away from the other animals. The goats were in three different areas of the pen, all eating, and Chickpea was standing near Dahlia. The family and their clinician stood outside the enclosure, observing their behavior and speaking as the animals.

> The Clinician/Kuzco started: "Hey Wally (mom). It's making me nervous that the goats are out there and we are in here. I can't see them. What are they doing!?"

> Daughter/Kronk: "I don't want to be out with them. They make me crazy."

> Dad/Duncan: "I heard that! What is wrong with us!?"

> Mom/Wally to Duncan: "Don't yell at them like that. They can spend time away from us if they want to."

> Dad/Duncan: "Why do you always take their side!? You never support me!"

> Daughter/Chickpea, to herself: "I don't know what their problem is, but I'm going to just stay over here and enjoy scratching myself against the feeder."

The point of this exercise is to be silly and maybe even loud. By exaggerating and externalizing the animals' thoughts and words, clients can see more clearly what they are doing and how it is affecting the others. In this brief interaction, you saw the family dynamics play out quickly. The clinician asked each family member to comment on how their animal helped or hurt the family. The next stage of the intervention would be for each member of the family to alter the narrative through the animals so that they each get more of what they need and want, while continuing to emotionally support the family system.

These interventions are just a sample of the many ways animals can be included in sessions with multiple people. Overall, animals provide a tremendous way for humans to witness and learn about relationships, communication styles, emotional responses, and many other dynamics of interacting with others.

REFERENCES

Duhl, F. J., Kantor, D., & Duhl, B. (1973). Learning space, and action in family therapy: A primer of sculpture. *Seminars in Psychiatry, 5*, 167–183.

Mehrabian, A. (1980). *Silent messages: Implicit communication of emotions and attitudes* (2nd ed.). Wadsworth Publishing.

Minuchin, S., & Fishman, H. C. (1981). *Family therapy techniques.* Harvard University Press.

Satir, V. (1972). *Peoplemaking.* Science and Behavior Books.

15

CATCHING THE MOMENT: LETTING ANIMALS LEAD

"You can learn so much from animals. They have this wonderful quality of being in the moment, and they help you spend time there."

—*EMMYLOU HARRIS*

Our intention for this book was to provide thoughtful ideas about how to engage clients and develop interventions for specific clients and mental health issues. This book has ideas and can be a helpful reference guide, but we do not claim that it is the complete picture. There are so many considerations and changing elements in AACP that this book is just the beginning. The true power and richness of AACP is discovered by each individual after you have practiced some of those initial interventions, learned to listen to the animals, and let the animals lead you in sessions. AACP is constantly evolving; every day, our team develops new interventions and creative ways to include animals and nature. In our experience, the most powerful and impactful interventions are those that happen due to spontaneous animal behaviors or interactions and a clinician's creative and therapeutic response. We want this for you as well—to find ways to be creative, flexible, spontaneous, and fun as you continue to practice AACP.

It is often helpful to think about AACP as a system, with a dynamic and ever-changing triad of relationships between client, animal(s), and therapist. Each of these parties has a separate and distinct relationship that is impacted by every other relationship within the triad. For example, the client's relationship with the therapist's dog will be influenced by the close and trusting relationship between the therapist and their dog. In turn, the therapist's relationship with the client will be affected by the client's interactions with the dog. However, if the same client and therapist were at a zoo with animals unknown to either, the way the client relates to an elephant would likely be unaffected by the therapists' relationship with this elephant. How the client views this elephant may not impact the clinician as powerfully.

If you include more than one animal in the AACP system, you have a complex relational milieu operating with almost unlimited possibilities. These different relationships are ripe with opportunity as they change moment to moment and are as unpredictable as the animals themselves. The animals are always acting and reacting to their environment and to the clients. Watching the animals' behavior can give you a unique insight into what may be happening with the client, well before you might see it yourself. For this reason, one of the most complex skills for an AACP therapist to develop is the ability to constantly scan the environment and the participants, ensuring safety, but also finding potential therapeutic moments where the animal is responding to the client. Another complex and equally important skill is to know how to manage those moments and handle them delicately and therapeutically.

YOUR ANIMAL'S UNIQUE SKILLS

Each therapy animal is unique but still genuine and honest in their reactions to humans. This may mean one animal goes toward a client who is upset, whereas another animal retreats. Knowing which animal to choose, with which client, on what day, is a complicated dance that gets easier over time, but is not a flawless process and may not have one right answer. Sometimes we have decided to work with a certain animal and client, planning a specific intervention, and the animal does not want to work that day, or the client refuses to engage. As AACP clinicians, it is our responsibility to adapt, find a new way to work with the client, and if possible, work with another animal or find a way to connect with nature. Though sometimes frustrating, these situations can also be therapeutically informative and powerful. We can use the information from the animal and the client to inform us about what is going on in the moment for each of these creatures and how it can impact therapy. For instance, if our dog goes to the door every time a certain client comes in, we need to pay attention to that information and understand what the dog might be noticing and picking up from that client. Or, if our client refuses to engage when we work with the horses, we need to explore where that resistance arises and how we might uncover and work through it. This process may happen internally for the clinician, or we can include the client in the discussion and wonder aloud what is happening. We can have honest, open discussions about what might be going on for the animal, or what we are noticing for the client, and use those discussions to move the therapeutic process forward.

The best way to illustrate how to "find the moment" with your client and animals is to provide some examples.

MAE

Mae was a 27-year-old divorced woman who periodically returned to therapy when she needed help with a particular situation. One of the largest ongoing issues for Mae was the lack of support in her life after her divorce and the high level of expectations she put on the few people who did support her. In one session, Mae was talking about her best friend "breaking up" with her because Mae was upset after her friend canceled a weekend away due to work obligations. Mae's friend was in the process of completing graduate school, working full time, and planning a wedding. Mae's friend had shared that Mae needed too much from her and she did not want to deal with her negativity.

During this discussion, our three-legged cat, Sigmund, was in the room. While Mae was talking, Sigmund crawled onto her and started to snuggle into her arms. He shifted several times in what seemed like a purposeful action aimed at creating a better "fit" between them. The clinician observed this and asked Mae what it felt like to have Sigmund snuggle and move into her body and space. The clinician had actually never seen Sigmund lay in that particular way on anyone, but both seemed comfortable and satisfied. The clinician shared how Sigmund seemed to intuitively learn how to move his body to match Mae's body; he was adjusting and shifting so that he could fit with someone else in a way that met both of their needs. They talked about this movement as an example of a reciprocal relationship, as both Mae and Sigmund were getting their needs met. Mae was unconsciously receiving comfort while also giving comfort and affection.

Sigmund then heard sounds outside the office window and jumped up to see what was happening, leaving Mae alone in the process. The clinician asked Mae how it felt to have him move away so quickly and she said it was, "Fine, I knew he was just curious." The therapist clarified that Mae was not disappointed. Within just another minute or so, Sigmund returned and cuddled Mae again. It seemed that because Mae could allow Sigmund the space to go away, he also felt free to return. The clinician asked Mae to process her relationship with Sigmund, the significance of it, and what he could teach her about her other relationships. The clinician noted that perhaps this interaction was a metaphor for Mae's relationships with other people. In this case, the clinician shared this insight with Mae, but that is not always essential, and allowing the client to reach their own interpretation is also quite powerful.

This was a very unique interaction. Because the clinician knew this client's primary issue at this point of therapy, she was able to help her learn how to develop and maintain close relationships without burning them out. The clinician was able to watch Sigmund for ways he might be able to contribute to that goal, and he did not disappoint. Animals truly seem to find ways to teach us what we need to learn, at the time we need to learn it. It is the clinician's job to help the client see those behaviors, interpret them, and learn from them.

SARAH

Sarah was an eight-year-old girl who came to therapy due to significant changes in her home life; in the past several months, her parents had divorced and her grandfather had died. Sarah had started to demonstrate signs of anxiety and depression, including school refusal, arguments with peers, tantrums at home, and sleep disturbances. However, she refused to talk with her parents about any of her thoughts or worries. During the first few sessions, Sarah requested to work with the rats and bonded closely with both of our female rats, spending time cleaning and rearranging their enclosure, holding them, and talking softly to them. After a two-week absence from therapy due to winter holiday, Sarah returned to session to find that one of the rats had died, due to an age-related health condition, similar to her grandfather's death.

Sarah was quite upset, but she was able to observe that our remaining rat, Ruby, was acting differently. Ruby did not come out to greet Sarah as she had done in the past and was curled in a ball in the corner of her enclosure. Sarah was initially annoyed and kept asking why Ruby would not say hi to her, commenting, "But she likes me. She always says hi. What is wrong with her?" The clinician said simply, "Hmm. Well, what changed for her?" Sarah was quiet a moment and then said "Oh. Yeah. I guess something big." Rather than interpreting Ruby's behavior for Sarah and explaining that Ruby might be sad, upset, or uncertain about her partner's absence, the clinician let Ruby's behavior speak for itself and allowed Sarah to recognize the reason behind it.

Sarah then asked what happened after the other rat died and the clinician explained how we had done a small service for her, planted a flower, and painted a special brick to help us remember her. They talked about special moments with the rat and Sarah was surprised that the clinician was open to discussing this, even if it was sad. Sarah noted that at her house, they never talked about her grandpa, even though it was really hard with him gone, and that she would feel a lot better if they could talk about missing him and how much they loved him. This led to a powerful discussion about not only Sarah's grandfather and what she missed and loved about him, but also how she could remember him in a tangible way. They worked to create a small token of remembrance of her grandfather that Sarah kept by her bed. In later sessions, they discussed how Sarah missed each parent when she was at the other's house, and how it felt like she could not talk about that. They created a plan to share these feelings with her parents, practicing together while Sarah held Ruby to stay calm. By allowing Ruby to behave as she needed and challenging Sarah to understand that behavior, the clinician was able to understand what was triggering Sarah's behaviors and help her heal.

MARK

Mark came to therapy for issues relating to his marriage and unhappiness with his career as a teacher. Several months of treatment had passed and Mark was talking about the same thing week after week. He seemed stuck with rehashing the weekly fights with his wife and conflicts with a challenging student. The clinician was becoming frustrated with his lack of progress and inability to go deeper into emotions. One session, they were walking outside when our male goat, Duncan, mounted our female goat, Dahlia. This is a normal animal behavior, though it can certainly make both clinicians and clients feel awkward in the moment. As the clinician was debating how to handle the situation, Mark laughed and said, "I know what we really need to talk about." Mark then disclosed that he struggled with sexual relationships as a result of flashbacks from childhood sexual abuse. He noted this was the first time he had shared this with anyone, personally or in therapy. The clinician was surprised and grateful that the goats' natural behavior had provided an avenue for Mark to reveal a significant issue that had been impacting his life. Perhaps the unabashed nature of the goats' behavior and the slight discomfort it provoked in Mark gave him the push to go one step further in his discomfort and share about his abuse. Or perhaps it triggered a deep awareness of his trauma and where he needed to go emotionally in order to heal. Or perhaps it was something else entirely; we do not always know. It does not necessarily matter how the animals' behavior inspires or motivates a client to share or act; what matters is that the clients respond to this genuine, natural behavior in a way that is therapeutic.

After this session and disclosure, Mark was able to discuss and process his abuse more freely and acknowledge the role it had played throughout his adult life. He was then able to integrate this experience into his self-concept and start making decisions in his life that changed how he functioned and related to those around him.

JOSH

Josh started therapy to address his highly volatile girlfriend, complicated family situation, and struggles with sobriety. He previously had a prescription drug problem, but was currently sober. He relied on his family for support, despite a tremendous amount of conflict with several family members. The clinician suggested that they have a session in the arena with the horses and asked Josh to determine which animals were most like the people in his life. He pointed to our feisty mini horse, Misty, as his girlfriend; our quarter horse, Cody, as his mother; and our mini horse, Stormy, as his father. The clinician asked Josh to go to the person/animal he most needed to be with at that moment. Josh walked over to Cody, but Cody walked away from Josh and into his paddock, where he stood on the other side of the fence and turned his back to Josh. When asked what he wanted to do, Josh said he wanted to go in after Cody and receive physical affection from Cody. The clinician indicated that he could try this, but when Josh entered the paddock, Cody again moved away and turned his back. The clinician noted, "Wow, what do you think is going on?" to which Josh stated, "This is just what my mom does. When I need her, she always has something else better to do and I feel left out in the cold." This was a powerful insight from Josh, who had previously refused to discuss his mother in sessions. The clinician asked Josh what he might do differently with Cody, and Josh decided to go back to the other side of the fence and give Cody space. He stood there quietly and practiced deep breathing as the therapist observed. After several minutes, Cody came out of his paddock, walked over to Josh, and nudged him with his soft nose.

Josh spent the remainder of the session petting Cody and processing the experience. He shared that he has chased people in his life, including his mother and girlfriend, causing them to retreat, physically or emotionally. His experience with Cody demonstrated the relational interactions that Josh kept repeating in his most significant relationships, which kept him feeling lost and alone. This interaction with Cody allowed Josh to see and feel how a new behavior on his part could lead to a better result.

FINAL THOUGHTS

The skills described in this section are advanced AACP interventions and are just a fraction of the interactions that clinicians see every day when they let the animals lead sessions. Many beginning clinicians will start with the style of interventions described in earlier parts of the book, but over time will feel more comfortable reading the system and integrating the spontaneous reactions into sessions. Our suggestion to newer clinicians of AACP is to continue to observe the interactions and reactions of the animals as sessions progress. The more you learn about and are open to this way of viewing interactions, the more you will see new and amazing opportunities to help your clients. The animals give tremendous feedback, and your job is to watch, listen, and then help the client understand the animals' communication. The clinician may want or need to change the course of the session if they see something happening with the animal that will be of value. It is vital to take advantage of the moment so that you can catch the animal's natural behavior in relation to the content or process taking place.

Integrating spontaneous reactions is a skill that requires that the clinician attend to multiple dynamics simultaneously: (1) the client's immediate situation; (2) the client's need at that specific moment; (3) the short-term goal for that session; (4) the client's long-term or overarching therapeutic goal; (5) the meaning of the animals' behavior; and (6) the animals' behavior in terms of what the client needs at that specific moment. In order to maintain the therapeutic relationship, the clinician must be aware of each of these elements, ensure safety, attend to the client, and hold the therapeutic space. A similar encounter could arise in two different sessions, and the clinician will need to modify their response and management according to the various elements. This work requires a great deal of comfort with the counseling process, the animals, and the client, with an awareness of how a client will respond to this type of spontaneous intervention. Throughout the process, the clinician also needs to notice subtle cues from the animal and envision the entire intervention and possible responses.

Often, when clients have worked with the animals for some time, they begin to independently recognize what the animals are telling them. We have heard several adolescents trying to walk a stubborn horse and comment, "Boy, I bet that's how my parents feel when they try to get me to do something!" They finally "got it," and all they need from us is a smile and understanding. There are countless ways that the animals engage with us, and us with them, so there are endless opportunities to work with clients in AACP. With this mindset, the list of interventions is truly endless.

You may have noticed that nearly all the interventions in this book involve the animals leading the session away from content and toward process. The animals are all about the process, the relationship, and the moment. This focus on the process is what can produce lasting change for clients. We hope that you discover the joy and countless possibilities when working with your own animals and clients, and that this experience enriches each of your lives.

PART 4

INTERVENTIONS BY TREATMENT GOAL

ABUSE	OVERARCHING GOAL: Client will process abuse and trauma and find ways to live free from its impacts.					
Working through childhood abuse is a long, involved process. The following interventions are geared primarily toward helping clients with the long-term impacts of abuse.						
Goals	Objectives	Intervention	Description	Animal(s)	Client(s)	Notes
Acknowledge Feelings Related to Abuse	Identify feelings	Animal stories	Clinician will share the animal's story, emphasizing elements that are connected or related to the client's story.	Any who has experienced abuse or trauma	All	In this intervention, you are sharing those aspects of your animal's life or history that may resonate powerfully with a client's life. This is also a good time to share an animal's picture album. You can ask the client to imagine how the animal felt then or how the animals feels now, and how they may have overcome their trauma. Clients of any age can be encouraged to talk to the animal, empathize, and let the animal know they support them.
	Grieve the loss of their previous self	Draw the change	Clinician asks the client to create several pictures of a therapy animal that has experienced abuse. The pictures may include how the client sees the animal now; the animal before the abuse; during the time of the abuse; and/or how the animal will look when they have resolved their past and feel healthy and strong.	Any who has experienced abuse or trauma	All	Clients can draw these images or create collages, using pictures cut from magazines. The themes you choose will depend on where both the client and animal are in resolving their abuse.
	Reduce aggression toward others	Name the animal's feeling	When an animal naturally shows frustration or aggression toward another animal, ask the client to imagine what the aggressor is feeling and to name the feeling for the animal. If safe and appropriate, the client can help calm the animal by giving the animal support and empathy.	Any animal who naturally gets frustrated or angry with other animals	All	This activity may be done from a distance if an animal is acting out, because ensuring client safety is very important. We will not let a client try to calm a very upset or dysregulated animal. This intervention can also be done watching animal videos, if a live animal is not available, and clients can discuss what those animals are thinking or feeling, and how they would try to calm them down if they could.
	Experience less shame	Talk about the imperfect animal	The clinician and client identify behaviors and attributes of an animal that are less than ideal, such as a cat who steals food, an odd looking guinea pig, or a dog who eats other animals' poop.	Any animal who has a behavior that is unappealing or an animal who looks "imperfect"	All	The client sees the clinician providing love and acceptance toward the animal, despite their behavior or flaws. The client can recognize the positives beyond these imperfections and cultivate compassion for the animal and in the process, compassion for themselves and begin to challenge their feelings of shame.

ABUSE	OVERARCHING GOAL: Client will process abuse and trauma and find ways to live free from its impacts.				
Working through childhood abuse is a long, involved process. The following interventions are geared primarily toward helping clients with the long-term impacts of abuse.					
Goals	Objectives	Intervention	Description	Animal(s)	Client(s)	Notes
Resolve Thoughts Related to Abuse	Feel a sense of empowerment	Walk a stubborn animal	Talk about the "victim stance" and then practice "acting as if" they are secure and confident. Explain how animals look for strength and clarity in a leader.	Any animal who may be more challenging to get to walk, such as equines or goats	All	Walking a large and/or stubborn animal, such as a horse, donkey, or goat can be very empowering, especially if that animal needs a confident person to lead them. Ideally, the animal will initially demonstrate some resistance, but listen to the client once the client is able to demonstrate their strength and intention.
	Put the responsibility for abuse on the perpetrator	Animal "Empty Chair"	In this intervention, the client is asked to provide a voice for the animal. The client speaks as though they were the animal and as if the animal's abuser were in the empty chair. Encourage them to emote and support the client as necessary to help them share as many thoughts, feelings, and consequences as possible. Afterward, it will be important to help the client to re-balance emotionally.	Any animal that has experienced abuse	All	This is not the traditional Empty Chair technique. The client is not speaking to the animal as if the animal were the abuser, as this may damage their bond with the animal. Instead they are speaking as the animal, which may allow them to have confidence and strength that they lack for themselves.
Rebuild Positive Sense of Self	Develop an increased self esteem	See section on Self Concept		All	All	
	Develop self-worth and self-concept	See section on Self Concept		All	All	

ABUSE OVERARCHING GOAL: Client will process abuse and trauma and find ways to live free from its impacts.

Working through childhood abuse is a long, involved process. The following interventions are geared primarily toward helping clients with the long-term impacts of abuse.

Goals	Objectives	Intervention	Description	Animal(s)	Client(s)	Notes
	Understand the concept of consent and practice giving and hearing consent	Gaining consent from animals	Ask the client to invite an animal to participate in an activity such as walking, grooming, or playing, and to observe how the animal displays consent—how the animal agrees to participate. If the animal refuses to engage, observe how that animal communicates their lack of consent.	All	All	We allow our animals to choose if and how they participate in sessions, which demonstrates to clients not only that our animals have a choice, but that we respect and embrace that choice.
	Develop the ability to state clearly when they do not consent	Saying "Yes" and "No"	Create an intervention where client must say "yes" and "no" to animal. For example: saying "yes" when the dog can jump up on couch and "no" when it cannot have food.	All	All	This intervention is about allowing the client to practice and hear their own voice saying "yes" and "no." Encourage the client to try different ways of saying the words that emphasize tones of voice, volume, levels of importance, and other verbal and nonverbal changes. The focus is not at all to be unkind or punish an animal, but to be able to set firm, clear, and reasonable boundaries.
Reducing Shame	Accept their flaws and understand they did not cause the abuse	Strange animal behavior	Observe animals that engage in strange, or funny behaviors and talk about if the animal feels or thinks about the behavior or how it looks.	All	All	Many animals engage in strange and even unappealing behaviors, such as eating poop, rolling in smells, and scratching/licking various body parts. Normalizing these behaviors can demonstrate to clients that we all have unusual quirks, but that those behaviors do not mean we are unworthy of love or safety. This can hopefully help reduce feelings of shame about themselves and their past abuse.
Regulate Emotions	React less intensely or reduce reactions to difficult situations and other triggers	Act, don't react	Engage with animals that are slower to warm up or are more conditional in their affection, such as cats or alpacas. Explore the client's feelings, thoughts and reactions that this behavior triggers and help the client explore reasons for the animals' behavior. See section on Behavior Regulation for more on this skill.	All, but particularly animals that are shy with new people, such as cats or alpacas	All	A common trait in clients who have experienced abuse is a quick reaction to triggers. These behaviors can create challenges in the client's life, so helping the client learn how to "act" instead of react in situations is a crucial part of their treatment. Animals that seem disinterested in engaging can help clients practice new ways of thinking and acting to certain triggers. They can understand that their initial feelings and reactions may be unproductive and find new ways to respond.

ADHD	OVERARCHING GOAL: Client will gain the ability to regulate their body and attend to tasks in a focused and calm manner.					

This goal is about "rehearsal" of new behaviors that can be developed and then practiced with the assistance of the animals. The client can get positive reinforcement from the animals for their pro-social and regulated behaviors. There is a great deal of overlap in this section with Behavior Regulation, so please review those interventions as well.

Goals	Objectives	Intervention	Description	Animal(s)	Client(s)	Notes
	Increase the time on a specific behavior or task	Animal Mirror	Client will mirror the behavior and speed of a slow or calm animal.	All	All	This intervention is especially good with calm animals, horses, and/or animals that stand still for long periods of time.
Increasing Attention	Increase the duration of attention span	Timed Activities	Decide a time limit for an activity with the animal and use a visual timer. This time can increase slightly each session.	All	Child or teenager	A manual timer is useful for this activity so the client can see the time elapsing. Fun animal timers are helpful for this intervention. If a client is avoiding therapeutic work by playing with the animal, you can also set limits for "work" and "play" and mark the time until they get to play with the animal.
Reducing Distractibility	Experience less distraction and develop the ability to focus on an activity	Staring contest	Client and animal stare at each other and see who breaks eye contact first.	Cat, dog, horse, or other animal that can make extended eye contact	Child	Some animals could be stressed by prolonged eye contact so should not do this activity; make sure you know how each of your animals responds to eye contact.
		The quiet game	Client attempts to be quiet longer than an animal.	A vocal animal	Child or teenager	This activity could leave clients feeling frustrated if working with a very quiet animal, so it is best when done with an animal that is "chatty" or makes frequent vocalizations.
Reducing Hyperactivity	Increase impulse-control	Animal Training	Client trains an animal to control or delay a behavior that normally would be impulsive, such as eating a treat.	Dog or any trainable animal	All	Clients can teach an animal to "leave it" or "wait" with a verbal and/or hand cue. This demonstrates how it both normal and difficult to resist impulses but that it can be done!
		Being Calm	Client will practice being calm with an animal.	Rabbit or other calm animal	All	This can be done with large or small animals who may retreat with loud, excitable clients but who respond well to quiet, calm behaviors. Engaging with the animals can be a powerful reward for clients who are able to calm their bodies.
		Slow-Walking	Client walks next to and matches the pace or a relatively slow animal.	Calm or slow animal	All	This is best done with a calm, slow animal, but can also be done with a more active animal and then compare how it felt to move with each animal.

ADHD	OVERARCHING GOAL: Client will gain the ability to regulate their body and attend to tasks in a focused and calm manner.					
	This goal is about "rehearsal" of new behaviors that can be developed and then practiced with the assistance of the animals. The client can get positive reinforcement from the animals for their pro-social and regulated behaviors. There is a great deal of overlap in this section with Behavior Regulation, so please review those interventions as well.					
Goals	Objectives	Intervention	Description	Animal(s)	Client(s)	Notes
	Increase ability to focus and follow directives	Staying with the Clinician	Client will demonstrate the ability to follow directions before interacting with animals.	All	All	This is an especially important intervention and one that we may do early in treatment. Knowing that the client can and will follow your directions is necessary in AACP to ensure animal and client safety. While we do not generally view animal interactions as a "reward," clients do need to demonstrate safety to "earn" the ability to be close or touch the animals. Animal interactions can also serve as a motivator for certain clients to control impulsive or risky behaviors.
Following Directions		"Simon says" with an animal	Clinician will ask the client and a trained animal to do behaviors they both can do, including "stay."	Dogs or any animals that can "stay" and know a few commands	Children or teens and adults who can be silly	This is a new variation on a traditional game, with a fun twist that allows the client and animal to practice paying attention to cues and responding appropriately. The client can also feel successful when they follow the "Simon says" directions and the animal does not!
		Red, Yellow and Green Light	Clinician gives instructions about walking slowly (yellow), quickly (green) and stop (red). Animal will follow the lead of the client. Roles can then be reversed and the client can give the instructions to clinician and animal.	Dog or other animal that will follow client's lead	Children or teens and adults who can be silly	You can add in other instructions/colors as well, such as dance (purple), sit down (blue), spin in circles (green), or many other variations. The goal is to help the child focus and remember instructions, while also having fun and being silly with the animal and clinician.
Executive Function-ing	Improve executive functioning	See section on Executive Functioning				

ANGER MANAGEMENT   OVERARCHING GOAL: Client will identify and express feelings of anger in a healthy manner.

Clients struggling with anger often need help identifying and then processing the emotion underlying the anger. This process may involve expressing new feelings and behaviors that can be practiced with the assistance of the animals. The client may also get positive reinforcement from the animals for expressing these feelings and prosocial behaviors.

Goals	Objectives	Intervention	Description	Animal(s)	Client(s)	Notes
Identify Underlying Feelings such as Fear, Hurt, Sadness, Anxiety	Understand the relationship between angry thoughts, feelings and behaviors	Observation	Observe how animals interact when angry, frustrated, or unhappy.	All	All	Since many animals' big responses are based in fear, this is a good way to teach how humans often react from fear as well. However, rather than acting genuinely, humans often hide our fearful responses behind angry behaviors.
	Identify steps leading to angry reaction	Observation	Observe animals in conflict and break down the sequence of events that led to the conflict. This is a foundation for some of the interventions to follow.	All	All	This intervention should be discussed with the client afterward in terms of how they see this pattern in themselves. If they can identify clear steps that lead to conflicts, they can use this in later interventions to interrupt behavior before it becomes volatile.
	Learn to identify and articulate feelings that trigger an angry reaction	Observation	Observe animals in conflict and give words to the feeling or thought the animal would have had that triggered their reaction.	All	All	Clients can do this intervention with live animals or watching videos. If done with live animals, ensure safety of humans and animals and stop the intervention/ interactions if safety is at all at risk. Allow the client to lead the interpretation process. It is the clinician's choice if they want to connect these conflicts to the client's issues or leave it in metaphor. If done with live animals, ensure safety of humans and animals and stop the intervention/interactions if safety is at all at risk.
	Learn to identify, challenge and replace faulty thoughts leading to angry reaction	Observation	Observe animals in conflict and discuss how this conflict could impact the animals' relationship. Ask client to help the animal challenge those thoughts or beliefs and find more functional thoughts or behaviors.	All	All	

ANGER MANAGEMENT

OVERARCHING GOAL: Client will identify and express feelings of anger in a healthy manner.

Clients struggling with anger often need help identifying and then processing the emotion underlying the anger. This process may involve expressing new feelings and behaviors that can be practiced with the assistance of the animals. The client may also get positive reinforcement from the animals for expressing these feelings and prosocial behaviors.

Goals	Objectives	Intervention	Description	Animal(s)	Client(s)	Notes
Communicate Feelings Instead of Acting Them Out	Verbalize emotions to communicate effectively	Speak for animal	Client will use words to voice what animal could "say" to the other about what they think or feel.	All	All	As above, clients can do this intervention with live animals or watching videos. The client should lead the process and it is the clinician's choice if they want to connect these conflicts to the client's issues or leave it in metaphor.
		Speak to animal	If situation occurs where client is angered by an animal's behavior, encourage healthy expression in words to the animal rather than acting out behaviorally.	All	All	If the client is frustrated or angry, ensure safety of all parties before processing. This may mean leaving an animal's space or putting an animal away before the client practices healthy verbal expression.
Manage Angry Feelings	Develop skills to interrupt an angry outburst and practice calming skills	Calm an animal	Client can use calming techniques specific to each animal. Client will interact with the animal in a way that helps the animal (and in turn the client) feel calmer. For example, deep pressure petting helps many animals feel calm, while other animals may benefit from distraction.	All	All	Make sure the animal is safe to be around before doing this intervention. A client should not be with a very upset or dysregulated animal. If it is safe, you can let the client use trial and error to find what works for the animal(s). Ask the client if they notice any difference in their own bodies as they calm the animal. Is this a way they would like to be calmed down or do they prefer something else?
	Verbalize alternatives to harmful behavior	"Talk" it out	Client will guide two animals in a "discussion" about what happened and how they can move forward as friends.	All	All	This can be done in the moment or after a client observes animals in conflict. Clinician can choose if they relate this issue to the client.

ANGER MANAGEMENT		OVERARCHING GOAL: Client will identify and express feelings of anger in a healthy manner.			
Clients struggling with anger often need help identifying and then processing the emotion underlying the anger. This process may involve expressing new feelings and behaviors that can be practiced with the assistance of the animals. The client may also get positive reinforcement from the animals for expressing these feelings and prosocial behaviors.					
Goals	Objectives	Intervention	Description	Animal(s)	Client(s)	Notes

Goals	Objectives	Intervention	Description	Animal(s)	Client(s)	Notes
Increase Healthy Communication	Practice new behaviors	Puppet Show	Work with animal puppets to create a story of the animals and practice new skills to resolve conflicts.	All	Child	This is a good option if you do not have access to live animals or if a client is not ready to work with live animals.
		Thought-stopping	Create a strategy including an animal which prevents escalation of a client's angry thoughts; for example, petting an animal or looking into the animal's eyes.	All	All	If the client has access to an animal at home, this is a good intervention to practice outside of sessions. Clients can also include an animal representation, such as a stuffed animal, either in session or at home.
		Practicing "No"	Client prevents the animal from doing something it wants, like having an extra treat or leaving an enclosed area.	All	All	Discuss how the animal manages their emotional state when denied what it wants. Is it a functional response or does it cause more issues? As with other interventions, it may be helpful to leave the discussion focused on animals or connect it to the client's experiences, depending on the client.
	Learn and practice assertive communication	Setting Boundaries with Animals	Teach about assertive communication and practice with animals that are pushy.	Pushy or aggressively friendly/playful animals	All	This is a good intervention with animals that have a hard time respecting boundaries and are invasive with clients' space. This can be anything from an overly friendly cat to a playful dog to a feisty goat.
		Walk a horse (with and without lead)	Help them practice an assertive tone of voice and recognize when the horse responds and follows them.	Horse or other equine	All	A horse that is a bit lazy or stubborn is especially helpful for clients to try to walk. In order to move the horse they will need to adopt an attitude of intention without being aggressive.
	Increase prosocial and responsible behaviors	Animal Care	Help feed, groom, and care for animals.	All	All	This helps client see what they can offer to others and also lets them see how others respond to them positively.
		Animal Enrichment	Work in session to create toys or other enrichment items for specific animal.	All	All	Clients get to see how they can help others and contribute positively, especially when they are regulated. Clients can "gift" or "dedicate" this item or space to the animal and feel pride and ownership.
	Accept responsibility for their actions	Observation	Observe animals in conflict and how the animals react to each other afterward. Discuss how the behavior impacts their relationship.	All	All	A good conversation here can also be about "fault" versus "responsibility" and how those terms can be similar but also different. We can discuss how to take responsibility for our behavior without saying a situation is entirely the fault of one person.

ANGER MANAGEMENT   OVERARCHING GOAL: Client will identify and express feelings of anger in a healthy manner.

Clients struggling with anger often need help identifying and then processing the emotion underlying the anger. This process may involve expressing new feelings and behaviors that can be practiced with the assistance of the animals. The client may also get positive reinforcement from the animals for expressing these feelings and prosocial behaviors.

Goals	Objectives	Intervention	Description	Animal(s)	Client(s)	Notes
Curb Angry Outbursts	Curb angry outbursts	Impulsive Animals	Teach an impulsive animal to curb their behavior.	Any animal with an impulsive behavior, positive or negative	All except those who may be endangered by an animals' impulsivity	This intervention first requires observation to learn the sequence of events that lead to an animals' impulsive behavior. For instance, our goat Lily gets overstimulated easily and then will want to "play" by headbutting. By noticing what causes the overstimulation, the client can then decide when is the most opportune time to redirect or train a new behavior. This can also be done with positive behaviors, such as a dog who wants to play constantly or a cat who jumps onto laps. The client simply needs to pay attention to nonverbal and environmental cues in order to determine when an action may occur.

ANXIETY   OVERARCHING GOAL: Client will be free of symptoms of anxiety.

There are many causes of anxiety. Before developing a treatment plan, it is important to understand the cause of anxiety, otherwise we can only work to reduce the symptoms. For many people, learning to untangle and express emotions and work through unresolved issues can help with the root cause of the anxiety. The interventions below focus on goals that can be addressed within therapy.

Goals	Objectives	Intervention	Description	Animal(s)	Client(s)	Notes
Identifying the cause of their anxiety	Understand the basis for anxiety	Psychoeducation about stress and anxiety in animals	Talk about the history of an animal that has anxiety and explore the possible reasons for their anxiety. Discuss how the animal manages this anxiety now and if they had to get support from others, either their humans or other animals.	Any animal with current or past anxious behaviors	All	Many animals, especially those that have been rescued, have dealt with anxiety or have some residual anxious current or past behaviors. This can be a good parallel to share with the client and normalize anxiety.
Identify feelings underlying anxiety *(cont. on next page)*	Identify underlying and suppressed emotions	Discuss and name animal emotions	While observing different animals, encourage the client to express what emotions the animal may be having at any given time, how they can tell, and how the animal is managing that emotion.	All	Teens & adults	Connect an animal's history to its current feelings or displays of anxiety so the client can see the relationship between past and present.
		Grooming	Comb out tangled manes or fur.	Equines, goats, dogs, or animals with long fur that gets tangled	All	"Tangles" can be used as a metaphor for the tangled emotions of the client. In addition, a good metaphor here is to compare "tangled" to the way that anxiety develops. Each strand of hair represents an issue, feeling, or problem that has been left unresolved. By ignoring these problems, the hair get so tangled and knotted that you cannot differentiate the strands anymore. The process of detangling and unraveling the hair helps determine what issues need to be resolved and how to work on each independently. The clinician can facilitate a discussion about what emotions/events are tangled, and therefore "unresolved" and how we can work to detangle them.

ANXIETY OVERARCHING GOAL: Client will be free of symptoms of anxiety.

There are many causes of anxiety. Before developing a treatment plan, it is important to understand the cause of anxiety, otherwise we can only work to reduce the symptoms. For many people, learning to untangle and express emotions and work through unresolved issues can help with the root cause of the anxiety. The interventions below focus on goals that can be addressed within therapy.

Goals	Objectives	Intervention	Description	Animal(s)	Client(s)	Notes
Identify feelings underlying anxiety	Identify how thoughts influence anxiety	Psychoeducation	Observe an animal with anxiety and talk about the relationship between the physiological, cognitive, behavioral and emotional components of the animal's anxiety.	Any animal with current or past anxious behaviors	All	Discuss how anxiety can impact many facets of our lives and the lives of our animals, but that we can work to change our thoughts. If we focus on a positive thought, our anxious thoughts cannot coexist with them.
		Reverse Projection	Ask the client how they think an animal views them and thinks about them.	All	All	This intervention can tell a clinician a lot about how the client thinks they are viewed and judged by others.
		Symptom Mapping	Watch an animal dealing with a mildly stressful situation and track/map the progression of symptoms you see.	All	All	Work with the client to imagine the animal's internal process before the anxiety is expressed through behavior.
Identification of triggers	Client will identify triggers for the animal	Observation	Discuss why an animal might be anxious, either in a situation or more generally. What situations, fears, or other feelings may underlly the animals's anxiety?	All	All	
Challenge fearful thinking and fears	Look at alternative ways of interpreting behavior	Helping an animal feel safe	Have client find a way to help anxious animal to feel safe and calmer.	All	All	We have done this with many of our newer rescued animals, in particular our feral barn cats. You can discuss how an animal's interactions with people helped change its perspective and move the animal away from fear. Encourage talk such as "you're safe," or "I'm not going to hurt you," that can later be incorporated into the client's self talk. Clients may be able to help acclimate an anxious therapy animal into a new space, if it is safe for all parties.

ANXIETY   OVERARCHING GOAL: Client will be free of symptoms of anxiety.

There are many causes of anxiety. Before developing a treatment plan, it is important to understand the cause of anxiety, otherwise we can only work to reduce the symptoms. For many people, learning to untangle and express emotions and work through unresolved issues can help with the root cause of the anxiety. The interventions below focus on goals that can be addressed within therapy.

Goals	Objectives	Intervention	Description	Animal(s)	Client(s)	Notes
Managing anxiety symptoms *(cont. on next page)*	Learn mindfulness strategies	See section on Mindfulness		All	All	Teaching mindfulness is a major task in dealing with chronic anxiety and depression. Clients learn that they can only have one thought at a time, and that their thoughts may trigger feelings of anxiety. Practicing a mindful activity moves the mind from the anxious thought to something external, or away from the anxiety. These techniques can then be used by the client at any time to move their thoughts away from their anxiety and onto something positive.
	Learn how to refocus attention to mitigate anxiety symptoms	Distraction	Get an anxious animal involved in play.	Any animal with current or past anxious behaviors	All	This intervention demonstrates how an animal can move beyond anxiety with distraction. This is a good fit for an animal that is easily distracted with a toy. We can process how this distraction and playfulness makes it hard to hold onto the anxious thoughts at the same time.
	Develop techniques that reduce anxiety symptoms *(cont. on next page)*	Exposure	Walk a challenging animal.	Horse, dog, goat, or any animal resistant to walking on lead	All	Help client to breathe and practice other anxiety-reduction techniques. Discuss how the animal may be reacting to or picking up on their anxiety and how calmness will facilitate the activity.
		Bilateral Stimulation	Bilateral Stimulation while walking.	All	All	As the client walks, they put their right hand on their left shoulder and their left hand on their right shoulder. Then, they alternate gently tapping each shoulder in a consistent rhythm or pattern. This stimulates the brain in a new way.

ANXIETY OVERARCHING GOAL: Client will be free of symptoms of anxiety.

There are many causes of anxiety. Before developing a treatment plan, it is important to understand the cause of anxiety, otherwise we can only work to reduce the symptoms. For many people, learning to untangle and express emotions and work through unresolved issues can help with the root cause of the anxiety. The interventions below focus on goals that can be addressed within therapy.

Goals	Objectives	Intervention	Description	Animal(s)	Client(s)	Notes
Managing anxiety symptoms (cont. on next page)	Develop techniques that reduce anxiety symptoms	Exposure	Go into an enclosure with a new or challenging animal.	Goats, alpacas, rabbits, ferrets, or any animal that feels slightly intimidating or new to the client, as long a they are safe and not overly stressed	All	Help client to set boundaries and feel brave while practicing anxiety-reduction techniques.
		Breathing techniques	Practice a breathing technique while resting a hand on an animal.	Calm animal	All	Client can focus on breathing while regulating with an animal.
		Build confidence	Engage in novel activities with animals to build a sense of confidence that is separate from their anxiety.	All	All	This ability to engage in novel activities and feel differently about one's self can help with developing a new self concept.
		Exposure therapy	Getting to know a new animal.	Calm animal	All	It is important to go slow with exposure because we want clients to feel safe. We do not recommend flooding or exposure if a client is not ready.
		Diaphramatic Breathing	While lying on their back, place a small animal or animal toy on a client's stomach and have the client breath deeply as they watch the animal rise and fall.	Small animal (guinea pig, rabbit, cat) or animal toy	All	This can be done with any deep breathing technique as long as the client is able to lay still and take long, slow breaths.
		Worry Time	Teach client to have 15 minute "worry time" each day when they dedicate time to worry about problems.	Client's pet or stuffed animal	All	The client dedicates specific time to think about all their anxiety provoking issues but agrees to put them aside once the time ends. Clients can sit with a pet or comfort item as they worry.

ANXIETY OVERARCHING GOAL: Client will be free of symptoms of anxiety.

There are many causes of anxiety. Before developing a treatment plan, it is important to understand the cause of anxiety, otherwise we can only work to reduce the symptoms. For many people, learning to untangle and express emotions and work through unresolved issues can help with the root cause of the anxiety. The interventions below focus on goals that can be addressed within therapy.

Goals	Objectives	Intervention	Description	Animal(s)	Client(s)	Notes
Managing anxiety symptoms	Identify realistic fears and create safety for an animal	Identifying and creating safe spaces	Help client to consider real threats to animals then help them identify an animal's safe space. Help clients determine and/or create their own safe space.	All	All	Help clients understand real threats (rather than imagined) and determine how to mitigate these threats and create safety. Help them understand measures you have already taken to ensure the animal's safety. Discuss how certain spaces can help animals and humans reset their anxious feelings and shift to a sense of calm.
Reduce symptoms of anxiety	Develop skills to calm their nervous system	Breathing with animal	Grooming and breathing with therapy animal.	All but especially powerful with large animals such as equines	All	Large animals are a good fit for this intervention because they are generally calm and breathe deeply. This intervention can also be done with a calm or sleeping animal, such as a dog or cat.
		Grounding	Grounding with animal or stuffed animal by holding close against abdomen.	All but small, calm animals work best	All	Deep pressure on the abdomen has a physiological effect of calming and helping the client to feel grounded. If an animal is not present, the client can hold a stuffed animal, backpack, jacket, or other small item against the abdomen.
		Petting Animal	Pet an animal while talking about anxiety.	All	All	The simple act of touching and petting an animal can reduce heart rate and blood pressure, while increasing oxytocin. These physiological impacts can reduce the physical cues of anxiety.
	Tune in and "borrow" calming influences from their environment	Being Part of the Herd	Client and clinician mingle with herd and mimic their general actions. Encourage the client to genuinely exist with the herd and feel protected.	Herd animals	All	This can be a very powerful intervention if a client can tune into the energy of the herd. This can also be done with couples and families or group sessions. We have done this intervention in our staff meetings to improve cohesion.

ATTACHMENT OVERARCHING GOAL: Client will learn to develop healthy attachments that feel safe, secure, and stable.

Attachment work is complicated and time-consuming, so while we cannot go into the full extent of an attachment treatment plan, these are some interventions to start the process. For many clients, including the animals in session provides a safer attachment figure than humans. Once the client can practice having a safe or positive attachment with an animal, the goal is to generalize that attachment to allow connection with other humans.

Goals	Objectives	Intervention	Description	Animal(s)	Client(s)	Notes
Reduce Physiological Reactivity (cont. on next page)	Experience feelings of safety and trust during sessions	Creating safety	Incorporating various animals into sessions to increase feelings of safety. Allow the client to lead the interactions and move at their own pace.	All	All	Once you have determined a client can safely be around your therapy animal(s), you can allow them to take the lead with interactions and how they engage with the animal. This allows them to feel in control and move at a pace that feels safe.
	Exposure to soothing, low frequency sounds	Purring cat	Encourage the client to pet the cat and listen to their purring.	Cat	All	Purring releases endorphins that help the client to feel safer. The vibration can also stimulate the vagus nerve.
	Practice staying in dysregulated states	Grounding	Grounding with animal or stuffed animal by holding close against abdomen.	All but small, calm animals work best	All	Deep pressure on the abdomen has a physiological effect of calming and helping the client to feel grounded. If an animal is not present, the client can hold a stuffed animal, backpack, jacket, or other small item against the abdomen.
	Experience an increase in oxytocin	Mutual gazing or petting	Client and animal will gaze into each other's eyes and/or client will pet the animal in a mindful way.	A calm animal that can make eye contact	All	Eye contact and physical interactions with animals, particularly dogs, releases oxytocin in humans. Oxytocin encourages social interaction, increasing trust, empathy, generosity, and inhibits stress-related activity. Oxytocin also modulates hyper-arousal, anxiety, and stress surrounding social relationships.

ATTACHMENT

OVERARCHING GOAL: Client will learn to develop healthy attachments that feel safe, secure, and stable.

Attachment work is complicated and time-consuming, so while we cannot go into the full extent of an attachment treatment plan, these are some interventions to start the process. For many clients, including the animals in session provides a safer attachment figure than humans. Once the client can practice having a safe or positive attachment with an animal, the goal is to generalize that attachment to allow connection with other humans.

Goals	Objectives	Intervention	Description	Animal(s)	Client(s)	Notes
Reduce Physiological Reactivity	Reduce the fight or flight impulse	Exposure	Discuss with the client which animals may trigger their feelings of fight or flight and then work toward intentionally, but safely, spending time with these animals.	All	All	This is an intentional activity with the client's awareness and understanding of the goal. This is not flooding, but a gradual exposure to things that activate the fight-flight impulse. This process is gradual and done with the client's permission and comfort level taken into careful account. You can also discuss which animals have stronger fight or flight reactions, such as predator vs. prey responses, and which they identify with more closely.
	Tolerate gradual physical closeness	Deep-petting	Practice slow, deep-petting to calm animal.	All	All	Often this deep petting is to calm "the animal" but serves to calm the client as well. It also helps create a relationship.
		Intentional touch	Ask client to decide about the amount of physical contact with each animal—be mindful and intentional about it.	All	All	See Mindfulness section for more details.
	Increase emotional intimacy	Animals accept me	Notice feelings of acceptance by animals.	All	All	Clients can observe and feel that the animals accept them, even when they are having various feelings and reactions.
		Observation of animal emotions	Observing animal interactions and how they express their emotions.	All	All	How do animals respond to certain situations? Do they all respond similarly or are there differences, and are some ways "better" than others?
		Observation of animal support system	Explore how animals have social support from other animals.	All	All	Explore how animals exist in social relationships and the benefits they derive from these bonds.
		Name that feeling	Name emotions they believe the animal is experiencing.	All	All	This helps clients identify and label various emotions.
		"Feeling felt"	An animal nudges the client's hand when the client needs touch.	Animal with this natural skill, often a dog	All	Client can see and physically feel that others notice and care about their emotional state.

ATTACHMENT   OVERARCHING GOAL: Client will learn to develop healthy attachments that feel safe, secure, and stable.

Attachment work is complicated and time-consuming, so while we cannot go into the full extent of an attachment treatment plan, these are some interventions to start the process. For many clients, including the animals in session provides a safer attachment figure than humans. Once the client can practice having a safe or positive attachment with an animal, the goal is to generalize that attachment to allow connection with other humans.

Goals	Objectives	Intervention	Description	Animal(s)	Client(s)	Notes
Animal as "Transitional Object"	Develop care and bonding relationships	Notice the animals' needs	Explore how animals ask for needs to be met.	All	All	Animals have lots of needs but no words to express these needs. How are they able to express their needs and get them met? What do we notice about the animals?
		Observe animal dynamics	Observe herd dynamics, including when one horse is taken away from the herd.	All	All	How do animals engage with each other and how does it change with different social configurations?
		What do I feel with whom?	Spend time with different animals to feel which they feel closer to and explore why they feel connected to certain animals.	All	All	Discuss what about each animal they connected with and/or what did not resonate with them. Talk about how we bond with certain individuals and not others and normalize that process.
Develop neural pathways *(cont. on next page)*	Practice cause and effect	Playing fetch	Play fetch with any animal that will engage in this game. Discuss the requirements of turn taking and cause and effect.	Dog or other animal that will play fetch	All	In cause and effect interventions, the client needs to see how their actions, or the actions of the animals, affect others. Clinicians will want to point out these relationships as they occur and try to develop interventions where the client's behavior impacts an animal. Talking about how the behavior specifically impacted the animal is important.
		Petting the animal	Pet any animal and see how they respond.	All	All	Pet any animal and see how they respond, physically and verbally. Do they make any noises or nonverbal cues that show enjoyment? This is a simple tracking of the cause and effect of the client's actions. For instance, if a client pets a cat and she purrs, you can note, "you pet the cat and she purred."
	Develop accountability	Animal care (feeding, watering)	Client helps with a caretaking task for the animal, such as filling a water bowl or helping the clinician feed the animals.	All	All	During this process, you can discuss how the animals rely on us and how the client is playing an important caretaking role for the animal.

ATTACHMENT

OVERARCHING GOAL: Client will learn to develop healthy attachments that feel safe, secure, and stable.

Attachment work is complicated and time-consuming, so while we cannot go into the full extent of an attachment treatment plan, these are some interventions to start the process. For many clients, including the animals in session provides a safer attachment figure than humans. Once the client can practice having a safe or positive attachment with an animal, the goal is to generalize that attachment to allow connection with other humans.

Goals	Objectives	Intervention	Description	Animal(s)	Client(s)	Notes
Develop neural pathways	Improve behavior through transitions	Animal transitions	Discuss how animals deal with transitions.	All	All	Discuss why transitions are hard, normalize that struggle, and discuss coping skills for transition. If animals are not stressed by transition, discuss why this may be the case and how they developed that resilience.
		Time for a change	Have clients notice when an animal is about to need a change from an activity.	All	All	This works well with playing fetch or other active games. Have the client notice when the animal is starting to get tired and decide when to end the activity. Process how the animal might feel when ending this fun, even if tired, and how the client can make it less difficult for the animal.
		Waking a sleeping animal to play	Have the client gently wake an animal that is sleeping then watch what it does to get ready to play.	All	All	Some therapy animals, such as rats, are nocturnal but also enjoy playing during the day. Discuss this dichotomy and how even fun activities can be hard and shifting modes can be difficult for everyone. This should only be done occasionally and if the animals can tolerate waking.
Improving Current Relation-ships *(cont. on next page)*	Parents will practice attachment	Psycho-education	Demonstrate healthy vs. unhealthy attachment styles with animals.	All	All	Look at the animals' relationships with each other and with humans. What are signs are healthy relationships and what are signs of unhealthy ones?
		Filial Therapy	Client and caregiver train an animal together. Model positive interaction for caregivers.	All	Child and caregiver	Rather than telling the parent what to do and how to interact, the clinician is showing them through action. The parent is able to see new behaviors and observe how their child responds.
		Animal play-time	Ask client and parents to create a playful activity for any animal of their choice. Have appropriate tools and props available. Explain about the importance of stimulation, enrichment and play time for the animal.	All	Family	This intervention models the kinds of interactions that caregivers can have with children. It also encourages reciprocity, sharing, problem-solving, communication and more. Good tools to include are cardboard boxes of various sizes, tubes, hula hoops and other small obstacles. This is a good creative activity for clinicians too!

ATTACHMENT   OVERARCHING GOAL: Client will learn to develop healthy attachments that feel safe, secure, and stable.

Attachment work is complicated and time-consuming, so while we cannot go into the full extent of an attachment treatment plan, these are some interventions to start the process. For many clients, including the animals in session provides a safer attachment figure than humans. Once the client can practice having a safe or positive attachment with an animal, the goal is to generalize that attachment to allow connection with other humans.

Goals	Objectives	Intervention	Description	Animal(s)	Client(s)	Notes
Improving Current Relationships	Practice rapprochement	The other-side of the door	This game is similar to peek-a-boo with an animal. The client will hide behind a door or wall and then suddenly reappear. Client and clinician will watch for the animal's reactions and provide care if the animal shows signs of stress.	Children	Children	Rapprochement is a developmental stage that is part of the separation-individuation process. It is a critical stage that is necessary for children to internalize caregivers/significant "objects" to reduce anxiety about going out on their own. This exercise demonstrates how animals are independent, but also benefit from the support of those around them. It can be beneficial to have a conversation about how we all need this type of connection to feel secure in the world. The animal should enjoy this game even though it may create mild anxiety (just as peek-a-boo does in young children).
	Develop reciprocity	Animal feelings	Explore animal feelings and empathic interaction.	All	All	Observe live animals or videos of animals and discuss how they may be feeling. Allow the client to lead the process and see if they are able to understand the animals' experience.
		You make me feel…	Build awareness of influence on others.	All	All	After an animal does something positive for the client, help them reflect on how that feels. Then have them do something nice for that same animal and ask the same question. How do they feel? How do they think the animal feels?
		We help each other	Explore how animals reciprocate with client.	All	All	Many animals want to engage with humans and even help them. Dogs are a great animal for this intervention because many truly seem to want to help humans.

BEHAVIOR REGULATION   OVERARCHING GOAL: Client will have the ability to calm themselves and manage their behaviors when their nervous system is in an aroused state.

Much of this goal is about "rehearsal" of new behaviors that can be developed and then practiced with the assistance of the animals. The client may also get positive reinforcement from the animals for their pro-social behaviors.

Goals	Objectives	Intervention	Description	Animal(s)	Client(s)	Notes
Identify dysregulation	Understand dysregulation and how it occurs	Observation of animals	Client and clinician will observe animals and notice when the animal becomes dysregulated. Discuss what they observe about the animal in this state compared to other states of being.	All	All	Not all animals show signs of dysregulation but most occasionally do, especially when stressed or unhappy. Often we will observe animals from a distance when they are dysregulated to ensure client and animal safety.
	Identify dysregulation in animals	Observation of animals	Client and clinician will observe animals and notice the behaviors that trigger and indicate the animal is dysregulated. Discuss what they observe about the animal in this state compared to other states of being.	All	All	This may happen when animals interact and pester each other. For instance, one of our alpacas often runs toward our goat, Lily, which dysregulates her and causes Lily to run toward her shelter. We can discuss what is going on for both animals and how they might both be feeling. Even though one animal instigates and the other responds, we can observe cues of dysregulation in both.
	Identify when an activity causes them to be dysregulated	Meeting a new animal	Meet a new, slightly pushy but safe animal that may cause mild stress for the client. Discuss what happened during the encounter and how the client felt.	Any animal with behavior that is mildly irritating, but not unsafe	All	This intervention requires a clinician to push the client a bit beyond their comfort zone as they tolerate some mild stress while remaining regulated. It is important to choose an animal that will not create too much discomfort for the client and cause them to want to avoid session.
Self-regulation	Recognize the benefit of regulation and learn ways to regulate	Would you rather...	Clinician will present client with a series of "would you rather" questions that have to do with their emotional state and subsequent behavior.	All	All	Ask the client various questions about animals and their lives. For instance, "would you rather be a horse being pushed away from its food by another horse, or a horse that has all the food it wants but lives alone." Or "would you rather be a cat who gets to play with all the toys or one who has to take turns but gets to play with other cats?"

287

BEHAVIOR REGULATION

OVERARCHING GOAL: Client will have the ability to calm themselves and manage their behaviors when their nervous system is in an aroused state.

Much of this goal is about "rehearsal" of new behaviors that can be developed and then practiced with the assistance of the animals. The client may also get positive reinforcement from the animals for their pro-social behaviors.

Goals	Objectives	Intervention	Description	Animal(s)	Client(s)	Notes
Self-soothing	Improve neurocep-tion	Finding friendly faces and soothing voices	Client chooses an animal whose face and vocalizations are soothing when the client wants to feel calm.	All that make noises	All	This exercise is based on Polyvagal Theory.
		Mirroring slow animal behavior	Client and clinician mimic the movements of an animal that moves slowly.	All but especially good with horses and animals that stand still for long periods of time	All	Clients learn to regulate their bodies in a fun way with an external focus.
		Build a relationship with a large therapy animal	Client learns to quietly spend time with a therapy animal and feel the relationship grow.	Equine or other large animal	All	This should be done only after client has reduced impulsivity and can be safe around a large therapy animal.
Behavior modula-tion *(cont. on next page)*	Demon-strate improved impulse control	Pausing dog play	Clinician will tell dog they are going to play fetch, but then decide dog has to wait a certain number of minutes. Client helps regulate or distract dog for that time, using a timer.	Dog who is anxious to play	All	Clients can help the dog regulate and be patient, thereby creating and practicing skills and ideas that they may be able to access in the future for themselves.
	Increase frustration tolerance	Walk an animal	Client uses a leash/lead to walk an animal.	All	All	This intervention is best done in stages, where a client starts with an animal that is eager or well behaved on a lead to get a sense of accomplishment and success. You can later move to work with animals that are more challenging in order to help the client practice new skills such as patience, frustration tolerance, and problem solving.
		Teaching a trick	Client teaches an increasingly challenging trick for the animals.	All	All	How does the animal handle learning new skills and manage harder demands? What behaviors do you see?

BEHAVIOR REGULATION   OVERARCHING GOAL: Client will have the ability to calm themselves and manage their behaviors when their nervous system is in an aroused state.

Much of this goal is about "rehearsal" of new behaviors that can be developed and then practiced with the assistance of the animals. The client may also get positive reinforcement from the animals for their pro-social behaviors.

Goals	Objectives	Intervention	Description	Animal(s)	Client(s)	Notes
Behavior modula- tion	Learn to delay grati- fication	Finish your work before dinner	Practice with animal completing a task before getting a treat.	All	All	How does the animal manage waiting for a treat?
		Kickball or soccer	Play kickball or soccer with dog.	Dog	All	This is fun but also involves turn taking and waiting.
	Practice Stop- Think-Act	Fetch	Play fetch in 3 steps. Ask dog to stop, sit and then throw the ball. Repeat.	Dog	All	It may be helpful to model these interventions first, es- pecially the "stop" before you begin the activity.
		Explain it to the animal	Ask client to assist with a mildly complex task, such as brushing a cat's teeth. Have the client stop the activity, tell the animal what they are going to do, and then per- form the action.	All	All	
	Reduce self-harm behaviors	Animal Self- Harm	Explore animals that self-harm, why the animals might engage in this behavior, and how we can help them.	Any animal with self-harming behavior	All	Often, animals will engage in behaviors that are coun- terproductive, such as overgrooming. They often do this as a self-soothing techniques or because of physical discomfort. We can share these stories with clients and discuss how we can help the animals learn and practice new soothing behaviors. We can also brainstorm how we can keep the animal safe or address their physical concerns, by changing their environment or taking them to a vet, for example.

BOUNDARIES OVERARCHING GOAL: Client will develop and maintain healthy boundaries and recognize and respect boundaries in others.

Animals usually set and maintain healthy boundaries, but often in different ways than humans. Watching how animals naturally communicate and enforce limits can lead to powerful discussions with clients.

Goals	Objectives	Intervention	Description	Animal(s)	Client(s)	Notes
Differenti-ation	Identify self from other	Animal Parts-Map then Self Parts-Map	Client will create or receive an outline drawing of an animal. They will use it to identify and then draw different aspects of the animal (e.g. Lily: playful, arthritis, pushy, friend to Dahlia, maternal to babies, etc.). Client will then create a self-outline or use other materials to create a parts map of themselves.	All	All	There are many ways to make parts maps, but often it is with a tracing of the client. One of our favorite ways is to use blank puzzle pieces; the client puts a characteristic or trait on each puzzle piece and then puts the puzzle together. Putting the puzzle together or leaving parts off represents aspects of self that are integrated or separated.
		Observing animals with differentiation from one another	Client and clinician will observe bonded animals as they engage in distinct behaviors.	Animals that live with other animals in pairs, groups, or herds	All	This is helpful to understand how we can be part of a group but also remain our own individual. For instance, our goats and rabbits are bonded but will often eat separately or have solo time in an enclosure. They are still bonded, but are able to behave as individuals.
Identifying ones' own limits	Identify when a situation feels unsafe	Boundary-busting animals	Client will engage with an animal that creates slightly stressful feelings.	Goats, horses or any other animal that may come "too close" or be overly friendly	Teens, Adults	This intervention is intended for clients to recognize slight discomfort when an animal gets in their space, but it also can feel uncomfortable to animals. Though therapy animals will generally not pose a risk to clients, the intervention should be carefully supervised and stopped if it appears the client or animal is overly stressed, truly afraid, or the situation seems unsafe.
		Stop and go game	Client and animal stand about 100' apart, facing each other. Client says "come" for animal to come over to them, then "stop" or "stay" when it feels like they are close enough.	Animal that knows "come", and "stop" or "stay"	All	The clinician may demonstrate this game first and/or choose to have the animal on a leash so that they can better manage the behavior and distance. The idea is for the client to reflect on what feels good and what feels "too close" and then to correct that distance.

BOUNDARIES	OVERARCHING GOAL: Client will develop and maintain healthy boundaries and recognize and respect boundaries in others.				
Animals usually set and maintain healthy boundaries, but often in different ways than humans. Watching how animals naturally communicate and enforce limits can lead to powerful discussions with clients.					
Goals	Objectives	Intervention	Description	Animal(s)	Client(s)	Notes
Setting Safe Boundaries	Set boundaries with others	Boundary-busting animals	Client will experiment to find a way to safely stop an animal from behavior that crosses boundaries or pushes limits of comfort or safety.	Goats, horses or any other animal that may come "too close" or be overly friendly	All	The clinician must know at least one way to get each animal to stop, back-up, move away, etc. Our best boundary-busting goat is learning "stay" and to push against a bright rubber ball placed between her head and the client. As with the above intervention, and any intervention that pushes some boundaries, this intervention should be carefully supervised and stopped if it appears the client is overly stressed, truly afraid, or the situation seems unsafe.
		Circle-sitting	The client sits inside a circle (e.g. drawn in dirt) and says "stop" or "stay" when an-imal gets to the drawn line.	Animal that understands "stop" or "stay"	All	This intervention helps clients set their own limits—they can determine the size of the circle and who they will allow inside with them.
Assertive-ness	Com-municate boundaries with asser-tive voice	Commands	Client will practice giving commands to an animal.	All	All	This may require coaching by the clinician. The idea is to help the client find their assertive voice when mak-ing requests of the animal.
		Lead-walking	Client will try various tones of voice and energy to get an animal to walk with them on a leash or lead rope.	All	All	This intervention works best when you have a lazy ani-mal, or at least one that requires a human to encourage them on a walk. You can start with an easy animal, then increase the challenge with a more stubborn one.

BOUNDARIES   **OVERARCHING GOAL: Client will develop and maintain healthy boundaries and recognize and respect boundaries in others.**

Animals usually set and maintain healthy boundaries, but often in different ways than humans. Watching how animals naturally communicate and enforce limits can lead to powerful discussions with clients.

Goals	Objectives	Intervention	Description	Animal(s)	Client(s)	Notes
Recognizing and Accepting Boundaries set by Others	Recognize when others are setting boundaries	"Take-a-break"	Identify when an animal needs to rest or take a break from an activity.	Animal that knows the command "take-a-break"	All	This command is helpful for animals who will play nonstop, to their own detriment. For instance, this command became necessary for Rupert, because he would play until he collapsed and needed a command to help him recognize and stop play for his health. As opposed to the direction used below ("that's it"), this is a temporary stop so the animal can rest or get water. Play can resume once the animal has rested, and clients can help determine when the animal is ready.
		"That's it"	Communicate to the animal when play time is over.	Animal that knows the command "that's it"	All	This is important when the animal needs to stop or if the human is done playing. For instance, it was useful with Rupert when a person was finished playing with him and was moving onto another activity. Both this command and "take a break" help the animal and client recognize when an animal needs to stop a particular behavior. It also helps to practice communicating the need to stop.
	Manage feelings when others set boundaries	Animal "Rejection"	When an animal chooses not to interact with the client, we notice this with clients and can explore the reasons behind this choice.	All	All	This is usually just the animal's choice to do something different. This choice may be prompted by the client's behavior, energy, emotion, or something entirely un-related to the client. The animal is not "judging" or "rejecting" the client, which is an important lesson for clients who read rejection in others' behaviors. How the client interprets this behavior and responds to it also gives the therapist valuable clinical information.

CRISES	OVERARCHING GOAL: Client will move through a crisis without developing debilitating symptoms.				
These interventions show how animals can assist clients in crisis situations. However, animals should never be put in a situation where they are at risk during a crisis.					
Goals	Objectives	Intervention	Description	Animal(s)	Client(s)	Notes

Goals	Objectives	Intervention	Description	Animal(s)	Client(s)	Notes
Arousal Modula-tion	Experience feelings of safety	Watch, touch, or pet a calm or sleeping animal	During this intervention, we are engaging the endocrine system by stimulating oxytocin and dopamine as the client observes or engages with an animal.	All	All	Engaging with an animal can release calming oxytocin and/or dopamine. The client can observe, be with, or pet the animal and try to calm their own body and mind.
	Reduce feelings of fear	Observe an animal in a new situation	The client will watch an animal and observe how they respond to a novel and potentially stressful situation.	All	All	Though we do not put our animals in unsafe situations, there are times they are in novel and/or mildly stressful situations, such as entering a new physical space or meeting a new animal. Clients can observe these situations and notice how the animal reacts. You can also have clients watch videos of animals in stressful situations if working with a live animal is not an option during a crisis.
	Reduce cortisol levels to improve stress-reduction	Practice managing stressful situations	Throughout therapy, the client will be exposed to different experiences that gently increase their stress.	All	All	This intervention is preventative and is practiced throughout the therapeutic process. This helps prepare the client's nervous system so that when a crisis does occur, the nervous system has some experience being calmed. It is important to stress a client only in small increments so that they can successfully accommodate the stress before moving onto gradually more stressful, but tolerable, interventions.
Move experience to the past	Consoli-date experience with context and environment	Remembering the feelings	Talk about sensory experiences and memory while petting an animal.	All	All	This is a combination of calming the nervous system while helping the brain to process and accept that the crisis experience is now in the past.

293

DEPRESSION   OVERARCHING GOAL: Client will be free from or learn to successfully manage symptoms of depression.

We want to help our clients let go of the patterns and thought processes that keep them feeling stuck. We can connect our animals' histories and past experiences to those of our clients by sharing how the animals have experienced sadness or depression and how they moved past those experiences.

Goals	Objectives	Intervention	Description	Animal(s)	Client(s)	Notes
Identifying Depressive Thought Processes	Gain awareness of the cause(s) of depression	Projection of animal depression	Clients may project depression onto an animal, so we can discuss what is causing that animal to feel depressed and how it could be alleviated.	All	All	Projection is an important tool in psychotherapy and clients will frequently project feelings, thoughts, motives, and other intentions onto the animals. This provides a great deal of information to the clinician about the client's struggles and perceptions of the world. Eventually, clients can try to help the animal find strategies to feel better.
	Identify patterns that keep clients stuck in depression	Projection of animal emotion and processes	Clinician can ask the client what they believe the animal is feeling and why.	All	All	Animals can likely feel sad or even simply look sad, regardless of their inner experience. Clients can interpret and share their thoughts and feelings about the animals.
	Challenge faulty beliefs	What is the animal thinking?	Using the feeling and thought patterns the client identified for the animal, encourage the client to challenge the animals' thought process.	All	All	The client is helping the animal with its problems and by proxy, the client is creating solutions and ideas for themselves.
Decrease Depressive Thoughts *(cont. on next page)*		Empty Chair	The client pretends that the animal is them and talks to the animal.	All, but can be helpful with those that will sit still	All	The client is talking to the animal as if the animal is them, externalizing the "self." Clients may say what they wish someone would say to them or what they would like to or imagine saying to themselves.

DEPRESSION	OVERARCHING GOAL: Client will be free from or learn to successfully manage symptoms of depression.				
We want to help our clients let go of the patterns and thought processes that keep them feeling stuck. We can connect our animals' histories and past experiences to those of our clients by sharing how the animals have experienced sadness or depression and how they moved past those experiences.					
Goals	Objectives	Intervention	Description	Animal(s)	Client(s)	Notes
Decrease Depressive Thoughts	Practice mindfulness to change depressive thoughts into neutral thoughts	See Mindfulness section		All	All	
	Move outside client comfort-zone	Catch that Animal!	"Catching" animals by approaching and putting a harness/lead on them, then walking them.	All	All	We are not encouraging a free for all, but rather a time for clients to move their bodies, find an animal, and safely get them on a leash or lead. This may involve running or playfulness, or it may involve slow, careful movements. Clients can experiment and clinicians are nearby to ensure safety.
	Externalize emotions	Paint your feelings	Paint feelings and thoughts onto paper, the ground, or an animal.	All	All	Clients can do art with the animals nearby, or some animals will tolerate being painted in small amounts. We only use non-toxic, washable paint and only do this with patient animals who are not bothered by the process.
Decrease depressive feelings	Move depressive thoughts and feelings to make room for other thoughts and feelings	Play with animals	Engage in light-hearted activities with animals.	All	All	Clients can pick what fun activities they want to do, as long as they are safe. The focus is on moving past depressive feelings and thoughts and finding some levity and joy.
		Run with animals	Just run and play!	Animals that like to run with humans—dogs, horses, goats, chickens	All	Do this with animals that will enjoy this activity and running will not frighten them. This is not about chasing animals, but inviting them to run with the client.

DEPRESSION OVERARCHING GOAL: Client will be free from or learn to successfully manage symptoms of depression.

We want to help our clients let go of the patterns and thought processes that keep them feeling stuck. We can connect our animals' histories and past experiences to those of our clients by sharing how the animals have experienced sadness or depression and how they moved past those experiences.

Goals	Objectives	Intervention	Description	Animal(s)	Client(s)	Notes
Dealing with Depressive Symptoms	Increase physical activity and movement	Walk or move with the animal	Encourage exercise by walking with an animal during session.	All	All	This can be done on a lead/leash or a client can simply walk around the pasture with an animal off lead. You can also do obstacle courses or active games.
	Help others to move focus outside oneself	Animal enrichment	Make something for an animal, such as a cat toy or a maze for the guinea pigs.	All	All	Give clients lots of materials and creative license to make fun items.
		Mindfulness	Mindfulness exercises with animal to externalize feelings—move focus away from feelings.	All	All	See Mindfulness section for more details.
	Deal with sleep challenges such as insomnia	Relaxing the animal	Pet an animal and focus on the animal's sleepiness.	All	All	Focus on petting an animal and helping it relax. Clients can try to find a special spot or petting style for each animal that helps it calm down. This activity moves the attention away from the client's own struggle to sleep. Any animal that can rest calmly is good for this intervention and it can be done in sessions or at home with a client's pet.
	Learn to receive support	Leaning on others	Build relationships with animals of client's choosing and practice leaning on them for support (physically and/or emotionally).	All especially equines	All	We can get support from animals emotionally, but doing this with large animal, such as horses or donkeys, can have multiple benefits, including helping client to feel truly physically supported.
	Experience an increase in oxytocin	Helping the animals	Find ways to make an animal's life more enjoyable, especially ones that the client thinks may feel sad or lonely.	All	All	Caregiving behavior stimulates the release of oxytocin which increases client's feelings of well-being. They can also choose what would help the animal which may stimulate creative thoughts or discussions about what may help the client feel better.
	Use distraction	Playing with animal	Focus on the moment and the playful activity with the animal. Concentrate on the feelings that it brings up.	All	All	As in mindfulness techniques, distraction moves the client's attention from feelings of hopelessness to the activity and interaction at hand. Try to keep the focus on the here-and-now and any positive feelings that are stimulated.

DEPRESSION	OVERARCHING GOAL: Client will be free from or learn to successfully manage symptoms of depression.

We want to help our clients let go of the patterns and thought processes that keep them feeling stuck. We can connect our animals' histories and past experiences to those of our clients by sharing how the animals have experienced sadness or depression and how they moved past those experiences.

Goals	Objectives	Intervention	Description	Animal(s)	Client(s)	Notes
Increasing Hope in the Future	Develop positive feelings of self-efficacy	Teach something new	Engage in novel activities with animals to build sense of confidence outside of depression (new self concept).	All	All	Learning new skills can help clients realize they are capable and help build self-worth.
	Understand that they can change their experiences	Training an animal	Clients choose a skill they would like to teach the animal and decide the necessary steps and items needed. Clinician observes and participates only if/when needed.	All	All	Clients develop and practice numerous skills when training an animal, such as problem solving, patience, frustration tolerance, goal setting, adjusting expectations, and managing success or failure. This process can provide clinicians with a lot of information about the client and can allow for new experiences and ways to tolerate stress.
		Walking a large or unique animal	Encourage exercise and new skills by walking an animal during session.	All, but especially equines, alpacas, and goats	All	Similar to the above intervention, walking a large or novel animal provides clients with new experiences and ways to practice various skills. When they are successful, they can also feel a tremendous sense of pride and accomplishment.
		Using a unique skill to help an animal	The client is encouraged to notice and then develop their special or unique skills with the animals.	All	All	As with the above interventions, clients can develop and practice unique skills that set them apart from others. They can develop a sense of themselves as special and capable. Clinicians may need to help the client recognize these unique skills.

EMOTIONAL REGULATION   OVERARCHING GOAL: Client will have a regulated nervous system.

Emotional regulation is usually developed as part of executive functioning during typical child development; however, clients have often not fully developed this skill. Being able to regulate the nervous system is vital if a client wants to live fully and happily. It is helpful if clients have a cognitive understanding of emotional regulation, but it is not essential. The Polyvagal Theory can be a useful way to approach this important issue. Animals often can regulate themselves or we can help them do so, which models and teaches clients about regulating their own bodies.

Goals	Objectives	Intervention	Description	Animal(s)	Client(s)	Notes
Identification of Escalating States	Recognize triggers of dysregulation	Observe triggers for animals	Identify what happens before an animal acts out.	All	All	Watch for behavioral cues that an animal is getting agitated and what happens if the animal is not able to regulate
		Teach calming signals	Tell the client about calming and stress signs that animals demonstrate. You can observe live animals or watch videos if live animals are not available.	All	All	Many animals use nonverbal cues, called calming signals, to communicate to other animals. It is fun and educational to watch animals demonstrate these cues to each other. Many animals, such as dogs, cats, and goats, display these cues regularly.
		Power struggles	Observe animals to witness their social dynamics and how they manage and respond to frustration and anger reactions.	All but particularly those that live in groups	All	How do animals negotiate social interactions? Are there fixed hierarchies or do they fluctuate? If dynamics change, what is the reason?
		Anger or Fear?	Observe a fearful or anxious animal. Does animal show "anger' or is this a secondary emotion to fear?	All	All	See Anger Management for more information.
		Observe animal regulation	Watch how an animal calms itself down in a stressful situation.	All	All	How does each animal calm down or self regulate when mildly stressed? Do they want to be alone or with another creature, human or animal?
		Take a break	Have the client identify when the animal needs to "take a break" when it is showing signs of stress or fatigue. Have them tell the animal to take a break or help the animal rest.	All	All	See Boundaries for more details.
		Tell it to the animal	Ask client to explain to a calm animal why they are angry.	All	All	Clients often find it easier to explain feelings to an animal. They can whisper it to an animal; even if you are not able to hear what they are saying, they are still practicing verbalizing their feelings.

EMOTIONAL REGULATION OVERARCHING GOAL: Client will have a regulated nervous system.

Emotional regulation is usually developed as part of executive functioning during typical child development; however, clients have often not fully developed this skill. Being able to regulate the nervous system is vital if a client wants to live fully and happily. It is helpful if clients have a cognitive understanding of emotional regulation, but it is not essential. The Polyvagal Theory can be a useful way to approach this important issue. Animals often can regulate themselves or we can help them do so, which models and teaches clients about regulating their own bodies.

Goals	Objectives	Intervention	Description	Animal(s)	Client(s)	Notes
Down-Regulation and Co-Regulation *(cont. on next page)*	Regulate the nervous system to be ready for counseling work	Quiet cuddling	When the client has been activated in session, sometimes it is best to encourage the client to quietly cuddle with their favorite animal until they can return emotionally to the room.	All	All	An animal's quiet calm and nonjudgmental presence is often the best way for a client to regulate and be ready to return to the hard work of therapy.
		You then Me	Self-soothing practice—pet an animal then use the same stroke on their own arms.	All	All	Client benefits from the animal's touch and practices gentle touch with themselves.
		Let's Play	Play enables the neural systems to down-regulate fight or flight mechanisms (Porges, 2015).	All	All	Just play! Examples include running, hula hooping, jumping rope, playing hide and seek, doing puzzles, making art, and many other creative ways to be playful.
	Regulate themselves through regulating an animal *(cont. on next page)*	Help the animal calm down	Calm stressed animal by using long, firm strokes down the animals back or horses flank.	All	All	Client benefits from the animal's touch and sensory regulation.
		Match the animal's breathing	Client puts ear on animal to hear their breathing.	All	All	Animals all have different respiratory rates, some are quite fast and some are slow. It is fun and informative for clients to match breathing and see what happens physically as they breathe in different ways.
		Grounding	Hold a small animal or stuffed animal firmly against solar plexus.	Small animal or stuffed animal	All	Holding a calm animal firmly against the chest and stomach can be very grounding. Not all animals like to be held in this way so a stuffed animal, purse, toy, or backpack can be used. This can also be taught for people to subtly do in public when anxious.
		Sing quietly to animal	Some clients process better via song or other alternative communication styles, so allowing them to express their feelings in various ways is helpful and they may feel less anxious or embarrassed when engaging with the animal.	All	All	Animals often calm down when clients sing to them and it may calm the client as well.

EMOTIONAL REGULATION

OVERARCHING GOAL: Client will have a regulated nervous system.

Emotional regulation is usually developed as part of executive functioning during typical child development; however, clients have often not fully developed this skill. Being able to regulate the nervous system is vital if a client wants to live fully and happily. It is helpful if clients have a cognitive understanding of emotional regulation, but it is not essential. The Polyvagal Theory can be a useful way to approach this important issue. Animals often can regulate themselves or we can help them do so, which models and teaches clients about regulating their own bodies.

Goals	Objectives	Intervention	Description	Animal(s)	Client(s)	Notes
Down-Regulation and Co-Regulation	Regulate themselves through regulating an animal	Slow as a snail	Practicing patience when animals are slow to do something.	Insects, other slow animals	All	Animals can be slow, but it is rewarding to engage with them once they arrive!
		What would you tell the animal?	Explore animal behaviors that help with their emotional regulation then explore what would help them.	All	All	Clients can project their issues onto the animal, which can make it easier to find solutions or discuss challenges.
		Walking	Any rhythmic activity with an animal can down-regulate the nervous system.	All	All	This is especially beneficial with large animals like horses and donkeys.
		Grooming	Grooming any animal and focusing on the sensory and calming input.	All	All	The physical process of grooming not only offers information about cause and effect information, but provides soothing sensory and physiological input.
		Petting	Petting any animal.	All	All	Same as above, with grooming; petting provides sensory and physiological input.
	Practice Mindfulness	See Mindfulness Section		All	All	
Using social engagement system to down-regulate	Reach out to someone in order to help down-regulate	Any direct interaction between client and animal	Engaging with an animal activates the social engagement system, which can then exercise neural pathways to develop more resilient neural circuits to regulate behavior.	All	All	Any interaction with the animal can provide these benefits.
		Looking at a caring face	Gaze at an animal who can look back with a happy face.	All	All	This intervention can be as simple as receiving positive input from another creature, or more complex, if you ask the client what the animal might be thinking or feeling.

EXECUTIVE FUNCTIONING

OVERARCHING GOAL: Client will have the foundation that allows them to make healthy choices and focus on goal-directed behaviors.

Executive Functioning (EF) skills are typically learned early in life and form the foundation for skills that are necessary to live a productive, successful life. Clients who grow up with abuse, trauma, neglect or in homes where parents do not provide adequate learning opportunities, may not develop EF and will encounter difficulties in later stages. Animals provide opportunities for clients to develop EF in new and fun ways. The purposeful interaction with the animals helps clients exercise necessary parts of the brain. There are multiple interventions for various goals, but there is a tremendous amount of overlap as clinicians often address multiple goals simultaneously.

Goals	Objectives	Intervention	Description	Animal(s)	Client(s)	Notes
Working Memory	Maintain thoughts in short term memory	Find hidden animal toys	Client looks in animal's area for the toys the animal has hidden.	Rabbits, ferrets or other animals that hide their toys	Children, teens	Very young clients can watch the animal hide their toys and then go find them.
		Hide animal toys	Client hides several of the animal toys or treats and encourages the animal to find them.	All that would look for toys or treats	Children, teens	Clients have to remember where they hid toys and watch the cause and effect process.
Flexible Thinking	Develop alternative solutions	Feeding animals	Client must find alternative ways to feed animals when something is missing or not available.	All	All	We do not always have the same ingredients for our animals' special meals. We may be missing a salad ingredient, so clients can problem solve by looking around the ranch, in the garden, or simply give the animal more of another ingredient. The goal is for the client to handle the dilemma while the clinician gently provides reminders of options if necessary.
		Organizing animals' living area	Client will arrange the animal's area so that it meets the animal's needs.	All	All	Clients can decide to rearrange, clean, or find other ways to reorganize an animal's space. This might mean moving hiding spots or feeding dishes for the small animals, or hay feeders for the goats, for example. Clients will need to problem solve and execute a plan.
Organization *(cont. on next page)*	Organize items in a way that is helpful to others, either the animals or clients	Organizing toys, animal's food areas, donation pantry, barn, tools, etc.	Client can move and organize supplies or other items in a way that makes them more accessible.	All	All	We have many areas at our ranch that require constant organization, including our food pantry, animal feed supplies, and garden supplies. Clients decide if they would like to reorganize or clean up a certain area and we support this activity, as it demonstrates caring and empathy for others and shows support for those around them. As in the above intervention, clients need to make a decision, create a plan, and follow through.

EXECUTIVE FUNCTIONING   OVERARCHING GOAL: Client will have the foundation that allows them to make healthy choices and focus on goal-directed behaviors.

Executive Functioning (EF) skills are typically learned early in life and form the foundation for skills that are necessary to live a productive, successful life. Clients who grow up with abuse, trauma, neglect or in homes where parents do not provide adequate learning opportunities, may not develop EF and will encounter difficulties in later stages. Animals provide opportunities for clients to develop EF in new and fun ways. The purposeful interaction with the animals helps clients exercise necessary parts of the brain. There are multiple interventions for various goals, but there is a tremendous amount of overlap as clinicians often address multiple goals simultaneously.

Goals	Objectives	Intervention	Description	Animal(s)	Client(s)	Notes
Organiza-tion	Rearrange obstacles in a deliberate way that is helpful to others, either animals or clients	Increasing and decreasing animal jumps in an organized way	Client will help set up increasingly taller items for animal(s) to jump on then reduce the height.	All that are willing to jump over hurdles	All	This can be used as part of the set-up for an obstacle course or other training exercise with animals.
Evaluating Priorities	Prioritize a hierarchy of actions	Restoring an animal's living area	Client will help put back together a large living area for the animal(s).	Any animal with a complex living area	All	Our rabbits and guinea pigs rooms have various rugs or materials on the ground with other items on top, such as toys and enclosures. After the animal's bedding is washed, clients can help you put the room back together. "What's next?" or "what is important?" are helpful questions to focus the client.
		Storytelling about an animal	Client makes up a story about an animal they care about.	All	Children and teens	Depending on the age of the child, the clinician can write down the words while the client draws the picture, or the client can do both. The clinician can prompt with "what happens next?" We have had great stories about our animals becoming heroes in the client's life or animals as representations of client family members.

EXECUTIVE FUNCTIONING

OVERARCHING GOAL: Client will have the foundation that allows them to make healthy choices and focus on goal-directed behaviors.

Executive Functioning (EF) skills are typically learned early in life and form the foundation for skills that are necessary to live a productive, successful life. Clients who grow up with abuse, trauma, neglect or in homes where parents do not provide adequate learning opportunities, may not develop EF and will encounter difficulties in later stages. Animals provide opportunities for clients to develop EF in new and fun ways. The purposeful interaction with the animals helps clients exercise necessary parts of the brain. There are multiple interventions for various goals, but there is a tremendous amount of overlap as clinicians often address multiple goals simultaneously.

Goals	Objectives	Intervention	Description	Animal(s)	Client(s)	Notes
Inhibitory Control	Curb impulses	Snail walk to food	Client puts a food item at a distance from an insect or small animal.	Slow-moving animals and insects	Children and teens	This can be done in the garden or in any place where little insects may be. The client has to wait patiently and not help the animal while the insect or animal moves toward the food.
		"Leave it"	Client and dog compete for who can last longer from grabbing a treat sitting in front of them.	Dogs	Children and teens	This is a variation on the marshmallow experiments by Walter Mischel. The treat should be something both the child and dog would enjoy—a marshmallow or piece of cheese often work—although parent approval is important before this intervention. The clinician sets a timer for increasingly longer time periods and asks the client and the dog to wait or "leave it" until the timer goes off. If the dog eats theirs first, the client gets two.
		Freeze	Client runs with animal and then suddenly stops and freezes, telling the animal to "stay." The last one to move "wins."	Dogs, goats, chickens	Children	Animals love to play chase and many can learn "stay." This intervention combines activities and helps children practice and witness impulse control.
Frustration Tolerance/ Widening the Window of Tolerance	Manage feelings of frustration without giving up	Walking a challenging animal	Client puts harness or lead on animal and walks to a destination.	All	All	In all these activities, it is important to increase the frustration level very slowly so that the client can master increasing amounts of time staying on task. The clinician can help the client stop, find ways to calm down, then return to the activity.
		Playing a mildly frustrating game or activity	Client must finish the game or activity before playing with their desired animal.	All	Children	It helps to explain to the clients why you are doing this intervention. It does not need to be a secret that they are learning to manage difficult feelings. Playing with the animal is the reward for completing a hard task.
		Waiting for the bug to move	Client will hold their hand still while a slow insect walks to its destination or walk next to a slow moving animal.	Slow insect or animal	All	Trying to get an insect or slow animal to move faster is an exercise in futility, so this intervention helps clients practice patience.

303

EXECUTIVE FUNCTIONING

OVERARCHING GOAL: Client will have the foundation that allows them to make healthy choices and focus on goal-directed behaviors.

Executive Functioning (EF) skills are typically learned early in life and form the foundation for skills that are necessary to live a productive, successful life. Clients who grow up with abuse, trauma, neglect or in homes where parents do not provide adequate learning opportunities, may not develop EF and will encounter difficulties in later stages. Animals provide opportunities for clients to develop EF in new and fun ways. The purposeful interaction with the animals helps clients exercise necessary parts of the brain. There are multiple interventions for various goals, but there is a tremendous amount of overlap as clinicians often address multiple goals simultaneously.

Goals	Objectives	Intervention	Description	Animal(s)	Client(s)	Notes
Perseverance	Remember a goal even when the goal is no longer in sight	Finishing a task	Client must finish a task before playing with their desired animal.	All	All	Children, teens, and some adults get bored easily, even when doing tasks they initiate, like feeding the animals. It is important to set a goal for completion of the task before engaging in a desired activity with an animal. Again, being with the animal is the simple reward.
		Teaching a trick to an animal	Client will work to train the animal and will need to notice when animal is losing attention and then determine what to do.	All	All	Animals, like humans, can stay focused on a training session for a limited amount of time. The client can notice when the animal has lost its focus, give the animal a break, decide how to help the animal refocus, then reinitiate the training session.
Staying Focused	Focus on a task	Imitating the animal	Client will imitate the animal's movements.	All	Children	This intervention is fun and silly as the client tries to imitate the animals, but can also work when the animal is staying still and the client is practicing regulation.
Initiating Tasks *(cont. on next page)*	Begin a task at the proper time without prompting *(cont. on next page)*	Build routines to start each session	Client and clinician will develop a routine for how they start each session.	All	All	This is the opposite of procrastination. We are helping clients learn to start and complete activities without excuses. Having a consistent activity that continues over each session provides this structure. Examples include saying hello to all the animals, getting water for the dog, watering a plant, or checking on the garden.

EXECUTIVE FUNCTIONING OVERARCHING GOAL: Client will have the foundation that allows them to make healthy choices and focus on goal-directed behaviors.

Executive Functioning (EF) skills are typically learned early in life and form the foundation for skills that are necessary to live a productive, successful life. Clients who grow up with abuse, trauma, neglect or in homes where parents do not provide adequate learning opportunities, may not develop EF and will encounter difficulties in later stages. Animals provide opportunities for clients to develop EF in new and fun ways. The purposeful interaction with the animals helps clients exercise necessary parts of the brain. There are multiple interventions for various goals, but there is a tremendous amount of overlap as clinicians often address multiple goals simultaneously.

Goals	Objectives	Intervention	Description	Animal(s)	Client(s)	Notes
Initiating Tasks	Begin a task at the proper time without prompting	Putting the animals to bed	Client and clinician have a pre-determined time each session when they help the animals to their enclosure.	All	All	The idea is for the clinician to do less prompting as the sessions continue and as the task gets more routine. Using a timer to signal the last 10 minutes of session can be the cue to initiate the action.
Problem-Solving		Animal puppet show	Client and clinician develop a puppet show where animals must solve a problem.	Any animal puppets	Children, preteens	Having a range of animal puppets helps clients identify one that resonates with them. The clinician should also have a puppet and initiate a story where there is a problem, perhaps similar to one the client has, or has had in the past. The clinician can prompt: "What should/ could we do?"
		Solving the animal's problems	Clinician describes a current problem that the animal has and client helps solve it.	All	Children, teens	There is usually a "problem" for at least one of our animals, from a health issue to something in the environment. Listening for the right problem/opportunity, the clinician can ask for the client's help to manage that problem. We do this frequently with our anxious animals and ask the clients to find ways to help them feel safer. We can also try to relate the issue to a client's challenges, deciding which parts of the issue to emphasize or share.
Time Management *(cont. on next page)*	Stay within an allotted time for various activities *(cont. on next page)*	10-minute play	Clinician and client determine several activities they would like to do in a session and each is completed in 10-minute increments.	All	Children, teens	The client can determine the order of activities, which helps create and evaluate priorities, or the clinician can set the order, often leaving the most valued activity for last. Using a timer, the clinician and client move from activity/animal to the next. The clinician should give minimal prompts about moving on and it is fine to occasionally remind clients of the final goal.

305

EXECUTIVE FUNCTIONING

OVERARCHING GOAL: Client will have the foundation that allows them to make healthy choices and focus on goal-directed behaviors.

Executive Functioning (EF) skills are typically learned early in life and form the foundation for skills that are necessary to live a productive, successful life. Clients who grow up with abuse, trauma, neglect or in homes where parents do not provide adequate learning opportunities, may not develop EF and will encounter difficulties in later stages. Animals provide opportunities for clients to develop EF in new and fun ways. The purposeful interaction with the animals helps clients exercise necessary parts of the brain. There are multiple interventions for various goals, but there is a tremendous amount of overlap as clinicians often address multiple goals simultaneously.

Goals	Objectives	Intervention	Description	Animal(s)	Client(s)	Notes
Time Management	Stay within an allotted time for various activities	Timed play with animal(s)	Clinician sets a timer for a certain amount of time that the client can interact with one animal.	All	Children	This is a good intervention for the animals as well, since it limits the amount of time the client is engaging a particular animal. This is helpful with animals that are older and/or semi-retired as they truly do need a limited amount of play and social interaction.
Planning, Setting and Meeting Goals	Set future goals	Animal training	Client helps clinician determine a skill to train the animal and the specific steps to complete this task.	All	All	As the animals learn basic behavior and tricks, the client can come up with ideas for more complex behaviors to train. The client can choose the skill and help determine the training steps and sequence in order to help the animal learn the trick (scaffolding). Ideas for complex tricks include opening a door, putting toys away, rolling over, and ringing a bell to go outside.
		Demonstrating for a caregiver or family member	Client demonstrates a trick with an animal they have trained.	All	Children, teens	It is so gratifying for clients to show caregivers their mastery and be rewarded by the caregivers' awe and respect. We have also had clients demonstrate their skills to classes or other groups.

FAMILY   **OVERARCHING GOAL: The family will have the ability to communicate effectively, support each other, and resolve conflicts.**

Animals can be integrated into family therapy in various ways, helping to keep the sessions fun and lighthearted, but also providing opportunities for new ways of interacting. Observing the animals' family configurations, how they interact, and how they accept differences can provide good modeling for families. The animals can also act as mirrors, reflecting the emotional temperature and dynamics within the family systems. While there may be difficult conversations in family therapy, these interventions can increase the family members' willingness to engage in therapy.

Goals	Objectives	Intervention	Description	Animal(s)	Client(s)	Notes
Identify Family Dynamics	Understand and identify family dynamics	Family Sculpture	Make a Family Sculpture with animals acting as family members.	All	All	This activity involves choosing an animal to represent each member of the family and then trying to move them into certain positions in a room or outdoor space. Family members can speak as the animals as they interact. Please read Virginia Satir for more details on Family Sculpting.
		Calming Signals	Teach the family about an animal's calming signals and have them observe the calming signals they see in a group of animals.	All	All	After observing animal calming signals, it can be fun to ask clients what calming signals they use. For example, a parent might take deep breaths whereas a child stomps her feet. It is useful for clients to understand how nonverbal cues communicate to other people, even unintentionally, and to help the recognize what family members are noticing.
		Herd dynamics	Ask family members to describe different animals in a group or herd. How do they compliment or cause stress for each other?	Any animals that live in a group or herd	All	Discuss how animals get along and how it can change over time. How do the animals manage this?
Improve Communication	Increase cooperation	Walking an animal	Walk a therapy animal or family pet together.	All, often a dog	All	This can be practiced in sessions and then done at home as a family activity.
	Develop activities that foster enjoyment together	Let's all Play!	This should be a creative play activity that involves all family members and a therapy animal or family pet.	All	All	This is a great activity to get families moving, energized, and having fun together. We love to play soccer and kickball with our therapy dogs and families can do this at home with pets as well.

FAMILY

OVERARCHING GOAL: The family will have the ability to communicate effectively, support each other, and resolve conflicts.

Animals can be integrated into family therapy in various ways, helping to keep the sessions fun and lighthearted, but also providing opportunities for new ways of interacting. Observing the animals' family configurations, how they interact, and how they accept differences can provide good modeling for families. The animals can also act as mirrors, reflecting the emotional temperature and dynamics within the family systems. While there may be difficult conversations in family therapy, these interventions can increase the family members' willingness to engage in therapy.

Goals	Objectives	Intervention	Description	Animal(s)	Client(s)	Notes
Decreasing Reactivity	Improve communication and problem solving between family members	Animal meal preparation	Prepare meals and feed animals together.	All	All	Families work together to gather ingredients and prepare meals for the animal. Cooperation, problem-solving, and turn-taking often need to occur when preparing multiple meals.
		Learn clicker training	Teach family the basics of clicker training. Have them work to master it together and then train an animal using the clicker.	All	All	Clicker training requires a lot of steps and coordination, so it can take a lot of teamwork and frustration tolerance, but can also be a very effective training method. Family members need to assign roles, problem solve, and work together.
		Train a human	A child/teen uses clicker training to train a caregiver.	All	All	The child/teen can choose a simple or silly task for the caregiver. This intervention requires a lot of coordination and patience, but also humor and levity, as it can be a tricky activity. The clinician often learns a lot about how the family interacts, communicates, solves problems, and handles frustration.
		Animal training	Family will train a therapy animal together.	All	All	This can be a tricky task and requires a lot of coordination, teamwork, and communication by the family. The clinician can learn a lot about how the family interacts, communicates, solves problems, and handles frustration.
		Obstacle course	Family will work to help an animal complete an obstacle course.	All	All	This can be a tricky task and requires problem-solving, patience, communication, frustration tolerance, and many other skills, while teaching the clinician a lot about how the family sets goals, communicates, solves problems, and handles frustration.

FAMILY	OVERARCHING GOAL: The family will have the ability to communicate effectively, support each other, and resolve conflicts.				
Animals can be integrated into family therapy in various ways, helping to keep the sessions fun and lighthearted, but also providing opportunities for new ways of interacting. Observing the animals' family configurations, how they interact, and how they accept differences can provide good modeling for families. The animals can also act as mirrors, reflecting the emotional temperature and dynamics within the family systems. While there may be difficult conversations in family therapy, these interventions can increase the family members' willingness to engage in therapy.					
Goals	Objectives	Intervention	Description	Animal(s)	Client(s)	Notes
Decreasing Reactivity	Decrease emotional reactivity	Conflict while keeping the animal asleep	Practice communication skills while keeping animal calm, asleep, and/or in the therapy room.	All but usually indoor animals such as cats, dogs, and rabbits	All	This intervention helps clients see how they communicate, both verbally and nonverbally, and the inadvertent impact they may have on those around them. During this time, the clinician can bring attention to the animal's response and discuss what the animal may be noticing. The clinician and clients can work toward keeping the animal calm and present in the room, even as difficult topics are being discussed.

FUN   OVERARCHING GOAL: The client will be able to find moments of fun and joy.

Animals are amazing at modeling how to let go, have fun, and make the most of each moment. These exercises are especially helpful for clients who feel emotionally shutdown or as though they have lost their spark. The animals provide spontaneous and contagious opportunities for fun and laughter, reminding clients that they are still capable of feeling joy.

Goals	Objectives	Intervention	Description	Animal(s)	Client(s)	Notes
Bringing Fun into their Life *(cont. on next page)*	Play spontaneously	Running with the animals	Client and clinician will run in a pasture and let animals run with or chase them.	Horses, donkeys, goats, chickens, dogs...any animal that will chase!	All	You can also do this intervention indoors with smaller animals. Rats will chase a client's hand or cats will chase a wand.
	Let go of ego and be silly	Mimicking animal noises	Client will mimic the various sounds the animal(s) make.	All	All	Some clients will feel silly and may resist doing this activity, but it certainly can elicit laughter. Clinicians can participate as well, especially if it helps a client let down their guard.
	Laugh freely	Watching the animals have fun	Observe animals being silly and having fun.	All	All	Animals are wonderful at being spontaneous and acting silly, both with humans and with each other. There are great videos online of rats laughing as they get tickled by a human. You can start this exercise by watching the video and then seeing which animals you can tickle!
		Animal Talk	Give dialogue to animal noises.	Animals that spontaneously make noises	All	This is fun with animals that are vocal, especially if their noises are silly, such as donkeys or ducks and chickens.
		Kickball	Playing kickball or soccer.	Dog or other animal that will chase a ball	All	Clients can watch an animal enjoy a simple activity and also move their own bodies, which can facilitate a change in mood.
		Observation of animal time	Explore how animals spend their free time.	All	All	This can be done with any animal, just watching quietly or discussing with the client what they notice.
		Observe animal play	Explore how and why animals play.	All	All	As above, this can be done with any animal, just watching quietly or discussing with the client what they notice. Clients can join the play if they choose.

FUN OVERARCHING GOAL: The client will be able to find moments of fun and joy.

Animals are amazing at modeling how to let go, have fun, and make the most of each moment. These exercises are especially helpful for clients who feel emotionally shutdown or as though they have lost their spark. The animals provide spontaneous and contagious opportunities for fun and laughter, reminding clients that they are still capable of feeling joy.

Goals	Objectives	Intervention	Description	Animal(s)	Client(s)	Notes
Bringing Fun into their Life	Exist in the moment	Observation	Observe animals in different conditions.	All	All	This is especially fun with outdoor animals in different weather conditions. For instance, our horses love the sun and the snow. On sunny days they will roll around in the warm dirt and in the snow they literally kick up their heels in joy. Our alpacas love to run in sprinklers. It is helpful to know your own animals' responses to different situations and allow clients to see the variations in behavior.
	Experience joy	Surprise attack of "joy"	Expose client to animals and natural experiences that spontaneously create feelings of joy in client.	All	All	This is what we call a "sideways intervention" because it is important not to explain the goal or to make too much out of this. The goal is for a client to be surprised by the feeling of joy that spontaneously occurs when they see something. The clinician can then point out that the client is still capable of internal "life" and "joy."
		What tickles you?	Clients identify what "tickles" an animal, i.e. makes them feel happy, silly, or joyful, then discuss what "tickles" the client.	All	All	This can be done after watching the rat tickling videos. If a client is uncomfortable with the idea of "tickling," another term can be substituted.

GRIEF	OVERARCHING GOAL: The client will work through feelings of grief and integrate the loss as a form of strength and resilience.					
Many animals have an intuitive understanding of how to support humans during grief. Simply petting an animal, especially one with whom the client has a relationship, can provide much needed and appreciated support. In many ways, the animal is acting as a surrogate for you or another human who would otherwise support the client physically and emotionally.						
Goals	Objectives	Intervention	Description	Animal(s)	Client(s)	Notes
Immediate Support after Loss	Share experience and feel listened to and understood	Pet a calm animal and share grief experience	Client simply sits with animal and shares as much or little as they feel comfortable.	All	All	Many therapy animals are eager to receive affection from clients and may be especially sensitive to those who are sad. If your therapy animal does not yet have this skill, they can still be present in different ways for the client, even just quietly sharing the space with the client. Animals can also learn simple commands that can more specifically support clients, such as "go to work" which means sitting next to and cuddling the client, or "lap," which means the animal puts their head or entire body on the client's lap.
		Share grief	The clinician can share an animal's experience of grief and loss, either of a home, human, or animal friend. The client can share their experience with the animal if they desire.	All	All	Many of our animals have changed homes and owners, or lost animal companions. Clients can feel connected to and understood when animals have had a similar experience.
		Hug an animal	If the animal is large enough and feels comfortable with this type of physical contact, the client can hold or lean on the animal for physical support.	All	All	Large animals, such as donkeys and horses, are wonderful for providing clients with support during grief. An equine that will tolerate being leaned on, held close, or cried upon is a valuable therapy partner! Large dogs are also helpful to lean on or lay next to when a client desires deep physical contact. Clients can also gently hold cats or smaller animals.
Understanding	Understand the process of grief	Psychoeducation	Talk about an animal's experience of loss.	All	All	As mentioned above, many of our animals have experienced grief. We can share these stories, while educating about and normalizing grief experiences.

GRIEF	OVERARCHING GOAL: The client will work through feelings of grief and integrate the loss as a form of strength and resilience.				
Many animals have an intuitive understanding of how to support humans during grief. Simply petting an animal, especially one with whom the client has a relationship, can provide much needed and appreciated support. In many ways, the animal is acting as a surrogate for you or another human who would otherwise support the client physically and emotionally.					
Goals	**Objectives**	**Intervention**	**Description**	**Animal(s)**	**Client(s)**	**Notes**
Remembering	Actively remember a loved one	Talk about the animal's loss	Talk about how an animal or animal family/herd deals with loss.	All	All	There is research that certain animals experience and have grief rituals. Share these stories with clients. You can also watch videos about grieving animals.
		Honoring the animal	Have a place and/or ritual to honor an animal that has died.	All	All	The unfortunate reality is that therapy animals will and do die. However, this provides an opportunity for clinicians to model how to deal with grief and loss and to allow the client to recognize and honor the loss.
		Write a story	Client writes a story about an animal that has lost a friend/family member.	All	All	This can be a made-up story or one about a real animal. The purpose is simply to practice discussing grief.
Long term Unresolved Grief	Recognize that others may be grieving	Goodbye my friend	Process the loss of a therapy animal.	All	All	Discussing loss and grief in a calm but compassionate way allows clients to process loss in a healthy, positive way and understand that death does not mean silence. We can share about and model our grief process with therapy animals.

MINDFULNESS   OVERARCHING GOAL: The client will develop mindfulness skills in order to help in times of stress and anxiety and enhance overall functioning.

Mindfulness skills can help with depression, anxiety, overall stress management, and other mental health issues. Mindfulness trains clients to focus their attention on pleasant or neutral thoughts rather than on the thoughts or feelings associated with depression or anxiety. Animals are naturally mindful, as they focus on the present moment, so interacting with and learning from the animals can be very powerful. The interventions below are only a small sampling of mindfulness activities.

Goals	Objectives	Intervention	Description	Animal(s)	Client(s)	Notes
Focus on the moment *(cont. on next page)*	Stay in and focus on the present moment	Grooming the animal	Grooming any animal and focusing on the sensory and calming input.	All	All	The physical process of grooming provides soothing sensory and physiological input and allows clients to focus on those sensations.
		Breathe with an animal	Client is near an animal, standing, sitting, or even laying down, and tries to match their breathing to the animal's breaths.	All	All	This works well with any animal, but particularly those that breathe slowly and deeply, especially if you are trying to help a client calm down.
		Find the animal's softest part	Pet an animal and gently explore the various textures of their fur.	All	All	As with grooming, this activity provides soothing sensory and physiological input and allows clients to focus on those sensations.
		Find the animal's favorite place to be pet	Pet an animal and watch how it responds; do responses vary depending on where it is pet?	All	All	How can you tell it is the animal's favorite part? How is the animal communicating to the client and how does the client feel, having made the animal feel good?
		Five senses with an animal	Client notices what they see, smell, hear, taste, and feel while with an animal or in nature.	All	All	Client focuses on their senses rather than any internal thoughts, feelings, or stressors.
		Noticing	Spend time outside, sitting or walking, as you and the client share the various things you see and notice.	All	All	There is not judgment or right/wrong when noticing. It is just what you and the client observe and share with each other.
	Move awareness away from disturbing thoughts *(cont. on next page)*	Walking in the animal's shoes	Walk with an animal and talk about what it is like from the animal's perspective.	All	All	It can be useful to discuss what the animal might notice differently. Clients and clinicians may move to the animal's level if they feel comfortable.
		Grounding on the ground	Client lay on their back, preferably outside if possible.	All	All	Laying on the grass or snow is an excellent way to bring a person back into their body and focus on physical sensations. This intervention can also be helpful for clients who are dissociating.

MINDFULNESS	OVERARCHING GOAL: The client will develop mindfulness skills in order to help in times of stress and anxiety and enhance overall functioning.				
Mindfulness skills can help with depression, anxiety, overall stress management, and other mental health issues. Mindfulness trains clients to focus their attention on pleasant or neutral thoughts rather than on the thoughts or feelings associated with depression or anxiety. Animals are naturally mindful, as they focus on the present moment, so interacting with and learning from the animals can be very powerful. The interventions below are only a small sampling of mindfulness activities.					
Goals	Objectives	Intervention	Description	Animal(s)	Client(s)	Notes
Focus on the moment *(cont. on next page)*	Move awareness away from disturbing thoughts *(cont. on next page)*	Belly-breathing with an animal	Client lays on their back while clinician places a small animal or stuffed animal on their stomach.	Small animal	All	It is fun to watch the animal go up and down on the client's stomach as they practice deep breathing. This can also be done with stuffed animals if there are not live animals present or the animals do not enjoy the activity.
		Describing the animal	Naming different qualities of the animal.	All	All	Clients focus on the animal and external stimuli, rather than internal stressors.
		Focus on the client's pet	The client brings pictures of and shares about their family pet(s).	All	All	This is a great way for clients to share an aspect of themselves with clinicians. The clinician not only learns about the animal, but about the client's attachments, values, and relational dynamics.
		Meditation with an animal	Demonstrate how to meditate with an animal quietly at feet or in lap.	All	All	This can be done with small animals inside sitting on/with the client, or outside with larger animals, sitting in the pasture.
		Contact with Earth	Standing, walking barefoot on earth/grass, etc. and feeling the sensory input and energy.	All	All	Client focuses on their senses rather than any internal thoughts, feelings, or stressors.
		Guided imagery	Develop a guided imagery with one of the client's favorite therapy animals involved in the story.	All	All	Client can imagine the animal or be with an animal during this intervention.
		Client listens as an animal eats	Client listens as an animal eats.	All	All	This is surprisingly calming and soothing as the animals eat their food and demonstrate quiet satisfaction.

MINDFULNESS	OVERARCHING GOAL: The client will develop mindfulness skills in order to help in times of stress and anxiety and enhance overall functioning.					
Mindfulness skills can help with depression, anxiety, overall stress management, and other mental health issues. Mindfulness trains clients to focus their attention on pleasant or neutral thoughts rather than on the thoughts or feelings associated with depression or anxiety. Animals are naturally mindful, as they focus on the present moment, so interacting with and learning from the animals can be very powerful. The interventions below are only a small sampling of mindfulness activities.						
Goals	Objectives	Intervention	Description	Animal(s)	Client(s)	Notes
Focus on the moment	Move awareness away from disturbing thoughts	Watching an insect move, walk, and eat	Closely observe an insect moving around their habitat and eating.	Insects	All	Client focuses on their senses rather than any internal thoughts, feelings, or stressors. Client can notice and appreciate the unique features of an insect that may be underappreciated.
		Observing nature		Nature	All	Client focuses on their senses rather than any internal thoughts, feelings, or stressors. Clients can also develop a sense of being part of a greater whole and perhaps put their own experiences or feelings in perspective.

NONVERBAL COMMUNICATION   OVERARCHING GOAL: Client will be able to read the nonverbal communication of others and understand their own nonverbal communication methods.

Humans communicate more with our nonverbal cues than with our words, but we often have a difficult time interpreting the nonverbal communication of others. Humans also use contradictory communication when we say one thing but our nonverbal communication says something else. These interventions help clients pay attention to and accurately interpret nonverbal communication. Because animals primarily use nonverbal communication with each other, they are wonderful models and partners with this goal.

Goals	Objectives	Intervention	Description	Animal(s)	Client(s)	Notes
Under-standing and De-ciphering Nonverbal Communi-cation *(cont. on next page)*	Identi-fy how others use nonverbal communi-cation *(cont. on next page)*	Teach and observe animal communica-tion	Client will learn about and observe animals using nonverbal communication and calming signals.	All	All	Almost all animals communicate nonverbally with each other. Turid Rugaas has written extensively about the calming signals of dogs in her book, On Talking Terms with Dogs. Calming signals in cats, horses, and other animals have also been identified. It is very powerful to observe animals or watch animal videos and notice how much they are able to communicate through body language.
		Observe the nonverbal communica-tion of differ-ent animals	Explore how animals use body language and sounds to communicate with other animals and with humans.	All	All	Some animals use different types of communication with humans than they do with animals. Explore how animals use nonverbal and verbal communication with each other and with humans.
		Learn how animals communicate with each other	After recognizing that animals use nonverbal communication with each other, ask the client to decipher what they think the animals are saying to each other.	All	All	What the client thinks animals are saying can be very informative about their own internal monologue and how they interpret others' behaviors. It can be fun when you have animals, such as chickens, that vocalize all at once, because the clinician and client can be silly and talk at the same time, making up what they think the animals are saying.
		Observe group animal dynamics	Discuss how the animal group or herd communicates with each other. Do they all use the same cues or do they differ depending on the animal?	Herd or groups of animals	All	Clients can observe nonverbal and verbal communication between animals. You can also discuss if animals communicate differently with members of their species and other animals, or if it changes depending on environment, context, or other circumstances.

NONVERBAL COMMUNICATION — OVERARCHING GOAL: Client will be able to read the nonverbal communication of others and understand their own nonverbal communication methods.

Humans communicate more with our nonverbal cues than with our words, but we often have a difficult time interpreting the nonverbal communication of others. Humans also use contradictory communication when we say one thing but our nonverbal communication says something else. These interventions help clients pay attention to and accurately interpret nonverbal communication. Because animals primarily use nonverbal communication with each other, they are wonderful models and partners with this goal.

Goals	Objectives	Intervention	Description	Animal(s)	Client(s)	Notes
Understanding and Deciphering Nonverbal Communication	Identify how others use nonverbal communication	Explore how animals sense the world around them	Explore how animals use different senses to listen and understand what's happening around them.	All	All	Horses are a great animal for this intervention since they seem to have a sixth sense of the world around them. It is not important that the client is correct about how the animals know what's going on, just that they recognize that there are many elements involved in communication.
		Observe how animals respond to them	Client will watch the animal's reaction to the client in various emotional or regulatory states.	All	All	This intervention is essential for clients who need to develop positive relationships. Animals' reactions to clients will change over time, depending on how the client acts and behaves. Exploring how the animals react helps start conversations about how client behavior impacts others in positive and negative way.
		Human calming signals	Discuss what human calming signals might be and how we could use them.	NA	All	Ask the client to find fun ways to communicate nonverbally with another human when they are wanting the situation to stay calm. Clinicians can practice with clients as appropriate.
		Observe the nonverbal communication of different humans	Observe other humans and identify nonverbal communication. This may involve going to public spaces and observing from a distance or watching videos without sound in order to identify nonverbal cues.	NA	All	Find an age-appropriate location, show, or video that has human (not cartoon) characters interacting. Clients can notice the different ways the humans interact and communicate nonverbally. The clinician can also ask the client to identify what certain body parts are communicating, such as the full body, mouth, eyes, posture, hand position, and gestures.
		Nature-talking	Observe nature at different points in time to observe how plants communicate what is happening to them and perhaps, what they need.	Plants	All	In most locales, plants change with the seasons. Plants also get weakened from pests, illness, lack of water, poor soil, or other stressors. Exploring the various ways that nature communicates to us and how that demonstrates the breadth of nonverbal communication.

NONVERBAL COMMUNICATION

OVERARCHING GOAL: Client will be able to read the nonverbal communication of others and understand their own nonverbal communication methods.

Humans communicate more with our nonverbal cues than with our words, but we often have a difficult time interpreting the nonverbal communication of others. Humans also use contradictory communication when we say one thing but our nonverbal communication says something else. These interventions help clients pay attention to and accurately interpret nonverbal communication. Because animals primarily use nonverbal communication with each other, they are wonderful models and partners with this goal.

Goals	Objectives	Intervention	Description	Animal(s)	Client(s)	Notes
Filters	Identify filters that clients use which may bias how they read others' nonverbal communication	Projection on the animals	While observing the animals' interactions, the clinician asks "what do you think is going on?"	All	All	With projection, clinicians can learn an incredible amount about what clients notice, how they interpret their observations, and how this impacts their interactions with others. Clinicians can use these projections and the information gained to focus treatment plans and interventions.
		Working with the client's story	A client's history and experiences may impact how they view events. Informed by the client's story and potential biases, the clinician can share real or hypothetical stories about therapy animals.	All	All	We all make assumptions about what we "hear" based on our past experiences. This is especially true with nonverbal communication. Using "what if…" the clinician superimposes the client's story onto an animal. Then, observing the animals' interactions with other animals, the clinician can ask: "What if ___ happened? Or "What do you think they believe ___ is saying to them?"
		Challenging the filter	After the above intervention is completed, clinician asks client "what else?" could the other animal(s) be communicating?	All	All	This borrows from CBT as the client projects onto the animals. You can take this intervention further by first finding the biases the client commonly uses and then challenging each of them. You can continue using CBT interventions to help change the automatic belief.

NONVERBAL COMMUNICATION   OVERARCHING GOAL: Client will be able to read the nonverbal communication of others and understand their own nonverbal communication methods.

Humans communicate more with our nonverbal cues than with our words, but we often have a difficult time interpreting the nonverbal communication of others. Humans also use contradictory communication when we say one thing but our nonverbal communication says something else. These interventions help clients pay attention to and accurately interpret nonverbal communication. Because animals primarily use nonverbal communication with each other, they are wonderful models and partners with this goal.

Goals	Objectives	Intervention	Description	Animal(s)	Client(s)	Notes
Speaking Nonverbally	Effectively communicate nonverbally	Train an animal using only hand signals	Client will teach an animal tricks using only hand signals.	All but especially dogs and cats	All	These interventions will highlight how clients use nonverbal communication with others, and how they can control these nonverbal cues to accurately convey what they want.
		Sharing small treats with a calm animal	Share a small, safe treat with an animal, such as fruit or cereal. The animal has to be in a calm and connected state in order to get the food.	All	All	Talk about how the animal regulates itself and what the smell of treats does to the animal's nervous system. How does the animal use nonverbal cues to show interest and ask for more treats?
	Modify nonverbal communication in order to be heard more effectively	Giving something good…	Give the animal a high value treat and watch them enjoy it in a calm and co-regulated state.	All	All	This activity has a lot of layers. The client can feel the joy of giving an animal a special treat and providing joy. You can also discuss the difference between the animal's outward behavior (lying down looking calm) and the animal's inner state (aroused, wanting more treats). You can discuss how the animal is able to use impulse control and how this may connect to the client's experiences; does the client ever look calm on the outside while feeling internally stressed or agitated?
		Getting a horse or large animal to walk	Client tries to walk a large animal as they focus on how to effectively communicate using their tone of voice and nonverbal cues.	Horse, donkey, alpaca	All	Horses and many large animals will not respond or follow directions if a client's internal state does not align with their nonverbal cues. Clients must practice and display congruence in order to be successful with this activity, which requires paying attention to and modifying their nonverbal behavior.

PTSD	OVERARCHING GOAL: Client will be reduce and ultimately be free from symptoms of post-traumatic stress disorder.				
Treating PTSD is a complex process. The animal can assist the clinician in providing a trauma-informed environment and be instrumental in helping the client identify, manage and eventually modify their reactions to triggers. Below are only a small set of the goals and objectives that can be implemented for clients with PTSD.					
Goals	Objectives	Intervention	Description	Animal(s)	Client(s)	Notes
Establish-ing Trust	Feel safe in the therapeutic relationship	Clinician is seen with their therapy animal	Therapy animal is present at all times, especially during intake and early sessions.	All	All	Simply being associated with an animal can enhance trust and increase positive feelings toward the clinician. As the client sees the animal engage with and trust the clinician, and sees the clinician treat the animal kindly, the client understands that the clinician is a person worthy of their trust as well.
		See Trust and Rapport section		All	All	
Availability for Treatment	Stay in the present moment	See Mindfulness section		All	All	
	Benefit from therapeutic touch	Cuddling, petting, sitting with an animal	Client chooses how to physically engage with an animal in a gentle way.	All	All	Any intervention where the client is physically engaging with the animal can provide physiological and emotional benefit, including release of calming hormones and reducing anxiety.
Managing Symptoms (cont. on next page)	Identify triggers (cont. on next page)	Projection	Client projects feelings onto animals.	All	All	This intervention allows clients to share their thoughts/feelings/reactions in an indirect way, which often feels safer to clients with PTSD. This also gives the clinician information about what the client is struggling with and how it impacts them.
		What happened before?	Client will observe an animal reacting to a certain situation and project what they believe happened in that animal's mind to trigger the reaction.	All	All	As with all the above intervention, this allows clients to share their thoughts/feelings/reactions in an indirect way, which often feels safer to clients with PTSD. This informs the clinician about the thoughts processes and trauma responses that the client experiences.

PTSD	OVERARCHING GOAL: Client will be reduce and ultimately be free from symptoms of post-traumatic stress disorder.					
Treating PTSD is a complex process. The animal can assist the clinician in providing a trauma-informed environment and be instrumental in helping the client identify, manage and eventually modify their reactions to triggers. Below are only a small set of the goals and objectives that can be implemented for clients with PTSD.						
Goals	Objectives	Intervention	Description	Animal(s)	Client(s)	Notes
Managing Symptoms	Avoid dissociation	Mindfulness	Focus on the animal's skin or fur.	All	All	Keeping clients focused on the present moment with a physical touch helps keep them from dissociating.
		Surprise	Let a small animal or insect climb up client's sleeve.	Small animal or insect	All	Because some clients will not like this sensation, make sure that they understand the intervention before beginning. This intervention can be a wonderful way to provide sensory input in a new way which also keeps the client present and focused.
		Smelling	Smell an animal's breath, paw, or other appropriate area of the body.	All	All	Animals' breath and paws can have unique and even soothing smells. Please make sure the animal is comfortable with this intervention.
		Kissed by an animal	Allow an animal to lick the client.	All	All	Some people do not like to be licked by animals so make sure to check with the client first.
	Identify emotions	The animal feels…	Identifying emotions of animals in different situations.	All	All	This can allow the clinician to see if a client notices an animal's behavior, what they do notice, and how they interpret it. Similar to above interventions, this allows the client to project and put thoughts/feelings onto another being, which can feel more accessible or safer than identifying their own feelings.
		Where in the body is the animal's feeling	The client indicates where in the body they think an animal is experiencing a feeling.	All	All	This can allow a client to notice how emotions can physically impact our bodies and can lead to a discussion about where the client carries emotion.
Moving Forward	Revisit images of traumatic event while feeling safe	Practice self-regulation skills	Client will use various skills to stay regulated as they verbally process their experience with clinician.	All	All	Clients can have the animals present to ground them and keep them in the present moment as they revisit a trauma. See Trauma and Emotional Regulation sections for more details.

RELATIONSHIPS OVERARCHING GOAL: Client will have the tools to identify healthy people and relationships and develop skills to cultivate healthy relationships.

Animals are powerful relationship motivators, as they give feedback about social skills in a clear but non-judgmental way. Animals clearly communicate their feelings of safety and require humans to build relationships thoughtfully. Clients learn how to behave and respond in ways that build trust and healthy relationships with the animals.

Goals	Objectives	Intervention	Description	Animal(s)	Client(s)	Notes
Establishing Safety	Reduce relationship stress by introducing The "Third Thing" (Winnicott, 1968)	Telling stories about the animals/client pets	The "Third Thing" or the "Third Object" is something that allows the client and clinician to make a connection on a human level. The purpose of introducing the third thing is to slowly help move the client toward issues with more difficult emotions. In AACP, the animal is the third thing and clients are able to focus on the animal to create safety within the therapeutic setting.	All	All	The function of this intervention is to draw attention away from the therapeutic relationship and/or areas of stress for the client. This intervention can include exploring a common interest outside the therapeutic relationship which allows for greater feeling of safety.
	Activate the neuroception of safety by activating the social engagement system	Observation	Client observes the safe, trusting interaction between clinician and animals.	All	All	Clients are able to see that the therapy animals trust the clinician, giving permission for the client to do so as well.
Trust	Engage in a trustworthy way with animals	Just Be with Me	Work on relational skills through building relationships with a variety of animals.	All	All	This intervention varies depending on client, animal, and clinician, but the focus is simply to let the client be with the animals and practice building a relationship with one or several animals.
Communication (cont. on next page)	Use clear communication	Talk to or train an animal	Practice speaking clearly or training an animal using a clear, strong tone of voice that is congruent with actions.	All	All	See Nonverbal Communication section and Verbal Communication section.

323

RELATIONSHIPS   OVERARCHING GOAL: Client will have the tools to identify healthy people and relationships and develop skills to cultivate healthy relationships.

Animals are powerful relationship motivators, as they give feedback about social skills in a clear but non-judgmental way. Animals clearly communicate their feelings of safety and require humans to build relationships thoughtfully. Clients learn how to behave and respond in ways that build trust and healthy relationships with the animals.

Goals	Objectives	Intervention	Description	Animal(s)	Client(s)	Notes
Communication	The client will read non-verbal cues from others	Observation of herd	Client will observe the herd or group dynamics.	Herd animals	All	See Nonverbal Communication section
	Demonstrate respectful listening	"What did they say?"	Client interprets and provides words for a chatty animal.	Vocal animals	All	Several of our animals are very vocal, so the client can listen to the animal's vocalizations and then try to translate what it said. The focus is about encouraging the client to listen to the animal's complete thought before responding. This intervention often leads to projection from the client onto the animal, which gives information to the clinician about the client's presenting issues.
Respect	Respect others boundaries	Practice respectful behavior with animals	Animals require different types of interactions and clients will need to learn and adapt.	All	All	See Boundaries section
		Practice appropriate greetings with animal	Animals also require different greetings and types of introductions to feel safe, so the client observes and practices different skills.	All	All	This is usually an intentional activity, so the client is aware of the goal. The client develops an understanding of how respect will help them build a relationship with the animal.
Empathy *(cont. on next page)*	Demonstrate empathy *(cont. on next page)*	Create a home	Client will set up the animal's home in a way that meets its needs.	All especially small animals	Children, teens	Clients choose what they feel is important to the animal, which provides information about their own needs and values.
		Help with feeding	Clients can help clinicians feed animals meals.	All	All	This intervention is useful for numerous goals, but in this case, the client is learning to help and meet the needs of another being.

RELATIONSHIPS OVERARCHING GOAL: Client will have the tools to identify healthy people and relationships and develop skills to cultivate healthy relationships.

Animals are powerful relationship motivators, as they give feedback about social skills in a clear but non-judgmental way. Animals clearly communicate their feelings of safety and require humans to build relationships thoughtfully. Clients learn how to behave and respond in ways that build trust and healthy relationships with the animals.

Goals	Objectives	Intervention	Description	Animal(s)	Client(s)	Notes
Empathy	Demonstrate empathy	Help with animal medical care	Some animals may need regular medication and clients can help prepare and even administer medication.	All	All	This intervention is clearly based on clinician discretion and animal safety, but when safe and appropriate, clients can help with this process. It can help clients feel a special bond with the animal and a sense of ownership over the animal's well being.
		Build awareness of emotional dysregulation	Notice how animal's emotional dysregulation impacts the animals around them.	All	All	Clients can observe an animal who is mildly stressed or frustrated and then discuss how the animals around them behave. How does one animal's behavior impact those around it?
			Notice how their own emotional dysregulation impacts the animals around them.	All	All	Clients with some self-awareness can notice when they are feeling stressed or frustrated and then discuss how the animals around them are responding and behaving. They can begin to understand how their behavior impacts others.
Improving attending skills *(cont. on next page)*	Demonstrate awareness of others' thoughts and feelings *(cont. on next page)*	Explore how animals build relationships	Observe the integration of new animals to the animals' group.	All	All	Animals that live in groups or herds may act stressed or slightly aggressive toward a new, prospective member of the group. This intervention is often done from a distance and may be mildly stressful for clients to observe but also very valuable.
		Observe herd dynamics	Notice how a herd or group of animals understands and supports each other.	All	All	This can be during a time of mild stress, as above, or perhaps during an activity. How does the herd engage and respond to each other?
		Observe the animals relate to each other	Observe the animals from a distance or the client can be part of the interaction.	All	All	This intervention is often good at the beginning of the treatment process, to help clients feel comfortable with and learn about the animals. It can also be done at parks or other venues if you do not have a group of animals and the client is comfortable going to a new location.

RELATIONSHIPS OVERARCHING GOAL: Client will have the tools to identify healthy people and relationships and develop skills to cultivate healthy relationships.

Animals are powerful relationship motivators, as they give feedback about social skills in a clear but non-judgmental way. Animals clearly communicate their feelings of safety and require humans to build relationships thoughtfully. Clients learn how to behave and respond in ways that build trust and healthy relationships with the animals.

Goals	Objectives	Intervention	Description	Animal(s)	Client(s)	Notes
Improving attending skills	Demonstrate awareness of others thoughts and feelings	Develop a special relationship with an animal	Work regularly with the animal in a calm way to create a special bond. Work toward having the animal approach and then accept touch from the client.	All but especially shy animals	All	Shy or slower to warm up animals are great for this intervention. One of our alpacas is great for this work, as he takes several sessions to warm up to clients. It often takes multiple sessions with clients waiting quietly and patiently offering his favorite treat, but eventually the alpaca will engage with those who are careful and respectful.
Reciprocity	Demonstrate give and take	Playing fetch	Play fetch with any animal that will engage.	Dog or another animal that will engage	All	Discuss the animal's enjoyment and how the client feels about bringing that happiness to the animal.
		Observe how animals share and get along	Observe the animals during a time when there is an item or items they want, such as food, treats, or toys.	All	All	Clients can observe how the animals navigate shared resources, whether it causes friction, and how they handle any conflict.
		Animal social support	Explore how animals receive social support from other animals.	All	All	This may focus just on the animals and a discussion about what social support looks like for animals. With some clients, you may also discuss the similarities and differences in social support between animals and humans.
		Animal emotional response	Notice how animals respond to the client in various situations or emotional states.	All	All	Pay attention to how each animal or animal type responds differently. Some may be bothered by strong emotions from the clients, others may not notice or care. Connect this to human relationships and how people may respond differently depending on how we present and engage with them, and different humans may have different capacities to support us.
		Observe how animals act in reciprocal ways with client	Discuss how animals engage with and support the client.	All	All	When and how do the animals know the client needs their support? How does it feel to the client to receive it?

RELATIONSHIPS **OVERARCHING GOAL: Client will have the tools to identify healthy people and relationships and develop skills to cultivate healthy relationships.**

Animals are powerful relationship motivators, as they give feedback about social skills in a clear but non-judgmental way. Animals clearly communicate their feelings of safety and require humans to build relationships thoughtfully. Clients learn how to behave and respond in ways that build trust and healthy relationships with the animals.

Goals	Objectives	Intervention	Description	Animal(s)	Client(s)	Notes
Dealing with Rupture *(cont. on next page)*	Resolve conflicts when they arise	What just happened?	Discuss a conflict or emotionally triggering situation while keeping the animal calm and in the room.	All	All	One of the most powerful ways to build a relationship with a client is through skillful handling of rupture and repair. This rupture or conflict can occur with an animal or with the clinician. If rupture happens with an animal, the clinician can bring attention to the animal's response to the conflict and perhaps model saying "sorry" or other ways to repair. The clinician can then help the client move through this process with the animal.
	Notice behavior that is counter-productive for relationships	What's going on?	Work with or observe a reactive animal and notice what the animal is responding to in various situations.	All	All	Ensure safety during this intervention, especially if an animal reacts strongly. This may mean observing and discussing from a distance. Discuss how the animal is responding, how this behavior may differ from other animals' responses, and the potential reasons behind this strong reaction.
		Fixing my part of the street	Practicing positive relationship-building with animal, with intentionality.	All	All	We cannot change how others respond, but we can modify our own behaviors, our "side of the street." Work with clients to modify or change behaviors that may be impacting the relationship with the animal and observe how the animal responds.
		Fetch x2	Throw one ball to two dogs—what are each thinking?	Dogs	All	It is helpful to do this intervention with one dog who loves fetch and one who is less interested. Discuss what is different for the dogs and how we can meet the needs of both.
	Work through old relational patterns	What does this remind you of?	Clinician sets up activity that allows client to replicate relational patterns.	All	All	Having multiple animals allows for a natural re-creation of relationship dynamics between the client and others, allowing for the opportunity to look more objectively at behaviors and allow for the client to adjust mental and neural states of tolerance.

RELATIONSHIPS OVERARCHING GOAL: Client will have the tools to identify healthy people and relationships and develop skills to cultivate healthy relationships.

Animals are powerful relationship motivators, as they give feedback about social skills in a clear but non-judgmental way. Animals clearly communicate their feelings of safety and require humans to build relationships thoughtfully. Clients learn how to behave and respond in ways that build trust and healthy relationships with the animals.

Goals	Objectives	Intervention	Description	Animal(s)	Client(s)	Notes
Dealing with Rupture	Let go of old wounds	How do animals handle "grudges"?	Discuss whether animals hold grudges.	All	All	Clients can observe animals in conflict, watch a video, or discuss hypothetically how animals respond to conflict and whether they hold grudges. If so, what does that look like and does it help the animal? If not, what might be the benefits?
	Address fear of abandonment	Discuss animal's loss	Share if an animal has lost a friend or family member and how they coped.	All	All	Many of our animals have changed homes and owners, or lost animal companions. Clients can feel connected to and understood when animals have had a similar experience.

RESILIENCE   OVERARCHING GOAL: Client will have resilience to manage life's challenges.

Building Resilience is a powerful therapeutic goal for clients of all ages. Resilience is usually formed in early childhood, but it can also be developed later in life. This is often a goal for teenagers whose home situation is intractable and unstable. Many teenagers in this situation may need to become more autonomous and create success on their own. The following goals are from the Seven C's Model of Resilience from the American Academy of Pediatrics (2006).

Goals	Objectives	Intervention	Description	Animal(s)	Client(s)	Notes
Confidence	Build confidence in their actions	Coax the animal	Client will use toys to coax a reluctant animal to interact.	Ferret, Alpaca other shy animal	All	This does not require that the animal engage if they do not want to, but it does give the client a chance to ask the animal to join session and find ways to make engagement appealing.
		Call me by name	Client teaches animal to come to them when they call their name.	All	All	While this is fairly easy with a dog, other animals can also learn to come when called. Try teaching a nontraditional animal, such as a cat, goat, or small animal to respond to their name.
Competence	Create a belief of self competence	Remembering the steps	Client will assist in a complex task, such as making a salad for a small animal.	All	All	Initially, the client may have the assistance of the clinician and a sheet of instructions. Over time, allow the client to take over the task completely and notice when they have mastered all the steps by memory.
		I grew that!	Client will plant a seed and watch its growth.	Plants	All	This is especially great when the client grows something they can then eat or admire, such as vegetables or flowers, and share with others.
Connection	Develop connections to supportive people	Practice connection with the animals	Client will develop a trusting relationship with an animal.	All	All	By starting with healthy relationships with animals, clients learn the skills needed to generalize to humans.
		Asking for help	Client will need to ask for help to complete a task.	All	All	We often do this intervention by asking a client to put on a horse's halter, but do not give them detailed instructions. We are creating a small amount of stress, watching how the client handles it, and then encouraging them to ask for help in completing a challenging task

RESILIENCE OVERARCHING GOAL: Client will have resilience to manage life's challenges.

Building Resilience is a powerful therapeutic goal for clients of all ages. Resilience is usually formed in early childhood, but it can also be developed later in life. This is often a goal for teenagers whose home situation is intractable and unstable. Many teenagers in this situation may need to become more autonomous and create success on their own. The following goals are from the Seven C's Model of Resilience from the American Academy of Pediatrics (2006).

Goals	Objectives	Intervention	Description	Animal(s)	Client(s)	Notes
Character	Demonstrate strong core values	Don't squish me!	Client will be nurturing to an "ugly" insect.	Insect	All	This can be done with an insect that humans generally think are "ugly" such as a cockroach or worm. Perhaps research a treat for that insect. Finding something the insect likes to eat, and watching the insects' face while it does, can change a client's perspective and open their mind to new possibilities.
		Let sleeping ferrets lie	Client will resist the urge to wake up a sleeping animal.	All	All	This intervention helps with patience, impulse control, and frustration tolerance. The clinician may need to provide the client some support so that the client can understand the value of this intervention.
Contribution	Engage in activities that help others	Giving animal medicine	Client assists in giving animal medication or is involved in animal's regular treatment regimen.	All	All	Many of our animals need medication or supplements and clients can help us prepare these or administer them when appropriate. Even helping put a fly mask on a horse can be a way to contribute and clients can see the direct effect of making the horse more comfortable. We like to say "it feels good to help" as a subtle way of encouraging the client to notice how helping feels internally rewarding.
		Teach an animal an important skill	Client will teach the animal a skill that will help its functioning.	All	All	Examples are helping an animal learn to walk on a lead, teaching an animal to tolerate getting its nails trimmed, helping the dog to put his toys away.
Coping *(cont. on next page)*	Develop skills to manage difficult situations in positive ways *(cont. on next page)*	Whoops, they escaped	Client assists in retrieving escaped animal.	All	All	This may happen as an accident if an animal gets out of an enclosure or it can be arranged before session intentionally, but only if safe for the animal. Helping the client to deal with a small amount of stress while simultaneously problem solving and taking action are excellent ways to develop coping skills.

RESILIENCE   OVERARCHING GOAL: Client will have resilience to manage life's challenges.

Building Resilience is a powerful therapeutic goal for clients of all ages. Resilience is usually formed in early childhood, but it can also be developed later in life. This is often a goal for teenagers whose home situation is intractable and unstable. Many teenagers in this situation may need to become more autonomous and create success on their own. The following goals are from the Seven C's Model of Resilience from the American Academy of Pediatrics (2006).

Goals	Objectives	Intervention	Description	Animal(s)	Client(s)	Notes
Coping	Develop skills to manage difficult situations in positive ways	Animal stayed at home	Client must accept that their favorite animal is unavailable due to illness, fatigue, or choice.	All	All	This intervention often happens naturally, if an animal is unavailable or does not want to work. The response of the clinician is important here. The client's initial reaction may be disappointment, but in talking about the reasons for the animal not coming to session, the clinician can model how they cope with the disappointment as well. This can be followed by an intervention that practices flexibility (see below).
Control *(cont. on next page)*	Control their behavior and accept the consequences of their actions *(cont. on next page)*	The animal doesn't want to play (with you)	Animal responds to a client's behavior that causes it to withdraw or remove affection.	All	All	This must happen organically since we do not believe in intentionally stressing our animals. If an animal does startle, ensure everyone's safety, then proceed with the client. This is a very important lesson for clients in realizing the impact of their behavior on others. It is critical that the clinician follow up the animal's withdrawal with a discussion about what just happened. Helping the client be reflective on their own behaviors and subsequent reactions starts to give them choices for future behaviors. Clinicians can also help clients check in with the animal and support ways to repair the relationship.

RESILIENCE	OVERARCHING GOAL: Client will have resilience to manage life's challenges.					

Building Resilience is a powerful therapeutic goal for clients of all ages. Resilience is usually formed in early childhood, but it can also be developed later in life. This is often a goal for teenagers whose home situation is intractable and unstable. Many teenagers in this situation may need to become more autonomous and create success on their own. The following goals are from the Seven C's Model of Resilience from the American Academy of Pediatrics (2006).

Goals	Objectives	Intervention	Description	Animal(s)	Client(s)	Notes
Control	Control their behavior and accept the consequences of their actions	You won't be seeing the animal(s) today	Client is not able to work with animals in session following previous inappropriate behavior toward animal.	All	All	This may be a follow-up to the intervention above. If the client is unable to read the animal's withdrawal behavior and continues to show unsafe behavior toward the animal, the subsequent session(s) should be without an animal. The client is learning that the animal's safety is a higher priority than the client's disappointment, but this is not about punishing the client. It is helping the client to understand that their choice of actions toward an animal has its consequences, including removal of the animal from sessions. The client can decide to choose differently and show the clinician through subsequent non-animal interactions that they are ready to try again and be safe with the animal(s).
Flexibility	Client will be able to shift to another action if something does not work	"Show me another way"	Client is asked to change their approach to something when it is unsafe or problematic.	All	Children	Ideally, this intervention precedes the ones listed above so that any behavior that could harm or frighten an animal is stopped early. This statement, "show me another way," is adapted from Synergistic Play Therapy and is a non-confrontational way of asking the client to find an alternative strategy for reaching their goal.
	Client will observe and understand agency	Finding alternative ways to get inside their home	Client blocks an animal's usual entrance to home.	All	Children	After blocking their usual entrance, clients can help create an alternate entrance to the animal's enclosure and watch how the animal figures out how to get inside. This should only be done with animals who will not be overly stressed by this change.

SELF-CARE

OVERARCHING GOAL: Client will have the skills and motivation to take care of their body, mind, and spirit.

Many clients have challenges with hygiene, eating, sleep, and general self-care activities, often as a result of their presenting issues. By asking the client to help care for the animals, we gently reinforce the importance of self-care without directly confronting the client.

Goals	Objectives	Intervention	Description	Animal(s)	Client(s)	Notes
Physical Care *(cont. on next page)*	Improve hygiene	Grooming animals to practice hygiene	Show client how to use the right brush for different types of brushing.	All	All	During the activity, discuss the importance of grooming and how it impacts the animal in positive ways, even if the animal does not always enjoy the activity.
		Observation of animal grooming behavior	Talk about how and why animals groom themselves.	All that groom (cat, rat, dog, rabbit)	All	Discuss not only the function of the grooming, but how it makes the animal feel, before, during, and after. Pay attention to the animal's body language during each step.
		Bathing an animal	Which animals need to be bathed and why?	All	All	Many animals will need to be bathed at some point and we can discuss the reasons and how the animals respond. Clients can assist in this process which can be very messy and very fun.
	Accept bodily functions	Mucking horse stalls	Work with the client to muck the horse stalls or arena to de-shame and normalize bowel movements.	Equine	All	We generally do not have clients muck the stalls for health reasons. However, we have had particular clients who request and love this activity, so we have allowed it with appropriate permissions and clinician participation. We do not ask clients to muck alone. Modeling washing up afterward is also an important aspect of this intervention.
		Observe animals eliminating	Animals go the bathroom when they need to, without shame; discuss this process with clients.	All	All	This is an intervention that happens spontaneously. Some animals prefer to eliminate in the same place, such as alpacas, rats, cats, and humans, whereas others just go when needed, such as dogs, goats, and horses. An interesting discussion is how and why these animals differ.

SELF-CARE   OVERARCHING GOAL: **Client will have the skills and motivation to take care of their body, mind, and spirit.**

Many clients have challenges with hygiene, eating, sleep, and general self-care activities, often as a result of their presenting issues. By asking the client to help care for the animals, we gently reinforce the importance of self-care without directly confronting the client.

Goals	Objectives	Intervention	Description	Animal(s)	Client(s)	Notes
Physical Care (*cont. on next page*)	Improve nutrition	Feeding animals to regulate weight and health	Client helps prepare meals for animals and feeds them.	All	All	Most clients love to feed the animals and there are many options for them to do so, including preparing food, chopping vegetables, and bringing food to the animals. Ensure safety when feeding, especially with the larger animals.
		Explore animal eating habits	Observe and/or discuss what animals eat and why.	All	All	This can be done with live animals or as a discussion without animals present. You can discuss what different animals naturally eat, what we feed them, if and how that differs and why.
		Emphasize eating routine for animals while feeding	Talk with client about the importance of a regular mealtime, location, and food type.	All	All	As above, this can be done with live animals or as a discussion without animals present. You can discuss why routine and consistency are important for the animals.
		Weigh small animals	Client weighs and writes weight on record to track changes.	All	All	This is especially good for our small animals. Some are older and have health issues and this is a regular part of our routine. By catching weight changes we can sometimes catch health problems early.

SELF-CARE	OVERARCHING GOAL: Client will have the skills and motivation to take care of their body, mind, and spirit.				
Many clients have challenges with hygiene, eating, sleep, and general self-care activities, often as a result of their presenting issues. By asking the client to help care for the animals, we gently reinforce the importance of self-care without directly confronting the client.					
Goals	Objectives	Intervention	Description	Animal(s)	Client(s)	Notes
---	---	---	---	---	---	---
Physical Care	Improve sleep	Observe how different animals sleep	Discuss sleep habits of animals and how each have different needs and preferences.	All	All	Watching animals sleep is also a calming behavior and can be added to the clients mental self-care list.
		Lay down next to the animal and try to "nap" together	Client can lay on the floor or ground and rest with an animal.	All	All	This can be practiced in session and also done at the client's home. If they do not have an animal, clients can do this with a stuffed animal.
		Sleep with calming animal	Practice sleeping with an animal in a way that is comfortable for everyone.	All	All	This is an at-home activity but clinicians can prepare the client for this during sessions, talking about which animal they like to sleep with and why and how to set up the space. You can discuss other soothing options if the client does not have an animal, such as a stuffed animal or pillows.
	Engage in physical activity	Walk or run with the animals	There are countless ways to get clients physically active in session, from running with horses to walking a dog.	All	All	Practice physical activity in session and find ways that feel fun and acceptable to the client. Some clients may love moving a lot, some may want to move slowly in the garden, but finding and embracing any movement is powerful. You can then discuss how to expand this movement beyond sessions.
Mental Self-Care	Learn to relax	Walk a dog before bed	Discuss the benefits of an evening walk for the client and animal.	All	All	This can be done in session to practice walking to calm down and then done with a client's pet at home. If clients do not have a pet, they can still go for a walk.
		Practice mindfulness with animal before bed	See Mindfulness section.	All	All	

SELF-CONCEPT   OVERARCHING GOAL: Client will develop a positive sense of who they are.

Having a positive self-concept is necessary if clients are going to make good choices in their lives, as our choices reflect who we believe we are. This may be one of the most powerful areas of change that AACP facilitates, because we can encourage clients to engage in various experiences and see new aspects of themselves. These are not just positive experiences, since learning who we are also involves accepting our limitations. Clients are able to see and feel that they are not defined by their problem and have the capacity to choose who they want to be, which is especially vital for clients who have struggled with addiction, trauma, or abuse. This is a small set of interventions that help develop self-concept but any new experience that clients have in therapy can also contribute to this goal.

Goals	Objectives	Intervention	Description	Animal(s)	Client(s)	Notes
Defining Self Beliefs	Identify beliefs about themselves	Animal Self-Statements	Client helps write a list of statements they believe the animal would make about themselves. Then they do the same for themselves using "I am…"	All	All	Starting with the animal self-statements is more accessible for many clients and can also be fun and silly. It also allows for projection and gives valuable information to the clinician.
	Develop mastery	Walk an Animal	Find mastery in walking a large animal, such as a donkey or horse, with a lead.	Large animal	All	Equines are large, strong, and often stubborn, so walking equines requires a new set of skills apart from simply holding a lead. This intervention simultaneously addresses many treatment goals, but mastering this demanding task can help build a positive self concept.
Finding Strengths in Mastery	Identify what they believe to be their ideal self	The perfect animal	Client will list traits of an animal they believe is perfect then list traits they want in themselves.	All	All	At some point the animal they have chosen will do something that is imperfect. Client can see this contradiction and try to work out if the animal is still perfect and if not, whether that is acceptable.
Finding Strengths in Mastery *(cont. on next page)*	Discover innate skills or talents *(cont. on next page)*	Lunging a Horse	Learn how to lunge a horse.	Horse	Teens or adults	Lunging involves harnessing and putting a long lead on a horse, and then asking the horse to move in a circle around you. This can be a challenging task and some horses are much more willing than others.
		Lead free walking	Learn how to guide a large animal without a lead.	Equine	All	You can do this with any animal but it is particularly challenging with a large animal such as an equine or alpaca. Clients need to determine how to convey their intention in new ways.

SELF-CONCEPT   OVERARCHING GOAL: Client will develop a positive sense of who they are.

Having a positive self-concept is necessary if clients are going to make good choices in their lives, as our choices reflect who we believe we are. This may be one of the most powerful areas of change that AACP facilitates, because we can encourage clients to engage in various experiences and see new aspects of themselves. These are not just positive experiences, since learning who we are also involves accepting our limitations. Clients are able to see and feel that they are not defined by their problem and have the capacity to choose who they want to be, which is especially vital for clients who have struggled with addiction, trauma, or abuse. This is a small set of interventions that help develop self-concept but any new experience that clients have in therapy can also contribute to this goal.

Goals	Objectives	Intervention	Description	Animal(s)	Client(s)	Notes
Finding Strengths in Mastery	Discover innate skills or talents	Animal Training	Client will train an animal to complete a trick or command.	All	All	Teaching the animal a new trick involves numerous skills and can address multiple treatment goals. When focusing on self-concept, clients are seeing and feeling that they are capable, can learn new skills, and can help others in the process.
		Trying New Things	Clinician will introduce new activities and experiences to the client.	All	All	The possibilities are endless with this intervention! These activities can be anything that the client has not done before. The idea is for the client to try new things and for the clinician and client to identify those things that come naturally, that they enjoy, and that can be nurtured as a part of therapy. Animals are usually a part of this process, but it can also involve being outside, going for a hike, or other activities without live animals.
		Any AACP activity that allows the client to see themselves in a different way	Gently challenge clients by encouraging them to interact with the animals in novel ways.	All	All	Creative, fun, and novel interventions allow clients to try new activities and behaviors and find skills or interests they did not know they had.

SELF-CONCEPT   OVERARCHING GOAL: Client will develop a positive sense of who they are.

Having a positive self-concept is necessary if clients are going to make good choices in their lives, as our choices reflect who we believe we are. This may be one of the most powerful areas of change that AACP facilitates, because we can encourage clients to engage in various experiences and see new aspects of themselves. These are not just positive experiences, since learning who we are also involves accepting our limitations. Clients are able to see and feel that they are not defined by their problem and have the capacity to choose who they want to be, which is especially vital for clients who have struggled with addiction, trauma, or abuse. This is a small set of interventions that help develop self-concept but any new experience that clients have in therapy can also contribute to this goal.

Goals	Objectives	Intervention	Description	Animal(s)	Client(s)	Notes
Self-Compassion	Accept imperfection	Letting the animal fail	Observe activities that tend to be typical for certain species and whether all members of the species have this skill.	All	All	This could be anything from a cat jumping to a dog retrieving; the purpose is to find an animal's "deficit" and process with the client. Does the animal seem to worry or care that they cannot do this activity as well as others? How does this impact the animal and their relationship with others? You may also discuss what we can learn from the animals and how we can learn to accept our own deficits and failures, or you can keep the focus simply on the animal.
		Any of the above activities	Allow mistakes and imperfection while doing AACP activities.	All	All	It is important to allow the client to make mistakes and even do poorly at some activities. The clinician helps the client to reframe and accept that humans are not perfect at everything, just as animals are not, and that is what makes us wonderful. You can also help the client keep trying, find new ways to approach activities, and celebrate their eventual success or growth.
	Care about themselves	Narrative Restructuring	Create a narrative about the animal.	All	All	If the animal had a difficult past, the client can create a story about who the animal is now and how their past experiences have helped them get there. Although the past has an influence, the animal is not defined by its past and can grow and change, just as humans can.

TRAUMA   OVERARCHING GOAL.: The client will process their past trauma and develop strengths and resilience.

Unresolved trauma can leave physical, emotional, behavioral, and spiritual wounds that negatively impact people in a myriad of ways. Traditional talk therapy may be important, but we have found that integrating the animals into this process can greatly support clients with their difficult emotions and memories. In addition, the animals can help the client to re-learn how to interact with the world and this experiential, re-learning process is a necessary step beyond talk therapy. Recovery from trauma is a complex process, so multiple other sections also address helpful aspects of trauma recovery, such as emotional regulation, grief, and PTSD.

Goals	Objectives	Intervention	Description	Animal(s)	Client(s)	Notes
Co-regulation / Down-Regulation	Regulate nervous system	Walking	Client engages in rhythmic walking with an animal.	Dog, alpaca, equine, goats, and other animals that will walk	All	Any rhythmic activity with an animal can down-regulate the nervous system. The physical process of walking, grooming, and petting provides soothing sensory and physiological input and allows clients to focus on those sensations.
		Grooming	Client engages in rhythmic brushing of an animal.	All	All	
		Petting	Client engages in rhythmic petting of an animal.	All	All	
	Process trauma memories	Share the animal's story	Introduce client to animals that have had trauma in their past.	Any animal that has experienced trauma	All	Allow clients to hear an animal's story and understand that while the traumatic memories play a role in the animal's life, they do not define it. Discuss how the animal may still be impacted by the trauma but also how they have moved on in various way.
	Consolidate memory	Animal memories	Tell the animal's story before adopted—discuss what kind of memories the animal might have.	Any animal that has experienced trauma	All	Clinician can share the animal's experience and discuss with the client what the animal may remember and how it may still impact the animal.
		Tell your story	Whisper in animal's ear what happened to them.	All	All	It is not important if the clinician can hear what the client says; the important element is that the client is sharing their story.
	Manage and diminish anxiety	The behavior tells the story	Observe anxious animals and relate the animal's behavior to their story.	All	All	See section on Anxiety

339

TRAUMA

OVERARCHING GOAL: The client will process their past trauma and develop strengths and resilience.

Unresolved trauma can leave physical, emotional, behavioral, and spiritual wounds that negatively impact people in a myriad of ways. Traditional talk therapy may be important, but we have found that integrating the animals into this process can greatly support clients with their difficult emotions and memories. In addition, the animals can help the client to re-learn how to interact with the world and this experiential, re-learning process is a necessary step beyond talk therapy. Recovery from trauma is a complex process, so multiple other sections also address helpful aspects of trauma recovery, such as emotional regulation, grief, and PTSD.

Goals	Objectives	Intervention	Description	Animal(s)	Client(s)	Notes
Positive Self-Identity	Move beyond identifying self with trauma	Who am I?	Client tells animals' story after their recovery from trauma.	All	All	This can be done verbally, in writing, or with art.
		My secret strengths	Notice what the client does well with the animal.	All	All	This is a strength based approach and the focus of this intervention is what the client does well with the animal and their successes in taking care of the animal.
	Stay in the moment	See section on Mindfulness				
Re-engagement with community	Return to normal functioning	Walk an animal in public	Take an animal for a walk in a park, neighborhood, or other safe place.	All	All	Clients can practice being in public and gradually move to interacting with people they may see on the walk. Clinicians can help process the client's anxiety or other powerful emotions while on the walk. It can be fun to have the client walk an unusual animal, such as a goat or cat, which can encourage more social interactions and levity.
Creating a safe space	Create a space for themselves to provide a sense of safety	Create a safe space for the animal	Clients choose what the animal needs to feel safe.	All	All	This allows clients to decide what is important for safety and informs the clinician about what the client may need for their own safety, either in sessions or at home.
Chronic Disruption of Co-Regulation	Change the response of their nervous system	Co-regulating with an animal	The client practices regulating with an animal that may also need to calm down. The focus can be on calming the animal and in the process, the client regulates as well.	All	All	S. W. Porges (2014) defines trauma as the chronic disruption of connectedness. Through developing predictable co-regulating connections, the client can begin to move out of the perceived danger zone.

TRUST AND RAPPORT OVERARCHING GOAL: Client will feel comfortable and develop trust in the clinician in preparation for more emotionally challenging psychotherapy.

Animals are wonderful for rapport-building. They can be the bridge between clinician and client until the client feels safe enough to trust the clinician.

Goals	Objectives	Intervention	Description	Animal(s)	Client(s)	Notes
Build Rapport	Client gets to know each animal	Introductions	Introduce client to animal(s) and encourage them to ask questions or share information about their experiences with animals.	All	All	We usually do this at the first or second session. It allows the client to connect with the animals and clinician and get to know our facility.
	Client learns the basics about each animal	Information sharing	Clinician shares basic information about each animal including species, age, gender.	All	All	During therapy we find an appropriate time to introduce aspects about the animal and animal's story that may be relevant to the client.
	Client experiences a positive emotion related to an animal	Sharing a fun or lighthearted moment with an animal	Demonstrate or watch with the client as a therapy animal does something silly.	All, but particularly nontraditional animals such as goats, alpacas, and chickens.	All	Finding something that allows the client to laugh can be especially helpful in breaking through anxiety, resistance, frustration, or other barriers to sharing or interest in therapy. It also allows the client to connect with you and the animal in an emotional and positive way. They will remember this special moment that made them laugh and it may be this moment that helps them return to their next session.
	Client shares about their own animals/pets	Client's pets	Ask client to share about their pets including telling stories and showing pictures. Clinician can consider if any client pets could provide intentional support for client.	All	All	This can be about current or past pets and allows the client to share and connect with a topic that feels safe to them. This also gives the clinician information about the client's experience with animals, how they view animals, and the role/value of animals in the home.

TRUST AND RAPPORT OVERARCHING GOAL: Client will feel comfortable and develop trust in the clinician in preparation for more emotionally challenging psychotherapy.

Animals are wonderful for rapport-building. They can be the bridge between clinician and client until the client feels safe enough to trust the clinician.

Goals	Objectives	Intervention	Description	Animal(s)	Client(s)	Notes
Build Trust *(cont. on next page)*	Client learns to trust clinician through interactions with the animals	Modeling caretaking behaviors	Interacting with your therapy animal in a positive, caring way and doing what is necessary to care for your animal.	All	All	This starts with the clinician naturally modeling caretaking and compassion for their own therapy animal. Clients can then assist in this caretaking. Even giving commands in a gentle way demonstrates love and compassion toward your animal.
		Demonstrating tricks	Show the client the tricks your therapy animal knows. The client can give the animal treats to reward their behavior.	All	All	This is different than allowing the client to train your animal because the client is observing what the animal already knows. This intervention is a good segue or introduction into letting the client train the animal in later sessions. Again, you are demonstrating a kind, trustworthy demeanor toward your animal thus modeling how you will treat and be able to care for the client. This also shows what expectations you have for how the client engages with your animal(s).
		Boundaries with animal handling	Client physically meets and interacts with animals and demonstrates their ability to safely interact with each animal.	All	All	The clinician is always near the client and may hold small animals as they encourage the client to touch and pet the animal, give treats, and engage in other gentle interactions. We have found that many of our clients actually feel relieved when we slowly develop relationships with the animals. This allows clients to see how we handle our animals, especially those animals new to the client. It also helps to build confidence and trust in themselves to be safe with the animal(s). We do not need to emphasize that we are setting boundaries. Rather, we can simply focus on the connection, saying something such as "let's get to know Rupert today!" This also models how relationships build slowly with small actions, not big interactions.

TRUST AND RAPPORT   OVERARCHING GOAL: Client will feel comfortable and develop trust in the clinician in preparation for more emotionally challenging psychotherapy.

Animals are wonderful for rapport-building. They can be the bridge between clinician and client until the client feels safe enough to trust the clinician.

Goals	Objectives	Intervention	Description	Animal(s)	Client(s)	Notes
Build Trust	Client learns to see elements of themselves through the animal's stories	Sharing information about the animal's history	At different stages of therapy, share elements about the animal's history, experiences, and past.	All	All	Having been rescued or re-homed, all of our animals have a complex history, which allows clients to connect with their stories. Even if your animal does not have a complicated story, there are often elements of their lives or personalities that can be shared in ways that allow clients to feel a special bond. For instance, information about your animal's favorite toys, animal friends, food preferences, dislike of baths, or other quirks can help clients find a connection. At the beginning stage of therapy it may be most useful to share just enough information so that the client can start to identify with them. For example, letting the client know that you adopted the animal from a shelter. Because this intervention is used primarily as a way to build rapport with the client, you can save more detailed information for the middle phase of therapy where a specific aspect of their story may be more helpful. For instance, in later sessions, you can share that your animal had been found wandering with a broken leg and was scared of people.
Inspire Commitment to Treatment *(cont. on next page)*	Clients develop caring feelings for animal(s) *(cont. on next page)*	Client helps provide for animal's needs	Client helps provide basic needs for the animal.	All	All	Clients can help with animals in so many ways, such as filling a water bowl/bottle, preparing an animal's meal, bringing food to the animal, or other basic caretaking needs. This is one of our client's favorite interventions, because it is fun and rewarding, but also helps clients feel invested in their relationship with the animals. Please make careful decisions about which animals can be fed by particular clients, as large animals may be a higher safety risk during feeding times.

TRUST AND RAPPORT **OVERARCHING GOAL: Client will feel comfortable and develop trust in the clinician in preparation for more emotionally challenging psychotherapy.**

Animals are wonderful for rapport-building. They can be the bridge between clinician and client until the client feels safe enough to trust the clinician.

Goals	Objectives	Intervention	Description	Animal(s)	Client(s)	Notes
Inspire Commitment to Treatment	Clients develop caring feelings for animal(s)	Hand-feeding animals	Client gives small food items to the animal of choice either by hand or in a food bowl.	All	All	It is helpful to know your animals' favorite treat foods and allow clients to give these to the animal, as it brings joy to everyone and enhances the relationship. Depending on the animal, you may want to use a special food bowl to prevent accidental finger nibbles!
		Hiding food for the animal to find	Client puts animals' treats in hiding places, either around a room or in their enclosure and encourages the animal to find them.	All	All	This activity provide enrichment for the animal and also gives them exercise as they run around looking for their food. It helps clients be creative about hiding places and encourage the animal to find the treats.
Encourage Session Attendance	Client will participate in animal enrichment activities	Build enrichment items to integrate in sessions	Client brainstorms and creates items that provide stimulation for animals.	All	All	Enrichment items can be anything that an animal will enjoy. These items can be complex or simple, but the focus is letting the client be creative, inventive, and use empathy to develop items that will be fun for the animal. Some examples include small socks filled with catnip for cats, PVC pipe or cardboard taped together as roads for small animals, or treats hidden under small box with piece of wood as a lever for a goat to step on to flip the box over.
		Clients develop a multi-step trick for animal to learn	Clients choose a trick and determine how to teach the animal.	All	All	Dogs are the most common animal to teach complex tricks, but most animals are capable of learning with sufficient time and patience. Allowing clients to choose the trick helps their investment in the training and encourages them to return each week to continue training. Complex tricks have several steps of training, which can provide a focus for successive sessions and numerous goal-setting and achievement tasks.

VERBAL COMMUNICATION   OVERARCHING GOAL: Client will be able to facilitate relationships through verbal expression of their thoughts and feelings.

At the heart of all good relationships is communication. Clients of all ages may need to learn or remember how to use their words to share important thoughts and feelings.

Goals	Objectives	Intervention	Description	Animal(s)	Client(s)	Notes
Understand Importance of Listening	Psycho-education about the importance of communication	Animals listen too	"Listen" to the animal—what is it saying how is it saying these things to you?	All	All	We start with listening for a reason: we often forget how important this part of communication is, especially for clients who have challenging relationships. This intervention focuses on verbal and nonverbal cues.
Improve Listening	Develop the ability to co-regulate	Touching an animal	While discussing or listening to something that may induce dysregulation, the client can touch or pet any animal that helps them feel calmer.	All	All	This intervention is often paired with psychoeducation about how touch can be soothing and how clients can incorporate touch when they feel dysregulated. It is helpful to explore how it is difficult to listen carefully and accurately when we are dysregulated.
	Practice active listening	What did the animal say?	The client gives words to any chatty animal.	Any vocal animal	All	Some animals are great at being vocal and "having conversations" with humans. With these animals, the client can create a conversation with the animal and practice good listening skills by repeating what they heard the animal say. It can also give clinicians insight into how clients engage with, interpret, and respond to others.
		Observation	Observe an animal and discuss how the animal demonstrates they are listening to you, the client, or other animals.	All	All	This works well with animals that will turn their heads or their ears to listen. It provides the opportunity for the animals to demonstrate how they communicate to each other that they are listening.
	Follow verbal directions	"Watch"	Teach and practice "watch" with dog.	Dog	All	This specific command is intended to get the attention of the dog by watching your face or eyes. It helps clients understand the importance of being focused on someone and being ready to listen.
		"Simon Says" with animal	Animal performs their tricks on cue.	All that know commands	All	This intervention is limited to tricks the animal already knows. Starting with "watch" is a great way to get the animal's attention and is a cue that a request will be following. Some clients, particularly children, may enjoy doing the tricks alongside the animal.

VERBAL COMMUNICATION   OVERARCHING GOAL: Client will be able to facilitate relationships through verbal expression of their thoughts and feelings.

At the heart of all good relationships is communication. Clients of all ages may need to learn or remember how to use their words to share important thoughts and feelings.

Goals	Objectives	Intervention	Description	Animal(s)	Client(s)	Notes
Improve Commu-nication Through Speaking *(cont. on next page)*	Increase communi-cation with others, such as parents and peers	Whispering to an animal	Client whispers thoughts and feelings into the ear of an animal.	All	All	It is not important if the clinician can hear what the client says; the important element is that the client is communicating with another being.
		Teaching animal tricks	Client can determine which animals they want to train and what they will ask them to do.	All	All	Often it is best to start with simple tricks for easily trainable animals, such as dogs, so clients do not get overly frustrated. Over time, you can work on more difficult skills and/or with harder to train animals.
		Teaching a dog to "speak"	Teach the dog to bark with a verbal cue then hand cue.	Dog	All	Though this can seem like an undesirable skill, teaching a dog to bark can actually help curb unwanted barking. It also shows the client that there are positive ways to communicate and less effective ways.
	Express thoughts and requests clearly	Walking an equine	Client practices walking an equine on a lead.	Equine	All	Equines are amazing to walk but can be challenging, so clients must use clear, assertive and intentional communication.
		Making clear requests of an animal	Client will use assertive voice and body language to work with a therapy animal.	All	All	Animals respond better and more reliably when a client is direct and assertive, rather than passive or overly stimulating. We can talk about the various ways to communicate and watch how the animal responds when the client tries new ways to communicate.
		Animal miscommuni-cations	Observing animals in their environments to view how they communicate and mis-communicate.	All	All	Animals communicate in many ways with other animals or humans and sometimes this communication is very subtle. How do animals respond when other animals or humans miss or misinterpret their communication? How does this impact the environment and the relationship?

VERBAL COMMUNICATION   OVERARCHING GOAL: Client will be able to facilitate relationships through verbal expression of their thoughts and feelings.

At the heart of all good relationships is communication. Clients of all ages may need to learn or remember how to use their words to share important thoughts and feelings.

Goals	Objectives	Intervention	Description	Animal(s)	Client(s)	Notes
Improve Communication Through Speaking	Express feelings clearly	Frustrating animal tasks	Ask client to complete a particular task with an animal then ask them to tell you what it was like.	All	All	How did the animal handle this frustration? What behaviors did you see and how could we have helped the animal? How did the client feel?
		Animal feelings	Client "reads" the feelings of the animals in various situations.	All	All	Clients often project their own internal thoughts and feelings onto the animal, which help them practice verbalizing and sharing. This also gives clinicians valuable information about the client's internal world.
	Use assertive communication	Tell me what to do	Client practices using assertive communication while trying to guide an animal's behavior.	All	All	We often talk about assertive communication and how that differs from passive or aggressive communication. How do the animals respond to each style and which is most effective?
		Yes-No Puppets	Clinician uses one puppet that says only "yes" while the client plays with another puppet that only says "no."	Any animal puppet	Children	This exercise gives the client practice saying powerful words and hearing their own voice. They can practice with different amplitudes and with different emphases. It can be both empowering and intimidating for the client.
	Verbalize (specific to selectively mute clients)	Engage with an animal in various ways	Using verbal cues, the client can play a game, teach a trick, praise, or talk to an animal.	All	All	Many clients who are nonverbal feel more comfortable talking to animals. They may speak inaudibly to clinicians but the important aspect is that they are speaking at all and practicing using words. Often, over time, they will begin to speak louder to the animal and perhaps even to the clinician eventually. All of these interventions encourage the client to verbalize without a direct request by the therapist.

ACKNOWLEDGMENTS

Thank you to the amazing team at Animal Assisted Therapy Programs of Colorado for supporting us in the writing of this book, sharing their experiences and client stories, working tirelessly for our clients and animals, and being a generally wonderful group of people. We could not have done any of this without you. Thank you to our clients, who trusted us and worked so hard to trust themselves. Thanks to all of our incredible therapy animals throughout the years, who taught us so much and helped bring our dreams to life.

—Linda and Ellen

This book and AATPC would never have been possible without my incredibly supportive husband, Jeff. He has had so many roles over the years, including property owner, financier, handyman, general contractor, and plumber. And most of all, thanks, Jeff, for trusting me and letting me chase my dream. I would also like to thank Ellen Winston who insisted on being a partner (when I thought I was hiring her). Ellen, you have always had my back, balanced me, said "no" to some of my crazier ideas, and translated me to the other staff when needed. I could not have asked for a better partner. To Nancy Parish-Plass, thank you for inspiring me and helping me bounce ideas around. Thank you Shlomit Flaisher-Grinberg for proofreading all the busy parts. Thank you Dr. Chris McFalls-Stegger for turning our data into meaningful information. And thank you to Jeffrey Kottler, my mentor and doctoral supervisor, who encouraged me to write and to think big.

Lastly, thank you Andrea, Alan, and the rest of the Purdue Press team for letting us share our passion in hopes to inspire more people to do this incredible work.

—Linda

It is hard to write acknowledgments, because there are so many people who have supported AATPC throughout the years, with donations, event attendance, referrals, visits to the ranch, and countless other ways. You helped us grow into what we are today.

Thank you to Linda, for trusting an inexperienced therapist with huge ambition, being willing to be my business partner, and managing so much at the ranch when I had to relocate. Who knew what we would create together! To her husband, Jeff, for helping us in innumerable ways, fixing anything and everything, and helping us bring AATPC to fruition. To my parents, for always supporting me and my dreams, even when it was difficult. I am so lucky to have you. To my sister, for challenging me, whether I liked it or not, and her fun and loving family. To Gail and Kip, for being staunch supporters of AATPC throughout the years, emotionally and financially. To all my pets for inspiring this passion, but especially Sasha, for being the best therapy dog, and to Luna, for getting me out for walks and runs every day and laying by my feet as I worked on this book. Finally, to my little owls—my wonderful, smart, silly, fierce, animal-loving daughters, Kenna and Shea—and to my husband, Ben, for being endlessly supportive, loving, thoughtful , and always making me laugh; you are everything I could ever ask for and more. I am grateful for all of you.

—Ellen

INDEX

Page numbers in italics indicate photos or tables.

ABOUT THE AUTHORS

Linda Chassman Craddock has been providing animal-assisted counseling and psychotherapy with clients for nearly 30 years. She is currently the cofounder and executive director of Animal Assisted Therapy Programs of Colorado (AATPC). Since 1995, Dr. Chassman has been integrating her cat Norman into her therapeutic work with youth and adults with complex trauma. Dr. Chassman is trained to conduct object relations psychotherapy for clients with ingrained issues and sees clients through a developmental lens. As well as being a licensed marriage and family therapist, Dr. Chassman has taught for over 14 years in graduate counseling programs in California and Colorado. Dr. Chassman's professional background includes being a psychotherapist, supervisor, researcher, writer, lecturer, and consultant. She has written several chapters for edited books on animal-assisted therapy and has spoken at conferences internationally. She lives with her husband and daughter, and dog, Rupert, three cats, and a rat, near Denver, Colorado. In her free time Dr. Chassman enjoys animal photography, gardening, and hiking.

Ellen Kinney Winston is the training director for AATPC, managing the international training and certification program in animal-assisted psychotherapy, overseeing and educating counseling professionals, consulting with international programs, and writing multiple book chapters (and now a book). Fueled by a desire to help both humans and animals, Winston cofounded Animal Assisted Therapy Programs of Colorado in 2010, helping to create the unique programs, recruit and train staff, conduct therapy sessions, and train professionals.

Winston is a Licensed Professional Counselor (LPC), a National Certified Counselor (NCC), and holds a BA in psychology, an MA in counseling psychology, a certificate in animals and human health, and a certificate in animal-assisted psychotherapy. Winston has counseling experience in a variety of settings, including residential treatment for adolescents, substance abuse treatment for adults, school counseling, Head Start centers, early childhood education centers and daycares, home-based family therapy, and private practice settings.

Winston lives in Portland, Oregon, with her husband, two daughters, and two rescue dogs; together they love to explore Oregon, camp, ski, mountain bike, run, rock climb, read, and go to the coast.

www.ingramcontent.com/pod-product-compliance
Lightning Source LLC
Chambersburg PA
CBHW071831270326
41929CB00013B/1958